Translations and Annotations
of
Choral Repertoire

Compiled and Annotated
by
Ron Jeffers

Volume I: Sacred Latin Texts

Printed by Cascade Printing Co., Corvallis, Oregon

ISBN 0-9621532-0-6 Hbd
ISBN 0-9621532-1-4 Pbk

e a r t h s o n g s
220 nw 29th street
corvallis, oregon 97330

this book is dedicated to my family

Becky, Alan, and Robin

and to

John Warren Owen

and

Howard Swan

*who helped me realize
how much words can mean*

thanks also to

The Monks of Mt. Angel Abbey
especially
Fr. Martin Pollard

Pamela J. Brown
Barbara Rohde
David Janower
Catherine Royer
David Hoang
Bonnie Hall
and
all who have offered advice and encouragement

T A B L E   O F   C O N T E N T S

S A C R E D   L A T I N   T E X T S

OTHER SACRED TEXTS

OTHER SACRED TEXTS

OTHER SACRED TEXTS

A P P E N D I C E S

This volume is addressed mainly to the practicing choral director, to the teachers and students of choral conducting, to professional and amateur choristers and to the avid listener. Music librarians, theorists, historians and composers -- and the general reader -- should also find it to be a valuable resource in a variety of ways. It represents what one choral conductor needed to know in order to explain these texts to a choir and to develop a personal understanding and interpretation of specific musical settings. A <u>literal</u> word-by-word translation was absolutely essential. The English paraphrases, the "syllabically-appropriate" translations for singing, and especially the poetic, rhymed translations were not enough; they were often much worse than nothing at all. A readable prose rendering was needed to restore the proper word order and to make the meaning clear. And a knowledge of the liturgical context to which these texts were appointed and for which much of the music was written was fundamental to a full understanding and appreciation of both the words and the music.

Compared to English, the Latin language is very succinct and economical. One word of Latin will often require two, three, or four English words to convey its literal meaning (to say nothing of its metaphorical, philosophical, or theological implications). My command of Latin was far short of what was required, but the need to know persisted and through the good graces of the Benedictine monks at Mt. Angel Abbey, a well-respected Latin teacher, various commentaries and previous translators, the translations and annotations of these texts have been compiled and offered to my colleagues in the profession.

The singers of art song and lieder discover early on how necessary it is to know the meaning and function of each and every word in a song; and opera singers soon realize the need to understand the dramatic context of a certain aria. Numerous reference works are now available to assist them in acquiring this essential information. But choral directors, whose need is just as great, search in vain for similar resources. Therefore you will find in this volume the literal word-by-word translation of each text side by side with a prose rendering which restores syntactical order and clarifies meaning:

Vérbum	cáro	fáctum	est	**The Word was made flesh**
Word	**flesh**	**made**	**was**	

<u>Both</u> the original Latin text and its prose translation should be printed in the program so that the meaning <u>and</u> the sounds of the original are available to the listener. This will help to place the focus on the original text rather than the translation. And since so many English words are derived from Latin roots, it is quite possible for the listener who has read or studied the translation prior to the performance to follow both the sounds and the meaning of the Latin text:

Crédo in únum Déum,	I believe in one God,
Pátrem omnipoténtem,	The Father almighty,
factórem coéli et térrae,	maker of heaven and earth,
visibílium ómnium, et invisibílium.	of all things visible and invisible.

It cannot be stated too strongly that singing in the original language is the *sine qua non* of fine choral music making. We must give the highest respect and honor to the virtually inseparable original marriage of sound and sense. Translation into the vernacular is necessary, but it should only be used as a tool to facilitate the understanding and appreciation the unique qualities and characteristics of the original language and culture.

Correct pronunciation is obviously essential. For often the sounds of the original text convey and express as much or more than the meaning of the words, especially in a musical setting. A thorough pronunciation guide (specifically oriented to the problems frequently encountered with these texts) has been provided, including the Austro-German variants that some composers had in mind when they conceived their musical settings.

Experience has repeatedly shown how important <u>context</u> is to a full appreciation and understanding of a work of art. The historical, social, political, philosophical, aesthetic, and stylistic context in which a piece of choral music is born must be the concern of every serious performer. The life and world of the composer shapes and informs every choral work to such a significant degree that one cannot begin to develop an understanding, let alone an interpretation, without this knowledge. For example, consider how important these factors are in *Ein Deutsches Requiem* by Brahms, in the Fauré *Requiem*, and in Benjamin Britten's *War Requiem*.

Appreciating the context in which these sacred Latin texts were written and performed means also knowing the liturgy of the Roman Mass and the Hours of Divine Office, the various seasons and feasts of the Liturgical Year, and the information which will be found in the Glossary of Terms. Knowledge of the history and structure of a given text also has great bearing on musical analysis, interpretation and performance. I can only hope that this information will be as useful and meaningful to you as it has been to me and my work.

There are many ways to use this book. Read it as a book, so that you get a sense of the larger context and not just information about a specific text. Read through the texts the way you read through music, looking for that special quality that resonates in your deepest places and is worthy of sharing with the members of the choir and the audience or congregation.

Become familiar with the Liturgical Year, the Hours of Divine Office, and the liturgy of the Mass and the Requiem Mass. Know the ecclesiastical season, the office or feast, and the liturgy to which the text is appointed. Introduce the piece to the choir in this way; use this information to enrich other remarks about the composer, historical period and musical structure that you may want to include in program notes or comments to the prospective listener.

Use the readings from the Gospel, Epistle, or Lesson as part of your presentation, or find musical settings of these related texts to program with the one you've already chosen. Program some pieces on the basis of their textual relationship in a single concert or over an entire year's program and let the juxtapositions, comparisons, and relationships speak to the performers and listeners.

Use the SELECTED SETTINGS Appendix to discover and perform settings of Latin texts with original settings of the corresponding English texts: *Absalom, fili mi* (Des Prez) with *When David heard* (Weelkes) or *David's Lamentation* (Billings). Program a group of different settings of the same Latin text:

1. spanning a large historical/stylistic time frame:

Ave Maria	Gregorian, Mode I
Ave Maria	W.A. Mozart
Ave Maria	J. Brahms
Ave Maria	I. Stravinsky

2. written within a single period or century:

Magnificat	A. Gabrieli	*Magnificat*	E. Rautavaara
Magnificat	G. Gabrieli	*Magnificat*	P. Chihara
Magnificat	C. Monteverdi	*Magnificat*	L. Berio

3. written by the same composer:

| *Jubilate Deo a 8* | G. Gabrieli | *Jubilate Deo a 5* | H.L. Hassler |
| *Jubilate Deo a 15* | G. Gabrieli | *Jubilate Deo a 14* | H.L. Hassler |

4. that emphasize different languages and cultures:

Ave Maria	T.L. Victoria	*Pater noster*	J. Handl	*De Profundis*	A. Schoenberg
БОГОРОДИЦЕ ДЕВО	Rachmaninoff	ОТЧЕ НАШЪ	I. Stravinsky	*De Profundis*	I. Lidholm
		Padre nosso	Villa-Lobos		
		Otčenáš	L. Janáček		

In choral music's beginning were the Words, carefully chosen words, as Stravinsky said, "that have been composed to precisely certain music at precisely certain places." Very rarely does a composer write a choral piece and then go in search of a suitable text. Most are like Samuel Barber, who once said: "When I write music for words, I try to immerse myself in the words and let the music flow from them." As performers we too must immerse ourselves in the words, in the sound and sense of the text and context, that we might become worthy channels through which these musical and poetic ideas might again be brought to life and communicated to others. To be the singer is not enough; we must become the song.

that these words
might become flesh
and dwell among us
full of grace and truth

Ron Jeffers
Corvallis, Oregon

The Liturgical Year

ADVENT
(preparation)

1st-2nd Sunday
Gaudete Sunday
Ember Days
4th Sunday

CHRISTMASTIDE
(celebration)

Christmas Day, Dec. 25
Circumcision, Jan. 1
Epiphany, Jan. 6
2nd-6th Sundays (varies)

SEPTUGESIMA
(penitence)

Septuagesima
Sexagesima
Quinquagesima

LENT
(preparation)

Ash Wednesday
1st-3rd Sunday
Laetare Sunday
Passion and Holy Week
Palm Sunday
Maundy Thursday
Good Friday
Holy Saturday

PASCHALTIDE
(celebration)

Easter Sunday
Low Sunday
2nd-5th Sundays
Ascension Thursday

TIME AFTER PENTECOST
(application)

Pentecost Sunday
Trinity Sunday
Corpus Christi
2nd Sunday
Sacred Heart
3rd-last Sunday

THE LITURGICAL YEAR

The liturgical context in which these Sacred Latin Texts appear cannot be understood or fully appreciated without some knowledge of the ecclesiastical cycle, the calendar of the Church year. Unlike the astronomical cycle with its four seasons of equal length and fixed beginning date, the Church year begins with the variable date of the First Sunday in Advent (from November 27 – December 3) and is divided into six periods of unequal length -- Advent, Christmastide, Septuagesima, Lent, Paschaltide, and the Time after Pentecost -- which are determined according to the dates of the three chief feasts of the year: Christmas, Easter, and Pentecost.

ADVENT is a time of *preparation* for the coming feast of Christ's Nativity on December 25. And, at the same time, it is a time of *penitence*, when one is mindful of the <u>second</u> coming and the day of judgement. It is also marked by *praise* and devotion to the Virgin Mother and the joyous "O antiphons" of *Gaudete* Sunday.

CHRISTMASTIDE *celebrates* Christ's Incarnation on Christmas Day, the feasts of St. Stephen (the first Martyr) and St. John the Evangelist, and Christ's Circumcision, his Holy Name, and his Epiphany or manifestations to the Gentiles in the person of the Magi and to others through his miracles and teachings.

SEPTUAGESIMA is the beginning of the *penitential preparation* for Easter during which the *Alleluia, Gloria in excelsis,* and *Te Deum* are not sung. This three-week period of prayer and penance continues into Lent, the most solemn time of mourning and sorrow. The number seventy refers to the period of the Babylonian Captivity and also symbolizes the period of our human sojourn on earth, but it does not literally mean "70 days before Easter." Quadragesima (Lent), beginning with Ash Wednesday, *is* 40 days before Easter Sunday, and the three Sundays before Ash Wednesday are called Quinquagesima, Sexagesima, and Septuagesima respectively.

LENT, which commences with Ash Wednesday, is a 40-day period of *fasting and penance* (recalling Christ's fast in the desert) in preparation for the commemoration of his Passion during Holy Week (Palm Sunday, Maundy Thursday, Good Friday, and Holy Saturday) which leads to the "solemnity of solemnities," the feast of the Resurrection on Easter morn.

PASCHALTIDE is a period of great *celebration and joy*, commemorating Christ's Resurrection and his establishment of the Church in the person of the Apostles during the 40-day period between the Resurrection and his Ascension. *Alleluia* is repeated after every antiphon, the *Gloria in excelsis* is sung at ferial masses, the *Te Deum* is heard daily at Matins, the *Vidi aquam* replaces the *Asperges* before the principal Sunday Mass, and the *Regina coeli LAETARE* replaces the *Angelus*.

The **TIME AFTER PENTECOST** is the longest period in the ecclesiastical cycle, sometimes lasting more than six months. Unlike the period from Advent to Pentecost, which represents a logical, historical cycle (from Christ's Incarnation to his Passion, Death, Resurrection, and Ascension and ending with the descent of the Holy Spirit on Pentecost), the Time after Pentecost consists of a series of unrelated but significant feasts. It is a time of *application*, a time when the Holy Spirit works through the lives and souls of the faithful to accomplish the mission of the Church on earth.

The ecclesiastical calendar is divided into two distinct parts: The Proper of the Time and the Proper of the Saints. The *Proprium Tempore* (Proper of the Time) is composed of the principal feasts of the year which are related to Christ's Incarnation and Redemptive Sacrifice and grouped in three cycles according to the major feasts of Christmas, Easter, and Pentecost. The calendar which follows lists those feasts along with selected feasts of the *Proprium Sanctorum* (Proper of the Saints) which are most relevant to the users of this volume. The list is long, but nowhere near complete, as virtually every day of the Church year is now devoted to feasts in honor of Christ, the Blessed Virgin Mary, the Angels, and the Saints.

THE ECCLESIASTICAL CALENDAR

The First Sunday of Advent

November	30	St. Andrew the Apostle
December	6	St. Nicholas of Myra
	7	St. Ambrose
	8	The Immaculate Conception of the Virgin Mary
	13	St. Lucy
	21	St. Thomas the Apostle
	24	Christmas Eve
	25	THE BIRTHDAY OF THE LORD JESUS CHRIST (Christmas)
	26	St. Stephen the First Martyr
	27	St. John the Evangelist
	28	The Holy Innocents
January	1	The Circumcision of Our Lord Jesus Christ
	6	THE EPIPHANY OF OUR LORD JESUS CHRIST
	24	St. Timothy
	27	St. John Chrysostom

Sunday between the Circumsion and the Epiphany: The Holy Name of Jesus
Monday within the octave of the Epiphany: The Holy Family

February	2	The Purification of the Blessed Virgin Mary (Candlemas)
	14	St. Valentine
	18	St. Simeon

Between February 4 and March 10: Ash Wednesday

March	7	St. Thomas Aquinas
	17	St. Patrick
	21	St. Benedict
	24	St. Gabriel the Archangel
	25	The Annunciation of the Blessed Virgin Mary (Ladyday)
	27	St. John of Damascus

Friday after Passion Sunday: The Compassion of the Blessed Virgin Mary
**Between March 22 and April 25 inclusive: THE RESURRECTION OF THE
LORD JESUS CHRIST (Easter)**

April	25	St. Mark the Evangelist

Third Wednesday after Easter: The Solemnity of St. Joseph

May	1	SS. Philip and James the Apostles
	3	The Finding of the Holy Cross
	27	St. Bede the Venerable

Forty days after Easter: The Ascension of the Lord Jesus Christ

Seven weeks after Easter: PENTECOST (Whitsunday)
The Sunday after Pentecost: The Most Holy Trinity
Thursday after Trinity Sunday: The Blessed Sacrament (Corpus Christi)
Second Friday after Corpus Christi: The Sacred Heart of Jesus

June	2	SS. Marcellinus, Peter, and Erasmus
	14	St. Basil the Great
	21	St. Aloysius Gonzaga
	24	The Birthday of St. John the Baptist
	29	St. Peter and St. Paul the Apostles
July	1	The Precious Blood of the Lord Jesus Christ
	2	The Visitation of the Blessed Virgin Mary
	25	St. James the Elder the Apostle
	29	St. Martha
	31	St. Ignatius Loyola
August	1	St. Peter in Chains
	6	The Transfiguration of the Lord Jesus Christ
	15	The Assumption of the Blessed Virgin Mary
	20	St. Bernard
	22	The Immaculate Heart of Mary
	24	St. Bartholomew the Apostle
	28	St. Augustine of Hippo
	29	The Beheading of St. John the Evangelist
September	8	The Birthday of the Blessed Virgin Mary
	12	The Holy Name of Mary
	14	The Exaltation of the Holy Cross
	15	The Seven Sorrows of the Blessed Virgin Mary
	17	The Imprinting of the Stigmata on St. Francis
	21	St. Matthew the Evangelist
	28	St. Wenceslaus
	29	St. Michael and All Angels (Michaelmas)
	30	St. Jerome
October	4	St. Francis of Assisi
	7	The Holy Rosary of the Blessed Virgin Mary
	11	The Motherhood of the Blessed Virgin Mary
	17	St. Margaret Mary
	18	St. Luke the Evangelist
	24	St. Raphael the Archangel
	28	SS. Simon and Jude the Apostles

Last Sunday in October: Lord Jesus Christ the King

November	1	All Saints
	2	The Commemoration of the Faithful Departed (All Souls' Day)
	9	The Dedication of the Archbasilica of the Saviour
	16	St. Gertrude
	18	The Dedication of the Basilicas of SS. Peter and Paul
	21	The Presentation of the Blessed Virgin Mary
	24	St. John of the Cross

The Hours of Divine Office

Psalmus V

Ení-te, exsultémus Dómino, jubí-lémus Dé-o sa-lutá-ri nóstro : prae-occu-pémus fá-ci-em é-jus in con-fessi- óne, et in psálmis jubi- lémus é- i.

Matins
Lauds
Prime
Terce, Sext, None
Vespers
Compline

THE HOURS OF DIVINE OFFICE

(*officium*, a service, duty)

Divine Office, "a duty accomplished for God," consists of the recitation of prayers at certain fixed hours of the day; it does not include the Mass and other liturgical ceremonies. The ancient Jewish custom of praying at midnight and the third (c. 9 a.m.), sixth (c. 12 noon), and ninth (c. 3 p.m.) hours was also observed by the Apostles (Acts 10:9, 16:25, etc.). The Christians borrowed not only the custom but also the content of these recitations: the recital or chanting of psalms, reading of the Old Testament, to which was soon added reading of the Gospels, Acts, and Epistles, and at times canticles composed or improvised by the assistants.

These elements gradually became the Mass of the Catechumens which preceded the celebration of the Eucharist. When the Eucharist was not celebrated, these recitations became independent offices and evolved by the end of the 6th century, under the strong codifying influence of Pope Gregory the Great (d. 604), into the Hours of Divine Office: **Matins, Lauds, Prime, Terce, Sext, None, Vespers,** and **Compline.**

MATINS

(*matuta*, goddess of the morning)

Matins, which comes from *Matuta*, the Latin name for the Greek goddess Leucothæ ("white goddess, goddess of the morning"), was originally said at dawn (now Lauds). The night–office, then known as "Vigils," was gradually combined with Matins, the latter serving as the closing part of Vigils. The name Matins was then later extended to the office of Vigils and subdivided into three Nocturns (one toward 9 p.m., another at Midnight, and the other at 3 a.m.) and the dawn office was given the name "Lauds" after the three *Laudate* psalms (Psalms 148–150) that are associated with it.

It has been, by virtue of its length, its position and content, the principal Office of the Church, notable for the variety and richness of its elements and distinguishing itself from the other Offices in the following ways:

    1. The first 108 Psalms (with a few exceptions) were recited each week (18 at Sunday Office and 12 at each ferial Office) with numerous Responses (the single precentor being answered by the choir instead of the antiphonic form of two choirs alternately reciting the psalms).

    2. The Lessons comprise the most important parts of the Old and New Testament, extracts from the Church Fathers, the legends of the Martyrs and the Saints, and extracts from all the Books of the Bible.

    3. It commences with a more solemn Invitatory (Psalm 94 [95] : "O come, let us sing unto the Lord") and closes, on certain days, with the Finale or *Te Deum* after the ninth lesson.

    4. The subdivision into three Nocturns (rarely observed except in some monasteries or for some of the more solemn feasts) is also unique.

LAUDS

(lauds, praises)

The Morning Office or Office of Aurora corresponding to **Lauds** is one of the most ancient offices and can be traced back to Apostolic times. Originally the word *Lauds* designated only the three *Laudate* psalms which are recited every day at the conclusion of this morning office. Gradually the name *Lauds* was applied to the whole office and the title *Matins* was given to the Night Office or Vigils. Lauds is thus the concluding nocturnal office, an office of great praise recited at dawn, recalling the memory of Christ's Resurrection and the bringing of light and illumination to a world of darkness.

The psalms used at Lauds, unlike those of Matins and Vespers, do not follow the order of the Psalter but rather are chosen because of their allusions to the break of day, the Resurrection of Christ, or the prayer of the morning. In addition, Psalm 50 [51] ("Have mercy upon me, O God"), Psalm 62 [63] ("O God, thou art my God; early will I seek thee"), and the three *Laudate* psalms (Psalm 148 – "Praise ye the Lord from the heavens," Psalm 149 – "Sing unto the Lord a new song," and Psalm 150 – "Praise God in his sanctuary") are sung every day.

Another distinguishing characteristic of this office are the seven Old Testament canticles which take place between Psalms 50 and 62 and the three *Laudate* psalms:

> On Sundays, the Canticle "Benedicite" (Daniel 3:57)
> On Mondays, the Canticle of Isaiah (Isaiah 12)
> On Tuesdays, the Canticle of Ezechias (Isaiah 38:10–20)
> On Wednesdays, the Canticle of Anna (I Kings 2:1–10)
> On Thursdays, the Canticle of Moses (Exodus 15:1–19)
> On Fridays, the Canticle of Habakkuk (Habakkuk 3:2–19)
> On Saturdays, the Canticle of Moses (Deuteronomy 32:1–43)

To these canticles the Roman liturgy adds, as the Finale to this office, the canticle of Zachary (Luke 1:68–79), commonly referred to as the *Benedictus* (from its first word).

The hymns of Lauds are also very ancient and they, too, generally celebrate the break of day, the Resurrection of Christ, and the spiritual light which He has made to shine on earth.

THE LITTLE HOURS OF DIVINE OFFICE

Prime, Terce, Sext, and **None** have come to be called The Little Hours of Divine Office. The fact that these hours originated as private prayers accounts for their being less solemn than the "greater hours" of **Lauds** and **Vespers** which were once the official worship of the whole people.

PRIME

(prima hora, first hour)

Prime is the second morning prayer, following the night office of Matins and the first prayer of Lauds at sunrise. It was first instituted at a Bethlehem monastery because the monks retired after Lauds and slept until nine in the morning (Terce); so, "to prevent an undue prolongation of sleep, the monks were called to choir at the hour of Prime [about 6 a.m.] and, after the recital of a few psalms, they were to work until Terce" (Cassian, c.392). This office was later adopted by St. Benedict (c.525) and the apportioning of the psalms was settled by Pius X in 1914.

The first part of the office is a prayer service consisting of a hymn and some psalms, a little chapter (*capitulum*) replacing the lesson, a responsory, *Kyrie eleison*, the *Pater Noster* and versicles, the confession of sins, and a prayer.

The second portion is a special service held in the chapter house of the monastery consisting, since the 9th century of the reading of the Martyrology (sometimes accompanied by the Necrology, the list of the anniversary commemoration of deceased brethren and benefactors) and prayers for the consecration of the day's work.

TERCE, SEXT, NONE

(tertia/sexta/nona hora, third/sixth/ninth hour)

The origin of **Terce, Sext,** and **None** is far more ancient than that of Prime, dating back to Apostolic times. It was customary among the Jews to offer private prayers at the third, sixth, and ninth hours of the day. Tertullian (c.200) states that "there should be no lax observation of certain hours [of prayer], those common hours that have long marked the divisions of the day -- the third, the sixth, and the ninth -- and which we may observe in Scripture to be more solemn than the rest."

TERCE (c. 9 a.m.) corresponds to the hour of Christ's condemnation to death; it is also associated with the mystical symbolism of the number three (the Trinity, the Trisagion or Thrice Holy, etc.). But it is its association with the descent of the Holy Spirit upon the Apostles at Pentecost (Acts 2:15) that gives Terce its special dignity and meaning.

SEXT (c. 12 noon) is the hour when St. Peter went up to pray (Acts 10:9) and, according to St. Ambrose, the time when the Divine light is at its fullest (cf. Psalm 118 [119] : 62). Abraham received the three angels, an image of the Trinity, at the sixth hour; Adam and Eve ate the fatal apple at this hour. But it was Christ's being crucified at this hour that made the deepest impact on the liturgy of Sext.

NONE (c. 3 p.m.) marked the close of the business day in ancient times; it was the time for the baths and the evening meal. St. Basil points out that the Apostles Peter and John went to pray at the Temple at the ninth hour. Amalarius compares the sinking of the sun at this hour to the lowering of man's spirit and his resistance to the temptation of the evil one. Others believe it is the hour when Adam and Eve were expelled from the Garden of Paradise. But it is the death of Christ that is mostly commemorated at this hour.

Thus the three final moments of Christ's passion -- condemnation, crucifixion, and death -- are associated with Terce, Sext, and None. St. Cyprian (*De oratione*) sees the three hours, each of which comes after a lapse of three hours, as an allusion to the Holy Trinity. They have all three been established as canonical hours since the 4th century. And although the liturgy has varied according to time and place (i.e., in certain countries, three psalms were assigned to Terce, six to Sext, and nine to None; others use three at each hour; etc.), the basic structure is the same: the *Deus in adjutorem* (Psalm 69 [70] : "Make haste, O God, to deliver me"), a hymn, three psalms, a short response, an oration, and the dismissal.

V E S P E R S

(*vespera*, evening, the evening meal)

Vespers, the evening service which consecrates the end of the day, is, together with Vigils, the most ancient Office known in the Church. It is derived from the *Lucernarium*, the Jewish blessing of lights that comes at the close of the Sabbath feast. The use of incense, candles, and other lights were originally connected with the Eucharistic agape, the common liturgical evening meal ("This is what thou shalt sacrifice upon the altar: Two lambs of a year old every day continually. One lamb in the morning and another in the evening" – Exodus 29:38-39); but eventually the agape was dropped and the *Lucernarium* became simply an appointed time of prayer. The blessing of the Paschal candle during the Easter Vigil and the offering of incense at the daily singing of the *Magnificat* at Vespers are the only remaining vestiges of this early custom.

The structure of Vespers has changed little since the 6th century: the introductory *Deus in adjutorum* (Psalm 69 [70] : "Make haste, O God, to deliver me") is followed by the singing of five antiphons and five psalms, a *capitulum*, a hymn with its versicle and response, the Canticle of Mary (the *Magnificat*, Luke 1:46-55) with its antiphon, the Collect of the day, and the dismissal (*Benedicamus Domino*).

The *Magnificat* is one of the most characteristic features of Vespers, a liturgical element it has retained throughout centuries without change, "a sign of the devotion which has always been paid to the Blessed Virgin in the Church." So, too, are the Vesper Psalms (Lucernal psalms): 109 [110] : *Dixit Dominus* ("The Lord said to my Lord"); 110 [111] : *Confitebor Tibi* ("I will praise you, O Lord, with my whole heart"); 111 [112] : *Beatus vir* (Blessed is the man who fears the Lord"); 112 [113] : *Laudate Pueri* ("Praise the Lord, ye children"); and 116 [117] : *Laudate Dominum omnes gentes* ("Praise the Lord, all ye nations").

The ancient hymns (c. 6th century) that have been consecrated to Vespers are all devoted to the praise of one of the days of the Creation: on the first day, Sunday, the hymn gives praise to the creation of light (*Lucis Creator Optime* ("O great Creator of light"); on the second day, Monday, to the separation of earth and the waters; on the third, to the creation of plants; fourthly, to the creation of the sun and moon; fifthly, to the creation of fish of the sea and the fowls of the air; and on Friday, to the creation of the beasts of the earth; Saturday is an exception: its hymn is in honor of the Blessed Trinity, because the Office of Sunday is then commencing.

St. Benedict (c. 525) had Vespers sung in his monasteries; Cassiodorus (c.540) refers to "the evening office of *Lucernarium*." And Amalarius, in the 9th century, speaks of singing Vespers on the eve of a major feast, a practice that survives today when I. Vespers are sung on the eve of a major feast and II. Vespers on the day of the feast.

COMPLINE

(completorium, ending; from *complere*, to complete)

Compline is the Office which completes the daily round of prayer and praise. The origins of this office date back to the 4th century monastic custom of saying private prayer in the dormitory before retiring (Eusebius; St. Ambrose; Cassian). St. Basil established an intermediate hour between Vespers and the night office at his retreat in Pontius (358–362). But it was St. Benedict, at the beginning of the 6th century, that gave the Office its name and invested it with its liturgical character and arrangement: three psalms (Psalms 4, 89 [90], and 132 [133]) to be sung straight on without an antiphon, a hymn (since the 16th century: *Te lucis ante terminum*, "To Thee, Creator of the day's last light"), the lesson, the versicle *Kyrie eleison*, the benediction, and the dismissal.

To this the Roman Church added a fourth psalm (Psalm 30 [31] : *In te, Domine, speravi*, "In thee, O Lord, have I hoped"), the reciting of the *Confiteor*, the response from Psalm 30 [31] ("*In manus tuas, Domine,* "Into thy hands, O Lord, I commend my spirit"), and the Gospel Canticle of Simeon, the *Nunc dimittis* ("Now let thy servant depart in peace").

The Office of Compline closes with the collect *Visita* ("Visit, we beseech thee, O Lord, this dwelling"), a blessing, and the Marian Antiphon appointed to the season which, more than half the year, is the *Salve Regina*.

8. TE lúcis ante términum, Rérum Cre- átor, póscimus,
Ut pro tú-a cleménti- a, Sis praésul et custódi- a.

Glossary of Terms

G L O S S A R Y   O F   T E R M S

Advent. (L *adventus*, a coming, approach, arrival) The beginning of the *Liturgical Year, a period of prayer in preparation for *Christmas, including four Sundays, the first being the one nearest to the feast of St. Andrew (Nov. 30). [see THE LITURGICAL YEAR]

Agnus Dei. (*Agnus Dei*, Lamb of God) The fifth and final portion of the *Ordinary of the *Mass; it is sung near the end of the Canon, between the Fraction (Breaking of the Bread) and the Communion antiphon. [see THE ROMAN MASS]

All Saints' Day. A feast commemorating all the saints of God, canonized or uncanonized, known or unknown, celebrated in the Western church on Nov. 1 (formerly called All Hallows' in England).

All Souls' Day. A solemn feast that commemorates all the Faithful departed; observed on Nov. 2 (or, if that falls on a Sunday, Nov. 3).

Alleluia. (Heb *halelû*, imperative of *hillel*, to praise + Jah, abbreviated form of *Jahvè*, God; praise ye Yahweh; praise to him who is. The present spelling is taken from the *Septuagint form Ἀλλελούϊα.) An ancient liturgical form of jubilation found frequently in the *Psalms, once in the Book of Tobit (13:18), and four times in Revelations (19:1, 3, 4, and 6, the well-known "Alleluia: for the Lord God omnipotent reigneth"). In the Roman Liturgy it is used after the *Gradual, before the Gospel, except from *Septuagesima Sunday to *Holy Saturday, in *Requiem Masses, on *Ember Days, and most *Vigils. It came into liturgical use quite early untranslated, like other Hebrew words *Amen, *Hosanna, and *Sabaoth. *Alleluia* is a liturgical mystical expression, an acclamation and ovation beyond grammatical explanation, "man's most ancient expression of devotion [and] monotheistic faith -- the true believer's primitive Credo, primitive doxology, primitive acclamation" (T.J. O'Mahony).

Alleluia-Verse. (*versus alleluiaticus*, Alleluiatic Verse) The third chant of the *Proper of the *Mass; it is sung immediately after the *Gradual, between the Epistle and the Gospel. From *Septuagesima to *Good Friday, on *Ember Days, some *Vigils, and at *Requiems it is replaced by the *Tract.

Amen. (Gr,L *amen*, verily; Heb. *amen*, verily, sobeit; from *aman*, to confirm) A solemn prayerful affirmation, acclamation of assent, or confirmation of one's own thoughts.

Angelus. The practice of honoring God and his Incarnation and commemorating the angel Gabriel's annunciation to the Blessed Virgin by saying three Hail Marys, some sentences, and a collect at morning, noon, and evening (all signalled by the ringing of the Angelus bell). The sentence begins: *Angelus Domini nuntiavit Mariae* ("The angel of the Lord declared unto Mary"), and thus the name. In *Paschal Time the *Regina coeli, laetare* ("Queen of heaven, rejoice") is recited instead of the Angelus.

Antiphon. (Gr *anti*, opposite of + *phone*, voice: *antiphona*) The antiphonal singing of a *psalm or *hymn, i.e., when alternate verses are sung by each side of the choir. This practice was attributed by Socrates to St. Ignatius, but Theodoret says it was begun at Antioch in Constantine's reign by the two monks Flavian and Diodorus. The earliest instance of the custom in the Latin Church associated with St. Ambrose (d. 397). Antiphons are also short verses sung before and after a *psalm or *canticle.

Antiphonal chants. The three chants (the *Introit, *Offertory, and *Communion) which are sung alternately by the choir to accompany the entrance or preparatory prayers, the offertory, and the cleansing of the vessels.

Antiphonary. A liturgical book containing the chant (*antiphons, *psalms, *hymns, etc.) of all sung parts of Divine *Office.

Antiphons of the Blessed Virgin Mary. Unlike the shorter *antiphons which serve to introduce and comment upon a *psalm or *canticle, these four chants are independent songs of considerable length and elaboration; each is said or sung after *Compline in the Divine *Office:

> *Alma Redemptoris Mater* – sung during *Advent until the *Purification of the Virgin Mary
> *Ave Regina Coelorum* – sung from then until Wednesday in *Holy Week
> *Regina coeli laetare* – sung from then until *Whitsun
> *Salve Regina* – sung from the *Octave of Whitsun until Advent

H.T. Henry notes that these four antiphons "run the gamut of medieval literary style, from the classical hexameters of the *Alma Redemptoris Mater*, through the richly-rhymed accentual rhythm and regular strophes of the *Ave Regina coelorum*, the irregular syntonic strophe of the *Regina coeli*, down to the sonorous prose rhythms (with rhyming closes) of the *Salve Regina*" (*Catholic Encyclopedia*).

Ascension, Feast of the.   A feast kept on the fortieth day after *Easter Sunday to commemorate Christ's ascent into heaven.

Ash Wednesday.   Now the first day of the forty days of *Lent (*Quadragesima), it was originally a 36-day fast ending on *Easter Day, but by adding the four days preceding the first Sunday of Lent, it became forty days, and accords with the fasts of Moses and Elias, and with that of Christ in the wilderness. It takes its name from the ceremony during which the priest blesses the ashes and then places them on the heads of each of the faithful saying: *Momento, homo, quia pulvis est, et in pulverem reverteris* ("Remember, man, that thou art dust, and unto dust thou shalt return").

Asperges, The.   (L *asperges*, thou wilt sprinkle) The ceremonial sprinkling of the people with holy water before the principal Sunday Mass during which the *antiphon *Asperges me, Domine* ("Thou wilt sprinkle me, O Lord") is sung and, from which, it takes its name. During Paschaltide it is replaced by the *Vidi aquam*.

Assumption, Feast of the.   The principal feast of the Blessed Virgin Mary which commemorates the taking into heaven of her soul and body (Aug. 15).

Benedictus.   (*Benedictus qui venit*, Blessed is he who comes) That portion of the *Mass which, along with the *Sanctus and *Hosanna forms the fourth part of the *Ordinary of the *Mass. It follows the Sanctus, and is itself preceeded and followed by the Hosanna; sometimes it is replaced or grouped with the motet **O salutaris hostia**. [see THE ROMAN MASS]

Breviary.   A book which, as its name implies, is an abridgement or compendium of the various books needed for the due performance of the Divine *Office, consisting of the *Psalter, the *Proper of the season, the *Proper of the Saints, the *Common, and certain special offices (i.e., the *Office of the Dead, etc.)

Canonical Hours.   The whole of the obligatory prayers which the Church appoints to be recited by clerics, beneficiaries, and "religious men and women who are bound by their rule to the office of choir" at the different *Hours of Divine *Office for each day; the book or collection of these prayers came to be known as the "book of hours."

Capitulum.   A little "chapter" -- a hymn with its versicle and response.

Catechumen.   (Gr *katekhouminos*, one instructed) A learner, one receiving instruction preparatory to being baptized and admitted into the Church (see *Mass of the Catechumens).

Christmas.   (OE *Cristes Maesse*, first found in 1038, or *Cristes-messe*, in 1131, Mass of Christ) Christ's Mass, the Feast of the Nativity of Jesus Christ. The actual date of Christ's birth is not known, but most scholars believe it was assigned the date of the winter solstice (Dec. 25 in the Julian calendar) as it gradually replaced the solar feast (*Natalis Invicti*, Birthday of the Invincible Sun) during the 4th century. The Feast of Christmas has three proper Masses, one at midnight, another at dawn, and on the day itself, going back to the custom originally practiced by a pope who celebrated a midnight mass in Rome's Liberian Basilica (where traditionally the manger of Bethlehem is preserved), a second in the nearby Church of Anastasia (whose feast falls on Dec. 25), and a third at the Vatican Basilica.

Christmastide.   The season of *Christmas, generally understood to extend from midnight of Christmas Eve to *Epiphany (Jan. 6). [see THE LITURGICAL YEAR]

Collects.   Prayers (at first, improvised, and, later, written) which are offered in the name of all the faithful; as these prayers usually sum up the main idea dominating a feast, the significance of a certain festival can be sought in them.

Common. All the *lessons, gospels, *antiphons, *responsories, and *versicles which are not reserved for a special occasion, but may be employed for a whole group of saints, including the Apostles, Evangelists, Confessors, Virgins, Holy Women, Martyrs, and the Blessed Virgin.

Communion. (1) The *antiphon recited by the priest after the ablutions; formerly sung while the people communicated, hence the name. (2) The eighth portion (*Lux perpetua luceat eis*, Light eternal shine upon them) of a musical setting of the *Requiem Mass (Mass for the Dead). [see THE REQUIEM MASS]

Compline. The concluding ("completing") *hour of the daily *office of the Roman Church, consisting of *lessons, *psalms, *a hymn, the *Pater noster* ("Our Father") and *Confitebor* ("I give praise to you, O Lord"), the *canticle of Simeon, *Nunc dimittis* ("Now let thy servant depart in peace"), a prayer, and the *antiphon of the day. [see THE HOURS OF DIVINE OFFICE]

Corpus Christi. (L *corpus christi*, the body of Christ) Established for the Thursday after *Trinity Sunday (the 8th Sunday after *Easter), its *Mass and *Office attributed to St. Thomas Aquinas, this solemn feast commemorates the institution of the *Holy Sacrament. [see **O sacrum convivium**]

Credo. (*Credo in unum Deum*, I believe in one God) The third part of the *Ordinary of the *Mass; it is sung or recited between the Gospel and the Offertory. The twelve central assertions of the Christian faith are articulated in the text known as the Nicene Creed. [see THE ROMAN MASS]

Doxology. (Gr *doxa*, opinion + *logia*, science, knowledge) The Greater Doxology or "ascription of glory"--the *Gloria in excelsis* ("Glory in the highest")--gradually assumed its place in the *Mass [see THE ROMAN MASS] and is said in all Masses, except those of the dead, of *ferias which do not occur in the *Paschal season (except *Maundy Thursday), or on the Sundays of *Advent or those Sundays from *Septuagesima to *Palm Sunday inclusive. The Lesser Doxology--the *Gloria Patri* ("Glory be to the Father")--is usually recited after each *psalm in the *office and after the *Judica* psalm (Ps.42 [43]) in the Mass.

Douay Bible. The Church's 16th-17th century translation of the Bible done from the Latin Vulgate, compared with Greek and Hebrew sources; it strives for accuracy rather than style.

Easter. The Sunday feast which celebrates and commemorates Christ's rising from the dead. The exultant *Alleluia is constantly repeated in the *Mass and Divine *Office, the *Vidi Aquam* replaces the *Asperges me, and the *Regina coeli* the *Angelus. (St. Bede derives the name from *Eastre*, a Teutonic goddess of dawn and spring.)

Ember Days. (from OE *ymbrendæg*, from *ymbrene*, circuit, anniversary + *dæg*, day) Three days set aside for fasting, abstinence, and prayer during each of the four seasons of the *Liturgical Year (called *Quattour Tempora* in the *Breviary and *Missal)--the Wednesday, Friday, and Saturday after the feast of St. Lucy (Dec. 13), the first Sunday of *Lent and *Pentecost, and the feast of the Holy Cross (Sept. 14).

Epiphany, Feast of the. (Gr *epiphaneia*, appearance, manifestation) The feast held on Jan. 6 which commemorates the manifestation of Jesus Christ to the gentiles in the persons of the Magi, his baptism in Jordan, and the first miracle of Cana. Sometimes referred to as Twelfth Night (after *Christmas).

Eucharist. (L *eucharista*, thanksgiving, thankfulness; from Gr *eucharistia*, gratitude) The true Body and Blood of Jesus Chirst, who is really and substantially present under the appearances of bread and wine, in order to offer himself in the sacrifice of the Mass and to be received as spiritual food in Holy Communion. It is called Eucharist, or "thanksgiving," because at its institution at the Last Supper Christ "gave thanks."

Euouae. The vowels of *seculorum, amen* (from *et in secula seculorum, amen*, and for generations of generations, amen) used for the various cadential formulas (*differentia*) found at the close of some gregorian chants.

Feria. (L *feria*, feast) The name given in the liturgical calendar to all days of the week except Sunday (*dies dominica*, the Lord's Day) and Saturday (*Sabbatum*, the Sabbath) on which no special ecclesiastical feast or *vigil is celebrated in the *Mass or Liturgy of the *Hours.

Forty Hours. A devotion in honor of the forty hours Christ spent in the tomb. After High Mass the Blessed Sacrament is exposed on the altar for forty hours while people come continuously to watch and pray.

Gaudete Sunday. (L *gaudete*, rejoice; from the Introit of the Third Sunday in *Advent, *Gaudete in Domino semper,* Rejoice in the Lord always, and again I say, rejoice) A day of rejoicing in a penitential season; rose-colored vestments may be worn, "the organ finds its voice" after two weeks of silence, and flowers may be placed on the altar.

Gentile. (ME, from L *gent-, gens*, nation) A person of a non-Jewish nation or faith.

Gloria. (*Gloria in excelsis Deo*, Glory to God in the highest) The second part of the *Ordinary of the *Mass, a hymn of praise sung immediately after the *Kyrie during the Entrance rite of the Roman Church. It is sung on all festal occasions, except the masses of the dead, the Sundays in *Advent, and those Sundays from *Septuagesima to *Easter inclusive. [see THE ROMAN MASS]

Gloria in excelsis. See *Doxology.

Gloria Patri. See *Doxology.

Good Friday. See *Holy Week.

Gradual. (L *gradus*, a step) An *antiphon sung after the Epistle, so called either because it used to be sung on the altar steps, or because it was sung while the deacon ascended the steps to sing the Gospel. In earlier times there were two *lessons before the Gospel, one from the Old Testament and the other the Epistle proper. The Gradual followed the first, and the *Alleluia or *Tract followed the second.

Greater Antiphons. See *O Antiphons.

Holy Saturday. See *Holy Week.

Holy Week. The week immediately preceding *Easter, from Passion (Palm) Sunday through Holy Saturday, during which the Church commemorates the death and burial of Christ--the Week of the Holy Passion.

> *Passion (Palm) Sunday.* The Sunday before *Easter, the first day in Holy Week, when Christ's triumphal entry in Jerusalem is commemorated by the blessing and procession of palms. The Mass itself concerns the Passion of Good Friday prophesied in the *tract for the day (Ps.21 [22] : "My God, my God, why hast thou forsaken me?").

> *Tenebrae.* (*tenebrae*, darkness) The name formerly given to the *Matins and *Lauds of the day which are usually sung on the Thursday, Friday, and Saturday of Holy Week. Various portions of the *office (the *Gloria Patri*, the *Antiphons of the Blessed Virgin Mary, etc.) are omitted in sign of sorrow; the *lessons of the first *nocturn are taken from the Lamentations of Jeremiah; and fifteen lighted candles are extinguished, one by one, at the conclusion of each *psalm till only one is left, signifying the growing darkness of the time when Christ the Light of the World was taken and crucified. The last candle is hidden, but not extinguished (signifying that death has no dominion over Christ), and then later brought out at the end of the *office.

> *Maundy Thursday.* (ME *maunde*, ceremony of washing the feet of the poor on Maundy Thursday; from OF *maundé*, L *mandatum*, command [cf. John 13:34]) The Thursday of Holy Week, the anniversary of the Lord's Supper, when Christ instituted the *Eucharist, the Sacrifice of the *Mass, and the sacrament of the priesthood. Only one Mass is offered, and that in the evening. The *hymn *Pange lingua* ("Sing, O tongue") is sung during the procession of the Blessed Sacrament to the Selpulchre or altar of repose,

recalling Christ's journey to the Mount of Olives following the Lord's Supper; the altars are stripped as Christ was stripped of His garments; the *Mandatum* or washing of the feet (from *Mandatum novum . . .*, A new commandment I give unto you--John 13:34; whence our English term Maundy Thursday) and the consecration of the Holy Oils follows.

Good Friday. This most sad and solemn day of the year commemorates the Passion of Christ as told in the Gospel of John. Prayers are offered for all conditions of men; the Improperia ("Reproaches") and the Trisagion are sung; the Blessed Sacrament is borne in procession while the *antiphons *Adoremus Te, Christe* ("We adore Thee, O Christ"), etc. are sung. This is followed by the *Pater Noster* ("Our Father") and Holy Communion, ending with the singing of three Post-communions.

Holy Saturday. The eve of Easter, a day of mourning for Christ in the tomb, until the vigil of the Resurrection in the late evening or during the night. This evening service begins with the blessing of the new fire which is used to light the Easter Candle which, marked with the sign of the Cross and adorned with five grains of incense representing the five glorious wounds of Christ, is then carried in solemn procession (*Lumens Christi*, Light of Christ) and used to light the candles of the celebrant and clergy and the lights of the church. At the *Gloria in excelsis*, the organ sounds and bells are rung for the first time since *Maundy Thursday, and the joyful *Alleluia peals forth after the Epistle. The *Agnus Dei, which was never added to this *Mass, and the Communion and Post-communion are simply replaced by the *lauds of the day.

Hosanna. (Heb *ho shi an a*, save me; an exclamation of joy) A shout of joy and triumph, presently heard twice at the Sanctus of the *Mass and on *Palm Sunday in imitation of the acclamations that accompanied Christ's triumphal entry into Jerusalem. [see THE ROMAN MASS]

Hours. The liturgical division of the day (founded on the ancient Roman divisions) into periods of approximately three hours each (the length varies depending on the seasons): *Prime (toward 6 a.m.), *Terce (toward 9 a.m.), *Sext (toward 12 noon), *None (toward 3 p.m.), *Vespers (toward 6 p.m.), and the Night *Vigils: *Matins (which is subdivided into three *Nocturns - 9 p.m., Midnight, and 3 a.m.) and *Lauds, which is to be recited at dawn. *Compline is recited at nightfall. (see THE HOURS OF DIVINE OFFICE)

Hymn. (L *hymnus*, song of praise) A religious poem, written in metre, sung or spoken in praise of God. Hilary of Poitiers (c.315-c368) is the first hymn writer whose hymns survive; others include Ambrose (340?-397), Gregory the Great (c.540-604), Venerable Bede (673-735), St. Bernard of Clairvaux (c.1090-1153), and St. Thomas Aquinas (c.1225-1274) who wrote *Lauda Sion* and *Pange lingua gloriosi*.

Immaculate Conception, Feast of the. The doctrine of the Immaculate Conception refers to the belief that the soul of the Virgin Mary was, at the first moment of its creation and infusion into her body, clothed in sanctifying grace and "preserved exempt from the stain of original sin." (It does not refer to the virgin birth of Christ or Mary.) The feast, under the title of "Conception of our Lady," was apparently not observed in the West much before the 11th century. In 1863 a new *Mass and *Office was provided and the word "Immaculate" added to the name; it is observed on Dec. 8.

Introit. (L *introitus*, entrance, from *intro-*, within + *ire*, to go) (1) The entrance or introductory rite of the *Mass, said at the beginning of the Mass as the clergy enters to the altar, consisting of an *antiphon (usually from the psalms), a psalm-verse, the *Gloria Patri*, and the antiphon repeated. (2) The opening movement (*Requiem aeternam dona eis*, Rest eternal grant unto them) of a musical setting of the *Requiem Mass, or Mass for the Dead. [see THE REQUIEM MASS]

Invitatory. The Invitatory psalm--Psalm 94 [95]: *Venite exultemus Domino* ("O come, let us rejoice before the Lord")--is sung at the beginning of *Matins on all days except the *Epiphany (where it appears as the third *nocturn) and the last three days of *Holy Week.

Jubilus.   The long, elaborate, joyful melismatic extension of the final syllable of the *Alleluia-Verse; it is related to the *jubilationes*, or *jubilare sine verbis* ("jubilations, to rejoice without words"), textless acclamations which were sung in fields and vineyards, on ships and during military campaigns from the 4th to the 6th centuries. "The Alleluia is short in word and long in neum, because that joy is too great to be expressed in words ... the *jubilus* at the end denotes the joy and love of the faithful" (Durandus). "We rejoice rather than sing ... and prolong the neums that the mind be surpirsed and filled with the joyful sound, and be carried thither where the saints rejoice in glory" (Rupert of Deut, 12th century).

Kyrie.   (*Kyrie eleison*, Lord have mercy upon us) The first part of the *Ordinary of the *Mass, a part of the opening Entrance rite of the Roman Church. It is sung immediately following the *Introit. [see THE ROMAN MASS]

Laudate Psalms.   The last three psalms of the *Psalter: Psalm 148 – *Laudate Dominum de caelis*, Psalm 149 – *Cantate Domino*, and Psalm 150 – *Laudate Dominum in sanctis ejus*. Called the *Laudate* psalms because the word *laudate* ("praise") functions like a leitmotiv in each of them, they are sung at the dawn office of *Lauds each day.

Lauds.   The concluding nocturnal office, an office of great praise recited at dawn recalling the memory of Christ's Resurrection and the bringing of light into a world of darkness. Composed of certain psalms and Old Testament *canticles, it derives its name from and is especially notable for the three *Laudate* psalms of praise (Psalms 148-150) which are said every day at the conclusion of this office. [see THE HOURS OF DIVINE OFFICE]

Lent.   (OE *lencten*, the spring season) The forty days (*Quadragesima) of penitence, prayer, and fasting from *Ash Wednesday to *Holy Saturday observed as a preparation for the passion, death, and resurrection of Jesus Christ. (For forty years the Israelites wandered, forty days Moses was on Mt. Sinai, Elias fasted, the Flood lasted, and Jesus Christ was in the wilderness of Judea.) Each day has its special *Mass (composed since the 7th and 8th centuries), very few feasts are observed, the organ is not played, the *Gloria in excelsis* and *Alleluia are omitted, etc.

Lessons.   Readings which follow the reading of the Holy Writ that are chosen from the Scriptures, commentaries of the Fathers (St. Augustine, St. Hilary, *et alia*) and other ecclesiastical writers to comment upon the passage of the Bible just previously heard.

Liber Usualis.   (L "Book of common practice or general use") The collection of prayers, lessons, and chants prescribed by the Council of Trent for most of the important services of the Roman Church; it was first issued by the Benedictines of Solesmes in 1896.

LU.   See *Liber usualis.

Mass.   (L *missa*, a form of *missio*, dismissal; from *mittere*, to send) The complex of prayers and ceremonies whose essential element is the celebration of the Holy Eucharist, a commemoration of the Last Supper of Christ and his Apostles. It is divided into two main parts: the Mass of the Catechumens (the Liturgy of the Word) and the Mass of the Faithful (the Celebration of the Eucharist). There were two solemn dismissals in the early liturgy--first, of the *catechumens after the Gospel and homily; next, of the faithful at the end of the service. The word for dismissal (*missa*) gradually came to denote the service from which the people were dismissed. There are many kinds of masses, some of the principal ones being the *Missa Solemnis (High Mass), *Missa bassa (Low Mass), *Votive Masses, the *Requiem Mass, etc. [see THE ROMAN MASS and THE REQUIEM MASS]

Mass of the Catechumens.   [see THE ROMAN MASS]

Matins.   The ancient Night Office, or *Office of the *Vigil, gradually became known as "Matins" and was subdivided into three *Nocturns (one towards 9 p.m., another at Midnight, and the other at 3 a.m.).   It is the principal Office of the Roman Church, characterized by the *responsorial singing of the Psalms, diverse and profound *Lessons, a solemn *Invitatory (Ps. 94 [95]), and, on certain days, the reciting or singing of the *Te Deum after the ninth lesson. [see THE HOURS OF DIVINE OFFICE]

Maundy Thursday.   See *Holy Week.

Missa bassa.   Low Mass, a Mass without music, the priest at least saying, not singing throughout. (Fr *Messe Basse*)

Missa Solemnis.   High Mass (missa alta), with incense, music, and the assistance of deacon and sub-deacon, etc.   It is usually sung. (Ger *Hochamt*)

Nocturns.   The three subdivisions of the night office of *Matins (9 p.m., Midnight, and 3 a.m.) which consist of the chanting of the psalms and the reading from Holy Scripture, the Law and the Prophets, the Gospel and the Epistle, and a short homily. [see THE HOURS OF DIVINE OFFICE]

None.   One of the "Little Hours" of Divine Office; celebrated at c. 3 p.m. [see THE HOURS OF DIVINE OFFICE]

O Antiphons.   (L *Antiphoniae majores*, the Greater Antiphons)   The seven antiphons to the *Magnificat* at *Vespers on the seven days preceding Christmas Eve, so-called because they each begin with the interjection "O" as they address the Messiah with a title inspired by the Old Testament [*O Sapientia*, O Wisdom - Ecclesiastes 24:5; *O Adonai*, O Sacred Lord - Exodus 6:13; *O Radix Jesse*, O Flower of Jesse's stem - Isaiah 11:10; *O Clavis David*, O Key of David - Apocalypse [Revelation] 3:7 (Isaiah 22:22); *O Oriens*, O Radiant Dawn - Zacharias 6:12; *O Rex Gentium*, O King of all nations - Aggeus 2:8; and *O Emmanuel* O Emmanuel - Isaiah 7:14; 8:8.

Offertory.   (1) An *antiphon which was sung while the faithful made their offerings of bread and wine for the *Mass, gifts for the support of the clergy, etc.   It also refers to the oblation of bread and wine by the priest made after the recitation of the Offertory *antiphon.   (2) The fourth movement (*Domine Jesu Christe*, Lord Jesus Christ) of a musical setting of the *Requiem Mass, or Mass for the Dead. [see THE REQUIEM MASS]

Office (Divine Office).   (*officium*, a service, duty)   The prayers and ceremonies for a particular day or feast, including *Mass and any other observances. [see THE HOURS OF DIVINE OFFICE]

Office of the Dead.   An *office for the repose of the souls of the dead, consisting of *Vespers, *Matins, and *Lauds.   It is obligatory only on *All Souls' Day, Nov. 2, and is also sung or said in choir on the day of death.

Octave.   (L *octava*, eighth)   The commemoration of a feast over a period of eight days, including the feast itself.   Only Easter and Christmas now have the Octave, which means no other feast will be celebrated during that time.

Ordinary of the Mass.   (*Ordinarium Missae*)   The parts of the *Mass that are mostly unchanging, namely the *Kyrie, *Gloria, *Credo, *Sanctus et *Benedictus, and the *Agnus Dei. [see THE ROMAN MASS]

Palm Sunday.   See *Holy Week.

Pasch.   (Gr form of Heb *pesakh*, passover)   The Jewish feast of the Passover which commemorates the passage of the destroying angel and the Christian feast of the Resurrection (usually referring to the whole *octave); the following Sundays until *Whitsun are referred to as "after the Pasch."

Paschaltide. The 56 days of rejoicing and jubilee from *Holy Saturday until *Vespers on the Saturday after *Whitsun, notable for the inclusion of the *Gloria* at *ferial masses, the additional *alleluias, the daily *Te Deum* at *Matins, the *Vidi aquam* replacing the *Asperges me*, and the *Regina coeli* being said instead of the Angelus. [see THE LITURGICAL YEAR]

Passion Sunday. See *Holy Week.

Penitential Psalms. A group of seven *Psalms (Pss. 6, 31, 37, 50, 101, 129, and 142 [Vulgate]) which are especially suitable for the use of penitents in that they express sorrow for sin and desire for pardon. As early as the 6th century these psalms were considered as forming a class by themselves. Innocent III (1198-1216) ordered their recitation in *Lent and later Pius V (1605-21) fixed the Fridays in Lent after *Lauds (except *Good Friday) as the time they should be said. Cassiodoris (d.565) interprets the number seven allegorically to indicate seven means by which sin is remitted: baptism, martyrdom, alms, forgiving others, conversion of a sinner, abundance of charity, and penance.

Pentecost. Fifty days (the 7th Sunday) after the Resurrection (*Easter); a feast which commemorates the Descent of the Holy Ghost upon the Apostles. [see Acts 2]

Precentor. The leader of a select group of monks (*schola cantorum*) who chant the more elaborate parts of liturgical music.

Prime. The morning *hour, a short *office at the beginning of the day (towards 6 a.m.) which consecrates the work of the day by the reciting of certain psalms and prayers concerning the work to come. [see THE HOURS OF DIVINE OFFICE]

Proper. The five parts of the *Mass that change from day to day depending on the liturgical season (*Proprium de Tempore*), the feasts of saints (*Porprium de Sanctis*), and other special days. The five parts are: the *Introit, *Gradual, *Alleluia-Verse (or *Tract), *Offertory, and *Communion. [see THE ROMAN MASS]

Proper of the Saints. That part of the *Breviary which contains the *lessons, *psalms and *antiphons for the feasts of the Saints. [see THE LITURGICAL YEAR]

Proper of the Season. A portion of the *Breviary which contains the *Office of the different liturgical seasons: *Advent, *Christmastide, *Septuagesima, *Lent, *Holy Week, paschal time and the time after *Pentecost. [see THE LITURGICAL YEAR]

Psalms, Book of. (L *psalmus*, from Gr ψαλμος, the usual *Septuagint translation of Heb *mizmôr*, song with stringed-music accompaniment) The 150 divinely inspired *hymns or poems (originally harp songs) which have formed the main part of the Liturgy of the *Hours of Divine *Office since apostolic times. David is the principal but not the sole author of the Psalms which, according to the *Vulgate, are divided into five sections (1-40, 41-71, 72-88, 89-105, and 106-150 [Vulgate numbering], each section closing with a doxology. (see *Vulgate)

Psalter. The most ancient and venerable portion of the *Breviary which consists of the 150 Psalms, arranged by the Roman church (since the 7th or 8th Century) in the following manner:

> *Psalms 1-108* (except Ps. 4, 5, 21-25, 42, 50, 53, 62, 64, 66, 89-92, and 94 which, because of their special aptitude are reserved for *Lauds, *Prime, and *Compline) are recited at *Matins.
>
> *Psalms 109-147* (except Ps.117, 118, and 142 which are reserved for other *hours) are recited or sung at *Vespers.
>
> *Psalms 148-150* (called the psalms of praise or *Laudes* because of the word "*Laudate*" which forms their leitmotiv) are recited at dawn in the concluding nocturnal *Office, which thus gets its name of *Lauds.

There are two principal Psalters, both translations by St. Jerome in the 4th century: the *Roman*, used at St. Peter's in Rome, St. Mark's, Venice, and Milan, and the *Gallican*, a later translation which was in common use before the complete revision of Divine *Office in 1970.

Purification of the Virgin Mary, Feast of the. A feast (Feb. 2) commemorating the ritual purification of the Virgin Mary in the Temple forty days after childbirth, according to Jewish law. It is also known as the Feast of the Presentation of Christ in the Temple and *Candlemas* (Candle Mass) because of the blessing, distribution, and procession with candles (Christ as "a light to enlighten the Gentiles" - Luke 2:32) which is part of this *office.

Quadragesima.   Any season of forty days' preparation by prayer and penance, but particularly the forty days before *Easter known as *Lent; the beginning of Lent, or *Ash Wednesday.

Requiem Mass.   A *Mass for the Dead, so called because of the opening words of the *Introit: *Requiem aeternam dona eis, Domine* ("Rest eternal grant to them, O Lord"). [see THE REQUIEM MASS]

Responsory.   A chant related to the *antiphon, in that a verse of a psalm, a sentence out of Holy Scripture, or a line by a liturgical author is sung responsively during Divine *Office; it differs in that the *precentor sings or recites a psalm and the choir or the faithful reply, repeating either one of the verses or the last words of the precentor.

Rogation Days.   (L *rogatio*, litany) The Monday, Tuesday, and Wednesday before the Feast of St. Mark on Apr. 25 (called the "Major Rogation") and those same days before *Ascension Day (the "Minor Rogation").   These three days of solemn supplication are so called because the Litany of the Saints is recited in the procession which takes place on each of these days.

Rubric.   (L *rubrica*, red earth; laws written in red) Directives or liturgical provisions printed in red to guide the clergy in the Eucharistic liturgy, the administration of sacraments, and the preaching of the Word of God. Some are obligatory, others are merely directive.

Sabaoth.   (Heb *sabaoth*, armies, hosts) A title which ascribes majesty, applied mainly to God as in the Sanctus of the *Mass (*Dominus Deus Sabaoth*, Lord God of Hosts).   It appears in the Old Testament no less than 282 times.   The full ascription *yhwh 'ĕlōhê ṣebā'ôt yiśrā'ēl*, "Yahweh, the God of the armies of Israel (I Samuel 17:45) conveys the concept of Israel's God seen as the supreme commander of its armies, a warrior who led the hosts of Israel into battle.   Later the term implies that Yahweh is also the God of the heavenly hosts and has sovereignity over all things.

Sanctus.   (*Sanctus, Sanctus, Sanctus*, Holy, Holy, Holy) The Trisagion (Thrice Holy) which, along with the *Hosanna and the *Benedictus, forms the fourth part of the *Ordinary of the *Mass.   It is also a part of the great hymn **Te Deum.** [see THE ROMAN MASS]

Secret.   One or more prayers, formerly said by the priest in a low tone, after the *Orate Fratres*. The prayer, normally only one, is now recited aloud and called the prayer *Super Oblata* ("over the offerings").

Septuagesima.   the third Sunday before *Quadragesima or *Ash Wednesday; the three-week period of preparation and penance preceding *Lent.

Septuagint.   L *septuaginta*, seventy) A pre-Christian Greek version of the Jewish Scriptures, commonly referred to as "LXX." The name is taken from the approximate number of its translators.

Sequence.   A medieval addition to the *Proper of the Mass which is sung following the *Alleluia-Verse and before the Gospel on certain special occasions.   There are five Sequences in use today: **Victimae paschali laudes** (*Easter), **Veni Sancte Spiritus** (*Pentecost), **Lauda Sion** (*Corpus Christi), **Stabat Mater** (Feast of the Seven Sorrows), and **Dies irae** (*Requiem Masses for the Dead).

Sext.   One of the "Little Hours" of Divine Office; it is observed at c. 12 Noon. [see THE HOURS OF DIVINE OFFICE]

Tenebrae.   See *Holy Week.

Terce.   One of the "Little Hours" of Divine Office; it is observed c. 9 a.m. [see THE HOURS OF DIVINE OFFICE]

Tract.   (L *tractatus*, a discussion, treatise) Verses of Scripture (replacing the *Alleluia) which comment on the *Gradual of the day in all Masses from *Septuagesima until *Holy Saturday. In the revised liturgy the tract is a *psalm with a *responsory. [see THE ROMAN MASS]

Trinity Sunday.   A feast in honor of the Most Holy Trinity observed on the 8th Sunday after *Easter, the next Sunday after *Pentecost.

Versicle. A short *responsory, usually taken from a psalm, which is commonly employed in Divine *Office after *lessons and the "Little Chapters" which take the place of lessons during the hours which have no special ones assigned to them; they belong to the category of liturgical acclamations or shouts of joy.

Vespers. The evening hour of Divine *Office which consecrates the end of the day. The singing of the five Lucernal or Vesper psalms with their antiphons and the Canticle of Mary (*Magnificat anima mea*) are the most characteristic features of this office. [see THE HOURS OF DIVINE OFFICE]

Vidi aquam. ("I saw water flowing from the right side of the temple"") The *hymn sung as an *antiphon in the Easter season in place of the *Asperges. [see Ezekiel 47]

Vigil. (L *vigilia*, a watching) Special offices and prayers (and, formerly, a fast) kept on the day and/or eve before a feast as a preparation for the feast itself.

Votive Mass. (L *votivus*, from *votum*, vow, vote) A Mass chosen for some special purpose and offered on any ordinary *ferial day in the year, outside of *Lent and *Advent, which does not require the *Mass of the day to be said.

Vulgate. (L *vulgata* [*editio*], popular, common [edition]) St. Jerome's 4th century authoritative Latin translation of the Bible from the original Hebrew, Aramaic, and Greek; its subsequent corrupted versions are now being compared and restored to its original form by the Benedictine order at the Abbey of St. Jerome in Rome. N.B. The numbering of the Psalms differs from that of the English Bible in the following ways:

Vulgate Psalms	1–9	=	English Psalms	1–9
Vulgate Psalms	10–145	=	English Psalms	11–146
Vulgate Psalm	146	=	English Psalm	147:1–ll
Vulgate Psalm	147	=	English Psalm	147:12–20
Vulgate Psalms	148–150	=	English Psalms	148–150

The Vulgate gives the English Psalm 10 the title *Psalmus X secundum Hebraeos* ("Psalm 10 according to the Hebrews). In this volume both numbers are frequently given to avoid confusion and to remind the reader of the different systems, expecially the reader doing research in Catholic commentaries and earlier writings. The Vulgate number is given first, followed by the Hebrew Psalter and King James, etc. number in brackets (Psalm 22 [23]).

Whitsun. (White Sunday) An Anglican term for *Pentecost, the seventh Sunday after Easter, so called because of the white garment worn by the babies baptized at that time.

LATIN PRONUNCIATION GUIDE

Since virtually all of the **SACRED LATIN TEXTS** in this volume have been appointed for use in the Roman Church, the Roman pronunciation of the liturgical Latin has been chosen for presentation here. First authorized by Pope Pius X (*Motu Proprio*) in 1903, this method was later published by the St. Gregory Guild in 1937 (*The Correct Pronunciation of Latin According to Roman Usage*), and "enlarged and newly edited" by William D. Hall in 1971 (*Latin Pronunciation According to Roman Usage*). The *Singer's Manual of Latin Diction and Phonetics* by Robert S. Hines is noteworthy for its linguistic thoroughness and its inclusion of the International Phonetic Alphabet (IPA) as a universally useful pronunciation guide. Another excellent summary, along with very insightful comments concerning the performance and interpretation of Plainsong, is given by the Benedictines of Solesmes in their introduction to the *Liber Brevior* of 1954. The principles set forth by these reknowned interpreters of the liturgical Latin repertoire have been chosen as the basis for this pronunciation guide.

V O W E L S

The six vowels in the Latin language are:

A   E   I   O   U   Y

In Latin, <u>unlike</u> English, all the vowel sounds should be pure and unchanging. Mixtures, impurities, and dipthongs are forbidden. "The vitally important element in this style," according to the Solesmes, "is the <u>rich</u>, <u>open</u>, <u>warm</u> sounds of the vowels **A** and **U**. The other elements will, to be sure, receive our close attention; but this one is primary and indispensable." The **O** is also problematical: both the "closed o" sound ([o]; lips too-rounded) and an "aw" sound that is too-open must be avoided; the correct sound is [ɔ], the "open o" of *w<u>a</u>rm*.

Written		**Pronounced**	**IPA**	**Incorrect Pronunciation**	**Transliterated**
A	=	*f<u>a</u>ther*	[α]	(never *f<u>aw</u>n* or *f<u>an</u>*)	ah
E	=	*f<u>e</u>d*	[ε]	(never *f<u>a</u>te*)	eh
I	=	*f<u>ee</u>t*	[i]	(never *f<u>i</u>t*)	ee
O	=	*f<u>ou</u>ght*	[ɔ]	(never *f<u>oe</u>*)	aw
U	=	*f<u>oo</u>d*	[u]	(never *f<u>oo</u>t*)	oo
Y	=	*f<u>ee</u>t*	[i]	(like **I** above)	ee

Examples:

Kýrie eléison,	Keé – *ree* – eh eh – léh – ee – šawn,
Glória in excélsis.	Gláw – *ree* – ah een eh – kshéhl – sees.
Crédo in únum Déum.	Kréh – daw een oó – noom Déh – oom.
Sánctus, Benedíctus qui vénit.	Sáhŋk – toos, Beh – neh – deék – toos kwee véh – neet.
Ágnus Déi, dóna nóbis pácem.	Áh – nyus Déh – ee, dáw – nah náw – bees páh – chehm.

Generally, when two vowels come together, each retains its own distinct sound and is treated as a separate syllable:

eléison	eh – léh – ee – šawn
fílii	feé – lee – ee
méi, áit	méh – ee, áh – eet

In some musical settings consecutive vowels are treated by the composer as one syllable and assigned to a single note, in which case they should be treated as "dipthongs," with the first vowel sound receiving the greatest duration and the second vowel introduced as a "vanishing vowel" just prior to the following syllable. For ensemble precision and clarity of diction these durations may be assigned rhythmic values, but they should not be articulated and heard as separate rhythmic entities.

AE/OE   should be pronounced as **E** ([ɛ] , "eh").

bónae voluntátis	báw – neh vaw – loon – táh – tees
ténebrae fáctae sunt	téh – neh – breh fáhk – teh soont
rex coeléstis	rrehks cheh – léh – stees
in saécula saeculórum	een séh – coo – lah seh – coo – láw – room

U   when preceded by **Q** or **NG** and followed by another vowel, is sung quickly (like the glide [w]) and is part of the same syllable as the vowel which follows:

qui, quae, quod, quam	kwee, kweh, kwawd, kwahm
únde flúxit sánguine	oón – deh floó – kseet sáhn – gwee – neh

Au/Eu/Ay are sung as dipthongs, with the greatest duration given to the first vowel, and the second vowel introduced just prior to the following syllable or word:

Laudáte Dóminum	Lah – *oo*dáh – teh Dáw – mee – noom
Víctimae pascháli láudes	Veék – tee – meh pah – skáh – lee láh – *oo*dehs

C O N S O N A N T S

If the purity of the Latin vowels is responsible for the warmth and rich vocal color of this venerable language, the consonants establish its essential character. Clean, quick articulation is essential; lyric diction is the rule. Double consonants should be prolonged and slightly suspended (like Italian), and, accordingly, the **D, T,** and **K** should not be strongly plosive as they are in English.

The following consonants are pronounced as they are in English:

B   D   F   K   L   M   N   P   Q   V

and the other consonants are pronounced as follows:

37

C is hard, like "k" in <u>k</u>ic<u>k</u> :

Cum Sán<u>c</u>to Spíritu	<u>K</u>oom	Sáhŋ<u>k</u> – taw	Speé – *ree* – too
Glori<u>c</u>ámus te	Glaw – *ree* – fee – <u>k</u>áh – moos		teh
Úbi <u>c</u>áritas	Oó – bee	<u>k</u>áh – *ree* – tahs	

except before **E, AE, OE, I, Y,** when it is like "ch" in <u>ch</u>ur<u>ch</u> :

Dóna nóbis pá<u>c</u>em	Dáw – nah	náw – bees	páh – <u>ch</u>ehm
des<u>c</u>éndit de <u>c</u>oélis	deh – shéhn – deet	deh	<u>ch</u>éh – lees
Rex <u>c</u>oeléstis	RRehks	<u>ch</u>eh – léh – stees	
In dúl<u>c</u>i júbilo	Een	doól – <u>ch</u>ee	yoó – bee – law

CC before the above vowels is pronounced "tch" (stopped "t"):

É<u>cc</u>e sa<u>c</u>érdos	Éh – <u>tch</u>eh	sah – <u>ch</u>éh*r* – daws

    but

In E<u>cc</u>lésiis	Een	Eh<u>k</u> – <u>k</u>léh – šee – ees
pe<u>cc</u>áta múndi	peh<u>k</u> – <u>k</u>áh – tah	moón – dee

SC before these same vowels is like "sh" in <u>sh</u>ell :

a<u>sc</u>éndit; de<u>sc</u>éndit	ah – <u>sh</u>éhn – deet; deh – <u>sh</u>éhn – deet	
sú<u>sc</u>ipe deprecatiónem	soó – <u>sh</u>ee – peh	deh – p*r*eh – cah – tsee – áw – nehm

CH is always like **K** :

<u>Ch</u>ríste eléison	<u>K</u>reé – steh	eh – léh – ee – sawn
Jésum <u>Ch</u>rístum	Yéh – šoom	<u>K</u>reé – stoom

G is hard, like the "g" in <u>G</u>od:

<u>Gl</u>ória Pátri	<u>Gl</u>áw – *ree* – ah	Páh – tree

except before **E, AE, OE, I,** when it is soft like the "g" in <u>g</u>em :

Pánis an<u>g</u>élicus	Páh – nees	ahn – <u>j</u>éh – lee – coos
Fílium uni<u>g</u>énitum	Feé – lee – oom	oo – nee – <u>j</u>éh – nee – toom

GN has the prepalatal sound found in Italian (so<u>gn</u>o), French (di<u>gn</u>e), and Spain (se<u>ñ</u>or), which is probably best rendered as "ny" :

Á<u>gn</u>us Déi	Áh – <u>ny</u>oos	Déh – ee
própter má<u>gn</u>am	práwp – tehr	máh – <u>ny</u>ahm
O má<u>gn</u>um mystérium	Aw máh – <u>ny</u>oom	mee – stéh – *ree* – oom
Ma<u>gn</u>íficat	Mah – <u>ny</u>eé – fee – caht	

H is <u>silent</u> as in *honest* (not *honey*) :

pax _hominibus	pahks ( )aw – meé – nee – boos	
et _homo factus est	eht ( )áw – maw fáhk – toos ehst	

except in the two Medieval glosses "*michi*" and "*nichil*" :

mi_hi; ni_hil meé – <u>k</u>ee; neé – <u>k</u>eel

PH has the sound of "f" :

per pro_phétas peh*r* p*r*aw – <u>f</u>éh – tahs

J is pronounced like the "y" in *you* (the glide [j]). Care must be taken to move quickly and completely through this sound to the purity of the following vowel:

Jubiláte Déo	<u>Y</u>oo – bee – láh – teh Déh – aw
Jésu Chríste	<u>Y</u>éh – šu K*r*eé – steh
et sémini é_jus	eht séh – mee – nee éh – <u>y</u>oos

and is sometimes written as an "i" :

Allelúi_a! Ahl – leh – loó – <u>y</u>ah!

PH is pronounced like "f" :

Chérubim et Séra_phim	Kéh – *r*oo – beem eht Séh – *r*ah – <u>f</u>eem
Pro_phetárum númerus	P*r*aw – <u>f</u>eh – táh – *r*oom noó – meh – *r*oos

R should be flipped with the tongue when it appears between two vowels or at the end of a word ([ɾ], herein transliterated as "*r*" – never the burred [r] as in American English), and should be rolled when it appears at the beginning of a word ([ř], herein transliterated as "*RR*" or "*rr*"). This consonant also requires special attention when combined with other consonants:

Mise_rére nóbis	Mee – šeh – *r*eh – *r*eh naw – bees
Per P_rophétas	Peh*r* P*r*aw – féh – tahs
Rex t_reméndae	*RR*ehks t*r*eh – méhn – deh
et _resur_réxit	eht *rr*eh – šoo – *rr*éh – kseet

it should not be introduced too early and thereby influence or modify the purity of the vowel which precedes it:

Ký_rie Keé – *r*ee – eh, **not** keé*r* – ee – eh

S

is hard as in _see_ (never _raise_) :

Sánctus	Sáhŋk – toos
Véni Sáncte Spíritus	Véh – nee Sáhŋk – teh Speé – ree – toos

except   when it comes between two vowels and is _slightly_ softened (š) :

Miserére méi, Déus	Mee – šeh – réh – reh méh – ee Déh – oos
invisibílium	een – vee – šee – beé – lee – oom
In paradísum	Een pah – rah – deé – šoom

SCH   is like the "sk" of _school_ :

Víctimae pascháli láudes	Veék – tee – meh pah – skáh – lee láh – oodehs

T

is hard as in _tea_, but not as plosive as it is in English:

Tu sólus altíssimus	Too sáw – loos ahl – teé – see – moos

TI   before a vowel and following any letter except **S, X,** or **T** is pronounced "tsee" :

Grátias ágimus tíbi	Gráh – tsee – ahs áh – jee – moos teé – bee
deprecatiónem nóstram	deh – preh – cah – tsee – áw – nehm náw – strahm
consubstantiálem Pátri	cawn – sub – stahn – tsee – áh – lehm Páh – tree

but

míxtio; mixtúra	meéks – tee – aw; meeks – toó – rah

TH   is always hard, like _tea_ :

únum sánctam Cathólicam	oó – noom sáhnk – tahm Cah – táw – lee – cahm
Dóminus Déus Sábaoth	Dáw – mee – noos Déh – oos Sáh – bah – awt

X

is pronounced like "ks" as in _tacks_ or _tax_ :

Rex treméndae	RRehks treh – méhn – deh
Júste Júdex	Yoó – steh Yoó – dehks

except   when it comes between 2 vowels and is _slightly_ softened ("ǩs") :

Díxit María	Deé – ǩseet Mah – reé – ah
láudat exércitus	láh – oodaht eh – ǩséhr – chee – toos
Exultáte Déo	Eh – ǩsool – táh – teh Déh – aw

XC   is pronounced as "ksk" before the vowels **O, A,** or **U** :

excogitáre; excusátus	eks – kaw – jee – táh – reh; eks – koo – šáh – toos

but when **XC** appears before **E, AE, OE, I,** and **Y** it becomes "ksh" :

in excélsis	een eh – kshéhl – sees

Y	is treated like the vowel **I** ([i], "ee").
Z	is pronounced like "dz" of *su<u>ds</u>* :

et cum Lá<u>z</u>aro	eht	coom	Láh – d<u>z</u>ah – raw

COMMON PRONUNCIATION PROBLEMS

As most directors have experienced far too often, the same problems seem to plague beginning choristers and inexperienced directors. Here are a few things to watch for:

A	often pronounced too far back in the throat instead of forward and open. Sing "ah" -- not "aw" (it is <u>not</u> "Awdoramus Te").
E	often too bright ("ay" instead of "eh"); sometimes even introduces the diphthong "ayee" (it is <u>not</u> "Adoramus Tayee").
I	sometimes pronounced "ih" instead of "ee" -- especially in the phrase <u>in</u> *excelsis*.
O	is often pronounced "oh" or "oh*oo*" (as a dipthong) instead of "aw" (it is <u>not</u> "Glohria")
U	often impure, towards *f<u>oo</u>t* or slightly "umlauted," especially if preceded by **J**. (*cujus, ejus*)
Y	sometimes heard as "ih" -- especially in the word *K<u>y</u>rie*.
AU	initial vowel not prolonged long enough before changing to [u].
AE/OE	often pronounced "ay" instead of "eh".
GN	one oftens hears a hard G, expecially in *Ma<u>gn</u>ificat* and *A<u>gn</u>us*.
H	is often pronounced (*<u>h</u>ominibus*); it should be <u>silent</u>, except *mihi* and *nihil*.
J	this sound must not be mixed in (remain) with the following [u] vowel; an impure umlaut sound often results.
R	is burred instead of flipped or rolled.
S	<u>not</u> Z, although *slightly* softened when it comes between two vowels.
TI	often pronounced "tee" instead of "tsee".
TH	should be "t", not "th"; listen to *Sabao<u>th</u>* and *ca<u>th</u>olicam* especially closely.
X	note the two exceptions to the "ks" pronunciation, expecially *excelsis* (*it is <u>not</u> ehks – chéhl – sees*).

However, the correct <u>pronunciation</u> is only one aspect of good diction. <u>Enunciation</u> and <u>articulation</u> are equally important. And even more important are the aspects of <u>syllable stress</u> and what Dorothy Uris (*To Sing in English*) calls "<u>sense stress</u>," emphasizing the message–bearing words more than others so that the meaning and emotional content of the text is clearly perceived by the listener.

Every two-syllable Latin word has its tonic accent or stress on the first syllable. In the other multi-syllable words, the tonic accent has been indicated (*Kýrie eléison*) and the <u>must</u> be observed if the phrasing and stylistic integrity of the piece are to be preserved. For most inexperienced musicians this matter of correct syllable stress becomes most problematical at cadence points, when the feminine endings, the graceful closures of the Latin [and German, etc.] are contradicted by an inordinate stressing of the final unaccented syllable, especially when the melodic line rises to the final note (*eléison*, **not** *eleisón;* *nóbis*, **not** *nobîs;* *Déo*, **not** *Deó*). Listen to the cadences in good performances of plainsong; let the graceful release of energy and and the lightening of vocal timbre be your guide.

"Good diction means good phrasing also, and the intelligent use of the Phraseological Accent [the "sense stress"]. For just as the tonic accent gives cohesion and life to the word, so the phraseological accent draws together the separate words into groups, and gives a tonic prominence and influence to the important word, phrase, and pause. Thus the listeners are made to understand the text; they feel that the [singer] understands it also." (*Liber Brevior*) Conveying the sense of a text, grouping it into its proper phrases, and varying the tonal inflections (those shifts of stress and emphasis which tone, tempo, articulation, dynamics, etc. can effect) depend upon the understanding of text and context. We must know each word's <u>pronunciation</u>, its literal and metaphorical <u>meaning</u>, and its <u>function</u> within the sentence, the poem, and the liturgy if our goal, as the Benedictines say, is to "cultivate a kindred spirit *in order to interpret aright* the accompanying melody."

AUSTRO - GERMAN   PRONUNCIATION   GUIDE

Austro-German Pronunciation of liturgical Latin becomes increasingly important as we strive to recreate stylistically authentic performances of music from the past. Exciting work has been done in the instrumental field. Fine performances and recordings of period instruments or replicas of authentic instruments are readibly accessible. The results are highly illuminating.

In the vocal/choral area some consideration has been given to these matters as well, particularly in terms of vocal technique (vibrato and timbre), the cultivation of coloratura capability and the countertenor voice, stylistic attention to matters of articulation and phrasing, and the employment of appropriately-sized choral forces for the work being performed. We are singing more and more of the choral masterworks *in their original languages*, but sometimes without proper pronunciation or adequate knowledge of the meaning of the text [see *Volume II: Foreign Language Texts*]. And we have only barely begun to consider various historical, cultural, or dialectical pronunciations of these texts as important elements of stylistic performance practice.

But is it not as essential as "authentic" instruments? What if Mozart expected to hear *Regina Coeli* with a hard "g," a "ts" for the "c," and the "oe" sung as the umlaut "ö" ? ("*RRe* - gee - nah Tsö - lee" is certainly <u>much</u> different than the "Ray - jee - nah   Chay - lee" we often hear.) Consider two different pronunciations of the word *Kyrie* : "Kee - *ree* - eh" according to Roman Usage, and "Kü - *ree* - e" according to the Austro-German pronunciation; and multiply that difference by the liturgical and polyphonic repetitions of the text. The degree of difference becomes stylistically significant.

One cannot state categorically that every choral piece written by a German or Austrian composer during, say, the Classical Period (or, additionally and more specifically, in Vienna, Salzburg, Cologne, etc.) was pronounced with these "Austro-German" variants. But the differences in vocal timbre and character, rhythmic vitality, articulation, and musical intensity are significant enough to warrant and inspire further investigative research and experimentation in rehearsal and performance.

Those wishing to explore this fascinating area should be guided by the following principles:

V O W E L S

A/I/U   are pronounced like the Roman Latin: [α], [i], [u]

E   is pronounced as the closed vowel [e] (not the dipthong [ei]) in accented syllables

      Déi; Jésu; unigénitum   [déi]; [jézu]; [unigénitum]

but as [ε] or schwa [ə] in most unaccented syllables:

      benedíctus; peccáta   [bɛnɛdíktus]; [pɛkkátα]

and as [e] or [ε] in single-syllable words, according to syntactical function:

      Et hómo fáctus est   [ɛt hómo fáktus est]
      Adorámus te   [αdorámus te]
      Rex coeléstis   [reks tsøléstis]

O   is pronounced as the closed vowel [o] (not the dipthong [ou])

      Glória; Crédo   [glóriα]; [krédo]

OE/AE   are pronounced as the umlauts "ö" [ø] and "ä" [e²]:

      Regina coéli laetáre   [regínα tsøli le²táre]
      et in saécula saeculórum   [ɛt in zé²kulα ze²kulórum]

Y   is pronounced as the umlaut "ü" [y] :

      Kýrie eléison   [kýrie eléizon]

C O N S O N A N T S

C   before the vowels **E, AE, OE, I** is pronounced as [ts] :

      dóna nóbis pácem   [dónα nóbis pátsɛm]
      benedícimus te   [bɛnɛdítsimus te]

G   is always hard [g], as in the word *get* :

Magníficat ánima méa	[mɑgnífikɑt ánimɑ méɑ]
Grátias ágimus tíbi	[grátiɑs ágimus tíbi]
Ágnus Déi	[ágnus déi]
Ex María Vírgine	[ɛks mɑría vírginɛ]

H   is pronounced:

hómo; homínibus	[hómo]; [homínibus]

QU   is pronounced as [kv] :

Quóniam tu sólus sánctus	[kvóniɑm tu zólus záŋtus]
Qui tóllis; qui sédes	[kvi tóllis]; [kvi zédɛs]

S   is pronounced as [z] before vowels, but as [s] before consonants and in final position:

Sánctus Dóminus Déus Sábaoth	[záŋtus dóminus déus zábɑot]
Et in spíritum sánctum	[ɛt in spíritum záŋtum]
in ecclésiam; únum baptísma	[in ɛkkléziɑm]; [únum bɑptísmɑ]
cum sáncto spíritu	[kum záŋto spíritu]
Jesum Christum	[jézum krístum]

T   is pronounced hard [t] , even before "i" ([ti], not [tsi]) :

con substantiálem	[kon zubstɑntiálɛm]
Póntio Piláto	[póntio piláto]
deprecatiónem; étiam	[dɛprɛkɑtiónɛm]; [étiɑm]
Grátias ágimus tíbi	[grátiɑs ágimus tíbi]

X   is pronounced [kz] when followed by a vowel and as [ks] when followed by a consonant or in final position:

Díxit María	[díkzit mɑría]
Exultáte Déo	[ekzultátɛ déo]
láudat exércitus	[láudɑt ɛkzértsitus]
Júste júdex ultiónis	[jústɛ júdɛks ultiónis]

XC   is pronounced [ksk] before **O, A,** or **U** ; but before **E** it becomes [ktz] :

Osánna in excélsis	[ozánnɑ in ɛktzélzis]

SACRED LATIN TEXTS
The Roman Mass

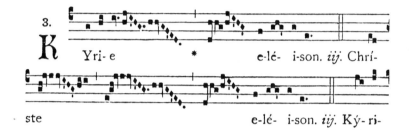

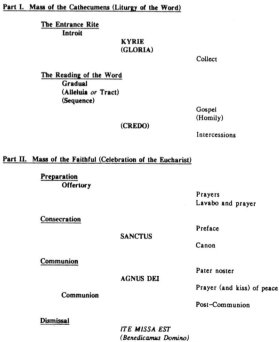

Part I. Mass of the Cathecumens (Liturgy of the Word)

The Entrance Rite
  Introit

  KYRIE
  (GLORIA)

  Collect

The Reading of the Word
  Gradual
  (Alleluia *or* **Tract)**
  (Sequence)

  Gospel
  (Homily)

  (CREDO)

  Intercessions

Part II. Mass of the Faithful (Celebration of the Eucharist)

Preparation
  Offertory

  Prayers
  Lavabo and prayer

Consecration

  Preface

  SANCTUS

  Canon

Communion

  Pater noster

  AGNUS DEI

  Prayer (and kiss) of peace

  Communion

  Post—Communion

Dismissal

  ITE MISSA EST
  (Benedicamus Domino)

  Blessing

THE ROMAN MASS

(L: *missa*; Fr: *messe*; Ger: *Messe*; It: *messa*; Sp: *misa*)

The Roman Mass is the complex of prayers and ceremonies whose essential element is the celebration of the Holy Eucharist, a commemoration of the Last Supper of Christ and his Apostles ("This do in remembrance of me" - Luke 22:19). The Mass is divided into two main parts: The Mass of the Catechumens (the Liturgy of the Word) and the Mass of the Faithful (the Celebration of the Eucharist).

The early Church called it *fractio panis* ("the breaking of the bread"), *coena dominica* ("the Supper of the Lord" - I Corinthians 11:20), *oblatio* ("sacrifice"), or *congregatio* ("the gathering together"). St. Ambrose (339-397) used the term *missa* ("dismissal") to refer to the end of the Mass of the Catechumens when the unbaptized were dismissed, or to denote the end of the Mass of the Faithful (*Ite, missa est* - "Go, [the mass] has been spoken"). The word *missa* was used later to refer to the dismissals of any type of service, and then it gradually became the term applied to the entire Eucharistic service about the time of Gregory the Great (d.604), and it was he who gave the Mass its most definite form up until that time. Elements from the Gallican Mass and the Ordinary that originated in the monastery of St. Gall in Switzerland were adapted to it in the 10th century, but it was the *Missale Romanum* of Pope Pius V that gave it universal shape and form in 1570.

The Mass of the Catechumens begins with the Entrance Rite, the **Introit**, a processional chant sung while the priests enter the sanctuary; the **Kyrie** and (on some days) the **Gloria in excelsis** follow; then comes the Collect, a prayer which summarizes the essential themes of the day, and the celebrant's greeting: *Dominus vobiscum* ("the Lord be with you") and the congregational response: *Et cum spiritu tuo* ("and with your spirit").

The Liturgy of the Word follows, with readings from the Epistles and the Gospels. The **Gradual** and **Alleluia-Verse** (sometimes the **Tract** and/or **Sequence**) are offered during this time as moments of reflection or meditation on the readings. A homily or short sermon then explicates the readings and relates it to the lives of those present and to the Eucharistic meal which is to come. On Sundays and major feasts the **Credo** (The Nicene Creed) is then sung, and the Mass of the Catechumens is concluded with intercessions and the Common Prayer of the Faithful.

The Mass of the Faithful begins with the **Offertory** antiphon which is sung while the gifts are brought to the altar. Preparations and offertory prayers are then followed by the *Lavaba* ("the washing of the hands") which leads to the Preface-Canon, the table blessing or Eucharistic Prayer, the high point of the Mass. The people (or choir) join and conclude the Consecratory Prayer with the **Sanctus** or Trisagion (The Thrice Holy).

It was Gregory the Great (d.604) who appointed the petitions of the **Pater Noster** to be the opening rite of the Communion Service; this universal prayer of the Christian Church is followed by the Embolism and the Fraction, or Breaking of the Bread. The **Agnus Dei**, introduced by Sergius I (d.701), was to be sung while the unleavened bread was being broken into pieces small enough for distribution. The Kiss of Peace and the partaking of **Communion** then followed. The Communion Antiphon, one of the "action chants" (like the Introit and the Offertory) was originally sung during the distribution of Communion. The celebration of the Roman Mass concludes with the dismissal **Ite, missa est** ("Go, [the mass] has been spoken") and the response *Deo Gratias* or *Benedicamus Domino*.

It is in High or Solemn Mass (*missa solemnis*) that most of the chants are sung, as opposed to the Low Mass (*missa lecta*) in which everything is read. Of particular interest to most readers are the principal musical portions of the Mass Liturgy and the way in which these pieces originally functioned in the liturgical context for which they were written or appointed. There are two main parts: the Ordinary (*Ordinarium Missae*), namely the **Kyrie, Gloria, Credo, Sanctus et Benedictus,** a n d **Agnus Dei** -- the parts that are mostly unchanging; and the Proper (*Proprium de tempore, Proprium Sanctorum, Commune Sanctorum*), the **Introit, Gradual, Alleluia-Verse, Sequence, Tract, Offertory,** a n d **Communion** -- those parts which are chosen according to the seasons of the Church Year, the feasts of saints, and other special days.

The plainsong melodies offer deep insights and give sensitive expression and inflection to these venerable texts and reward serious study. Even the short excerpts from the beginnings of each chant can be instructive: they immediately seek to establish the character and mood of a given text. Originally simple and unadorned, they gradually became more ornate under monastic influence until they could only be sung by the trained *schola cantorum*. Early polyphonic settings first used the texts of the Propers, but composers soon realized that the fixed chants of the Ordinary, unlike the Propers which were assigned to specific feasts, could be performed throughout the liturgical year; and thus the first musically unified settings appeared. One of the greatest, and the first to be composed by a single composer, was the *Messe de Nostre Dame* by Guilliame de Machaut in the 14th century. The various parts of this musical unity were still performed separately (except for the Kyrie and Gloria), *in their liturgical contexts*, not consecutively as most concert presentations do today. We could certainly enrich our concert experience of these pieces if we would find an imaginative way of presenting them that somehow recreates a vivid sense of their original context and function.

Various techniques were employed for unifying the musical settings, including the use of a recurring *cantus firmus* (e.g., Lionel Power's *Mass Alma Redemptoris Mater*), basing the polyphonic pieces on a well-known plainsong (Josquin's *Missa pange lingua*), or by using the technique of the so-called "Parody Masses," which are based on a pre-existing polyphonic piece (Victoria's *Missa O Magnum Mysterium*). "Music associated with the Mass in the Middle Ages and early Renaissance was of crucial importance in the development of both monophonic and polyphonic styles; in the 15th century, the polyphonic Mass Ordinary, unified by purely musical means, became a genre in its own right and one of the seminal forms of European art music" (Ruth Steiner, *New Grove Dictionary*).

These polyphonic settings also became more and more elaborate and occasioned the reforms decreed by the Council of Trent in 1562 which officially banned all "seductive and impure" secular melodies from church use and ordered that the text be made once again intelligible to the congregation. Thus this form declines after 1600, even though Bach, Mozart, Haydn, Beethoven, . . . and Stravinsky were to make memorable settings of the Ordinary texts. Other more recent settings include those of Vaughan Williams, Hindemith, Poulenc, and Duruflé, as well as various Folk Masses (*Missa Luba, Missa Criolla*) and Bernstein's theatrical setting.

To enumerate these settings in the **Selected Settings of the Latin Texts** would be an overwhelming task and of questionable value to the reader and user of this book [Palestrina wrote 104 Masses!, Lassus: 53, Obrecht: 24, Victoria and Josquin: 20]. For as Louise Cuyler has written: "No form, save the symphony from the Viennese Classical period onward, has been so long-lived, popular and inspiring of great music. To enumerate major Mass composers is virtually to call the role of the musically elite, through the eighteenth century. Even works like Bach's so-called *B-minor Mass* and Beethoven's *Missa Solemnis*, which are not judged to be "liturgical" by present standards, have taken their inspiration from the ancient texts of the Ordinary, as have the Masses of various contemporary composers."

THE ORDINARY OF THE MASS

KYRIE

(Κυριε ελεησον, *Kyrie eleison*, Lord have mercy)

Kýrie	eléison,	*repeat,*	*repeat*		Lord have mercy,	*repeat, repeat*
Lord	**have mercy,**	" ,	"			
Chríste	eléison,	*repeat,*	*repeat*		Christ have mercy,	*repeat, repeat*
Christ	**have mercy,**	" ,	"			
Kýrie	eléison,	*repeat,*	*repeat*		Lord have mercy,	*repeat, repeat*
Lord	**have mercy,**	" ,	"			

This acclamatory supplication -- its brief invocation and petition being similar to Psalm 6:3 ("Have mercy on me, O Lord, for I am weak") and Psalm 40 [41] : 5,11 ("O Lord, be thou merciful unto me . . . But thou, O Lord, have mercy on me") -- is found in pagan antiquity and in 4th century Jerusalem. In the 5th century Pope Gelasius I (492-6) substituted a litany for the common Prayer of the Church and the Greek form was retained as the people's response. The litany was then moved to the beginning of the Mass, retaining the same Greek form, Κυριε ελεησον, (*Kyrie eleison*), that is still used today. The second portion (*Christe eleison*) was added by Pope Gregory I (d.604).

The *Ordo of St. Amand* of the 8th century is the first evidence of the *Kyrie* consisting of the familiar nine acclamations. Its tripartite A–B–A structure, with each part having its own intrinsic tripartite structure, has been attractive and inspirational to composers throughout history, from the earliest plainsong to the present day. Some of the earliest plainsong chants, like the *Kyrie* of the *Missa pro Defunctis*, uses the same melody for all acclamations except the last: AAA AAA AAA'. Other common forms are: AAA BBB AAA; AAA AAA BBB; AAA BBB CCC; ABA CDC EFE.

Liturgical context: The **Kyrie** is the first part of the Ordinary of the Mass rite; it is sung immediately following the Introit.

GLORIA

(*Gloria in excelsis*, Glory to God in the highest)

Glória	in	excélsis	Déo.		Glory to God in the highest.
Glory	**in**	**highest**	**to God.**		
Et	in	térra	pax		And on earth peace
And	**on**	**earth**	**peace**		to all those of good will.
homínibus	bónae	voluntátis.			
to men	**of good**	**will.**			

Laudámus   te.   Benedícimus   te.
We praise   thee.   We bless   thee.

Adorámus   te.   Glorificámus   te.
We worship   thee.   We glorifiy   thee.

We praise thee. We bless thee.
We worship thee. We glorify thee.

Grátias   ágimus   tíbi
Thanks   we give   to thee

propter   mágnam   glóriam   túam.
because of   great   glory   thy.

We give thanks to thee
according to thy great glory.

Dómine   Déus,   Rex   coeléstis,
Lord   God,   King   of heaven,

Déus   Páter   omnípotens.
God   Father   almighty.

Lord God, Heavenly King,
God the Father almighty.

Dómine   Fíli   unigénite,   Jésu   Chríste.
Lord   Son   only begotten, Jesus   Christ.

Lord Jesus Christ, the only begotten Son.

Dómine   Déus,   Agnus   Déi,
Lord   God,   Lamb   of God,

Fílius   Pátris.
Son   of Father.

Lord God, Lamb of God,
Son of the Father.

Qui   tóllis   peccáta   múndi,
Who   take away   sins   of world,

miserére   nóbis.
have mercy   on us.

Qui   tóllis   peccáta   múndi,
Who   take away   sins   of world,

súscipe   deprecatiónem   nóstram.
receive   supplication   our.

Thou who takest away the sins of the world,
have mercy upon us.
Thou who takest away the sins of the world,
receive our prayer.

Qui   sédes   ad   déxteram   Pátris,
Who   sit   at   right hand   of Father,

miserére   nóbis.
have mercy   on us.

Thou who sittest at the right hand of the Father,
have mercy upon us.

					For Thou alone art holy.
Quóniam	tu	sólus	sánctus.			Thou alone art the Lord.
For	**thou**	**alone**	**holy.**			Thou alone art the most high, Jesus Christ.

Tu	sólus	Dóminus.
Thou	**alone**	**Lord.**

Tu	sólus	Altíssimus,	Jésu	Chríste.
Thou	**alone**	**most high,**	**Jesus**	**Christ.**

Cum	Sáncto	Spíritu		With the Holy Spirit
With	**Holy**	**Spirit**		in the glory of God the Father. Amen.

in	glória	Déi	Pátris.	Amen.
in	**glory**	**of God**	**Father.**	**Amen.**

The **Gloria in excelsis** is an early prose hymn whose origins have been traced back to a "morning prayer" in the Apostolic Constitution (c.380) and to a Greek version of the 2nd century. It is, along with the *Te Deum*, one of the *psalmi idiotici*, a psalm-like text composed by an individual rather than being taken from the Biblical Psalter. The first extant Latin version appears in the *Bangor Antiphonary* (c.690), but it differs significantly from the version we have today which is first found in Frankish sources of the 9th century. It is found in the Roman rite by the 6th century, but was generally reserved for special occasions (especially Christmas) and omitted during Advent and from Septuagesima to Easter.

It is known as the *hymnus angelicus* since it begins with the angelic hymn sung at Christ's nativity ("Glory to God in the highest, and on earth peace among men of good will" – Luke 2:14). And it is also called the Greater Doxology or "Ascription of Glory" (as distinguished from the Lesser Doxology, the *Gloria Patri*). Along with the Credo, it is one of the longest texts of the Ordinary, consisting of the following sections:

1. *hymnus angelicus*
2. acclamations: *Laudamus ... benedicimus ... adoramus ... glorificamus*
3. invocations: *Domine Deus . . .*
4. petitions: *miserere . . . suscipe*
5. doxology: *Quoniam . . .*

This hymn of praise addresses itself to each Person of the Holy Trinity: God the Father (*Gloria in excelsis Deo ...*), God the Son (*Domine Fili unigenite ...*), and, briefly, to the Holy Spirit (*Cum Sancto Spiritu ...*).

Liturgical context: The **Gloria** is the second part of the Ordinary of the Mass, a hymn of praise sung immediately after the Kyrie during the opening Entrance rite; it is sung on all festal occasions, except the masses of the dead, the Sundays in Advent, and those Sundays from Septuagesima to Easter inclusive. Neither is it included in the votive Masses, except those of the Angels and the Blessed Virgin on Saturday. The *Gloria in excelsis Deo* is intoned by the celebrant, and the remaining text is sung by the choir.

CREDO

(Credo in unum Deum, I believe in one God)

Crédo in únum Déum,
I believe in one God,

I believe in one God,

Pátrem omnipoténtem,
Father almighty,

The Father Almighty,
maker of heaven and earth,
and of all things visible and invisible.

factórem coéli et térrae,
maker of heaven and of earth,

visibílium ómnium, et invisibílium.
visible of all things, and invisible.

Et in unum Dóminum Jésum Chrístum,
And in one Lord Jesus Christ,

And I believe in one Lord, Jesus Christ,
the only begotten Son of God,
born of the Father before all ages.
God from God, Light from Light,
True God from true God.
Begotten, not made,
of one substance with the Father
by whom all things were made.
Who for us and for our salvation
came down from heaven.

Fílium Déi unigénitum.
Son of God only begotten.

Et ex Pátre nátum ante ómni saécula.
And of Father born before all ages.

Déum de Déo, lúmen de lúmine,
God from God, light from light,

Déum vérum de Déo véro.
God true from God true.

Génitum, non fáctum,
Begotten, not made,

consubstantiálem Pátri:
of one substance with Father,

per quem ómnia fácta sunt.
by whom all things made were.

Qui propter nos hómines,
Who for us men,

et propter nóstram salútem
and for our salvation

descéndit de caélis.
descended from heavens.

Et   incarnátus   est   de   Spíritu   Sáncto
And made flesh was of   Spirit   Holy

And was incarnate by the Holy Spirit
of the Virgin Mary. And was made man.

ex María Vírgine. ET HOMO FACTUS EST.
of Mary Virgin. And man   made   was.

Crucifíxus étiam pro nóbis sub Póntio Piláto:
Crucified also for us   under Pontius Pilate,

Crucified also for us under Pontius Pilate,
he suffered, and was buried.

pássus,   et   sepúltus   est.
suffered,   and buried   was.

Et resurréxit tértia díe,
And he rose   third   day,

And on the third day he rose again,
according to the Scriptures.
He ascended into heaven and
he sits at the right hand of the Father.
He shall come again with glory
to judge the living and the dead;
and of his kingdom there will be no end.

secúndum   Scriptúras.
according to   Scriptures.

Et   ascéndit   in   caélum:
And he ascended into heaven,

sédet   ad   déxteram   Pátris.
he sits   at   right hand   of Father.

Et íterum ventúrus   est cum glória,
And again going to come he is with glory,

judicáre   vívos   et   mórtuos:
to judge   living   and dead;

cújus   régni   non   érit   fínis.
of whose kingdom not will there be   end.

Et   in Spíritum Sánctum
And in Spirit   Holy

And I believe in the Holy Spirit,
the Lord and Giver of life,
who proceeds from the Father and the Son
who together with the Father and the Son
is adored and glorified,
who spoke to us through the Prophets.

Dóminum,   et   vivificántem:
Lord,   and   lifegiver

qui ex   Pátre   Filióque   procédit.
who from Father and Son   proceeds.

Qui   cum   Pátre,   et   Fílio
Who with Father   and   Son

simul   adorátur   et   conglorificátur:
together is adored   and   glorified,

qui locutus est   per   Prophétas.
who   spoke   through   Prophets.

Et	únam,	sánctam,	cathólicam		And I believe in one, holy, catholic
And	**one,**	**holy,**	**catholic**		and Apostlic Church.

et	apostólicam	Ecclésiam.
and	**Apostolic**	**Church.**

Confíteor	únum	baptísma		I confess one baptism
I confess	**one**	**baptism**		for the remission of sins.

in	remissiónem	peccatórum.
for	**remission**	**of sins.**

Et	expécto	resurrectiónem	mortuórum.		I await the resurrection of the dead,
And	**I expect**	**resurrection**	**of dead.**		and the life of the world to come. Amen.

Et	vítam	ventúri	saéculi.	Amen.
And	**life**	**to come**	**of age.**	**Amen.**

The **Credo,** the longest text of the Mass Ordinary, was the last to be added, being finally incorporated into the Roman Mass in 1014 when the German Emperor Henry II required it of Pope Benedict VIII. The twelve articles of belief, the central assertions of the Christian faith, are traditionally ascribed to the Twelve Apostles who are said to have composed this Creed on the day of Pentecost while still under the direct influence of the Holy Spirit (see Acts 2:1-13). As early as the 2nd century the Roman form of this text compares closely with those of St. Irenaeus in southern Gaul and Tertullian of distant Africa, suggesting that, if not itself drawn up by the Apostles, the early form of the Creed was at least based on an outline which dates back to the Apostolic age.

This early form of the text, known as the Apostles' Creed, appears in very early times as part of the baptismal rite which featured a separate confession to each Person of the Holy Trinity [this explains the first person singular – *Credo,* I believe – which may seem unfitting today for congregational recitation; see also: Acts 8:36-37 and Matthew 28:19].

The present form of the Creed is based on the Nicean (or Nicea-Constantinople) version, which was approved by the Council of Nicea in 325. It was introduced to the eucharistic liturgy in Constantinople (early 6th century), in Spain (by the Council of Toledo, 589), and later into the Gallican rite in France, when Alcuin, Charlemagne's liturgical advisor, appointed a new Latin translation made by Paulinus of Aquileia in 796 to be sung between the Gospel and the Offertory. Pope Benedict VIII then introduced it into the Roman rite in 1014 at the insistence of the German Emperor Henry II.

The text has been an inspiration to composers throughout history, with its larger three-part form A B_ C (*Patrem... Filium... Spiritum Sanctum...*) offering a compelling larger structural organization [compare the Kyrie – A B A, and the Gloria – A B_ c], and the general ascriptions of A and C balancing nicely with the extended Christological specifics of B. In addition, the closing dogmatic assertions of *unum Ecclesiam* and *unum baptisma* find joyous release in the concluding *et expecto resurectionem ... et vitam. Amen!*

What a range of concepts and feelings! rich and abundant contrasts that sustain its considerable length and offer endless opportunities for "word-painting" and musical variety (e.g., *unum, visibilium/invisibilium, descendit,* the mystical *et incarnatus/ET HOMO FACTUS EST, crucifixus, sepultus, resurrexit, ascendit, sedit, iterum, judicare, vivos/mortuos, regni, unam, expecto, resurrectionem/mortuorum, vitam, Amen.*). Compare the more limited possibilities in this regard of the Kyrie, Sanctus-Benedictus, Agnus Dei, and even the Gloria; compare the Credo settings of Josquin's *Pange lingua,* Bach's *B-minor Mass,* Schubert's *G Major Mass,* Beethoven's *Missa Solemnis,* etc. to begin to appreciate the imagination and creativity these concepts and images have inspired. The large formal structure encourages the necessary unity and balance and the internal richness offers almost endless variety and contrast.

Liturgical context: The **Credo** is the third part of the Mass Ordinary and is sung in the Roman rite between the Gospel and Offertory. The celebrant intones the *Credo in unum Deum,* and the remainder is sung or recited by the choir or congregation.

SANCTUS

(*Sanctus, Sanctus, Sanctus* – Holy, Holy, Holy)

Sánctus,	Sánctus,	Sánctus,		Holy, Holy, Holy,
Holy,	**Holy,**	**Holy,**		**Lord God of Hosts.**

Dóminus Déus Sábaoth.
Lord God of Hosts.

Pléni	sunt	coéli	et	térra	Heaven and earth are full
Full	**are**	**heaven**	**and**	**earth**	**of thy glory.**

glória túa.
of glory thy.

Hosánna	in	excélsis.	Hosanna in the highest.
Hosanna	**in**	**highest.**	

BENEDICTUS

(*Benedictus qui venit,* Blessed is he who comes)

Benedíctus	qui	vénit	Blessed is He who comes
Blessed	**who**	**comes**	in the name of the Lord.

in	nómine	Dómini.
in	**name**	**of Lord.**

Hosánna	in	excélsis.	Hosanna in the highest.
Hosanna	**in**	**highest.**	

The **Sanctus** or Trisagion ("Thrice Holy") is the culmination of the prayers of thanksgiving offered by the celebrant in the Preface, an actual continuation of his final words: "The heavens and the heavenly hosts together with the blessed Seraphim in triumphant chorus unite . . . saying:" and the people (or choir) then join with "Holy, Holy, Holy . . ." These words are adapted from the words of the cherubim in Isaiah 6:3 :

> "And one cried unto the other, and said, Holy, Holy, Holy is the Lord
> of hosts: the whole earth is full of his glory" [Heb: "his glory is the fulness of
> the earth"].

which are echoed in the Apocalypse [Revelations] 4:8 :

> "And the four beasts had each of them six wings about him; and they
> were full of eyes within: and they rest not day and night, saying: Holy, Holy,
> Holy, Lord God Almighty, which was, and is, and is to come."

The Trisagion is found in the Hebrew liturgy as early as the 2nd century, in the Gallican rite by 529 (Council of Vaison), and in the Roman rite by the 7th century; it is found almost universally in every Christian rite, east or west. It preceeds the Canon, the most solemn portion of the Mass, the point at which the celebrant offers up the prayers and sacrifices of all the Faithful.

Sabaoth is a title which ascribes majesty, referring mainly to God. It appears in the Old Testament no less than 282 times. The full ascription *yhwh 'ĕlōhê sebāôt yiśrā'ēl*, "Yahweh, the God of the armies of Israel" (I Kings [Samuel] 17:45), conveys the concept of Israel's God seen as the supreme commander of its armies, a warrior who led the hosts of Israel into battle. Later the term implies that Yahweh is also the God of the heavenly hosts and has sovereignty over all things.

The **Benedictus** follows the **Sanctus** and is itself preceded and followed by the **Hosanna**. The text is from Matthew 21:9, where Christ's triumphal entry into Jerusalem is greeted with:

> "Hosanna to the Son of David: Blessed is he that cometh in the name
> of the Lord; Hosanna in the highest."

which is, in turn, based on Psalm 117 [118]:26 :

> "Blessed is he that cometh in the name of the Lord: we have blessed
> you out of the house of the Lord."

This psalm was recited by the Hebrews on the Feast of the Tabernacles during the procession around the altar. On the seventh procession of the seventh day of this feast, rejoicing when the trumpet sounded as the priest reached verses 25–26, the people would wave palms and willows and shout: *O Domine, salvum fac; O Domine, bene prosperare. Benedictus qui venit in nomine Domini!* (O Lord, let me be saved; O Lord, cause me to prosper well. Blessed is he who comes in the name of the Lord") The Hebrew word for *salvum fac* was "hoshi'a na"; and thus the seventh day of the feast became known as the Great Hosanna and the word itself became a shout or exclamation of joy, triumph, and exultation. [cf. Matthew 21:15; Mark 11:9–10; John 12:13]

Liturgical context: The **Sanctus** is the fourth part of the Mass Ordinary, the culmination of the celebrant's Preface which is recited or sung by the people (or choir). It also appears in the great hymn *Te Deum.* The **Benedictus** follows, preceded and followed by the **Hosanna**, just prior to the Canon; it is sometimes replaced or grouped with the motet *O salutaris hostia* ("O Redeeming Sacrifice"). The **Hosanna** is also heard on Palm Sunday during the distribution of the palms and as part of the solemn procession.

A G N U S   D E I

(*Agnus Dei*, Lamb of God)

Agnus   Déi,
Lamb   of God,

Lamb of God,
who takest away the sins of the world,
have mercy upon us.

qui   tóllis   peccáta   múndi:
(you)who take away   sins   of world,

miserére   nóbis.
have mercy   on us.

Agnus   Déi,
Lamb   of God,

Lamb of God,
who takest away the sins of the world,
have mercy upon us.

qui   tóllis   peccáta   múndi:
(you)who take away   sins   of world,

miserére   nóbis.
have mercy   on us.

Agnus   Déi,
Lamb   of God,

Lamb of God,
who takest away the sins of the world,
grant us peace.

qui   tóllis   peccáta   múndi:
(you)who take away   sins   of world,

dóna   nóbis pácem.
grant   us   peace.

The text of the **Agnus Dei** is found embedded in the ancient chant of the Roman and Ambrosian rites, the *Gloria in excelsis*:

> "*Agnus Dei, Filius Patris,*
> *Qui tollis peccata mundi,*
> *miserere nobis;*
> *Qui tollis peccata mundi,*
> *Suscipe deprecationem nostram;*
> *Qui sedes ad dexteram Patris,*
> *miserere nobis.*"

It is also attributed to John the Baptist who was questioned by the priests and Levites from Jerusalem concerning whether or not he was the Christ, and why he was baptizing others:

"Why, then, dost thou baptize, if thou art not the Christ, nor Elias, nor the Prophet?

John said to them in answer: I baptize with water; but in the midst of you there has stood one whom you do not know. . .

The next day John saw Jesus coming to him, and he said: Behold, the Lamb of God, who takes away the sin of the world!" (John 1:25-26, 29)

In early times the **Agnus Dei** was used in the Litanies at the end of the Mass (like the **Kyrie** at the beginning), and it survives in that form in the litanies of Holy Saturday and the Rogation Days. It was incorporated into the liturgy by Pope Sergius I (687-701) as a *confractum*, a chant to accompany the Fraction or breaking of the bread. When leavened bread was used, this activity took a considerable amount of time; but now, with unleavened bread, it takes only a few moments, and the **Agnus Dei** has come to be associated with the Kiss of Peace or the distribution of Communion.

The petition *miserere nobis* was originally unchanging (as it is still on Maundy Thursday when the Kiss of Peace is not given); it was repeated as necessary to accompany the Fraction. But during the 10th-12th centuries the three-fold form became established and the *dona nobis pacem* replaced the third *miserere nobis*. In the Requiem Mass the third line becomes: *dona eis requiem sempiternam* ("Grant them rest everlasting").

Liturgical context: The **Agnus Dei** is sung near the end of the Canon, following the passage *Haec commixto* ("May this mixture and consecration of the Body and Blood of our Lord Jesus Christ be to us who receive it effectual unto eternal life. Amen."), between the Fraction and the Communion antiphon. It is the fifth and final portion of the Mass Ordinary and the only one that is changed when sung as part of the Requiem Mass where the final *dona nobis pacem* is replaced by *dona eis requiem sempiternam.*

THE PROPER OF THE MASS

Unlike the unchanging portions of the Ordinary of the Mass (the Kyrie, Gloria, Credo, Sanctus et Benedictus, and Agnus Dei), the five parts of the Proper vary from Mass to Mass depending on the season of the liturgical year (*Proprium de Tempore*), the feasts of saints (*Proprium de Sanctis*), and other special days. The five parts of the Proper are: the **Introit, Gradual, Alleluia Verse** (or **Tract**), **Offertory**, and **Communion.** They were in general use by 500 A.D., and fully standardized by Pope Gregory the Great (d.604) by the late 6th century.

The Propers fall into two categories: chants that follow a lesson (**Gradual** and **Alleluia**), and those that accompany a liturgical action (the **Introit**, sung during the entrance of the clergy; the **Offertory**, sung during the bringing of offerings to the altar; and the **Communion**, sung during the distribution of the Host to the Faithful).

Another changing part of the Proper of the Mass is the singing of the five major Sequences on certain occasions: *Victimae paschali laudes* (Easter and Easter Week), *Veni Sancte Spiritus* (Trinity Sunday), *Lauda Sion* (Corpus Christi), *Stabat Mater* (Feasts of the Seven Sorrows), and the *Dies irae* (Mass for the Dead). The Sequence, sung after the Gradual and Alleluia, just before the Epistle and the Gospel, was added to the liturgy during the Middle Ages.

INTROIT

(*introitus*, entrance; *antiphona ad introitum*, entrance chant)

The **Introit** is the first item of the Proper of the Mass, one of the so-called "action chants" which is sung by the *schola* to accompany the entrance of the clergy into the church at the beginning of the Mass. It consists of an antiphon, a verse, the *Gloria Patri*, and the repetition of the antiphon. The texts are usually taken from the psalms, but those for the most important feasts are often from elsewhere in the Bible; for instance, *Puer natus est* ("A boy is born"), the Introit antiphon for the III Mass of the Nativity, is from Isaiah 9:6. Like *Puer natus est*, most Introits announce the dominant theme of the Feast.

GRADUAL

(*Graduale*, from *gradus*, a step)

Unlike the other three "action chants" of the Proper (the Introit, Offertory, and Communion) which are sung to accompany a liturgical action, the **Gradual** is sung for its own sake as a commentary on the Lesson or Epistle which has just been recited during the Liturgy of the Word. The name *Gradual* comes from the fact that the soloist originally chanted the psalm from an elevated place, the step (*gradus*) of the ambo where the subdeacon had just read the Epistle.

Originally whole psalms were sung by a soloist and the people answered each verse with a refrain. The text now consists of two verses, usually taken from the same psalm, but sometimes the second verse is chosen from another psalm or book of Scripture, and some are from non-liturgical sources (i.e., the *Dolorosa et lacrymosa* and *Virgo Dei* from the feast of Seven Sorrows and the first verse of the Gradual for Requiems: *Requiem aeternam . . .*). Other non-psalmodic texts include: *Ecce sacerdos, Omnes de Saba, Christus factus est,* and *Locus iste.*

ALLELUIA - VERSE

The **Alleluia-Verse** (or Alleluiatic Verse, *versus alleluiaticus*) is the third part of the Proper of the Roman Mass and is sung immediately following the Gradual, between the Epistle and the Gospel during the Liturgy of the Word. Following the long melismatic extension of the final syllable of the *Alleluia* (called the *Jubilus*), a verse from the psalms or a fragment of a Christian poem was added (c. 8th century); the *Alleluia* is then repeated. From Septuagesima to Good Friday, on Ember Days and at Requiems, the Alleluia-Verse is replaced by the Tract.

TRACT

(tractus, a drawing through)

The **Tract** (*psalmus tractus*) is the second psalm sung between the Epistle and the Gospel during the Liturgy of the Word. It replaces the **Alleluia-Verse** during times of penitence and mourning (from Septuagesima to Good Friday, Ember Days, some Vigils, and in Requiems). It is called *Tractus* because it is sung straight through without any responses by the choir (*in uno tractu*, in one coursing through), as distinguished from the responsorial nature of the Gradual which preceeds it. In the Middle Ages the Tract was known as a "chant of grief," which Hugh of St. Victor interpreted as the "laments of the saints which were <u>drawn</u> up from the depths of their hearts." The texts are almost always a few verses chosen from a psalm.

SEQUENCE

(sequentia, that which follows)

Not officially listed as one of the five parts of the Proper of the Mass, the **Sequence** is liturgically "proper" in the sense that each of the existing Sequences is associated with a particular season or feast; it is, then, one of the "changing" or variable portions of the Roman Mass, as distinct from the fixed portions of the Ordinary.

In its early period (850-1050) the Sequence was basically a syllabic text added to the pre-existing melodic melismas of the Alleluia *jubilus*, a "memory aid" that reduced the long ecstatic melismas to a completely syllabic style which was mostly unrhymed and of irregular meter, but consistent in syllabic correspondence within the double versicles (paired isorhythmic couplets sometimes called *prosa* or "prose"). Notker Balbulus of St. Gall (c.840-912) is often cited as the "inventor" of this style even though he called the collection of his works "hymns" (*Liber hymnorum*, Book of Hymns) and describes his inspiration as coming from a Norman Antiphonary brought to St. Gall c.885 by a refugee from the Abbey of Jumièges. Other possible sources are Saint-Benoît sur Loire, Toul, and Lâon.

A transitional stage follows (1050-1150) in which the Sequence begins to evidence increased rhythmic regularity and a greater frequency of rhyme. And the melody, although it may borrow its *Incipit* from an existing chant, is composed freely thereafter to go with the newly-created text, a procedure that allows for much greater expression than the earlier process of underlaying (syllabic) text to a pre-existing (melismatic) melody. [see *Victimae paschali laudes*]

In the final period (1150-1300) the Sequence became regular rhymed verse with a symmetry that was almost predictable and, if not progressive, at least popular. Adam of St. Victor and the other Victorine poets developed this later sequence to its definitive form which consists of parallel strophes of symmetrical construction and progressive repetitions of paired lines (double versicles) which both have the same melody (*aa bb cc dd ...*), as opposed to the verses of a hymn which are all identical in structure and sung to the same music.

The Sequence is a medieval addition to the Proper of the Mass which is sung immediately following the Alleluia-Verse and before the Gospel on certain special occasions. Of the thousands of medieval Sequences, four survived the reforms of the Council of Trent (1545-1563), and the fifth (the *Stabat Mater*) was reinstated by Pope Benedict XIII in 1727. Sr. Marie Girten (in Nicholson, *Dictionary of Plainsong*) gives a sensitive analysis and insightful listing of the five great Sequences in use in the Roman Church today: "*Victimae paschali* of Easter, full of restrained triumph; *Veni Sancte Spiritus* of Pentecost, with a distinct mystical element both in words and music; *Lauda Sion* of Corpus Christi, solemn and doctrinal in tone; *Stabat Mater* for the feast of the Seven Sorrows of the Blessed Virgin Mary, a contemplation of the 'passion' of Our Lady and an expression of tender sympathy; and the *Dies irae* in Masses for the dead, redolent of great awe combined with confidence."

OFFERTORY

(*offertorium*, offering; from *offere*, to bring before, present)

The **Offertory** is the beginning of the Mass of the Faithful (the Celebration of the Eucharist). Originally the offerings were the bread and wine that were to be consecrated for the Eucharistic meal, and they were brought in procession to the altar in silence. The singing of a psalm or offertory chant during this action was introduced at Carthage by St. Augustine (d.430) as early as the 4th century.

Liturgically it is one of the five parts of the Proper, those portions of the Mass which change according to the season or particular feasts. It is one of the "action chants" (like the Introit a n d Communion), an antiphonal chant sung to accompany a liturgical action, in this case, the bringing of the gifts to the altar.
The Offertory chants are very elaborate and melismatic, often expressing great joy and praise (*Jubilate..., Benedicite..., Laudate...*); or, during some seasons (i.e., Lent), they are more restrained and prayerful. The texts are taken mostly from the book of Psalms, chosen according to the feast of the day or related in some way to the text of the Introit or the Gospel reading. Many of these other texts are "old Latin" translations of parts of the Bible, and "may be earlier than the 5th century."

COMMUNION

(*communio*, a sharing in common, uniting together)

Communion originally consisted of the recitation of a psalm, with the *Gloria Patri*, and was sung to fill the time needed by the clergy for the distribution of the Host. Thus, like the Introit and the Offertory, it is one of the "action" chants of the Proper of the Mass which is sung to accompany a liturgical action and which changes according to the particular feast, liturgical season, or the purpose for which the Votive Mass is being offered. The texts were chosen from the psalms or from texts composed for the particular occasion. By the 12th century only the antiphon remained, and it was sung after the Communion. The one exception is in the Requiem Mass (the Mass for the Dead) where the *Lux aeterna* is followed by the verse *Requiem aeternam*.

SACRED LATIN TEXTS
The Requiem Mass

Intr.
6.

R Equi-em * aetér- nam dó-na é- is   Dómi-

ne :   et lux perpé-tu- a   lúce- at   é-   is.

"It is my conviction that in certain words of ancient origin
the inner meaning is revealed,
not in semantics, but in their sounds."
(Harry Somers)

THE REQUIEM MASS

(*Missa pro Defunctis*, Mass for the Dead)

The Requiem Mass, "one of the most beautiful and expressive in the Roman Missal," is of very ancient origin. In pre-Apostolic times the Jews prayed that the immortal souls of the just might have *requiem aeternam* ("rest eternal"), and sources from the 2nd century mention this celebration of the Eucharist, as do the New Testament apocryphal Acts of John and the writings of Tertullian from the 3rd century.

The Requiem Mass is celebrated *In commemoratione Omnium Fidelium Defunctorum* ("in memory of all the faithful departed") on All Soul's Day (November 2), and is also, strictly speaking, neither a Common Mass or a Votive Mass, but the one appointed by the Roman Church to be sung on the day or anniversary of the death or burial of a Christian, and also on the third, seventh, or thirtieth day after the burial.

The name *Requiem* (which is taken from the first word of the Introit: *Requiem aeternam ...* , Rest eternal ...) is used to refer to the Mass itself and to musical settings of the text (i.e., Verdi's Requiem). Liturgically, a Requiem is distinguished from the Common or Votive Masses in the following ways: the psalm *Judica me* (Psalm 42 [43] : "Judge me, O God") is omitted from the beginning; the *Gloria in excelsis* and the *Credo* are not said; the joyous Alleluia-Verse is replaced by the Tract *Absolve, Domine, animas omnium fidelium defunctorum* ("Absolve, O Lord, the souls of all the faithful departed"); the Sequence *Dies Irae* ("Day of wrath" – a long, extremely powerful depiction of the chaos and terror of the Last Judgement) is appointed to be sung in the first Mass of All Soul's Day, funeral masses, and anniversary Requiem masses; and the Kiss of Peace is omitted since Communion is not given in this rite.

Like other Masses appointed for special occasions, the Collect and the readings from the Epistle and the Gospel are chosen with sensitivity and care. The following texts are the ones appointed for the three Masses for All Soul's Day:

I. *Epistle:* "Behold I tell you a mystery: we shall indeed rise again, but we shall not all be changed ... at the last trumpet ... Death is swallowed up in victory ... thanks be to God ... " (I Corinthians 15: 51–57).

   Gospel "... And they who have done good shall come forth unto resurrection of life; but they who have done evil unto the resurrection of judge-ment" (John 5: 19–29).

II. *Epistle:* " ... it is therefore a holy and wholesome thought to pray for the dead, that they might be loosed from their sins" (II Machabees 12: 42–46).

   Gospel: " ... For this is the will of my Father who sent me, that whoever be-holds the Son, and believes in him, shall have everlasting life, and I will raise him up on the last day" (John 6: 37–40).

III. *Epistle:* "And I heard a voice from heaven saying, Write: Blessed are the dead who die in the Lord henceforth. Yea, says the Spirit, let them rest from their labors, for their works shall follow them" (Apocalypse [Revelation] 14:13).

   Gospel: "... He that eateth my flesh, and drinketh my blood, hath everlasting life: and I will raise him up on the last day" (John 6: 51–55).

The liturgy follows the same order as the Common Mass [see THE ROMAN MASS] with the exceptions noted above; but two additional texts have been frequently set by composers as part of the Requiem which liturgically belong to the *Exequiarum Ordo* or Burial Rite: the first is the *Libera me* ("Deliver me, O Lord"), a responsory which is sung after the Mass, before the "absolution" of the corpse; and the second, the antiphon *In paradisum* ("May the Angels lead you into Paradise") which is sung while the coffin is being carried to the grave.

In its actual form the Requiem Mass and the Office of the Dead can be traced back to the ninth or eighth century, even though some prayers and a service for the dead existed long before that time (St. Ambrose speaks of the celebration of funeral masses in Rome in the 4th century). All Soul's Day, the feast for the commemoration of the dead, was instituted by St. Odo of Cluny in 998, but it wasn't until the 13th century, when the doctrine of Purgatory was universally accepted, that Masses for the dead became common. The sequence *Dies irae* was the last portion to be added, first appearing in an Italian Dominican Missal of the 14th century and in French Missals of the 15th century before being incorporated into the Roman Missal promulgated by Pope Pius V in 1570 by order of the Council of Trent (1545-1563). The *Missa pro Defunctis* is a "Mass for the *defunctis*," the "finished," those who have finished the course of life or existence; hence, the departed, the dead. Its liturgical order is not always observed by composers in their musical settings; movements are sometimes omitted entirely, or combined in part with other movements, or repeated for musical purposes. These choices always offer insights into the ways a particular composer is thinking musically, theologically, and philosophically and are well worth careful attention.

THE REQUIEM MASS

Introit	*Requiem aeternam* ("Rest eternal grant unto them")
Kyrie	*Kyrie eleison* ("Lord, have mercy")
Gradual	*Requiem aeternam* ("Rest eternal grant unto them")
Tract	*Absolve, Domine* ("Absolve, O Lord, the souls of the faithful departed")
Sequence	*Dies irae* ("Day of wrath")
Offertory	*Domine Jesu Christe* ("Lord Jesus Christ")
Sanctus	*Sanctus, Sanctus, Sanctus* ("Holy, Holy, Holy")
Benedictus	*Benedictus qui venit* ("Blessed is he who comes")
Agnus Dei	*Agnus Dei* ("Lamb of God")
Communion	*Lux aeterna* ("May light eternal shine on them")
Responsory	*Libera me, Domine* ("Deliver me, O Lord")
Antiphon	*In paradisum* ("May the Angels lead you into paradise")

(*introitus*, entrance)

Réquiem aetérnam dóna éis, Dómine:
Rest   eternal   grant to them,   Lord;

Rest eternal grant to them, O Lord,
and let perpetual light shine upon them.

et   lux   perpétua   lúceat   éis.
and light perpetual let shine on them.

Te   décet   hýmnus Déus in Zíon,
Thee befits   hymn   God in Zion,

A hymn befits thee, O God in Zion.
and to thee a vow shall be fulfilled
in Jerusalem.

et   tíbi   redétur
and   to thee   shall be fulfilled

vótum   in   Jerúsalem:
vow   in   Jerusalem.

exáudi oratiónem méam,
Hear   prayer   my,

Hear my prayer,
for unto thee all flesh shall come.

ad   te   ómnis cáro   véniet.
to thee   all   flesh shall come.

(*Repeat*: Réquiem aetérnam . . . lúceat éis)   (*Repeat*: Rest eternal . . . shine upon them.)

The Requiem Mass takes its name and much of its general character (the 14th century addition of the *Dies irae* sequence notwithstanding) from the first word of the **Introit**: *Requiem aeternam dona eis, Domine* ("Rest eternal grant unto them, O Lord"). The source of this text is found in IV Esdras ("the Apocalypse of Esdras"), an uncanonical apocryphal book which "is reckoned among the most beautiful productions of Jewish literature. Widely known in the early Christian ages and frequently quoted by the Fathers (especially St. Ambrose), it may be said to have framed the popular belief of the Middle Ages concerning the last things" (C.L. Souvay). It is also the source of other liturgical texts: the response *lux perpetua lucebit sanctis tuis*, the introit *Accipite jucunditatem*, the *Modo coronantur* of the Office of the Apostles, and the *Crastina die* for Christmas eve.

Esdras, a "second Moses," is credited with the organization of the synagogues and the determination of the books hallowed as canonical among the Jews, but he is not the author of IV Esdras. The main body of the book (Chapters 3-14) is ascribed to an unknown Jew from the first century (c. 97 A.D.), but the passage containing the *requiem aeternitates* and *lux perpetua* is from Chapter 2, verses 34 and 35, a portion of the introductory and concluding chapters which shows evident traces of Christianity and is ascribed to the 3rd century (c. 201-268):

Ego Esdras praeceptum accepi a Domino	I, Esdras, received a command from the Lord
in monte Oreb, ut irem ad Israel;	on Mount Oreb, that I might go to Israel.
ad quos cum venirem, reprobaverunt me,	When I came to them, they rejected me,
et respuerunt mandatum Domini;	and cast out the commandment of the Lord.
ideoque vobis dico, gentes quae auditis,	Therefore I say to you, nations who hear,
et intelligitis: Expectate pastorem vestrum,	and understand: Expect your shepherd,
<u>requiem aeternitatis dabit vobis</u>,	<u>he will give you eternal rest</u>,
quoniam in proximo est ille,	since he is near at hand,
qui in fine saeculi adveniet.	he who will come at the end of the age.
Parati estote ad praemia regni,	Be prepared for the rewards of the kingdom,
quia <u>lux perpetua</u> in lucebit vobis	because <u>perpetual light</u> will shine on you
per aeternitatem temporis.	throughout all eternity.

And we also read in Isaiah 58:10-11:

Cum effuderis esurienti animam tuam,	When thou shalt pour out thy soul to the hungry,
et animam afflictam repleveris,	and shalt satisfy the afflicted soul,
orietur in tenebris lux tua,	thy light shall rise up in darkness,
et tenebrae tuae erunt sicut meridies.	and thy darkness shall be as the noonday.
<u>Et requiem tibi dabit Dominus semper</u>,	<u>And the Lord will give thee rest continually</u>,
et implebit splendoribus animam tuam,	and will fill thy soul with brightness,
et ossa tua liberabit ...	and deliver thy bones ...

One of the tenets of the ancient Jewish faith was that after death the immortal soul of the just went to sleep with their fathers. For them, in a sense, the Introit is "Requiem enough." They have offered prayers since pre-Apostolic times that the dead might have eternal <u>rest</u>.

"But <u>I will sleep with my fathers</u>, and thou shalt take me away out of this land, and bury me in the buryingplace of my ancestors" (Genesis 47:30).

"So David <u>slept with his fathers</u>, and was buried in the city of David" (III Kings [I Kings] 2:10).

" ... He sent [a] sacrifice to be offered for the sins of the dead, thinking religiously concerning the resurrection, (for if he had not hoped that they that were slain should rise again, it would have seemed superfluous and vain to pray for the dead,) and because he considered that <u>they who had fallen asleep with godliness</u> had great grace laid up for them. It is therefore a holy and wholesome thought to pray for the dead, that they may be loosed from sins" (II Machabees 12:44-46).

"For if the dead do not rise, neither has Christ risen; and if Christ has not risen, vain is your faith, for you are still in your sin. Hence <u>they also who have fallen asleep</u> with Christ, have perished ... But as it is, Christ has risen from the dead, the first-fruits of <u>those who have fallen asleep</u>" (I Corinthians 15:16-18, 20).

The second portion of the Introit--the antiphon--is taken directly from Psalm 64 [65] : 2-3, and it too is echoed elsewhere in the Holy Scriptures:

"Offer to God the sacrifice of praise: and pay thy vows to the most High" (Psalm 49 [50] : 14).

"And there shall be month after month, and sabbath after sabbath: and all flesh shall come to adore before my face, saith the Lord" (Isaiah 66:13).

KYRIE

(Κυριε ελεησον, *Kyrie eleison*, Lord have mercy)

Kýrie	eléison,	*repeat,*	*repeat*	**Lord have mercy,** *repeat, repeat*
Lord	**have mercy,**	" ,	"	

Chríste	eléison,	*repeat,*	*repeat*	**Christ have mercy,** *repeat, repeat*
Christ	**have mercy,**	" ,	"	

Kýrie	eléison,	*repeat,*	*repeat*	**Lord have mercy,** *repeat, repeat*
Lord	**have mercy,**	" ,	"	

This acclamatory supplication -- its brief invocation and petition being similar to Psalm 6:3 ("Have mercy on me, O Lord, for I am weak") and Psalm 40 [41]: 5,11 ("O Lord, be thou merciful unto me . . . But thou, O Lord, have mercy on me") -- is found in pagan antiquity and in 4th century Jerusalem. In the 5th century Pope Gelasius I (492-6) substituted a litany for the common Prayer of the Church and the Greek form was retained as the people's response. The litany was then moved to the beginning of the Mass, retaining the Greek form, Κυριε ελεησον (*kyrie eleison*), as it still does today. The second portion (*Christe eleison*) was added by Pope Gregory I (d.604).

The *Ordo of St. Amand* of the 8th century is the first evidence of the *Kyrie* consisting of the familiar nine acclamations. Its tripartite A–B–A structure, with each part having its own intrinsic tripartite structure, has been attractive and inspirational to composers throughout history, from the earliest plainsong to the present day. Some of the earliest plainsong chants, like the *Kyrie* of the *Missa pro Defunctis*, uses the same melody for all acclamations except the last: AAA AAA AAA'. Other common forms are: AAA BBB AAA; AAA AAA BBB; AAA BBB CCC; ABA CDC EFE.

Liturgical context: The **Kyrie** of the Requiem Mass is the portion of the opening Entrance rite which is sung following the Introit *Requiem aeternam*.

SEQUENCE

(*sequentia*, that which follows)

Díes	írae,	díes	ílla,
Day	**of wrath,**	**day**	**that,**

Day of wrath, that day
shall dissolve the world into embers,
as David prophesied with the Sibyl.

Sólvet	saéclum	in	favílla:
shall dissolve	**world**	**into**	**embers,**

Téste	Dávid	cum	Sibýlla.
witness	**David**	**with**	**Sibyl.**

Quántus	trémor	est	futúrus,
How great	**trembling**	**there is**	**going to be,**

How great the trembling will be,
when the Judge shall come,
the rigorous investigator of all things!

5 Quando	júdex	est	ventúrus,
when	**judge**	**is**	**going to come,**

Cúncta	stricte	discussúrus!
all things	**strictly**	**about to investigate!**

Túba	mírum	spárgens	sónum
Trumpet	**wondrous**	**sending out**	**sound**

The trumpet, spreading its wondrous sound
through the tombs of every land,
will summon all before the throne.

Per	sepúlchra	regiónum,
through	**tombs**	**of regions,**

Cóget	ómnes	ante	thrónum.
will summon	**all**	**before**	**throne.**

10 Mors	stupébit,	et	natúra,
Death	**shall be stunned,**	**and**	**nature,**

Death will be stunned, likewise nature,
when all creation shall rise again
to answer the One judging.

Cum	resúrget	creatúra,
when	**will rise again**	**creation,**

Judicánti	responsúra.
(the one) judging	**to answer.**

Líber	scríptus	proferétur,
Book	**written**	**will be made known,**

A written book will be brought forth,
in which all shall be contained,
and from which the world shall be judged.

In	quo	tótum	continétur,
in	**which**	**all**	**shall be contained,**

15 Unde	múndus	judicétur.
from which	**world**	**shall be judged.**

Júdex   ergo   cum   sedébit,
Judge   therefore   when   will sit,

Quíd-quid   látet   apparébit:
whatever   lies concealed   will be revealed,

Nil   inúltum   remanébit.
nothing (wrong)   unavenged   shall remain.

When therefore the Judge is seated,
whatever lies hidden shall be revealed,
no wrong shall remain unpunished.

Quid   sum   míser   tunc   dictúrus?
What   am I   wretch   then   to say?

20 Quem   patrónum   rogatúrus?
Which   protector   going to ask for,

Cum   vix   jústus   sit   secúrus.
when   scarcely   just man   is   secure?

What then am I, a poor wretch, going to say?
Which protector shall I ask for,
when even the just are scarcely secure?

Rex   treméndae   majestátis,
King   of fearful   majesty,

Qui   salvándos   sálvas   gratis,
who   the saved   save   freely,

Sálva   me   fons   pietátis.
save   me   fount   of pity.

King of terrifying majesty,
who freely saves the saved:
Save me, fount of pity.

25 Recordáre   Jésu   píe,
Remember   Jesus   merciful,

Quod   sum   cáusa   túae   víae,
that   I am   cause   of your   sojourn,

Ne   me   pérdas   ílla   díe.
not   me   cast out   that   day.

Remember, merciful Jesus,
that I am the cause of your sojourn;
do not cast me out on that day.

Quaérens   me,   sedísti   lássus:
Seeking   me,   you sat   weary;

Redemísti   crúcem   pássus:
you redeemed   Cross   having suffered.

30 Tántus   lábor   non   sit   cássus.
Such great   labor   not   be   futile.

Seeking me, you sat down weary;
having suffered the Cross, you redeemed me.
May such great labor not be in vain.

Júste   júdex   ultiónis,
Just   judge   of vengeance,

Dónum   fac   remissiónis,
grant   gift   of remission,

Ante   díem   ratiónis.
before   day   of reckoning.

Just Judge of vengeance,
grant the gift of remission
before the day of reckoning.

Ingemísco, tamquam   réus:
I groan,   like   guilty one;

35 cúlpa   rúbet   vúltus   méus:
guilt   reddens   face   my.

Supplicánti   párce   Déus.
Supplicant   spare   God.

I groan, like one who is guilty;
my face blushes with guilt.
Spare thy supplicant, O God.

Qui   Maríam   absolvísti,
Who   Mary   absolved,

Et   latrónum   exaudísti,
and   thief   heeded,

Míhi   quoque   spem   dedísti.
to me   also   hope   have given.

You who absolved Mary [Magdalene],
and heeded the thief,
have also given hope to me.

40 Préces   méae   non   sunt   dígnae:
Prayers   my   not   are   worthy;

Sed   tu   bónus   fac   benígne,
but   you   good   grant   kindly,

Ne   perénni   crémer   ígne.
not   everlasting   I burn   in fire.

My prayers are not worthy,
but Thou, good one, kindly grant
that I not burn in the everlasting fires.

Inter   óves   lócum   praésta,
among   sheep   place   of eminence,

Et   ab   haédis   me   sequéstra,
and   from   goats   me   separate,

45 Státuens   in   párte   déxtra.
stationing   on   hand   right.

Grant me a favored place among thy sheep,
and separate me from the goats,
placing me at thy right hand.

69

Confutátis   maledíctis,
confounded   accursed,

When the accursed are confounded,
consigned to the fierce flames:
call me to be with the blessed.

Flámmis   ácribus   addíctis,
to flames   harsh   consigned,

Vóca me   cum   benedíctis.
call   me   with   blessed.

Oro   súpplex   et   acclínis,
I pray   kneeling   and suppliant,

I pray, suppliant and kneeling,
my heart contrite as if it were ashes:
protect me in my final hour.

50 Cor   contrítum quasi cínis:
heart contrite   as if ashes:

Gére   cúram   méi   fínis.
bear   care   of my   end.

Lacrimósa   díes   ílla,
Tearful   day   that,

O how tearful that day,
on which the guilty shall rise
from the embers to be judged.
Spare them then, O God.

Qua   resúrget   ex   favílla,
on which shall rise from   embers,

Judicándus   hómo réus.
to be judged   man   guilty.

55 Húic   érgo   párce Déus.
Him   therefore spare   God.

Píe   Jésu Dómine,
Merciful Jesus Lord,

Merciful Lord Jesus,
grant them rest.

dóna   éis   réquiem.
grant   to them rest.

Commonly ascribed to Thomas of Celano, the 13th century Franciscan friar and biographer of St. Francis of Assisi (1182-1226), the sequence **Dies irae** is most probably of earlier origin, having been found in manuscripts dated c. 1250-55 and, according to Inguanez, to one "perhaps" of the 12th century. Thomas, whose authorship is a late attribution (14th century), may have reworked an earlier text. H.T. Henry considers "very probable the conjecture usually entertained by hymnologists, that the *Dies irae* was composed by a Franciscan in the 13th century" (*Catholic Encyclopedia).*

The form of the present text suggests that the original was probably seventeen three-line stanzas in length and that the last six lines were later additions, the first four of those lines (beginning at line 52: *Lacrimosa dies illa*) having been taken verbatim from a 12th century *trope* on the responsory *Libera me*, and the last two lines (*Pie Jesu, Domine ...*) being an added concluding prayer. Thus the structure of the poem consists of 17 three-line stanzas in accentual, trochaic meter with two-syllable rhymes:

> 1. *Dí-es̆ í-raĕ, dí-es̆ íl-lă,*
>   *Solvet saeclum in favilla:*
>   *Teste David cum Sibylla.*

followed by 3 couplets: the first two having two-syllable rhymes, and the last being assonant and catalectic:

> 18. *Lacrimosa dies illa,*
>   *Qua resurget ex favilla,*
>
>   *Judicandus homo reus.*
> 19. *Huic ergo parce Deus.*
>
>   *Pie Jesu Domine,*
>   *dona eis requiem.*

The structural and expressive closure of the first seventeen stanzas gives further credence to this theory. The ending two-syllable rhymes are never the same in consecutive stanzas (*illa, futurus, sonum, natura*, etc.) until the strong assonance found in the final two of these first seventeen stanzas (*maledictis, acclinis*). The dramatic denouement is expressed in the final words of these last six lines, the penitent's final plea: *Maledictis addictis; benedictis. Acclinis: cinis . . . finis. ([When] Accursed are consigned; [voca] blessed. Supplicant: ashes . . . finis.)*

The source of the present text is found in the Prophecy of Sophonias (Soph. 1:15-16), also known as Zephaniah (a contemporary of Jermias), which was written in the beginning of the reign of Josias (641-610 B.C.):

> *Dies irae, dies illa,*   Day of wrath, that day,
> *dies tribulationes et angustiae,*   a day of tribulation and distress,
> *dies calamitatis et miseriae,*   a day of calamity and misery,
> *dies tenebrarum et caliginis,*   a day of darkness and obscurity,
> *dies nebulae et turbinis*   a day of clouds and whirlwinds,
> *dies tubae et clangoris.*   a day of the trumpet and alarm.

The Rev. John Julian, writing in his monumental *Dictionary of Hymnology* (1925), states that "the hold which this Sequence has had upon the minds of men of various nations and creeds has been very great. Goethe uses it ... in his *Faust* with great effect."

Carefully selected portions of the Sequence appear in Scene XX, when Margaret is attending the Requiem for her slain brother Valentine. Earlier Faust, in his search for a meaningful earthly existence, had cursed "whatever entices and snares the souls with vision vain ... high ambition ... apparition ... name, and fame ... possession ... indulgent leisures ... Hope ... Faith ... And Patience most of all!" But his divine philosophical struggles produced nothing tangible, and his egoistic impatience weakens him and he offers his soul to Mephistopheles, confident that the devil cannot "with rich enjoyment fool [him]"

71

into losing the wager. Mephistopheles unsuccessfully tempts him with base debaucheries and then tries restoring his youth and tempting him with the love of a poor young maiden, Gretchen [Margaret], by wooing her himself with jewels that she supposes to have come from Faust [the "Jewel Song"]. Gretchen [am Spinnrade] surrenders herself to Faust ("a living sin am I! Yet--all that drove my heart thereto, God! was so good, so dear, so true!") and becomes the Stabat Margaret, praying to the Mater Dolorosa for comfort and intercession. Her brother Valentine, a soldier, enraged at her shameful act, engages the suitor and Mephistopheles in a duel and is killed by Faust. Margaret, *tristis et afflicta*, her own soul pierced by the sword of her grief (Luke 2:35), is in the Cathedral, attending the Byronic Requiem, when, overcome by her sorrow and shame, she bids a Bacchanalian adieu (translation by Bayard Taylor):

MARGARET.

Woe! woe!
Would I were free from the thoughts
That cross me, drawing hither and thither,
Despite me!

CHORUS.

Dies irae, dies illa,
Solvet saeclum in favilla!
(*Sound of the organ.*)

EVIL SPIRIT.

Wrath takes thee!
The trumpet peals!
The graves tremble!
And thy heart
From ashy rest
To fiery torments
Now again requickened,
Throbs to life!

MARGARET.

Would I were forth!
I feel as if the organ here
My breath takes from me,
My very heart
Dissolved by the anthem!

CHORUS.

Judex ergo cum sedebit,
Quidquid latet, apparebit,
Nil inultum remanebit.

MARGARET.

I cannot breathe!
The massy pillars
Imprison me!
The vaulted arches
Crush me! -- Air!

EVIL SPIRIT.
Hide thyself! Sin and shame
Stay never hidden.
Air? Light?
Woe to thee!

CHORUS.
Quid sum miser tunc dicturus?
Quem patronum rogaturus,
Cum vix justus sit securus?

EVIL SPIRIT.
They turn their faces,
The glorified, from thee:
The pure, their hands to offer,
Shuddering, refuse thee!
Woe!

CHORUS.
Quid sum miser tunc dicturus?

MARGARET.
Neighbor! Your cordial!
(She falls in a swoon.)

Julian also notes that this great Sequence "furnishes a grand climax to Canto vi. in Sir Walter Scott's *Lay of the Last Minstrel*." This "greatly admired" condensed rendering consists of only twelve lines:

That day of wrath, that dreadful day,
When heaven and earth shall pass away,
What power shall be the sinner's stay?
How shall he meet that dreadful day?

When, shrivelling like a parchèd scroll,
The flaming heavens together roll;
When louder yet, and yet more dread,
Swells the high trump that wakes the dead:

Oh, on that day, that wrathful day,
When man to judgment wakes from clay,
Be Thou the trembling sinner's stay,
Though heaven and earth shall pass away.

The **Dies Irae** "is a sublime and awesome portrayal of the Last Judgement and of the emotion aroused in the Christian at the prospect of the end of all things" (Parrish); it is "the chief glory of sacred poetry and the most precious treasure of the Latin Church" (Daniel), "solitary in its excellence" (Coles), and "remarkable for its fine technique and sublime inspiration" (Cabrol). It brings out "some of the violent powers of the Latin language -- the solemn effect of the triple rhyme which has been likened to blow following blow of the hammer on the anvil -- the confidence of the poet in the universal interest of his theme, a confidence which has made him set out his matter with so majestic and unadorned a plainness as at once to be intelligible to all -- these merits, with many more, have given the *Dies Irae* a foremost place among the masterpieces of sacred song" (Trench).

Like other Sequences [see THE PROPER OF THE MASS: SEQUENCE] the text is set syllabically and its inherent power and drama have inspired a wide-ranging melodic setting. But the structure of the plainsong is not like other sequences: the form of its first seventeen stanzas, *aa bb cc; aa bb cc; aa bb c* , followed by *d e f* differs greatly from the "progressive" form of other sequences: *aa bb cc dd ee ff etc.* This unusual degree of internal repetition in the *Dies irae* has contributed greatly to its power and popularity.

One other musical comment worth noting, since the plainchant melody has been employed so frequently by later composers (from Berlioz's *Symphonie fantastique* to 20th century works by Pizzetti, Dallapiccola, and Penderecki), is that the melody is also taken from the responsory *Libera me*:

Liturgically, this Sequence was early employed in private prayers and as an Advent hymn, heralding the One who is coming to judge the world. It is found in 13th century Franciscan Missals, and Julian notes its appearance in a 14th century Dominican Missal written apparently for use at Pisa. It was included in the Requiem Mass in Italy from the 14th century and in French Missals of the 15th century. It survived the reforms of the Council of Trent (1545-1563) and finally became a part of the Roman Missal in 1570 under Pope Pius V.

"No hymn in any language has been honored by so many translations" (Britt) [over 300 in English, 90 in German, and no less than 18 by Abraham Coles (who maintained that "no single version can reflect the totality of the original"), 9 by W.W. Nevin, and 6 by Samuel Duffield]. Saintsbury (*Flourishing of Romance*) praises the efficacy of its "rhyme, alliteration, cadence, and adjustment of vowel and consonant values [which] all receive perfect expression in it . . . Fortunately there is not ever likely to be lack of those who ... will hold these wonderful triplets ... as nearly or quite the most perfect wedding of sound to sense that they know."

Berlioz writes to Humbert Ferrand: "I am at work on a requiem ... I am finishing the *Prose de morts* today, beginning with the *Dies Irae* and ending with the *Lacrymosa*; it is sublimely gigantic poetry. I was intoxicated with it at first, but afterwards I managed to get it under; I have mastered my subject [!], and I now think that my score will be passably grand" [indeed!].

And James Mason Neale (*Medieval Hymns*, 1867) gives it his highest acclamation: "[The hymn *Pange lingua gloriosi*] contests the second place among those of the Western Church with the *Vexilla Regis*, the *Stabat Mater*, the *Jesu Dulcis Memoria*, the *Ad Regius Agni Dapes*, the *Ad Supernum*, and one or two others, leaving the *Dies Irae* in its unapproachable glory."

Notes:

1. *Dies irae, dies illa.*

A direct quote from the Prophecy of Sophonias (Zephaniah) written during the reign of Josias (641-610 B.C.): Sophonias 1:15.

2. *Solvet saeclum in favilla.*

"A fire shall go before him, and shall burn his enemies round about" (Psalm 96 [97] : 3). "But the day of the Lord will come as a thief; at that time the heavens will pass away with great violence, and the elements will be dissolved with heat, and the earth, and the works that are in it, will be burned up" (II Peter 3:10). *In favilla* may be rendered "into dust" ("Earth to earth, ashes to ashes, dust to dust" – *Book of Common Prayer*) or "into embers."

3. *Teste David cum Sibylla.*

"The Sybilline verses [were] second only to sacred Scriptures in prophetic authority ... the two being regarded as parallel lines of authority, the Church's and the world's, and consenting witness to the same truths" (Trench, in Julian, *Dictionary of Hymnology*). [The "suspicious" variant readings of some manuscripts, *Teste Petro cum Sibylla*, refer to II Peter 3:7-13, Peter's prophecy of the ultimate destruction of the world by fire.]

4. *Quantus tremor est futurus.*

"And there will be ... men fainting for fear and for expectation of the things that are coming on in the world" (Luke 21:25-26).

5. *Quando judex est venturus.*

Et iterum venturus est cum gloria, judicare vivos et mortuos ("And he shall come again with glory, to judge the living and the dead" -- ORDINARY: CREDO, The Nicene Creed).

6. *Cuncte stricte discussurus.*

"But I tell you, that of every idle word men speak, they shall give account on the day of judgement" (Matthew 12:36) - every detail of everyone's life. "And they were judged each one, according to their works" (Apocalypse [Revelation] 20:13). *Discussurus* is a fut. part. describing *judex*; literally: "When the Judge who is about to examine all things strictly is going to come."

7. *Tuba mirum.*

"A day of the trumpet and alarm" (Sophonias [Zephania] 1:16). "Behold, I tell you a mystery: we shall all indeed rise, but we shall not all be changed -- in a moment, in the twinkling of an eye, at the last trumpet. For the trumpet shall sound, and the dead shall rise incorruptible and we shall be changed" (I Corinthians 15:51-52). "And he will send forth his angels with a trumpet and a great sound, and they will gather his elect from the four winds, from one end of the heavens to the other" (Matthew 24:31).

8. *Per sepulchra regionem.*

"And the sea gave up the dead that were in it, and death and hell gave up the dead that were in them" (Apocalypse [Revelation] 20:13).

9. *Coget omnes ante thronum.*

"And I saw a great white throne and the one who sat upon it; from his face the earth and heaven fled away, and there was found no place for them" (Apocalypse [Revelation] 20:11].

10. *Mors stupebit.*

"But when this mortal body puts on immortality, then shall come to pass the word that is written, Death is swallowed up in victory! O death, where is thy victory? O death, where is thy sting?" (I Corinthians 15:54-55).

10. *et natura.*

"Let the heavens rejoice, and let the earth be glad, let the sea be moved, and the fulness thereof: the fields and all things that are in them shall be joyful" (Psalm 95 [96] : 11).

13. *Liber scriptus.*

"And I saw the dead, the great and the small, standing before the throne, and scrolls were opened. And another scroll was opened, which is the book of life; and the dead were judged out of those things that were written in the scrolls, according to their works" (Apocalypse [Revelation] 20:12).

15. *Unde mundus judicetur.*

"And they were judged each one, according to their works" (Apocalypse [Revelation] 20:13). *Unde*, "from which source" (Britt).

17. *Quidquid latet.*

"And he knoweth not that the eyes of the Lord are far brighter than the sun, beholding round about all the ways of men, and the bottom of the deep, and looking into the hearts of men, into the most hidden parts" (Ecclesiasticus 23:28).

18. *Nil inultum.*

"For God did not spare the angels when they sinned, but dragged them down by infernal ropes to Tartarus [hell], and delivered them to be tortured and kept in custody for judgment. Nor did he spare the ancient world ... " (II Peter 2:4-5).

19. *miser.*

The "impious and the sinner" (I Peter 4:18).

21. *Cum vix justus sit securus.*

And if the just man scarcely will be saved, where will the impious and the sinner appear?" (I Peter 4:18).

22. *Rex tremendae majestatis.*

"And then they shall see the Son of Man coming upon a cloud with great power and majesty" (Luke 21:27). *Tremendae*, "tremendous," in the sense of fearful, dreadful, terrifying.

23. *Qui salvandos salvas gratis.*

salvandos, those who are (predestined) to be saved will be saved *gratis*, freely, by his grace.

31. *Judex judex ultionis.*

"Revenge is mine, and I will repay them in due time" (Deuteronomy 32:35); "The Lord is a jealous God, and a revenger: the Lord is a revenger, and hath wrath: the Lord taketh vengeance on his adversaries, and he is angry with his enemies" (Nahum 1:2).

34. *Ingemisco.*

"For we know that all creation groans and travails in pain until now. And not only it, but we ourselves also who have the first-fruits of the Spirit -- we ourselves groan within ourselves, waiting for the adoption as sons, the redemption of our body" (Romans 8:22-23).

37. *Mariam . . . absolvisti.*

Mary Magdalene, one of the natives of the prosperous fishing village of Magdala on the Sea of Galilee, was one of "certain women who had been cured of evil spirits and infirmities" who accompanied Jesus and the Twelve Apostles and "provided for them out of their means" (Luke 8:1-3). She is recorded as: standing by the cross with Mary, Christ's mother and Mary of Cleophas, and the disciple John (John 19:25 *et al.*); being the first witness to the resurrection (Mark 16:9); and being the one chosen by

Christ to report his resurrection to the disciples (John 20:16-18). She is not to be confused with Mary of Bethany (Matthew 26:6-13) or the penitent sinner (Luke 7:36-50) [see J.E. Fallon, *New Catholic Encyclopedia*].

      . . . "Wherefore he said to her, Thy sins are forgiven" (Luke 7:49).

38. *latronum exaudisti.*

      One of the robbers crucified with Jesus mocked and abused him, saying "If thou art the Christ, save thyself and us." The other, to whom tradition has given the name Dismas, rebuked him and said to Jesus, "Lord, remember me when thou comest into thy kingdom. And Jesus said unto him, Amen I say to thee, today thou shalt be with me in paradise" (Luke 23:39-43).

44. *ab haedis me sequestra.*

      "And before him will be gathered all the nations, and he will separate them one from another, as the shepherd separates the sheep from the goats" (Matthew 25:32).

45. *in parte dextra.*

      "And he will set the sheep on his right hand, but the goats on the left" (Matthew 25:33). *Domini Fili unigenite, Jesu Christe . . . Qui sedes ad dexteram Patris* ("Lord Jesus Christ, the only-begotten Son . . . who sits at the right hand of the Father" – Ordinary of the Mass: Gloria)

47. *Flammis acribus addictis.*

      "Then he will say to those on his left hand, Depart from me, accursed ones, into the everlasting fire which was prepared for the devil and his angels" (Matthew 25:41).

50. *Cor contritum quasi cinis.*

      "A sacrifice to God is an afflicted spirit: a contrite and humbled heart, O God, thou wilt not despise" (Psalm 50 [51] : 19). "I had heard of thee by the hearing of the ear, but now my eye sees thee; therefore I despise myself, and repent in dust and ashes" (Job 42:5-6).

53. *ex favilla.*

      May be rendered "from the dust" ("ashes to ashes, and dust to dust") – meaning when the dead shall rise; or "from the embers" – if all is reduced to embers by the final holocaust, then it would mean that the now living and the dead will all rise together,

57. *dona eis requiem.*

      The penitent petition of the Introit, Gradual, *Dies Irae, Agnus Dei, Lux aeterna, Libera me,* and *In paradisum* of the Requiem Mass; taken from the uncanonical apocrypha known as the Book of IV Esdras (2:34) and Isaiah 58:11 - "And the Lord shall give thee rest continually." The souls of the just were immortal, according to ancient Jewish faith, and "slept with their fathers" eternally; prayers for "eternal rest" have been offered by generations of generations. [see Introit above]

Liturgical context: **Dies irae** is the Sequence on All Soul's Day (November 2); in Masses celebrated on the occasion or anniversary of a death or burial; and also on the third, seventh, or 30th day after burial; and, optionally, in daily or votive masses for the dead. It is one of the five major Sequences in liturgical use today [the others being *Lauda Sion, Stabat Mater, Veni Sancte Spiritus,* and *Victimae paschali laudes*].

OFFERTORY

(*offertorium*, offering, the presenting of gifts)

Dómine Jésu Chríste, Rex glóriae,
Lord Jesus Christ, King of glory,

líbera ánimas ómnium fidélium defunctorum
liberate souls of all faithful departed

de poénis inférni et de profúndo lácu:
from pains of hell and from deep pit;

Lord Jesus Christ, King of glory,
liberate the souls of all the faithful departed
from the pains of hell and from the deep pit;

líbera éas de óre leónis,
deliver them from mouth of lion,

ne absórbeat éas tártarus,
not let swallow them hell,

ne cádant in obscúrum:
not let them fall into darkness,

deliver them from the lion's mouth;
let not hell swallow them up,
let them not fall into darkness:

sed sígnifer sánctus Míchael
but standard-bearer holy Michael

repraeséntet éas in lúcem sánctam:
let bring them into light holy

but let Michael, the holy standard-bearer,
bring them into the holy light,

Quam olim Abrahae promisísti,
which once to Abraham you promised,

et sémini éjus.
and to seed his.

which once thou promised to Abraham
and to his seed.

Hóstias et préces tíbi,
Sacrifices and prayers to thee,

Dómini, láudis offérimus:
Lord, of praise we offer.

tu súscipe pro animábus íllis,
thou receive for souls of those

quárum hódie memóriam fácimus:
whose today memory we recall:

Sacrifices and prayers of praise,
O Lord, we offer to thee.
Receive them, Lord, on behalf of those souls
we commemorate this day.

78

fac	éas,	Dómine,	
Grant	**to them,**	**Lord,**	

Grant them, O Lord,
to pass from death unto life,

de	mórte	transíre	ad	vítam.
from	**death**	**to pass**	**to**	**life.**

Quam	olim	Abrahae	promisísti,
which	**once**	**to Abraham**	**promised,**

which once thou promised to Abraham
and to his seed.

et	sémini	éjus.
and	**to seed**	**his.**

The text for the **Offertory** was formerly a prayer that was recited for the sick who were *about* to die; it was later adopted into the Requiem Mass for the Dead. This accounts for the variant readings of some translations in which *defunctorum* is rendered as "dying" instead of "departed," and *libera* as "preserve from" instead of "deliver."

Sed leads us from darkness into light, a dramatic change often reflected in musical settings of this text. Theologically, Michael the archangel is not the one sent by God to lead souls *in lucem sanctam*, but he is depcted variously as "the great prince, who standeth for the children of thy people" (Daniel 12:1), as "fiercely disputing with the devil about the body of Moses" (Jude 1:9. Satan wished to use his body to seduce the Jewish people into the sin of hero-worship. See the apocryphal book on the assumption of Moses.), as the victorious leader of his angels in the battle "with the dragon and his angels" (Apocalypse [Revelation] 12 : 7-9), and as the angel with the "golden censer": "And there was given to him much incense, that he might offer it with the prayers of all the Saints ... and the prayers of the saints went up before God from the angel's hand" (Apocalypse [Revelation] 8 : 3-4. *Hostias et preces tibi.*). These deeds are commemorated on the feast of St. Michael and all angels on September 29. [Heb mîkā'ēl, Who is like God?]

The Promise to "Abraham and his seed" is found in the Book of Genesis:

"And I will make of thee a great nation, and I will bless thee, and I will magnify thy name and thou shalt be blessed" (Genesis 12:2).

"This is my covenant which you shall observe, between me and you, and thy seed after thee: ... Sara thy wife shall bear thee a son, and thou shalt call his name Isaac, and I will establish my covenant with him for a perpetual covenant, and unto his seed after him" (Genesis 17:10,19).

"And in thy seed shall all the nations of the earth be blessed, because thou hast obeyed my voice" (Genesis 22:18).

"And I will multiply thy seed like the stars of heaven: and I will give to thy posterity all these countries: and in thy seed shall all the nations of the earth be blessed" (Genesis 26:4).

SANCTUS

(Sanctus, Sanctus, Sanctus, Holy, Holy, Holy)

Sánctus,	Sánctus,	Sánctus,		**Holy, Holy, Holy,**
Holy,	**Holy,**	**Holy,**		**Lord God of Hosts.**

Dóminus	Déus	Sábaoth.
Lord	**God**	**of Hosts.**

Pléni	sunt	caéli	et	térra	**Heaven and earth are full**
Full	**are**	**heaven**	**and**	**earth**	**of thy glory.**

glória	túa.
of glory	**thy.**

Hosánna	in	excélsis.	**Hosanna in the highest.**
Hosanna	**in**	**highest.**	

BENEDICTUS

(Benedictus qui venit, Blessed is he who comes)

Benedíctus	qui	vénit	**Blessed is he who comes**
Blessed	**who**	**comes**	**in the name of the Lord.**

in	nómine	Dómini.
in	**name**	**of Lord.**

Hosánna	in	excélsis.	**Hosanna in the highest.**
Hosanna	**in**	**highest.**	

The **Sanctus** or Trisagion ("Thrice Holy") is the culmination of the prayers of thanksgiving offered by the celebrant in the Preface, an actual continuation of his final words: "The heavens and the heavenly hosts together with the blessed Seraphim in triumphant chorus unite . . . saying:" and the people (or choir) then join with "Holy, Holy, Holy," words which are adapted from the praises of the two seraphim found in Isaiah 6:3 :

"And one cried unto the other, and said, Holy, Holy, Holy is the Lord of hosts: the whole earth is full of his glory" [Heb: "his glory is the fulness of the earth"].

which we hear again in Revelations 4:8 :

> "And the four beasts had each of them six wings about him; and they
> were full of eyes within: and they rest not day and night, saying: Holy, Holy,
> Holy, Lord God Almighty, which was, and is, and is to come."

The Trisagion is found in the Hebrew liturgy as early as the 2nd century, in the Gallican rite by 529 (Council of Vaison), and in the Roman rite by the 7th century; it is found almost universally in every Christian rite, east or west. It preceeds the Canon, the most solemn portion of the Mass, the point at which the celebrant offers up the prayers and sacrifices of all the Faithful.

Sabaoth (Heb *sabaoth*, armies, hosts) is a title which ascribes majesty, referring mainly to God. It appears in the Old Testament no less than 282 times. The full ascription *yhwh 'ĕlōhê sebā'ôt yiśrā'ēl*, "Yahweh, the God of the armies of Israel" (I Kings [Samuel] 17:45) conveys the concept of Israel's God seen as the supreme commander of its armies, a warrior who led the hosts of Israel into battle. Later the term implies that Yahweh is also the God of the heavenly hosts and has sovereignty over all things.

The **Benedictus** follows the **Sanctus** and is itself preceded and followed by the **Hosanna**. The text is from Matthew 21:9, where Christ's triumphal entry into Jerusalem is greeted with:

> "Hosanna to the Son of David: Blessed is he that cometh in the name
> of the Lord; Hosanna in the highest."

which is itself based on Psalm 117 [118]:26 :

> "Blessed is he that cometh in the name of the Lord: we have blessed
> you out of the house of the Lord."

This psalm was recited by the Hebrews on the Feast of the Tabernacles during the procession around the altar. On the seventh procession of the seventh day of this feast, rejoicing when the trumpet sounded as the priest reached verses 25–26, the people would wave palms and willows and shout: *O Domine, salvum fac; O Domine, bene prosperare. Benedictus qui venit in nomine Domini!* (O Lord, let me be saved; O Lord, cause me to prosper well. Blessed is he who comes in the name of the Lord") The Hebrew word for *salvum fac* was "*hoshi'a na*"; and thus the seventh day of the feast became known as the Great Hosanna and the word itself became a shout or exclamation of joy, triumph, and exultation. [cf. Matthew 21:15; Mark 11:9–10; John 12:13]

Liturgical context: The **Sanctus** one of the parts of the Ordinary of the Mass which is retained in the Requiem Mass. It is the culmination of the celebrant's Preface to the Eucharistic meal which is recited or sung by the people (or choir). The **Benedictus** follows, preceded and followed by the **Hosanna**.

AGNUS DEI

(*Agnus Dei*, Lamb of God)

Agnus Dei, **Lamb of God,**	**Lamb of God,** **who takest away the sins of the world,** **grant them rest.**
qui tollis peccata mundi, **(you)who take away sins of world,**	
dona eis requiem. **grant them rest.**	
Agnus Déi, **Lamb of God,**	**Lamb of God,** **who takest away the sins of the world,** **grant them rest.**
qui tóllis peccáta múndi, **(you)who take away sins of world,**	
dóna éis réquiem. **grant them rest.**	
Agnus Déi, **Lamb of God,**	**Lamb of God,** **who takest away the sins of the world,** **grant them rest everlasting.**
qui tóllis peccáta múndi, **(you)who take away sins of world,**	
dóna éis réquiem sempitérnam. **grant them rest everlasting.**	

The text of the **Agnus Dei** is found embedded in the ancient chant of the Roman and Ambrosian rites, the **Gloria in excelsis:**

> *"Agnus Dei, Filius Patris,*
> *Qui tollis peccata mundi,*
> *miserere nobis;*
> *Qui tollis peccata mundi,*
> *Suscipe deprecationem nostram;*
> *Qui sedes ad dexteram Patris,*
> *miserere nobis."*

It is also attributed to John the Baptist who was questioned by the priests and Levites from Jerusalem concerning whether or not he was the Christ, and why he was baptizing others:

> "Why, then, dost thou baptize, if thou art not the Christ, nor Elias, nor the Prophet?
> John said to them in answer: I baptize with water; but in the midst of you there has stood one whom you do not know. . .
> The next day John saw Jesus coming to him, and he said: Behold, the Lamb of God, who takes away the sin of the world!" (John 1:25-26, 29)

82

In early times the **Agnus Dei** was used in the Litanies at the end of the Mass (like the **Kyrie** at the beginning), and it survives in that form in the litanies of Holy Saturday and the Rogation Days. It was incorporated into the liturgy by Pope Sergius I (687–701) as a *confractum*, a chant to accompany the Fraction or breaking of the bread. When leavened bread was used, this activity took a considerable amount of time; but now, with unleavened bread, it takes only a few moments, and the **Agnus Dei** has come to be associated with the Kiss of Peace or the distribution of Communion.

The petition *miserere nobis* was originally unchanging (as it is still on Maundy Thursday when the Kiss of Peace is not given); it was repeated as necessary to accompany the Fraction. But during the 10th–12th centuries the three-fold form became established and the *dona nobis pacem* replaced the third *miserere nobis*. [N.B. in the Requiem Mass the third line becomes: *dona eis requiem sempiternam* ("Grant them rest eternal")]

Liturgical context: The **Agnus Dei** is sung near the end of the Canon, following the passage *Haec commixto* ("May this mixture and consecration of the Body and Blood of our Lord Jesus Christ be to us who receive it effectual unto eternal life. Amen."), between the Fraction and the Communion antiphon. It is the fifth and final portion of the Mass Ordinary and the only one that is changed when sung as part of the Requiem Mass where the final *dona nobis pacem* is replaced by *dona eis requiem sempiternam*.

COMMUNION

(*communio*, a sharing in common, uniting together)

Lux aetérna lúceat éis, Dómine:
Light eternal let shine on them, Lord,

Cum sánctis túis in aetérnum:
With saints your for eternity;

quia píus es.
for merciful you are.

Réquiem aetérnam dóna éis, Dómine,
Rest eternal grant to them, Lord,

et lux perpétua lúceat éis.
and light perpetual may shine on them.

May light eternal shine upon them, O Lord, in the company of thy saints forever and ever; for thou art merciful.

Rest eternal grant to them, O Lord, and let perpetual light shine upon them.

The antiphon *Lux aeterna* echoes the *lux perpetua* of the Introit, a situation which has suggested musical recapitulation to some composers. It also brings to mind the ancient custom of lighting candles during the Mass for the Dead. These were used not only to illumine some of the early subterranean burial places, but as a symbolic prayer for light.

The **Communion** of the Requiem Mass holds a special place in the history of the liturgy in that it preserves the custom of having a verse (*Requiem aeternam*) follow the antiphon, a practice retained elsewhere only in the Introit.

RESPONSORY

(*responsoria*, responsory, reply)

Líbera me, Dómine, de mórte aetérna,
Deliver me, Lord, from death eternal,

in díe ílla treménda:
on day that of terror:

Quando coéli movéndi sunt et térra:
when heavens to be moved are and earth,

Dum véneris judicáre saéculum per ígnem.
when you come to judge world by fire.

Deliver me, O Lord, from death eternal,
on that dreadful day:
when the heavens and the earth shall quake,
when thou shalt come
to judge the world by fire.

Trémens fáctus sum égo, et tímeo
Trembling made am I, and I fear

dum discússio vénerit,
until judgement should come,

atque ventúra íra.
also coming wrath.

I am seized by trembling, and I fear
until the judgement should come,
and I also dread the coming wrath.

Díes ílla, díes írae,
That day, day of wrath,

calamitátis et misériae,
of calamity and misery,

díes mágna et amára valde.
day momentous and bitter exceedingly,

Dum véneris judicáre saéculum per ígnem.
When you come to judge world by fire.

O that day, day of wrath,
day of calamity and misery,
momentous day, and exceedingly bitter,
when thou shalt come
to judge the world by fire.

Réquiem aetérnam dóna éis, Dómine:
Rest eternal grant to them, Lord,

et lux perpétua lúceat éis.
and light perpetual let shine on them.

Eternal rest grant to them, O Lord,
and let perpetual light shine upon them.

The **Libera me** is not part of the liturgical Requiem Mass, but a responsory sung after the Mass during the Burial Rite while the coffin is sprinkled with holy water and incensed. Like the Communion it contains two portions of text from previous movements and, indeed, it is often treated musically as a "reprise" of the *Dies Irae*. This situation has strongly influenced composers to set it as part of a "Requiem," especially those who have chosen to place it as the final movement of a large scale work. In addition to structural closure, it also provides the potential for great musical contrast and a final return to the opening sentiments and character of the Introit with which the Requiem Mass begins: *Requiem aeternam dona eis . . .* ("Rest eternal grant to them . . .").

ANTIPHON

In paradísum dedúcant te Angeli:
Into paradise may lead you Angels;

May the angels lead you into paradise;
May the Martyrs welcome you upon your arrival,
and lead you into the holy city of Jerusalem.

in túo advéntu suscípiant te Mártyres,
upon your arrival welcome you Martyrs,

et perdúcant te in civitátem
and lead you into city

sánctam Jerúsalem.
holy Jerusalem.

Chórus Angelórum te suscípiat,
Choir of angels you may welcome,

May a choir of angels welcome you,
and, with poor Lazarus of old,
may you have eternal rest.

et cum Lázaro quondam páupere
and with Lazarus once poor,

aetérnam hábeas réquiem.
eternal have rest.

The **In paradisum** is sung after the Requiem Mass and the Rite of Absolution (*Libera me*) while the coffin is being carried to the grave along with the *Benedictus* (the Canticle of Zachary, Luke 1:68-79) and some Psalms (Psalm 129 [130] : *De profundis* ("Out of the depths have I cried to thee") and Psalm 50 [51] : *Miserere mei, Deus* ("Have mercy upon me, O God").

The Gospel reading for the Mass on the Day of Death or Burial is interestingly related to this antiphon which will be sung later. It records the conversation of Martha (the sister of Lazarus) and Jesus in which Martha states her faith in Christ and in the resurrection of the dead on the last day. And "Jesus said unto her: I am the resurrection and the life: he that believes in me, even if he dies, shall live" (John 11:25). Shortly thereafter Mary and Martha and Jesus go to Lazarus's tomb and Jesus calls him forth from the dead, a miracle that won him many followers and also convinced the Sanhedrin that he must be put to death (John 11:20-53).

Thus the Gospel recalls the events of the Lazarus who was raised from the dead, but the antiphon refers to *Lazaro quondam paupere*, the poor man Lazarus who, though he ate crumbs from the rich man's table, "was borne away into Abraham's bosom; but the rich man also died and was buried in hell" (Luke 16:19-31). [Gr *lazoros*, from Heb *'el'azar*, God has helped]

SACRED LATIN TEXTS
Other Sacred Texts

"Plainsong being vocal and Latin music, neither its rhythm nor its melody can be rightly appreciated or sung apart from the meaning of the text, the correct pronunciation of the words, and their proper grouping into phrases. In other words, there must be good diction. No Choir should attempt to sing a melody before reading the text correctly and fluently. Nor is a knowledge of music sufficient; one must somehow understand the Latin text and its liturgical content and cultivate a kindred spirit in order to interpret aright the accompanying melody." (*Liber Brevior*, 1954)

"I will sing with the spirit, and I will sing with the understanding also."
(I Corinthians 14:15).

"There is a certain hidden power, as I learnt by experience, in the thoughts underlying the words themselves; so that, as one meditates upon the sacred words and constantly and seriously considers them, the right notes, in some inexplicable manner, suggest themselves quite spontaneously." (William Byrd)

ABSALOM   FILI   MI

Vulgate: II Kings [Samuel] 18:33

Fíli   mi   Absalom!   Absalom   fíli   mi!
Son   my   Absalom!   Absalom   son   my!

O my son Absalom, Absalom my son!

Quis   míhi   tríbuat
Who   to me   grants

Who grants to me
that I might die for you?

ut   égo   móriar   pro   te,
that   I   may die   for   you?

Absalom   fíli   mi!   fíli   mi   Absalom!
Absalom   son my!   son   my   Absalom!

O Absalom my son, my son Absalom!

Text of setting by Josquin Des Prez

Absalon,   fíli   mi,   fíli   mi,   Absalon!
Absalom,   son   my,   son   my,   Absalom!

Absalom, my son, my son, Absalom!

Quis   det
Who   grants

Who grants
that I might die for you?

ut   moriar   pro   te,
that   I may die   for   you?

fíli   mi   Absalon,
son   my   Absalom,

O my son Absalom,

Non   vívam   últra,
Not   I may live   longer,

That I might live no longer,
but go down into hell weeping.

sed   descéndam   in   inférnum   plórans.
but   may go down   into   hell   weeping.

Absalom was the third of six sons born to King David in Hebron (II Kings [Samuel] 3:2–5); his mother was Maacha, daughter of Tholmai, King of Gessun. Known in his youth for his "faultless beauty" and "the luxurious wealth of his hair," he grew increasingly ambitious and began to seek ways in which he could become heir to his father's throne. [See II Kings [Samuel], Chapters 13–18, for a detailed account of his life.] He killed Amnon, David's eldest son, after Amnon had wronged Thamar, the beautiful sister of Absalom, and then alienated himself from his father David who had refused to punish Amnon for the deed.

Gradually Absalom acquired a sympathetic group of conspirators (15:12), declared himself ruler of Hebron (15:13), whereupon King David and his loyal followers took flight. A battle was eventually "fought in the forest of Ephraim. And the people of Israel were defeated there by David's army, and a great slaughter was made that day of twenty thousand men" (18:6-7). David had ordered that his son Absalom be spared (18:5); but during the battle Absalom's "head caught hold of the oak, and he was taken up between the heaven and the earth; and the mule that was under him went away" (18:9). While hanging there, his long hair became entangled in the foliage, and, before he could extricate himself, Joab, one of David's generals, thrust three darts into his heart.

When David heard that Absalom was slain, he was inconsolable, and "he went up to his chamber and wept. And as he went, he said: O my son Absalom, my son, my son, Absalom! would to God I had died for thee, O Absalom, my son, my son!" (18:33)

"And the victory that day was turned into mourning unto all the people" (19:2). "And they took Absalom and cast him into a great pit in the forest, and they laid an exceeding great heap of stones on him" (18:17).

Source: The text of **Absalom, fili mi** is taken from II Kings [Samuel] 18:33.

AD DOMINUM CUM TRIBULARER

Grad. 5.

AD Dómi- num, * dum tribu-lá- rer,

Ad Dóminum cum tribulárer,	In my distress I cried to the Lord,
To Lord when I was distressed,	**and he heard me.**

clamávi: et exaudívit me.	
I cried: and he heard me.	

Dómine, líbera ánimam méam	O Lord, deliver my soul
Lord, deliver soul my	**from lying lips and a deceitful tongue.**

a lábiis iníquis	
from lips lying	

et a língua dolósa.	
and from tongue deceitful.	

The Epistle for the Sunday with the Octave of Corpus Christi [see *O sacrum convivium*] is taken from I John 3:13-18: "Do not be surprised, brethren, if the world hates you. We know that we have passed from death to life, because we love the brethren: he that loveth not, abideth in death . . . let us not love in word nor in tongue, but in deed and truth." The Gradual **Ad Dominum con tribularer** (Psalm 119 [120]:1-2) immediately follows and is concluded by the joyous Alleluia Verse with its *jubilus* from Psalm 7:2: "O Lord my God, in thee have I put my trust: save me from all them that persecute me, and deliver me. Alleluia."

Litrugical context: **Ad Dominum con tribularer** is the Gradual for the Sunday within the Octave of Corpus Christi.

ADESTE FIDELES

A D-éste fidé-les, laéti, tri- umphántes : Vení-te, ve-

Adéste fidéles, laéti, triumphántes:
Approach faithful, joyful, triumphant:

Veníte, veníte in Béthlehem:
Come, come to Bethlehem:

Nátum vidéte Régem Angelórum:
New-born see King of Angels:

Veníte, adorémus, veníte, adorémus,
Come, let us adore, come, let us adore,

veníte adorémus Dóminum.
come let us adore Lord.

Approach ye faithful,
ye joyful and triumphant:
Come, O come to Bethlehem:
See the new-born King of Angels:

O come, let us adore the Lord.

Cantet nunc Io
Sing now joyfully

Chorus Angelorum;
Choir of Angels;

Cantet nunc aula caelestium,
Sing now court of celestials,

Gloria in excelsis Deo.
Glory in highest to God.

Sing joyfully now,
Choir of Angels,
Sing now you celestial hosts.
Glory in the highest to God.

Ergo qui natus
Therefore who born

Die hodierna
This day

Jesu, tibi sit gloria,
Jesus, to you be glory,

Patris aeterni
of Father eternal

Verbum caro factum.
Word flesh made.

Therefore to you
who is born this day,
Jesus, to you be the glory,
Eternal Word of the Father
made flesh.

91

William Studwell (*Christmas Carols*) ascribes this hymn to John Francis Wade (1711–1786), stating that both the lyrics and the music were probably written in Douai, France, between 1740–43 and that the text was published in 1760 and the music in 1782. It has also been ascribed to St. Bonaventura, but it is not found in any edition of his works.

Liturgical context: **Adeste Fideles** is a hymn that has been used at Benediction at Christmastide in France and England since the close of the 18th century.

ADORAMUS TE, CHRISTE

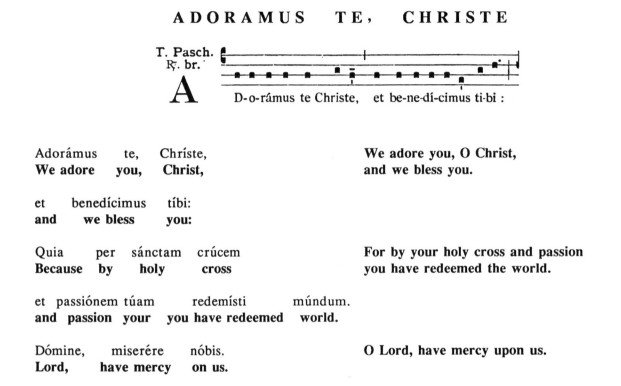

| Adorámus | te, | Chríste, | | We adore you, O Christ, |
| **We adore** | **you,** | **Christ,** | | and we bless you. |

| et | benedícimus | tíbi: | |
| **and** | **we bless** | **you:** | |

| Quia | per | sánctam | crúcem | | For by your holy cross and passion |
| **Because** | **by** | **holy** | **cross** | | you have redeemed the world. |

| et | passiónem túam | redemísti | múndum. |
| **and** | **passion your** | **you have redeemed** | **world.** |

| Dómine, | miserére | nóbis. | | O Lord, have mercy upon us. |
| **Lord,** | **have mercy** | **on us.** | |

The Church's devotion to the Holy Cross is represented in the Liturgy by the rite of Good Friday (the Adoration of the Cross, the *Improperia*, the hymns *Crux fidelis* and *Pange lingua – certaminis*, and the great processional hymn *Vexilla regis*) and by the feasts of the Finding of the Holy Cross (May 3) and the Exaltation of the Holy Cross (September 14). Two texts from the Office of these latter two feasts relate directly to **Adoramus te, Christe** which is sung as a short response during Vespers. One is the Gradual, from Phillipians 2:8-9 [see *Christus factus est*]:

> "He humbled himself, becoming obedient to death, even to death on a cross. Therefore God also has exalted him and has bestowed upon him the name that is above every name."

and the other is the Introit, from Galatians 6:14 :

> "God forbid that I should glory save in the cross of our Lord Jesus Christ: in whom is our salvation, life, and resurrection: by whom we are saved and delivered. *Alleluia. Alleluia.*"

Liturgical context: **Adoramus te, Christe** is a short Responsory sung during Vespers before the Hymn on the Feast of the Finding of the Holy Cross (May 3) and the Exaltation of the Holy Cross (September 14).

ALMA REDEMPTORIS MATER

Ant.
5.

A L- ma * Redemptó-ris Má- ter, quae pér-

| Alma | Redemptóris | Máter, | Loving Mother of the Redeemer, |
| **Loving** | **of Redeemer** | **Mother,** | who remains the accessable Gateway of Heaven and Star of the Sea, |

quae pérvia caéli pórta mánes,
who accessable of heaven gate (you)remain,

et stélla máris, succúre cadénti,   Give aid to a falling people
and star of sea, succour falling,   that strives to rise;

súrgere qui cúrat pópulo;
to rise who strives people;

Tu quae genuísti natúra mivánte,   O Thou who begot thy holy Creator,
You who begot nature marvelling,   while all Nature marvelled,

túum sánctum Genitórum,
your holy Creator,

Vírgo prius ac postérius,   Virgin before and after
Virgin before and after,   receiving that "Ave" from the mouth of Gabriel,

Gabriélis ab óre súmens íllud Ave,
of Gabriel from mouth receiving that "Ave",

peccatórum miserére.   have mercy on sinners.
sinners have mercy.

Hermanus Contractus (1013-1054), a monk of Reichenau, poet and composer of sequences, is generally credited as the author of this Marian Antiphon, but recent scholarship finds the evidence insufficient. The antiphon is found in a Munich manuscript probably of the 13th century and in a *Sacrum Breviary* of the 14th century.

Sung repeatedly during each of the church year's four seasons at the close of the day, the Marian Antiphons became very well known. The popularity of **Alma Redemptoris Mater** in England is evidenced by Chaucer's use of it in the *Prioress's Tale* which is based wholly on a legend connected with its recitation by the "Litel Clergeon":

> "This litel childe his litel book lerninge,
> As he sat in the scole at his prymer,
> He *Alma redemptoris* herde singe,
> As children lerned hir antiphoner;
> And, as he dorste, he drough hym ner and ner,
> And herkned ay the wordes and the note,
> Till he the firste vers coude al by rote."

The tale continues by explaining how the child mastered the words and the music of the Antiphon, how he sang it in the public streets and was murdered by the Jews for so doing, and the subsequent results.

Mary, the Mother of the Redeemer; heaven's portal, through which Christ passes from heaven to earth and whose intercession can open the gates of heaven for mortals; star of the sea [see *Ave maris stella*]; the immaculate Virgin mysteriously giving birth to her own Creator; Virgin before and after Gabriel's annunciation [see *Ave Maria* and Luke 1:28 – "Hail, full of grace . . ."] -- have mercy on sinners.

Liturgical context: **Alma Redemptoris Mater** is one of the four Marian Antiphons [see also: *Ave, Regina caelorum, Regina coeli,* and *Salve Regina*]. It is sung at the end of Compline from the Vespers of Saturday before the first Sunday of Advent to the second Vespers of the Purification (Feb. 2).

ANGELUS   AD   PASTORES   AIT

3. Ant.
7. d

ANge-lus * ad pastóres á- it : Annúnti-o vóbis

Angelus ad pastóres áit:	The angel said to the shepherds:
Angel to shepherds said:	
Annúncio vóbis gáudium mágnum,	I bring you tidings of great joy,
I announce to you joy great,	for unto you is born this day
	the Saviour of the world. Alleluia!
quia nátus est vóbis hódie	
because born is to you today	
Salvátor múndi. Allelúia.	
Saviour of world. Alleluia!	

"And there were in the same country shepherds abiding in the field, keeping watch over their flock by night. And, lo, the angel of the Lord came upon them, and the glory of the Lord shone round about them: and they were sore afraid. And **Angelus ad pastores** *ait: Annuncio vobis gaudium magnum . . .* "

The first antiphon for Lauds of Christmas Day is *Quem vidistis, pastores?* ("Whom did you see, shepherds?") and the third antiphon, which folows the singing of *Jubilate Deo* ("Rejoice in God, all the earth") is **Angelus ad pastores** (Luke 2:8–11).

Liturgical context: **Angelus ad pastores** is the third antiphon for Lauds of Christmas Day.

ASCENDIT DEUS

Offert.
1.

A-scéndit * Dé- us in ju- bi- la- ti-
ó- ne, Dó- mi- nus in vó- ce túbae, al- le- lú-ia.

Ascéndit	Déus	in	jubilatióne,	**God is ascended amid jubilation,**
Is ascended	**God**	**in**	**jubilation,**	**and the Lord to the sound of the trumpet.**
				Alleluia!

et	Dóminus	in	vóce	túbae.
and	**Lord**	**to**	**sound**	**of trumpet.**

Allelúia.
Alleluia!

     Ascendit Deus (Psalm 46 [47]:6) was originally sung after an Israelite victory to describe how the God of the Covenant, enthroned upon the ark, was borne to Mount Sion amid the acclaim of his people and the sound of trumpets ("And David and all the house of Israel brought the ark of the covenant of the Lord with joyful shouting, and with sound of trumpet" -- II Kings [Samuel] 6:15). In the liturgy of the Roman Church it is sung at Mass on the Feast of the Ascension in commemoration of Christ's Ascension into heaven according to Mark 16:19, Luke 24:51, and Acts 1:2,9. Mount Olivet is the traditonal site of the Ascension (see Acts 1:12); the same place where Christ suffered the agony in the garden is become the site of jubilee and rejoicing.

     Ascendit Deus appears as an Alleluia Verse response to the Epistle for the day which is St. Luke's account of the Ascension in Acts 1:1-11. The final verse of this passage (v.11 - "Man of Galilee, why do you stand looking up to heaven? This Jesus who has been taken up from you into heaven, shall come in the same way as you have seen him going up to heaven.") is also used in the Introit along with another verse from Psalm 46 [47] (v.1 - "O clap your hands, all ye nations: shout unto God with the voice of joy.") which is very similar in character to the **Ascendit Deus**.

     Note well the difference between **Ascendit Deus** ("God is ascended") and *Assumpta est Maria* ("Mary is taken up"); God ascends according to his own will, just as he wills to "yield up" his spirit (*emisit spiritum*) at the moment of his death on the cross.

Liturgical context: **Ascendit Deus** is the Alleluia Verse response to the Epistle in the Mass for the feast of the Ascension and a short antiphon for Terce of the feast of the Most Holy Rosary of the Blessed Virgin Mary (October 7).

ASPERGES ME, DOMINE

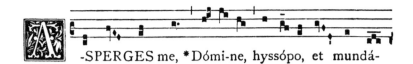

-SPERGES me, *Dómi-ne, hyssópo, et mundá-

Aspérges	me	Dómine	hyssópo,	**You will sprinkle me with hyssop, O Lord,**
You will sprinkle	**me**	**Lord**	**with hyssop,**	**and I shall be cleansed;**

et	mundábor:
and	**I shall be cleansed;**

lavábis	me,	**you will wash me,**
you will wash	**me,**	**and I shall be made whiter than snow.**

et	super	nivem	dealbábor.
and	**more than**	**snow**	**I shall be made white.**

The hyssop plant was used by the ancient Hebrews in many of their purification rites. These ritual sprinklings included the cleansing of persons healed from leprosy (Leviticus 14:4-6, 49-57) and the sprinkling of the doors with the blood of the paschal lamb to avoid the sword of the "destroying angel" (Exodus 12:21-23). The Asperges of the Roman Liturgy, the ceremonial sprinkling (*aspersis aquae*) of the congregation with holy water, is a symbolic spiritual cleansing of the soul, preparing the faithful since the 10th century for the Eucharistic meal of the Mass which is to follow. It is sung with the fourth penitential psalm (**Miserere mei, Deus**, Psalm 50 [51] : "Have mercy upon me, O God") and the *Gloria Patri*, except during Paschaltide when it is replaced by the *Vidi aquam* and Psalm 117 [118] (*Confitemini Domino*, "O give thanks unto the Lord").

Liturgical context: **Asperges me, Domine** is the antiphon sung during the Asperges, the ceremonial sprinkling of the congregation with holy water before the principal Mass on Sunday, except during Paschaltide when it is replaced by the *Vidi aquam*.

ASSUMPTA EST MARIA

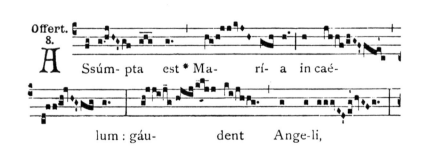

Offert. 8.

H Ssúm- pta est *Ma- rí- a in caé-

lum : gáu- dent Ange-li,

I	Assúmpta	est	María	in	caélum:
	Taken up	**is**	**Mary**	**into**	**heaven:**

Mary is taken up into heaven:
All the Angels rejoice:
Joyfully they bless the Lord.

	gáudent	Angeli,
	rejoice	**Angels,**

	laudántes	benedícunt	Dóminum.
	praising	**they bless**	**Lord.**

II	María	Vírgo	assúmpta	est
	Mary	**Virgin**	**taken up**	**is**

The Virgin Mary is taken up
to the heavenly bridal chamber,
in which the King of Kings
sits on his starry throne.

	ad	aethéreum	thálamum,
	to	**heavenly**	**bridal chamber,**

	in	quo	Rex	régum
	in	**which**	**King**	**of kings**

	stelláto	sédet	sólio.
	on starry	**sits**	**throne.**

III	In	odórem	unguentórum	tuórum	cúrrimus:
	To	**fragrance**	**of ointments**	**your**	**we run:**

Into the fragrance of your ointments we run:
the young women have loved you exceedingly.

	adolescéntulae	dilexérunt	te	nimis.
	young women	**have loved**	**you**	**exceedingly.**

IV	Benedícta	fília	tu	a	Dómino:
	Blessed	**daughter**	**you**	**by**	**Lord:**

You are blessed, daughter, by the Lord:
because, through you,
we have received the fruit of life.

	quia	per	te
	because	**through**	**you**

	frúctum	vítae	communicávimus.
	fruit	**of life**	**we have received.**

V	Pulchra	es	et	decóra,
	Beautiful	**are**	**and**	**comely,**

You are beautiful and comely,
O daughter of Jerusalem:
formidable as an army set in array.

	fília	Jerúsalem:
	daughter	**of Jerusalem:**

	terríbilis	ut	castrórum	ácies	ordináta.
	terrible	**as**	**of armies**	**array**	**ordered.**

Nothing certain is known concerning the date, year, and manner of the death of the Blessed Virgin Mary, though dates assigned to it vary from 3 to 15 years after Christ's Ascension. The belief in her corporeal assumption was first founded on various apocryphal writings from the 4th and 5th centuries, and later formulated by various church fathers, including the following excerpt from the writings of John of Damascus:

"St. Juvenal, Bishop of Jerusalem, at the Council of Chalcedon (451 A.D.), made known to the Emperor Marcian and Pulcheria, who wished to possess the body of the Mother of God, that Mary died in the presence of all the Apostles, but that her tomb, when opened, upon the request of St. Thomas, was found empty; wherefrom the Apostles concluded that the body was taken up to heaven."

Belief in the corporeal assumption is universal today in both the East and the West, and is commemorated by the Roman Church on "our Lady's greatest feast," the Feast of the Assumption (August 15). The Lesson for the Mass of that day is taken from the writings of Jesus, the son of Sirach, in the Book of Wisdom called Ecclesiasticus: "And I shall abide in the inheritance of the Lord . . ." (Ecclesiasticus 24:11-20). The text for the Gradual is taken from Psalm 44 [45] : 5, 11-12 ("a canticle for the Beloved"), and the Gospel tells of Christ's visit to the home of Mary and Martha, when "Martha was busy about much serving" but Mary "seated herself at the Lord's feet, and listened to his word." "Mary," Jesus said, "has chosen the best part, and it will not be taken from her" (Luke 10:38-42), words which are echoed with greater significance in the Communion antiphon which follows the Offertory **Assumpta est Maria**.

The first portion of the text is appointed for the Offertory of the Mass and, along with the second portion (*Maria Virgo assumpta est . . .*), is also used as a short Responsory for Sext and None. During II. Vespers of the Feast of the Assumption all five portions of the text are employed, each serving in turn as the antiphon for one of the five Vesper psalms (Psalms 109, 112, 121, 126, and 147 [Vulgate]).

It may well be that the concluding verse of the Lesson ("I gave a sweet smell like cinnamon and aromatical balm, I yielded a sweet odour like the best myrrh" – Ecclesiasticus 24:20) and the verses which follow (24:21-27) suggested the additional paraphrases of the Canticle of Canticles for the second, third, and fifth portions of the text. Compare the following passages from the Canticles with the text of **Assumpta est Maria**:

"Let him kiss me with the kiss of his mouth: for thy breasts are better than wine, smelling sweet of the best ointments. Thy name is as oil poured out: therefore young maidens have loved thee. Draw me: we will run after thee to the odour of thy ointments. The king hath brought me into his storerooms: we will be glad and rejoice in thee, remembering thy breasts more than wine: the righteous love thee. I am black but comely, O ye daughters of Jerusalem" (Canticles 1:2-4).

"Thou art beautiful, O my love, sweet and comely as Jerusalem: terrible as an army set in array" (Canticles 6:3).

and compare Elizabeth's greeting to the Blessed Virgin during the Visitation to the fourth portion of the **Assumpta est Maria**:

"Blessed art thou among women, and blessed is the fruit of thy womb!" (Luke 1:42)

Liturgical context: **Assumpta est Maria** is sung as the Offertory for the Feast of the Assumption (August 15). [See also *Tota pulchra es Maria*, where "the virgin daughter of Jerusalem" is similarly praised.]

AVE DULCISSIMA MARIA

Áve,   dulcíssima María,   Hail, O sweetest Mary,
Hail,   sweetest   Mary,   true hope and life,
                                    sweet refreshment!
véra   spes   et   víta,
true   hope   and   life,

dúlce   refrígerium!
sweet   refreshment!

O María,   flos   vírginum,   O Mary, thou flower of all virgins,
O Mary,   flower of virgins,   pray for us to Christ, O Mary.

óra,   pro nóbis, Jésum, O María.
pray, for   us,   to Jesus, O Mary.

Gesualdo's penchant for extremes is reflected in his choice and musical setting of this ecstatic version of the **Ave Maria**. Sensual imagery and language (*dulce refrigerium, flos virginum*) and Italian exuberance (*dulcissima Maria, O Maria . . . O Maria*) have transformed the "Hail Mary" into a very personal expression of religious devotion.

AVE MARIA

Ave   María,   grátia   pléna: **Hail Mary, full of grace,**
Hail   Mary,   of grace   full: **the Lord is with thee,**

Dóminus   técum,
Lord   with you,

benedícta tu   in   muliéribus,   **blessed art thou among women,**
blessed   you among   women,   **and blessed is the fruit of thy womb, Jesus.**

et benedíctus frúctus véntris   túi, Jésus.
and blessed   fruit of womb your, Jesus.

Sáncta María, Máter Déi,
Holy Mary, Mother of God,

óra pro nóbis peccatóribus,
pray for us sinners,

nunc et in hóra mórtis nóstrae. Amen.
now and at hour of death our. Amen.

Holy Mary, Mother of God,
pray for us sinners,
now and at the hour of our death. Amen.

The text of this venerable antiphon of the Blessed Virgin, the best known of the Marian prayers, is historically divided into three parts. The first portion consists of the opening salutation of the Angel Gabriel with which he greeted the Blessed Virgin on the day of the Annunciation (Luke 1:28). The second part is the divinely inspired greeting of St. Elizabeth uttered during the Visitation:

> "And [Mary] entered the house of Zachary and saluted Elizabeth. And it came to pass, when Elizabeth heard the greeting of Mary, that the babe in her womb leapt. And Elizabeth was filled with the Holy Spirit, and cried out with a loud voice, saying, Blessed art thou among women and blessed is the fruit of thy womb!" (Luke 1:40-42).

The third and final portion, the addition of the holy name and the final petition for intercession, first appeared c. 1440 with Bernadine of Sienna and was fixed in its present form by Pope Pius V in the *Breviary* of 1568.

The "Angelic salutation" was first used as a greeting and usually accompanied by some external gesture of homage (a genuflection or inclining of the head). As early as the 6th century it is found in a Syrian ritual attributed to Severus, the Patriarch of Antioch (c. 513), and also in the writings of Andrew of Crete and John of Damascus (d. 749). The use of these words as a devotional formula probably has its source in certain versicles and responsories used in the Little Office of the Blessed Virgin which began to develop during the 11th century; and in the 12th century Abbot Baldwin, Archbishop of Canterbury, wrote: "To this salutation of the Angel, by which we daily greet the most Blessed Virgin, with such devotion as we may, we are accustomed to add the words, 'and blessed is the fruit of thy womb,' by which clause Elizabeth at a later time, on hearing the Virgin's salutation to her, caught up and completed, as it were the Angel's words."

During the 14th and 15th centuries it was customary for those who privately recited the *Ave* to add some personal petition at the end, usually that of the sinner asking for pardon and especially for help at the hour of death. The present form of the *Ave* (identical except for the omission of the final word *nostrae*) is found in 1495 in the writings of the Italian religious reformer Giralamo Savanarola (1452-1498), and, as noted above, was finally incorporated into the *Roman Breviary* of 1568.

The gestures of homage that accompanied its early use as a greeting, and the gradually increasing number of repetitions (the 12th century saint, Aibert of Crespin, is said to have recited 150 Hail Marys daily, 100 with genuflections and 50 with prostrations) led to its employment as a penitential excercise which was sometimes practiced to even greater extremes than the one mentioned above. "A certain woman from the crowd" said to Jesus: "Blessed is the womb that bore thee, and the breasts that nursed thee. But he said: Rather blessed are they who hear the word of God and keep it" (Luke 11:27-28).

Liturgical context: The **Ave Maria** is found in the *Liber Antiphonarius* of St. Gregory the Great (d. 604) as an antiphon for the Fourth Sunday in Advent. The Mass for this feast begins with the beautiful Introit from Isaiah 45:8, *Rorate coeli* ("Drop down dew, ye heavens, from above, and let the clouds rain the just; let the earth be opened and bud forth a Saviour"). The Epistle for the day is taken from I Corinthians 4:1-5 and speaks of the time when "the Lord comes, who will both bring to light the things hidden in darkness and make manifest the counsels of hearts." And the Gospel from St. Luke 3:1-6 recounts the prophecy of Isaiah 40:3-5, "the voice of one crying in the wilderness, prepare ye the way of the Lord." The *Credo* and the offertory antiphon **Ave Maria** follow.

The words of the Archangel Gabriel with which the text begins naturally suggest that it also be sung as part of the feasts of the Annunciation (March 25) and the Immaculate Conception (December 8). As part of the first of these two feasts, the **Ave Maria** has been sung since the 8th century as the offertory antiphon following the *Credo* and the Gospel account of the Annunciation from Luke 1:26-38.

The feast of the Immaculate Conception, known in the East as early as the 8th century and in the West soon thereafter, begins with the Introit from Isaiah 61:10, *Gaudens gaudebo* ("I will greatly rejoice in the Lord, and my soul shall be joyful in God"), words very similar to those which the Blessed Virgin herself sings in the *Magnificat* (Luke 1:46-55). The Lesson, the passage from the Book of Wisdom (Proverbs 8:22-35), relates so meaningfully to this feast: "The Lord possessed me in the beginning of his ways, before he made anything, from the beginning ... before the earth was made. The depths were not as yet, and I was already conceived." The Gradual that follows (from Judith 13:23, "Blessed art thou, O daughter, by the Lord the most high God, above all women on the earth") with its verse from the Canticle of Canticles (Canticle 4:7, *Tota pulchra es*, "Thou art all fair, Maria, and there is in thee no stain of original sin"). The **Ave Maria** is again appointed as the offertory antiphon, following the Creed and the Gospel reading from St. Luke 1:26-28, the same account of Gabriel's annunciation with which the **Ave Maria** begins.

These words are also heard during the II Vespers of the feast of the Most Holy Rosary of the Blessed Virgin Mary (October 7) when they are sung as the third antiphon with Psalm 121 [122], *Laetatus sum*, ("I <u>rejoiced</u> at the words which were said unto me, we shall go into the house of the Lord"), again recalling the Canticle of Mary found in Luke 1:46-55. In addition to these occasions, the **Ave Maria** is also sung in other Masses of the Blessed Virgin Mary throughout the year.

> Can one say enough about how meaningful the liturgical context is to the full appreciation and understanding of these texts? Each is so beautifully appointed to a particular feast, amplified and enriched by the other texts in the liturgy, and so intimately wedded to its function within the Mass or Office. Surely this liturgy, refined and tempered by centuries of use and service to the human race, is one of the shining glories and lasting cultural achievements of the Western Church.

AVE MARIS STELLA

Hymn. 1.

A-ve má-ris stélla, Dé- i Má-ter álma, Atque

Ave, máris stélla,
Hail, of sea star,

Déi Máter álma,
of God Mother loving,

Atque semper Vírgo,
and also always Virgin,

Félix caéli pórta.
happy of heaven portal.

Súmens íllud Ave
Receiving that "Ave"

Gabriélis óre,
of Gabriel from mouth,

Fúnda nos in páce,
confirm us in peace,

Mútans Evae nómen.
changing of Eve name.

Sólve víncla réis,
Break chains of sinners,

Prófer lúmen caécis,
bring light to blind,

Mála nóstra pélle,
evils our drive away,

Bóna cúncta pósce.
Good things all ask for.

Mónstra te ésse mátrem,
Show thyself to be mother,

Súmat per te préces,
May he accept through thee prayers,

Qui pro nóbis nátus
who for us born

Túlit ésse túus.
willed to be your.

Hail, Star of the Sea,
Loving Mother of God,
And Virgin immortal,
Heaven's blissful portal!

Receiving that "Ave"
From the mouth of Gabriel,
Reversing the name of "Eva,"
Establish us in peace.

Break the chains of sinners,
Bring light to the blind,
Drive away our evils,
And ask for all good things.

Show thyself to be a mother,
That, through thee,
He may accept our prayers,
He who, born for us,
Chose to be your Son.

Vírgo	singuláris,			O incomparable Virgin,
Virgin	**unique,**			Meek above all others,
				Make us, freed from our faults,
Inter	ómnes	mítis,		Meek and chaste.
above	**all**	**meek,**		

Nos   cúlpis   solútos,
us   from faults   absolved,

Mítes   fac   et   cástos.
gentle   make   and   chaste.

Vítam   praésta   púram,   Keep our life pure,
Life   keep   pure,   Make our journey safe,
                                   So that, seeing Jesus,
Iter   pára   tútum,   We may rejoice together forever.
journey make   safe,

Ut   vidéntes   Jésum,
that   seeing   Jesus,

Sémper   collaetémur.
forever   we may rejoice.

Sit   laus   Déo   Pátri,   Let there be praise to God the Father,
Be   praise to God Father,   And glory to Christ the most High,
                                   And to the Holy Spirit,
Súmmo   Chrísto   décus,   And to the Three be one honor. Amen.
to highest Christ   glory,

Spirítui   Sáncto,
to Spirit   Holy,

Tríbus   hónor   únus.   Amen.
to Three honor   one.   Amen.

The authorship of this Vesper hymn has been ascribed to the Cistercian monk St. Bernard of Clairvaux (c.1090-1153), but it is first recorded in a manuscript found in the Abby of St. Gall (Switzerland) dating from the 9th century. Cardinal Tommasi ascribes it, without sufficient evidence, to Fortunatus, bishop of Poitier (d. 609). This ancient hymn is one of the few unrevised hymns in the Roman Breviary.

The name Mary, according to St. Bernard, "is said to mean 'star of the sea' . . . Indeed most aptly is she compared to a star; for as a star sheds its beams without any decay on its part, so the Virgin brought forth her Son without any damage to her virginity" (*Roman Breviary*). She is heaven's happy portal, through which Christ passes on his way to earth, and the one by whose intercession mortals may enter the gates of heaven. The *Ave* (*Ave Maria*; "Hail, full of grace . . ." (Luke 1:28)) of Gabriel's annunciation "reverses" the name of "Eve" (*Eva*, wife of Adam). "May Mary change *Eva*, a curse, into *Ave*, a blessing" (Britt).

Liturgical context: **Ave maris stella** is the Vesper hymn employed for the many feasts of the Blessed Virgin Mary.

AVE, REGINA COELORUM

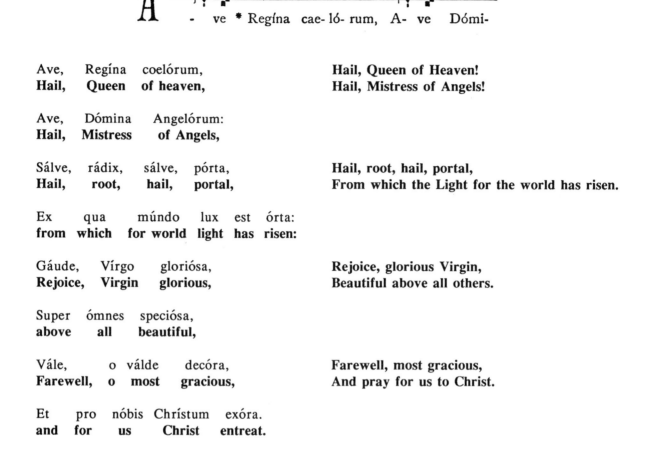

Ave, Regína coelórum, **Hail, Queen of heaven,**	Hail, Queen of Heaven! Hail, Mistress of Angels!
Ave, Dómina Angelórum: **Hail, Mistress of Angels,**	
Sálve, rádix, sálve, pórta, **Hail, root, hail, portal,**	Hail, root, hail, portal, From which the Light for the world has risen.
Ex qua múndo lux est órta: **from which for world light has risen:**	
Gáude, Vírgo gloriósa, **Rejoice, Virgin glorious,**	Rejoice, glorious Virgin, Beautiful above all others.
Super ómnes speciósa, **above all beautiful,**	
Vále, o válde decóra, **Farewell, o most gracious,**	Farewell, most gracious, And pray for us to Christ.
Et pro nóbis Chrístum exóra. **and for us Christ entreat.**	

The author of this Marian Antiphon is unknown, but it dates at least from the 12th century where it is found in St. Alban's Book of Hours. It is said to have been introduced into the Divine Office by Clement VI in the 14th century.

Notes:

> *radix.* "And there shall come forth a rod out of the root of Jesse" (Isaiah 11:1) and "There shall be a root of Jesse, and he that shall rise to reign over the Gentiles" (Romans 15:12). [see also *Virga Jesse floruit*]. The Blessed Virgin Mary was of the house of David who was the son of Jesse.

> *porta.* Mary is the portal through which Christ passed on his way to earth and the one whose intercession can open the gates of heaven for mortals. [see *Alma Redemptoris Mater, Regina Coeli,* and *Salve Regina*]

> *vale.* This antiphon is sung at the end of Compline at the close of the day; the Offices are completed, and the Choir is about to leave.

Liturgical context: **Ave Regina coelorum** is one of the four Marian Antiphons (the others being *Alma Redemptoris Mater, Regina Coeli,* and *Salve Regina*); it is sung at the end of Compline from February 2 (Candlemas Day) until Wednesday in Holy Week.

AVE VERUM CORPUS

- ve vérum * Córpus ná-tum de Ma-rí- a Vírgine :

Ave **Hail**	vérum **true**	Córpus, **Body,**	

Hail, true Body,
born of the Virgin Mary,

nátum **born**	de **of**	María **Mary**	Vírgine: **Virgin:**

Vere **Truly** pássum, **has suffered,**

Who has truly suffered,
was sacrificed on the cross for mortals,

immolátum **was sacrificed** in crúce **on cross** pro **for** hómine: **mankind:**

Cújus **Whose** látus **side** perforátum, **was pierced,**

Whose side was pierced,
whence flowed water and blood:

unda **whence/water** flúxit **flowed** sánguine: **blood:**

Esto **Be** nóbis **for us** praegustátum **foretaste**

Be for us a foretaste (of heaven)
during our final examining.

in **in** mórtis **of death** examine. **weighing.**

O Jésu dúlcis, O Jésu píe,
O Jesu sweet, O Jesu pious,

O Jesu sweet, O Jesu pure,
O Jesu, Son of Mary,
have mercy upon me.　Amen.

O Jésu Fíli Maríae,
O Jesu Son of Mary,

miserére méi. Amen.
have mercy on me. Amen.

This short Eucharistic hymn is said to have been written by either Pope Innocent III (1198-1216) or Pope Innocent IV (1243-1254). It has been used liturgically during Benediction, during the Offertory of the Mass, and as a private devotion during the Elevation of the Host (a part of the Mass introduced only in the 12th century). This hymn has been associated primarily with the votive Mass of the Most Holy Sacrament and the feast of Corpus Christi ("Body of Christ").

The text of **Ave verum corpus** commemorates Christ's redemptive Sacrifice, and especially focuses on the great symbol of Baptism: the pouring forth of water from his pierced side. Ezekiel's Old Testament vision of Baptism (see *Vidi aquam*, "I saw water flowing from the right side of the temple"), St. John's account of the fulfillment of this prophecy during the Crucifixion (John 19:34), the prophecy of Zacharias ("And I will pour out upon the house of David, and upon the inhabitants of Jerusalem, the spirit of grace, and of prayers: and they shall look upon me, whom they have pierced"), and St. John's Apocalyptic vision of the River of Life ("a river of the water of life, flowing forth from the throne of God and of the Lamb" – Apocalypse [Revelation] 22:1) are all recalled in this Eucharistic sequence. [N.B. *unda* (water, or stream) also poetically implies *unde* (whence).

BEATUS VIR

Tract.
8.

B E- á- tus vir, * qui tímet Dó- mi-

1 Beátus vir qui tímet Dóminum,
Blessed man who fears Lord,

Blessed is the man who fears the Lord,
who delights in his commandments.

in mandátis éjus vólet nímis.
in commandments his takes pleasure much.

2 Pótens in térra érit sémen éjus,
Powerful on land shall be seed his,

His seed shall be mighty upon the earth;
the generation of the righteous
shall be blessed.

generátio rectórum benedicétur.
generation of righteous shall be blessed.

3 Glória et divítiae in dómo éjus,
Glory and riches in house his,

Glory and prosperity shall be in his house;
and his justice endures from generation
to generation.

et justítia éjus mánet
and justice his remains

in saéculum saéculi.
from generation to generation.

4 Exórtum est in ténebris lúmen réctis,
Risen has in darkness light for upright,

A light has risen in the darkness
for the upright: one who is
merciful, compassionate, and just.

miséricors et miserátor et jústus.
merciful and compassionate and just.

5 Jucúndus hómo, qui miserétur et cómmodat,
Happy man, who sympathizes and shares,

Happy is the man
who sympathizes and shares,
who chooses his words with discretion:

dispónet sermónes súos in judício.
chooses words his with discretion.

6 Quia in aetérnum non commovébitur.
Because for eternity not shall he be moved.

Because he will not be troubled for eternity;
the just man shall be
in everlasting remembrance.

7 In memória aetérna érit jústus,
In memory eternal will be just man,

He shall not fear evil tidings;
his heart is ready to hope in the Lord.

ab auditióne mála non timébit.
from hearing evil not shall he fear.

Parátum cor éjus speráre in Dómino.
Prepared heart his to hope in Lord.

8 Confirmátum est cor éjus;
Strengthened is heart his;

Non commovébitur
Not shall he be shaken

donec despíciat inimícos súos.
until he looks down upon enemies his.

His heart is strengthened;
he shall not be shaken
until he looks down upon his enemies.

9 Dispérsit, dédit paupéribus,
He shares, he gives to poor,

justítia éjus mánet
justice his endures

in saéculum saéculi.
from generation to generation.

Cornu éjus exaltábitur in glória.
Horn his shall be exalted with glory.

He disperses, he gives to the poor;
his justice endures from generation
to generation.
His horn shall be exalted with honor.

10 Peccátor vidébit et irascétur,
Transgressor will see and be angered,

déntibus súis frémet et tabéscet:
with teeth his will gnash and waste away.

desidérium peccatórum períbit.
desire of wicked shall perish.

The wicked will see, and be angered;
he will gnash with his teeth, and waste away.
The desire of the wicked shall perish.

Beatus vir (Psalm 111 [112]) is a companion piece to Psalm 110 [111], *Confitebor tibi, Domine*: both are written by the same author; both are "alphabetical psalms" in the original, consisting of 22 clauses, each beginning with a different letter of the Hebrew alphabet in regular order; they share common phrases (*et justitia ejus manet in saeculum saeculi; misericors et miserator Dominus/misericors et miserator et justus*); and the closing thought of Psalm 110 ("The fear of the Lord is the beginning of wisdom") segues into the beginning of Psalm 111 ("Blessed is the man who fears the Lord").

The text divides into five main parts, the first verse being an introductory "rule for living" -- fear the Lord; keep his commandments. The next strophe (verses 2-3) speaks of the rewards of the virtuous: their family shall increase and have wealth and prosperity. God, the light, he who is merciful, compassionate and just, shall protect the generous man who excercises good judgement (verses 4-6a). The just man need not fear evil tidings or the violence of his enemies (verses 6b-8). And finally (verses 9-10) the just shall be exalted for ever, but the wicked shall perish.

Liturgical context: **Beatus vir** is one of the five Lucernal or Vesper psalms; it is sung after the third antiphon at Sunday Vespers. The first three verses are also set as a Tract following the Gradual *Ecce sacerdos* ("Behold a great priest, who in his days pleased God") in the Common appointed for the Mass of a Confessor or Bishop.

BENEDICAMUS DOMINO

5. Benedicámus Dó- mi-no.

| Benedicámus | Dómino. | | Let us give praise unto the Lord. |
| Let us give praise | to Lord. | | |

| Déo | dicámus | grátias. | Let us give thanks unto God. |
| To God | let us say | thanks. | |

Benedicamus Domino is the concluding formula in the Latin rite for Divine Office, and later it also served as an alternate concluding formula for the Mass, replacing the *Ite, missa est* ("Go, the dismissal is made") on those penitential Sundays when the *Gloria in excelsis* was not said. In Divine Office it is sung at the close of Lauds and Vespers and near the close of Compline, just prior to the concluding Marian Antiphon.

The hymn *O Filii et Filiae*, sung after Vespers on Easter Sunday, incorporates this versicle and its respond in its final two stanzas:

> *In hoc festo sanctissimo*
> *Sit laus et jubilatio*
> *BENEDICAMUS DOMINO. Alleluia.*
>
> *De quibus nos humillimas*
> *Devotas atque debitas*
> *DEO DICAMUS GRATIAS. Alleluia.*

CANTATE DOMINO

Intr. 6. Cantáte Dómi- no * cánti-cum nó- vum, alle-

| Cantáte | Dómino | cánticum | novum, | Sing to the Lord a new song, |
| Sing | to Lord | canticle | new, | sing to the Lord all the earth. |

| cantáte | Dómino | omnis | terra. | |
| Sing | to Lord | all | earth. | |

| Cantáte | Dómino, | et | benedícite | Sing to the Lord, |
| Sing | to Lord, | and | give praise | and bless his name: |

| nómini | ejus. | |
| to name | his. | |

Annuntiáte	de	die	in	diem	Proclaim his salvation from day to day.
Announce	**from**	**day**	**to**	**day**	

salutáre	ejus.
salvation	**his.**

Annuntiáte	inter	gentes	Declare his glory among the nations,
Make known	**among**	**nations**	his wonders among all people.

glóriam	ejus,
glory	**his,**

in	ómnibus	pópulis	mirabília	éjus.
among	**all**	**people**	**wonders**	**his.**

Quóniam	magnus	Dóminus	For the Lord is great
Because	**great**	**Lord**	and greatly to be praised;
			he is to be feared above all gods.

et	laudábilis	nimis;
and	**to be praised**	**greatly;**

terribílis	est	super	omnes	deos.
to be feared	**he is**	**above**	**all**	**gods.**

Cantate Domino canticum novum (Psalm 95 [96] : 1–4), the Introit for the 4th Sunday after Easter, gives the day its name "*Cantate* Sunday," much the same as the first word of the Introits for the third Sunday in Advent and fourth Sunday of Lent give those days the names of *Gaudete* and *Laetare* Sunday respectively. These names were commonly known in the Middle Ages and were used in secular affairs as well as ecclesiastical.

The *Canticum Novum* also greets the birth of the promised Messiah on Christmas Day during the III Nocturn of Matins when it follows the antiphon *Laetantur caeli* ("Let the heavens rejoice and the earth exult before the face of the Lord -- because he has come"). Advent, the time of preparation and penitence, is over: *venit*, he has come! *Cantate Domino canticum <u>novum</u>*, the Old Law gives way to the New, the Prophecies are fulfilled. *Benedicite! Annuntiate!*

CHRISTUS FACTUS EST

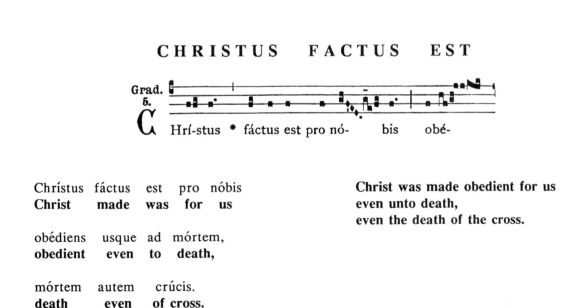

Chrístus	fáctus	est	pro	nóbis	Christ was made obedient for us
Christ	**made**	**was**	**for**	**us**	even unto death,
					even the death of the cross.

obédiens	usque	ad	mórtem,
obedient	**even**	**to**	**death,**

mórtem	autem	crúcis.
death	**even**	**of cross.**

Propter quod	et	Déus	exaltávit	íllum,	Therefore God also has exalted him,
For	which also	God	has exalted	him,	and given him a name
					which is above every name.

| et | dédit | ílli | nómen, |
| and | given | him | name, |

| quod | est | super | ómne | nómen. |
| which | is | above | every | name. |

Maundy Thursday is the great feast of the Holy Eucharist (*Feria in Coena Domini* – the fifth feast [of Holy Week] in honor of the Supper of our Lord), the commemoration of Christ's first institution of the Blessed Sacrament. It was the only feast in honor of the Holy Eucharist until 1264 when Pope Urban IV established the feast of Corpus Christi ("Body of Christ") to focus solely on this event. [see *O sacrum convivium*]

The Epistle for Maundy Thursday (I Corinthians 11:20-32) recounts Christ's institution of the new Pasch of the Holy Eucharist with his disciples and also warns against the abuse of unworthy partaking of the Eucharist: "But let a man prove himself -- Put your own selves to test, whether you are in the faith, prove yourselves -- and so let him eat of that bread and drink of the cup" (I Corinthians 11:28; II Corinthians 13:5). The gradual **Christus factus est** (Phillipians 2:8-9) follows.

Notes:

> *obediens . . . usque ad mortem.*
> "And he [Christ], Son though he was, learned obedience from the things that he suffered" (Hebrews 5:8). "Father, if it is possible, let this cup pass away from me; yet not as I will, but as thou willest" (Matthew 26:39).

> *Deus exaltavit illum.*
> The first verse of the motet speaks of the things Christ did for humankind; the second of what the Father did for him. Christ, to his disciples: "All power in heaven and on earth has been given to me" (Matthew 28:18).

> *super omne nomen.*
> "the working of [God's] mighty power, which he has wrought in Christ in raising him from the dead, and setting him at his right hand in heaven above every Principality and Power and Virtue and Domination -- in short, above every name that is named, not only in this world, but also in that which is to come" (Ephesians 2:19-21). [see *Jesu, dulcis memoria*]

Liturgical context: **Christus factus est** is the Gradual for the Mass on Maundy Thursday. In shortened form it serves as an antiphon sung after the Benedictus and other parts of Divine Office on Maundy Thursday and Good Friday.

CONFITEBOR TIBI, DOMINE

1. Confitébor tíbi Dómine in tóto cór-de mé- o * in con-

1 Confitébor tíbi, Dómine,
I will praise you, Lord,

in tóto córde méo;
with whole heart my;

in consílio justórum, et congregatióne.
in council of just, and congregation.

I will praise you, O Lord,
with my whole heart;
in the council of the just,
and in the congregation.

2 Mágna ópera Dómini,
Great works of Lord,

exquisíta in ómnes voluntátes éjus.
excellent by all choices his.

Great are the works of the Lord,
made excellent by all his choices.

3 Conféssio et magnificéntia ópus éjus;
Praiseworthy and magnificent work his;

et jústitia éjus mánet
and justice his remains

in saéculum saéculi.
from generation to generation.

His work is praiseworthy and magnificent;
and his justice continues
from generation to generation.

4 Memóriam fécit mirabílium suórum,
Remembrance he has made of wonders his;

miséricors et miserátor Dóminus.
merciful and gracious Lord.

He has made a remembrance of his wonders;
being a merciful and gracious Lord.

5 Escam dédit timéntibus se.
Food he gave to those fearing him.

Mémor érit in saéculum
Mindful he will be for generations

testaménti súi.
of covenant his.

He provided food for those that fear him.
He will be forever mindful of his covenant.

6 Virtútem óperum suórum
Power of works his

annuntiábit pópulo súo.
he will make known to people his.

The power of his works
he will make known to his people.

111

7 Ut   det   íllis
   So that   he may give   them

   hereditátem   géntium:
   inheritance   of Gentiles:

   ópera   mánuum   éjus
   works   of hands   his

   véritas   et   judícium.
   truth   and   good judgement.

> So that he may give them
> the inheritance of the Gentiles:
> the works of his hands
>
> are truth and good judgement.

8 Fidélia   ómnia   mandáta   éjus,
   Trustworthy   all   commandments   his,

   confirmáta   in   saéculum   saéculi,
   confirmed   from   generation   to   generation,

   fácta   in   veritáte   et   aequitáte.
   created   in   truth   and   equity.

> All his commandments are trustworthy,
> confirmed from generation to generation,
> created in truth and equity.

9 Redemptiónem   mísit   Dóminus
   Salvation   has sent   Lord

   pópulo   súo;
   to people   his;

   mandávit   in   aetérnum
   he has set down   for   eternity

   testaméntum   súum.
   covenant   his.

   Sánctum   et   terríbile   nómen   éjus:
   Holy   and   terrible   name   his:

> The Lord has sent salvation to his people;
> he has mandated his covenant for ever.
> Holy and terrifying is his name:

10 Inítium   sapiéntiae   tímor   Dómini;
   Beginning   of wisdom   fear   of Lord;

   intelléctus   bónus ómnibus
   understanding   good   to all

   faciéntibus   éum.
   practicing   it.

   Laudátio   éjus   mánet
   Praise   his   endures

   in   saéculum   saéculi.
   from generation   to generation.

> The beginning of wisdom
> is the fear of the Lord;
> All who practice this fear
> have a good understanding.
> His praise endures
> from generation to generation.

Confitebor tibi, Domine (Psalm 110 [111]) is closely connected to the psalm which follows: both were written by the same author, they share similarities of phrase and structure [see *Beatus vir*], and together they sing the praise and greatness of the works of Jehovah (*Confitebor*) and the greatness, the works, and the rewards of "those that fear him and keep his commandments" (*Beatus vir* – "Blessed is the man who fears the Lord"). "The fear of the Lord is the beginning of wisdom . . . and the knowledge of the holy is prudence" (Proverbs 9:10).

Liturgical context: **Confitebor tibi, Domine** is one of the five Lucernal or Vesper psalms; it is sung at Sunday Vespers following the second antiphon *Magna opera Domini* ("Great are the works of the Lord").

CONFITEMINI DOMINO

| Confitémini | Dómino | quoniam | bónus: | | **Praise ye the Lord for he is good:** |
| Give praise | to Lord | because | good: | | **because his mercy endures for ever.** |

| quoniam | in | saéculum | misericórdia | éjus. |
| because | for | generation | mercy | his. |

At the beginning of Mass on Holy Saturday, after the *Kyrie*, the Litanies, and the Collect for the day, the Lesson from Paul's Epistle to the Colossians is said:

> "Brethren: If you be risen with Christ, seek the things that are above, not the things that are upon the earth. For you are dead, and your life is hid with Christ in God. When Christ shall appear, who is your life, then shall you also appear with him in glory" (Colossians 3:1–4).

After the Epistle the priest solemnly intones the *Alleluia*,

L-le-   lú-   ia.

which he sings thrice, each time upon a higher tone; the choir repeats it after him in the same manner, and after the third time adds the verse:

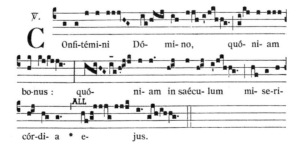

quoniam bonus, quoniam in saeculum misericordia ejus.

This psalm (Psalm 117 [118]) is also appointed as the first psalm of the Office of Prime on Sunday, and the first verse is the joyous response of the Alleluia-Verse which follows the Lesson from James 5:16-20 at the beginning of the Mass of the Litany of the Saints.

DE PROFUNDIS

De profúndis clamávi ad te, Dómine;
Out of depths I have cried to thee, Lord;

   Out of the depths I have cried to thee, O Lord;
   O Lord, hear my voice.

Dómine, exáudi vócem méam.
Lord, hear voice my.

Fíant áures túae intendéntes
Let be ears your attentive

   Let thy ears be attentive
   to the voice of my supplication.

in vócem deprecatiónis méae.
to voice of supplication my.

Si iniquitátes observáveris, Dómine,
If iniquities will have marked, Lord,

   If thou, O Lord, will have marked iniquities,
   Lord, who will withstand?

Dómine, quis sustinébit?
Lord, who will withstand?

Quía ápud te propitiátio est;
But with you forgiveness is;

   But with you there is forgiveness:
   and on account of your law
   I have waited for you, O Lord.

et propter légem túam
and on account of law your

sustínui te, Dómine.
I have waited for you, Lord.

Sustínuit ánima méa in vérbo éjus;
Has relied soul my in word his;

   My soul trusts in his word:
   my soul hopes in the Lord.

sperávit ánima méa in Dómino.
has hoped soul my in Lord.

A custódia matutína usque ad nóctem,
From watch morning up to night,

   From the morning watch even until night,
   Let Israel hope in the Lord.

spéret Israel in Dómino;
let hope for Israel in Lord;

quia apud Dóminum misericórdia,
For with Lord mercy,

   For with the Lord there is mercy,
   and with him there is plenteous redemption.

et copiósa apud éum redémptio.
and plenteous with him redemption.

Et ípse rédimet Israel
And alone he shall redeem Israel

   And he shall redeem Israel
   from all its iniquities.

ex ómnibus iniquitátibus éjus.
from all iniquities its.

King David, "the sweet psalmist of Israel," exhorted those who were to follow after him with his famous last words: "He that ruleth over Israel must be just, ruling in the fear of God" (II Kings [Samuel] 23:3). But the period from David's reign to that of Hezekiah was one of degeneracy and decay. Dazzled by Solomon's glorious monarchy Israel began to forget the Theocracy on which it was founded, and the time soon came when the psalmist cried out: "The godly man ceaseth. . . the wicked walk on every side, . . . the vilest of the sons of men are exalted" (Psalm 12:1,8). The time of the Babylonian captivity, the long exile from Jerusalem, and the fall of the Temple was at hand.

Shortly after this period, **De Profundis**, one of the fifteen "songs of ascents," was written [authorship unknown]. The songs of ascents or "degrees" (*L canticum graduum*, song of steps), the "songs of the goings up," are the songs of the exiled Hebrew nation, the pilgrim psalter of a people "going up" from captivity to the holy city of Jerusalem. They are acclamations *de profundis*, pilgrim odes of those who once again "lift their eyes unto the mountains" (Psalm 120 [121] : 1), trusting that "they who sow in tears shall reap in joy" (Psalm 125 [126] : 5), and hoping in the Lord, "for with the Lord there is mercy, and with him there is plenteous redemption. And he will redeem Israel from all its iniquities" (Psalm 129 [130] : 7–8).

De Profundis, Psalm 129 [130], is the sixth of the seven Penitential Psalms (the others being: Psalms 6, 31, 37, 50, 101, and 142 [Vulgate]), so called because they express sorrow for sin and desire for pardon. Used by penitents since the 6th century, Innocent III ordered their recitation during Lent and Pius V later fixed the Fridays in Lent after Lauds as the time they should be said.

Composers from Josquin Des Prez and Orlandus Lassus to Arnold Schoenberg, Knut Nystedt, Arvo Pärt, and Ingvar Lidholm have all made personal and particularly expressive choral settings of this psalm which Moses Buttenweiser summarizes in the following way:

> "The gospel of the pardon of sin is proclaimed in this profound psalm
> with a noble simplicity that cannot be surpassed. The psalm . . . stands out as
> *sui generis* because there is no mention whatever in it of physical suffering and
> misery, whether personal or general, though we may be sure that there was no
> lack of these at the time it was written."　　　　　　　　(The Psalms, p. 650)

Liturgical context: **De profundis** was traditionally sung in the Roman Church every Wednesday at Vespers, at II. Vespers of Christmas, at the beginning of the funereal rites (along with Psalm 50 [51] *Miserere mei* and the antiphon *Si iniquitatis*), in the Office of the Dead at Vespers and the end of Lauds, as a Tract on Septuagesima Sunday, and as the Offertory on the 23rd Sunday after Pentecost.

DEO   DICAMUS   GRATIAS

Déo	dicámus	grátias.	**Let us give thanks unto God!**
To God	**let us say**	**thanks.**	

Deo dicamus gratias is the respond employed at the conclusion of Divine Office or the Mass, following either the familiar dismissal *Ite, missa est* ("Go, [the mass] has been spoken") or the versicle *Benedicamus Domino* ("Let us give praise to the Lord"). [see also *Benedicamus Domino*]

DIES SANCTIFICATUS

Llelú- ia. * *ij.* ℣. Dí-

es sancti- ficátus illúxit nó-   bis :

Díes	sanctificátus	illúxit	nóbis:
Day	**made holy**	**has dawned**	**for us;**

A holy day has dawned for us;
come, nations, and worship the Lord,
for today a great light has descended to earth.

veníte	géntes	et	adoráte Dóminum:
come	**nations**	**and**	**worship Lord,**

quia	hódie	descéndit
because	**today**	**has descended**

lux	mágna	in	térris.
light	**great**	**to**	**earth.**

Haec	díes,	quam	fécit	Dóminus:
This	**day,**	**which**	**has made**	**Lord;**

This is the day which the Lord has made;
let us rejoice exceedingly and be glad in it.

exultémus		et	laetémur in	éa.
let us exult		**and**	**be glad in**	**it.**

"For behold, darkness shall cover the earth, and a gloom shall come over the people: but the Lord shall arise upon thee, and his glory shall be seen upon thee. And the Gentiles shall walk in thy light, and kings in the brightness of thy rising" (Isaiah 60:2-3).

"A light has risen in the darkness for the upright" (Psalm 110 [111] : 4), "to be a light to enlighten the Gentiles, and to be the glory of thy people Israel" (Luke 2:32).

And, from the Epistle of the Third Mass for Christmas Day: "God ... has spoken to us by his son ... who, being the brightness of his glory and the image of his substance, has effected man's purgation from sin" (Hebrews 1:1-12). The Gradual *Viderunt omnes* then says: "All the ends of the earth shall see the salvation of our God; *jubilate*, rejoice!" The Alleluia-Verse which follows, *Dies sanctificatus*, continues: "A holy day has dawned for us; *adorate*, adore, worship!" This text echoes the thoughts of the Epistle and effects a transition to the Gospel which is from the first chapter of John: *In principio erat Verbum*, "In the beginning was the Word."

The opening portion of the text is non-scriptural, "probably from old Byzantium," as the chant melody appears in an early manuscript in the Vatican library with both a Latin and a Greek text accompanying it. In its fuller form, with the *Haec dies* from Psalm 117 [118] : 24 appended, this text appears in the liturgy of the Feast of the Circumcision as a Responsory after the second lesson of the first Nocturn of Matins.

DIXIT DOMINUS

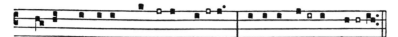

1. Dí-xit Dóminus Dómino mé- o:* Séde a déxtris mé- is.

1 Díxit   Dóminus   Dómino   méo:
  Said   **Lord**   **to Lord**   **my:**

  Séde   a   déxtris   méis,
  Sit   **at**   **right hand**   **my**

  donec   pónam   inimícos   túos
  until   **I shall make**   **enemies**   **your**

  scabéllum   pédum   tuórum.
  stool   **of feet**   **your.**

The Lord said unto my Lord:

Sit at my right hand
until I make your enemies
your footstool.

2 Virgam   virtútis   túae
  Rod   **of power**   **your**

  emíttet   Dóminus ex Síon:
  shall send forth   **Lord** **from** **Zion;**

  domináre in médio inimicórum tuórum.
  rule   **in** **midst** **of enemies**   **your.**

The sceptre of your power
the Lord shall send forth from Zion:
Rule thou in the midst of your enemies.

3 Técum   princípium in díe virtútis túae,
  With you   **power** **on** **day** **of might** **your,**

  in splendóribus   sanctórum:
  in   **splendor**   **of holy ones;**

  ex   útero   ante   lucíferum
  from   **womb**   **before**   **light–bringer**

  génui   te.
  I have begotten   **you**

The power to rule is with you
on the day of your strength,
in the splendor of the holy ones:

I have begotten you from the womb
before the rising of the day–star.

4 Jurávit   Dóminus,
  Has sworn   **Lord,**

  et   non   poenitébit   éum:
  and   **not**   **will repent**   **of it:**

  Tu es sacérdos in   aetérnum
  You **are** **priest** **for**   **eternity**

  secúndum   órdinem   Melchísedech.
  according to   **order**   **of Melchisedech.**

The Lord has sworn an oath,
and will not repent of it:

You are a priest for ever,
after the order of Melchisedech.

5 Dóminus   a   déxtris   túis,
Lord   **at right hand   your,**

    confrégit   in   díe   írae   súae   réges.
    destroys   on   day   of wrath   his   kings.

The Lord at your right hand
destroys kings on the day of his wrath;

6 Judicábit   in   natiónibus,
He shall judge   among   heathen,

    implébit   ruínas,
    he shall pile up   ruins;

    conquasábit   cápita   in   térra   multórum.
    he shall shatter   heads   on   land   of many.

He shall judge among the heathen;
he shall pile up ruins
and scatter skulls on many lands.

7 De   torrénte   in   vía   bíbet,
Of   torrent   in   way   he shall drink;

    proptérea   exaltábit   cáput.
    therefore   he shall lift up   head.

He shall drink of the torrent in his way;
therefore he shall lift up his head.

Dixit Dominus (Psalm 109 [110]) is one of the five Lucernal or Vesper psalms which have been a characteristic feature of the office of Vespers for many centuries. The opening phrase, *Dixit Dominus ... sede a dextris meis*, is also used as an antiphon at Sunday Vespers, as an *Incipit* preceding the chanting of the entire psalm.

This psalm is closely related to Psalm 2 ("Why do the nations rage?"), each of them being a Messianic song based on Nathan's prophecy of the permanence and universality of the kingdom of David (see II Kings [Samuel] 7:8-17).

Notes:

    1. *Dixit Dominus Domino meo.*
        Dominus, Yahweh, speaking through his oracle to *Domino meo*, my lord, my sire (as in Genesis 23:6 - "My lord, hear us, thou art a prince of God among us"), the Messiah.

    1. *Sede a dextris meis.*
        In pre-Islamic Arabia the viceroy sat at the right hand of the king and took precedence next to him. A position of honor; the Messiah as second only to Him that sent him.

    1. *scabellum pedum.*
        Your footstool, your subject and servant. The victorious king placed his foot on the necks of his vanquished foes. (Joshua 10:24)

    2. *Virgam virtutis.*
        "Thou shalt rule them with a rod of iron" (Psalm 2:9).

    3. *principium.*
        The Messiah is by birth heir to the house of David and ruler over Sion.

4. *Juravit Dominus.*

"I have sworn to David my servant ... I will build up thy throne unto generation and generation ... I will cut down his enemies ... and my truth and mercy shall be with him ... And I will make him my firstborn, high above the kings of the earth ... Once I have sworn my holiness I will not lie unto David: his seed shall endure for ever" (Psalm 88 [89] : 4-5, 24-36).

4. *Melchisedech.*

"Melchisedech the king of Salem ... the priest of the most high God" (Genesis 14:18); God's promise "implies that priesthood and royalty shall be united in the person of the Messiah, as it was in the ancient priest-king in Salem" (Buttenwieser).

5-6. *confregit reges, judicabit, implebit, conquasabit ...*

"[The Lord] shall speak to them in his anger, and trouble them in his rage ... [he] will trample the nations in [his] wrath, smash them in fury, and spill their blood upon the earth ... [and] break them in pieces like a potter's vessel" (Psalm 2:5; Isaiah 63:3; Psalm 2:9).

7. *De torrente bibet ... exaltavit caput.*

"For thus saith the Lord: Behold I will bring upon [Jerusalem] as it were a river of peace, and as an overflowing torrent the glory of the Gentiles, which you shall suck" (Isaiah 66:12). "The children of men shall put their trust under the covert of thy wings. They shall be inebriated with the plenty of thy house; and thou shall make them drink of the torrent of thy pleasure. For with thee is the fountain of life" (Psalm 35 [36] : 8-10). The Messiah shall lift up his head in triumph over the kings of the earth.

DIXIT MARIA

| Díxit | María | ad | Angelum: | Mary said to the Angel: |
| Said | Mary | to | Angel: | |

| Ecce, | ancílla | Dómini: | Behold the handmaid of the Lord; |
| Behold, | handmaid | of Lord; | Be it done unto me according to your word. |

| fíat | míhi | secúndum | vérbum | túum. |
| be it done | to me | according to | word | your. |

119

The angel Gabriel's Annunciation to the Virgin Mary is recounted in Luke 1:26-38. He greets her with the *Ave Maria, gratia plena* ("Hail Mary, full of grace") and explains that she "shall conceive and bring forth a son" and "call his name Jesus." Mary asks, "How shall this happen, since I do not know a man? And the angel answered and said unto her, The Holy Spirit shall come upon thee and the power of the Most high shall overshadow thee; and therefore the Holy One to be born shall be called the Son of God . . . for nothing shall be impossible with God." And *Dixit Maria ad Angelus: Ecce, ancilla Domini . . . fiat mihi secundum verbum tuum*, thus expressing her complete surrender (in faith) to God's will.

The liturgy for the Feast of the Annunciation (March 25), one of the most ancient feasts celebrated in honor of the Blessed Virgin (dating back to the 5th century in the East and to the 8th century in the West), prescribes that the above account from the Gospel of St. Luke be read along with the prophecy of Isaiah: "Behold a virgin shall conceive, and bear a son, and his name shall be called Emmanuel. He shall eat butter and honey, that he may know to refuse the evil, and the choose the good" (Isaiah 7:10-15). Heard also in this Mass are the *Ave Maria* and *Virga Jesse floruit* texts combined to form the Alleluia and its Verse, the salutation *Ave Maria* repeated for the Offertory, and Isaiah's prophecy (*Ecce, Virgo concipiet*, "Behold a virgin shall conceive") sung as the Communion antiphon. Later that day, at Vespers, the words of Mary from **Dixit Maria** are employed as the antiphon for the fifth psalm, *Lauda Jerusalem* (Psalm 147 [147:12-20] - "Praise the Lord, O Jerusalem"). The short *capitulum* from Isaiah 7:14-15 follows, along with the Marian Antiphon for the season, *Ave Maris Stella* ("Hail, Star of the Sea").

DUO SERAPHIM CLAMABANT

Dúo	Séraphim	clamábant,		The two Seraphim proclaimed,
Two	**Seraphim**	**proclaimed,**		one to the other:

álter	ad	álterum:
one	**to**	**other:**

Sánctus,	Sánctus,	Sánctus,		Holy, Holy, Holy,
Holy,	**Holy,**	**Holy,**		Lord God of Hosts.
				The whole earth is full

Dóminus	Déus	Sábaoth.		of his glory.
Lord	**God**	**of Hosts.**

Pléna	est	ómnis	térra
Full	**is**	**whole**	**earth**

glória	éjus.
of glory	**his.**

Tres sunt qui testimónium	There are three
Three are who testimony	who give testimony in heaven:
	the Father, the Word, and the Holy Spirit;
dant in coélo.	and these three are one.
give in heaven.	

Páter, Verbum, et Spíritus sánctus	
Father, Word, and Spirit Holy	

et hi tres únum sunt.	
and these three one are.	

Laus et perénnis glória	Praise and continuing glory
Praise and continuing glory	be to God the Father and the Son
	and the Holy Spirit now and forevermore.

Déo pátri cum fílio,
to God Father with Son,

sáncto símul paracléto
holy at same time Paraclete

in sempitérna sécula.
for everlasting generations.

"In the year that King Uzziah died, I saw the Lord sitting on a throne, high and lifted up, and the train of his robe filled the temple. Above it stood the seraphim; each one had six wings: with two he covered his face, with two he covered his feet, and with two he flew. And one cried to the other and said: Holy, holy, holy is the Lord of hosts; the whole earth is full of his glory."

This opening of the account of Isaiah's vocational vision (Isaiah 6:1–3) uniquely and specifically describes these celestial beings in the court of Yahweh and favors the opinion that they are only two in number, continually crying the Trisagion or Thrice Holy "one to the other." The name "seraphim" comes from the Hebrew verb meaning "to burn," a reference to the one seraph's purifying of Isaiah by touching his mouth with a live coal (Isaiah 6:6–7). The remainder of the text is probably a medieval gloss with an appended doxology.

ECCE SACERDOS

1. Ant.
7. c

Cce sacérdos mágnus, *qui in di- ébus sú- is plá-

Écce sacérdos mágnus,
Behold priest great,

qui in diébus súis plácuit Déo.
who in days his pleased God.

Behold a great priest,
who in his days pleased God.

Non est invéntus símilis ílli
Not was found like to him

There was none found like unto him
who kept the law of the Most High.

qui conserváret légem Excélsi.
who kept law of Most High.

Ideo jurejurándo fécit íllum Dóminus
Therefore oath made him Lord

Therefore by an oath the Lord made him
to increase among his people.

créscere in plébem súam.
to increase among people his.

Benedictiónem ómnium géntium dédit ílli,
Blessing of all nations he gave to him,

He gave him the blessing of all nations,
and confirmed his covenant upon his head.

et testaméntum súum confirmávit
and covenant his he confirmed

super cáput éjus.
upon head his.

Sacerdótes Déi, benedícite Dóminum:
Priests of God, bless Lord:

Priests of God, bless the Lord:

Sérvi Dómini, hýmnum dícite Déo.
Servants of Lord, hymn say to God.

Ye servants of the Lord,
recite a hymn to your God.

Sérve bóne et fidélis,
Servant good and faithful,

Good and faithful servant,
enter into the joy of your Lord.

íntra in gáudium Dómini túi.
enter into joy of Lord your.

The Mass *Statuit* of the Confessor Pontiff takes its name from the first word of the Introit *Statuit ei Dominus* ("He made to him a covenant of peace, and he made him prince [of the sanctuary], that the dignity of the priesthood should be to him for ever. *Alleluia.* O Lord, remember David, and all his meekness. *Gloria Patri.*"). Thus begins the Mass in which those Confessors who were not Martyrs (those who confessed their faith by their penance, zeal and sanctity, and suffered for Christ's sake but were not killed because of their witness) are commemorated and praised.

The text for **Ecce sacerdos**, like the opening of the Introit, is taken from the Book of Wisdom written by Jesus the Son of Sirach of Jerusalem; it is called Ecclesiasticus, a name which comes from a Greek word that signifies a preacher. Jesus, who "has written in this book the doctrine of wisdom and instruction" (50:29) concerning all manner of things, turns, in Chapter 43, to the praise of the wonderful works of God, and, in Chapters 44-50, to the hymn of praise for the holy fathers, the venerable *Hymnum Patrum* from which the text of **Ecce sacerdos** is taken.

The composition of the text for the Lesson of this Mass has been carefully selected and edited from Chapters 44 and 45, converting the praise of specific persons into general ascriptions that could be applied to all "such as have borne rule in their dominions, men of great power, ruling over the present people, and by the strength of wisdom instructing the people in most holy words" (44:3-4). This tasteful gleaning can perhaps be best appreciated by a comparison of the Ecce sacerdos text with the original passages from Ecclesiasticus which are used for the Lesson:

	Ecclesiasticus	**Ecce sacerdos**

. . . .

44:7 *Omnes...in diebus suis habentur in laudibus.*

**Ecce sacerdos magnus
qui in diebus suis**

44:16 *Enoch placuit Deo, et translatus est ...*

placuit Deo

44:20 *Abraham magnus pater multitudinis gentium,
et non est inventus similis illi in gloria;
qui conservavit legem Excelsi,
et fuit in testamento cum illo.*

**Non est inventus similis illi
qui conservaret legem Excelsi.**

44:22 *Ideo jurejurando dedit illi gloriam in gente sua,
crescere illum quase terrae cumulum*

**Ideo jurejurando fecit illum Dominus
crescere in plebem suam.**

44:25 *Benedictionem omnium gentium dedit illi Dominus,
et testamentum suum confirmavit
super caput Jacob.*

**Benedictionem omnium gentium dedit illi,
et testamentum suum confirmavit
super caput ejus.**

[The Lesson continues with selected portions of 44:26,27 and 45:3,6,8,19,20]

The Gradual **Ecce sacerdos** is sung immediately after the Lesson, and is itself followed by the Alleluia-Verse *Tu es sacerdos* ("Thou are a priest for ever, according to the order of Melchisedech") from Psalm 109 [110]. [see *Dixit Dominus*] After Septuagesima, the Tract *Beatus vir* ("Blessed is the man who fears the Lord, who delights exceedingly in his commandments") is sung instead of the Alleluia-Verse. The Gospel which follows is the parable of the talents from Matthew 25:14-23, which concludes: "Well done, good and faithful servant; because thou hast been faithful over a few things, I will set thee over many; enter into the joy of thy Lord." This is the text on which the final portion of **Ecce sacerdos** is based.

At II. Vespers the entire **Ecce sacerdos** text is divided into five parts (*Ecce sacerdos, Non est inventus, Ideo jurejurando, Sacerdotes Dei,* and *Serve bone et fidelis*) and employed as the antiphons for each of the five Vesper psalms. The first four psalms appointed are from the group of five Lucernal psalms long associated with the office of Vespers (Psalm 109, *Dixit Dominus*; Psalm 110, *Confitebor*; Psalm 111, *Beatus vir*; and Psalm 112, *Laudate Pueri* [Vulgate]). But the fifth and final psalm, which is sung with the antiphon *Serve bone et fidelis*, is Psalm 131 [132], *Memento, Domine* ("Remember, O Lord, thy servant David, and all his meekness"), chosen for its obvious praise of one of the holy fathers, and the particular appropriateness of verses 9 ("Let thy priests be clothed with justice, and let thy saints rejoice") and 16 ("I will clothe her priests with salvation, and her saints shall rejoice with exceeding great joy").

Liturgical context: **Ecce sacerdos** is the Gradual for the Mass *Statuit* of the Confessor Pontiff. The text, divided into five parts, is also employed for the antiphons of the Vesper psalms at II. Vespers of the same feast.

EXSULTATE DEO

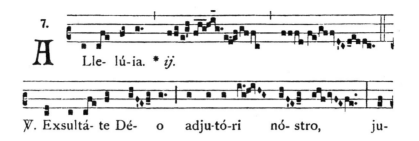

7.
A Lle- lú-ia. * *ij.*

℣. Exsultá- te Dé- o adju-tó-ri nó- stro, ju-

| Exsultáte | Déo, | adjutóri | nóstro, | **Rejoice greatly to God our helper,** |
| **Rejoice** | **to God,** | **helper** | **our,** | **shout for joy to the God of Jacob.** |

| jubiláte | Déo | Jácob. |
| **shout for joy** | **to God** | **of Jacob.** |

| Súmite | psálmum, | et | dáte | týmpanum | **Take up a psalm, and bring the timbrel** |
| **Take** | **psalm,** | **and** | **bring** | **timbrel** | **and the sweet psaltery with the harp,** |

| Psaltérium | jucúndum | cum | cíthara |
| **psaltery** | **sweet** | **with** | **harp** |

| Buccináte | in | neoménia | túba | **Blow the trumpet on the new moon,** |
| **Blow** | **on** | **new moon** | **trumpet** | **on the notable day of your solemnity.** |

| Insígni | díe | solemnitátis | véstrae. |
| **Notable** | **day** | **of solemnity** | **your.** |

The Epistle for the Mass of the Eleventh Sunday after Pentecost is St. Paul's testimony of the Resurrection (I Corinthians 15:1–10) which concludes: "And last of all, as by one born out of due time, he was seen also by me. For I am the least of the apostles and am not worthy to be called an apostle, because I persecuted the Church of God. But by the grace of God I am what I am, and his grace in me has not been fruitless." The Gradual *In Deo speravit* follows:

"In God hath my heart confided, and I have been helped; and my
flesh hath flourished again; and with my will I will give praise to him. Unto
thee have I cried, O Lord: O my God, be not thou silent; depart not from me."
(Psalm 27 [28] : 7,1) --

words which could have been uttered by either the Risen Lord or an Apostle giving thanks for God's grace. The joyous Alleluia–Verse follows, celebrating the Resurrection with the exuberant praise of the opening verses of **Exsultate Deo** (Psalm 80 [81]) which recalls the text of the Gradual (Psalm 27 [28] : 7a) and summons the musicians for the feast of thanksgiving.

The religious observance of the New Moon, the beginning of the lunar cycle which determined Israel's calendar, was much like the sabbath: a day of rest, rejoicing, and festive religious rites.

"On the first days of your months you shall sound the trumpets over
the holocausts and the sacrifices of peace offerings, that they may be to you a
remembrance of your God." (Numbers 10:10)

The New Moon festival of the seventh month was given special solemnity:

> "And the Lord spoke to Moses, saying: Say to the children of Israel: The seventh month, on the first day of the month, you shall keep a sabbath, a memorial, with the sound of trumpets, and it shall be called holy." (Leviticus 23:23-24)

> "The first day also of the seventh month shall be venerable and holy unto you; you shall do no servile work therein, because it is the day of the sounding and of trumpets." (Numbers 29:1)

The trumpet used for this special day (later to be known as Rosh Hashanah, or New Year's Day) was the shofar or wild goat's horn, an instrument reserved for high religious observances.

The superscription in the Vulgate for **Exsultate Deo** (Psalm 81 [82]) is "for the winepresses," signifying that this psalm was to be sung at this same feast of Tabernacles (also called the feast of Booths) after the gathering in of the vintage.

Liturgical context: **Exsultate Deo** is the Alleluia-Verse for the 11th Sunday after Pentecost.

EXSULTATE JUSTI

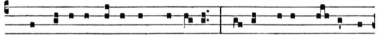

Ps. Exsultá-te jústi in Dómi-no : * réctos décet col-laudá-

Exsultáte	jústi	in	Dómino:
Rejoice	**just**	**in**	**Lord:**

Rejoice in the Lord, O ye just:
Praise is fitting for the upright.

réctos	décet	collaudátio.
for upright	**it is fitting**	**to praise.**

Confitémi	Dómino	in	cíthara,
Give praise	**to God**	**upon**	**harp,**

Give praise to God upon the harp,
play upon the ten-stringed psaltery.

in	psaltério	décem	chordárum	psállite	ílli.
upon	**psaltery**	**of ten**	**strings**	**play**	**to him.**

Cantáte	éi	cánticum	nóvum,
Sing	**to him**	**song**	**new,**

Sing to him a new song,
Sing skillfully with a strong voice.

béne	psállite	éi	in	vociferatióne.
well	**sing**	**to him**	**in**	**strong tones.**

These opening verses of Psalm 32 [33] constitute a general call to praise, the words *canticum novum* ("new song") suggesting to many a recent victory over the nations (verses 10 and 12) as the occasion for yet another song of thanksgiving.

The first verse has been employed as the psalm-verse for a number of introits: *Sapientiam sanctorum* ("Wisdom of the saints") for the Common Mass of Many Martyrs; *Misericordias Domini* ("The mercy of the Lord") for the second Sunday after Easter; *Gaudeamus omnes* ("Let us all rejoice in the Lord") for the Feast of All Saints (November 1); etc. The antiphon and psalm itself are appointed to be said at None.

Notes: Related scriptural references:
    Exsultate justi: Psalm 31 [32]:11; *decet collaudatio:* Psalm 146 [147]:1; *psalterio decem chordarum:* Psalm 143 [144]:9; *canticum novum:* 39 [40]:3; *bene psallite:* I Kings [Samuel] 16:17. *In vociferatione* is read by some as "among shouts of gladness."

GLORIA PATRI

1. Gló-ri- a Pátri, et Fí-li- o, et Spi-rí-tu- i Sáncto. *

Glória	Pátri,	et	Fílio,	**Glory be to the Father, and to the Son,**
Glory	**to Father,**	**and**	**Son,**	**and to the Holy Spirit.**

et	Spirítui	Sáncto.
and	**Spirit**	**Holy.**

Sicut	érat	in	princípio,	**As it was in the beginning,**
As	**it was**	**in**	**beginning,**	**is now, and ever shall be,**
				world without end. Amen.

et	nunc,	et	sémper,
and	**now,**	**and**	**always,**

et	in	saécula	saéculorum.	Amen.
and	**for**	**generations**	**of generations.**	**Amen.**

The **Gloria Patri** (the *doxologia minor*, or Lesser Doxology) is usually recited after each psalm employed in Divine Office and after the *Judica* psalm (Psalm 42 [43], "Judge me, O God") in the Mass. It also occurs after canticles and is used frequently in extra-liturgical services, such as the Rosary. Like the Greater Doxology, the *Gloria in excelsis*, its joyous nature excludes it from occasions of mourning such as the last three days of Holy Week, and also from the Office of the Dead where it is replaced by the *Requiem aeternam* and the *Et lux perpetua*.

The tradition of closing a psalm with a doxology, first ordered by St. Benedict in his *Rule* of 525, comes from the tradition of the Synagogue where ancient rites and hymns concluded with a similar formula (e.g., *tibi est gloria in saecula saeculorum. Amen.*). Each book of the Psalter also ends with a doxology (see the final verses of [Vulgate] Psalms 40, 71, 88, 105, and Psalm 150, the end of the fifth book and final psalm in the Psalter, which is itself regarded as "wholly a doxology.").

The first portion of the text, which dates from the 3rd or 4th century, was probably modeled on the formula for baptism ("baptizing them in the name of the Father, and of the Son, and of the Holy Spirit" – Matthew 28:19) where the Trinity is named in parallel order. Earlier doxologies were addressed to God the Father, or to Him *through* the Son, or to Him *in* or *with* the Holy Spirit. The concluding words, *Sicut erat in principio . . .* , are of late origin. Their inclusion is often cited as a protest against Arianism's denial of the Son's eternity, *sicut erat* being at first interpreted to mean "as he [*Filius*] was *in principio* (John 1:1), as opposed to the common belief today that understands *Gloria* as the referent of *erat* ("As it [glory] was in the beginning . . .").

HAEC DIES

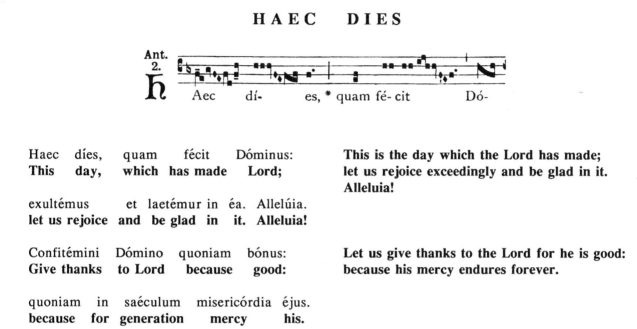

Haec díes, quam fécit Dóminus:
This day, which has made Lord;

This is the day which the Lord has made;
let us rejoice exceedingly and be glad in it.
Alleluia!

exultémus et laetémur in éa. Allelúia.
let us rejoice and be glad in it. Alleluia!

Confitémini Dómino quoniam bónus:
Give thanks to Lord because good:

Let us give thanks to the Lord for he is good:
because his mercy endures forever.

quoniam in saéculum misericórdia éjus.
because for generation mercy his.

The Lesson for Easter Sunday Mass is from Paul's letter to the Corinthians:

"Purge out the old leaven, that you may be a new dough,
as you really are without leaven. For Christ, our Passover, has
been sacrificed. Therefore let us keep festival, not with the old
leaven, nor with the leaven of malice and wickedness, but with the
unleavened bread of sincerity and truth" (I Corinthians 5:7-8).

The Gradual **Haec dies** follows as a commentary on this reading, and is itself followed by the venerable Sequence for Easter Day, *Victimae paschali laudes* ("To the Paschal Victim let Christians offer their praises").

The **Haec dies** (Psalm 117 [118]:24,1) is also found, in shortened form, as the 2nd Antiphon for the office of Vespers on Easter Day.

Notes:

exultemus.
From *exultare*: exult, rejoice exceedingly, revel (lit. spring up as in a dance).
laetemur.
From *laetare*: rejoice, feel joy, be joyful/glad.

HODIE CHRISTUS NATUS EST

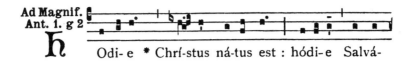

Ad Magnif.
Ant. 1. g 2

ℏ Odi- e * Chrí-stus ná-tus est : hódi- e Salvá-

| Hódie | Chrístus | nátus | est: | | Today Christ is born; |
| Today | Christ | born | is; | | today the Saviour has appeared; |

| hódie | Salvátor | appáruit: |
| today | Saviour | has appeared; |

| hódie | in térra | cánunt | Angeli, | today the Angels sing, |
| today | on earth | sing | Angels, | the Archangels rejoice; |

| laetántur | Archángeli: |
| rejoice | Archangels; |

| hódie | exsúltant | jústi, | dicéntes: | today the righteous rejoice, saying: |
| today | exult | righteous, | saying: | Glory to God in the highest. Alleluia! |

| Glória | in | excélsis | Déo, | allelúia. |
| Glory | in | highest | to God, | alleluia. |

The liturgy of II. Vespers on Christmas Day is yet another example of the great sensitivity and artistry with which the Church has appointed certain texts to particular feasts and functions. The antiphons for each of the five Vesper psalms are not only taken from the psalm with which they are associated, but the particular verses chosen relate each psalm directly to the implications of the joyous event of Christmas Day:

> 1. Ant. *Tecum principium:* "The power to rule is with you on the day of your strength, in the splendor of the holy ones: I have begotten you from the womb, before the rising of the day-star." (*Dixit Dominus*)

> 2. Ant. *Redemptionem misit Dominus:* "The Lord has sent salvation to his people; he has set down his covenant for eternity." (*Confitebor*)

> 3. Ant. *Exortum est:* "A light has risen in the darkness for the upright: one who is merciful, compassionate, and just." (*Beatus vir*)

> 4. Ant. *Apud Dominum misericordia:* "With the Lord there is mercy, and with him is plentiful redemption." (*De Profundis*)

> 5. Ant. *De fructis ventris:* "Of the fruit of thy womb I will set upon thy throne." (*Momento David*)

A short *capitulum* from Hebrews 1:1-2 with its versicle and response *Notum fecit Dominus* ("The Lord has made known his salvation. Alleluia!") follows:

> "God, who at sundry times and in divers manners spoke in times past to the fathers by the prophets, last of all, in these days, hath spoken to us by his Son, whom he hath appointed heir of all things, by whom also he made the world."

Hodie Christus natus est (a paraphrase of Luke 2:11,13–14 and Psalm 32 [33] : 1) then follows as the antiphon to the textual climax of the Vesper office, the exultant Canticle of the Blessed Virgin Mary, *Magnificat anima mea* ("My soul magnifies the Lord, and my spirit rejoices in God my Saviour").

IN DULCI JUBILO

In dúlci júbilo   In sweet rejoicing
In **sweet** **rejoicing**   **now sing and be joyful.**

Nun *singet* *und* *seit* *froh.*
Now **sing** **and** **be** **joyful.**

Unsers *Herzens* *Wonne*   **Our heart's delight**
Our **heart's** **delight**   **lies in the manger,**

liegt in *praesepio,*
lies **in** **manger,**

und *leuchtet* *als* *die* *Sonne*   **and shines like the sun**
and **shines** **as** **the** **Sun**   **in his mother's lap.**

mátris in *grémio.*
of mother **in** **lap.**

Alpha es et O.   **Thou art Alpha and O,**
Alpha **you are** **and** **O.**   **the beginning and the end.**

The author of **In dulci jubilo** is not certainly known, but it may have been the 14th century German and Dominican mystic Heinrich Suso (d.1366) who, according to legend, wrote the tune and the words after he had danced with the angels and sung the song with them. John Mason Neale's free paraphrase of these lines is the well-known English carol *Good Christian Men, Rejoice*.

The original text exhibits a technique known as "farsing" (from *farcire*, to stuff): the interpolation or insertion of the vernacular into set texts, which is sometimes defended as being a vernacular exposition for the laity.

The tiny child, our heart's delight, lying in his mother's lap, is the ALPHA and OMEGA, the beginning and the end (A and Ω are the first and last letters of the Greek alphabet).

"I am the first, and I am the last, and besides me there is no God." (Isaiah 44:6)

"I am Alpha and Omega, the beginning and the end, saith the Lord, which is, and which was, and which is to come, the Almighty." (Apocalypse [Revelation] 1:8)

IN ECCLESIIS

In ecclésiis benedícite Dómino.
In assemblies bless Lord.

  Alleluia!

In ómni lóco dominatiónis,
In every place of dominion,

benedic, ánima méa, Dóminum.
bless, soul my, Lord.

  Alleluia!

In Déo salutári méo
In God salvation my

et glória méa.
and glory my.

Déus, auxílium méum
God, help my

et spes méa in Déo est.
and hope my in God is.

  Alleluia!

Déus méus, te invocámus,
God my, you we call upon,

te adorámus.
you we worship.

Líbera nos, sálva nos,
Deliver us, save us,

vivífica nos.
enliven us.

  Alleluia!

Déus, adjútor nóster, in aetérnam.
God, helper our, for eternity.

  Alleluia!

In the congregations bless the Lord.

  Alleluia!

In every place of his dominion,
bless the Lord, O my soul.

  Alleluia!

In God is my salvation and my glory.
God is my help, and my hope is in God.

  Alleluia!

My God, we call upon you,
we worship you.
Deliver us, save us, give us life.

  Alleluia!

God is our helper for ever and ever.

  Alleluia!

The inclusion of **In Ecclesiis** in this volume of sacred Latin texts is based on the merits and popularity of Giovanni Gabrieli's setting of it which is found in Book II of his *Sacrae Symphoniae*, Venice, 1615. G. Wallace Woodworth's introduction to the G. Schirmer edition and the remarks and continuo realization in Apel and Davidson's *Historical Anthology of Music* (H.A.M. #157) contain much food for thought and practice.

Woodworth makes the following comment about the text itself: "The text of *In ecclesiis* illustrates the independence of the ritual at St. Mark's, and suggests by its non-liturgical and episodic structure that it may have been expecially arranged for a grand ceremonial occasion in the Church of St. Mark." And grand it must have been, as Thomas Coryat's first-hand description from 1608 clearly testifies:

"Sometimes there sung sixteene or twenty men together, having their master or moderator to keepe them in order; and when they sung, the instrumentall musitians played also. Sometimes sixteene played together on their instruments, ten Sagbuts, foure Cornets, and two Violdegambaes of an extraordinary greatnesse; sometimes tenne, sixe Sagbuts and foure Cornets; sometimes two, a Cornet and a treble violl . . ."

The text consists mostly of paraphrases and quotations form the Psalms, as the few following examples will serve to illustrate:

"Bless the Lord, all ye his hosts: you ministers of his that do his will. Bless the Lord, all his works: in every place of his dominion, O my soul, bless thou the Lord." (Psalm 102 [103] : 21-22)

"Bless the Lord, O my soul: and let all that is within me bless his holy name." (Psalm 102 [130] : 1)

"The Lord is my helper and my protector: in him hath my heart confided, and I have been helped . . . The Lord is the strength of his people, and the protector of the salvation of his annointed." (Psalm 27 [28] : 7,8)

"Rejoice to God our helper: sing aloud to the God of Jacob." (Psalm 80 [81] : 2)

"Our God is our refuge and strength: a helper in troubles, which have found us exceedingly." (Psalm 45 [46] : 2)

IN MONTE OLIVETI

Resp. 8.

IN món- te * Olivé- ti o-rá- vit ad

| In mónte Olivéti | On Mount Olivet |
| **On mount Olivet** | **he prayed to the Father:** |

| orávit ad Pátrem: |
| **he prayed to Father:** |

| Páter, si fíeri pótest, | Father, if it is possible, |
| **Father, if be done it can,** | **let this cup pass from me.** |

| tránseat a me cálix íste. |
| **let pass from me chalice this.** |

| Spíritus quidem prómptus est, | The spirit indeed is willing, |
| **Spirit indeed ready is,** | **but the flesh is weak:** |

| cáro autem infírma: |
| **flesh but weak:** |

| fíat volúntas túa. | thy will be done. |
| **be done will your.** |

The three psalms appointed to the I. Nocturn of Matins for Maundy Thursday could not be better chosen to set the scene for the tragic events of this day:

Psalm 68 [69], *Salvum me fac, Deus* – "Save me, O God"
Psalm 69 [70], *Deus in adjutorium* – "O God, come to my assistance"
Psalm 70 {71], *In te, Domine* – "In thee, O Lord, have I hoped"

The first Lesson for this office is taken from Lamentations 1:1–5. The superscription in the Vulgate and verse 5 are as follows:

"And it came to pass, after Israel was carried into captivity, and Jerusalem was desolate, that Jeremias the prophet sat weeping, and mourned with this lamentation over Jerusalem, and with a sorrowful mind, sighing and moaning, he said:

"Her adversaries are become her lords, her enemies are enriched: because the Lord hath spoken against her for the multitude of her iniquities: her children are led into captivity: before the face of the oppressor."

In monte Oliveti (taken from Matthew 26:39, 41–42) is the Responsory to this first Lesson of the I. Nocturn on Maundy Thursday.

JESU, DULCIS MEMORIA

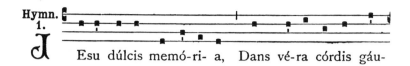

Hymn. 1.

Esu dúlcis memó-ri- a, Dans vé-ra córdis gáu-

JÉSU,	dúlcis	memória,	
Jesus,	**sweet**	**thought,**	

JESUS, how sweet the very thought,
Giving true joy to the heart,
But sweeter than honey and all else
Is His presence.

Dans	véra	córdis	gáudia:
Giving	**true**	**of heart**	**joy,**

Sed	super	mel	et	ómnia
But	**above**	**honey**	**and**	**all**

Ejus	dúlcis	praeséntia.
His	**sweet**	**presence.**

Nil	cánitur	suávius,
Nothing	**is sung**	**more lovely,**

Nothing more melodious is sung,
Nothing more delightful is heard,
Nothing sweeter is ever thought,
Than Jesus, the Son of God.

Nil	áuditur	jucúndius,
Nothing	**is heard**	**more delightful,**

Nil	cogitátur	dúlcius,
Nothing	**is thought of**	**sweeter,**

Quam	Jésus	Déi	Fílius.
Than	**Jesus**	**of God**	**Son.**

Jésu	spes	paeniténtibus,
Jesus	**hope**	**for penitents,**

Jesus, hope of the penitents,
How kind you are to petitioners!
How good you are to those that seek!
But what more to those that find you!!

Quam	píus	es	peténtibus!
How	**kind**	**you are**	**to petitioners!**

Quam	bónus	te	quaeréntibus!
How	**good**	**you**	**to seekers!**

Sed	quid	inveniéntibus?
But	**what**	**to those finding you!!**

Nec	língua	válet	dícere,
No	**tongue**	**is able**	**to say,**

No tongue can tell,
No written word can express:
The one who has experienced you can believe
What it might be to love Jesus.

Nec	líttera	exprimére:
No	**word**	**to express:**

Expértus	pótest	crédere,
Experienced one	**is able**	**to believe**

Quid	sit	Jésum	dilígere.
What	**may be**	**Jesus**	**to love.**

Sis	Jésu	nóstrum	gáudium,	May Jesus be our glory,
May be	**Jesus**	**our**	**glory,**	He who will be our reward:
				May our glory be in you,
Qui	es	futúrus	praémium:	Throughout all eternity.
(You)who	**are going to be**		**reward:**	

| Sit | nóstra | in | te | glória, |
| **Be** | **our** | **in** | **you** | **glory,** |

| Per | | cúncta | semper | saécula. |
| **Throughout** | | **all** | **always** | **ages.** |

This "*Jubilus* on the name of Jesus" (the name **JESUS** is found in thirty of its forty-two stanzas) is generally ascribed to St. Bernard of Clairvaux (c. 1090-1153), but the real author appears to be an anonymous Cistercian who lived at the close of the 12th century. James Mearns, in his article in Julian's *Dictionary of Hymnology*, calls it "the finest and most characteristic specimen of St. Bernard's 'subjective loveliness,' and in its honied sweetness vindicates his title of *Doctor mellifluus*." And Dr. Schaff (*Christ in Song*) finds it to be "the sweetest and most evangelical hymn of the Middle Ages."

The angel appeared to Joseph in a dream, saying: "Fear not to take unto thee Mary thy wife: for that which is conceived in her is of the Holy Ghost. And she shall bring forth a son, and thou shalt call his name **JESUS**." (Matthew 1:20-21) And the angel Gabriel announced to the virgin Mary: "Behold, thou shalt conceive in thy womb, and bring forth a son, and shalt call his name **JESUS**." (Luke 1:26-33) "And when eight days were accomplished for the circumcising of the child, his name was called **JESUS**, which was the name given him by the angel before he was conceived in the womb." (Luke 2:21)

In the 15th century a liturgical feast of the Holy Name was granted to the Franciscan order, based on a devotion written by Saints Bernadine of Siena and John Capistran; in 1721 it was extended to the whole Western Church. The name **JESUS** is the Latin form of the Greek Ἰησοῦς, which is derived for the Hebrew *Jehoshua* (Josue) and means "Yahweh is salvation." Christ, from the Greek Χριστὸς, meaning "the Annointed One," is the Messias, the expected Redeemer ("The spirit of the Lord is upon me, because the Lord has annointed me" - Isaiah 61:1), the king who was to come. Thus, "Christ" is His official title, while **JESUS** is His ordinary name ("Jesus the Christ").

Jesus "became obedient unto death, even the death of the cross. Wherefore God also hath highly exalted him, and given him a name which is above every name: That at the name of Jesus every knee should bow, of things in heaven, and things in earth, and things under the earth." (Philipians 2:8-10) "O Lord our Lord, how excellent is thy name in all the earth." (Psalm 8:1)

Liturgical context: **Jesu, dulcis memoria** is the Vesper hymn for the Feast of the Holy Name of Jesus which is celebrated on the Sunday between the feast of the Circumcision (Jan. 1) and Epiphany (Jan. 6), or on Jan. 2 if there is no such Sunday.

JUBILATE DEO

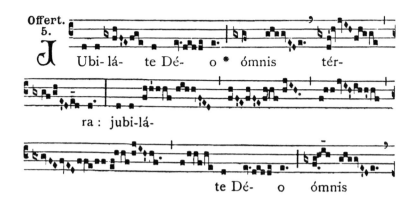

Offert. 5.

Ubi-lá- te Dé- o * ómnis térra : jubi-lá-
te Dé- o ómnis

1 Jubiláte   Déo,   ómnis   térra;
  Sing joyfully to God,   all   earth;

   servíte Dómino in   laetítia.
   serve   Lord   with   gladness.

   Introíte in conspéctu éjus in exultatióne.
   Enter   into presence his with jubilation.

Sing joyfully to God, all the earth;
serve the Lord with gladness.
Enter into his presence with great joy.

2 Scitóte quóniam Dóminus ípse est Déus;
  Know   that   Lord   alone is God;

   ípse fécit nos, et non ípsi nos;
   he   has made us, and not ourselves we;

   pópulos éjus, et óves páscuae éjus.
   people his, and sheep of pasture his.

Know that the Lord alone is God;
he has made us, and not we ourselves;
we are his people,
and the sheep of his pasture.

3 Introíte pórtas éjus in confessióne,
  Enter   gates his with thanksgiving,

   átria éjus in hýmnis; confitémini ílli.
   courts his with   praise; give thanks to him.

   Laudáte nómen éjus:
   Praise   name   his:

Enter into his gates with thanksgiving,
and into his courts with praise;
give thanks to him. Praise his name:

4 quóniam suávis est Dóminus;
  for   gracious is Lord;

   in aetérnum misericórdia éjus,
   for eternity   mercy   his,

   et   usque in generatiónem
   and continually for generations

   et generatiónem véritas éjus.
   and generations truth his.

for the Lord is gracious;
his mercy is everlasting,
and his truth endures for all generations.

Jubilate Deo omnis terra (Psalm 99 [100]) is appointed to be said at Lauds on feast days, following Psalm 92 [93] *Dominus regnavit* ("The Lord hath reigned; he is clothed with beauty") and preceding Psalm 62 [63] *Deus, Deus meus* ("O God, my God"). The Canticle of the Three Children (Daniel 3:57-58,56), the *Laudate* Psalm 148 *Laudate Dominum de caelis* ("Praise ye the Lord from the heavens"), and the Canticle of Zachary (the *Benedictus*, Luke 1:68-79) also follows it in this office. At Lauds on Christmas Day it is followed by the *jubilate* of the antiphon *Angelus ad Pastores ait*.

On the Sunday within the octave of Epiphany **Jubilate Deo** is the Offertory which follows the Gospel account of the child Jesus in the Temple (Luke 2:41-52), and it is also heard as the verse of the Alleluia which follows the Gradual *Benedictus Dominus* (Psalm 71 [72] : 18,3). The same *Jubilate* text also serves as the Alleluia verse for the votive Mass for the Propagation of the Faith, following the Lesson from Ecclesiasticus 36:1-19 and the Gradual *Confiteantur tibi populi Deus* (Psalm 66 [67] : 6-8, "Let all the people praise thee, O God").

> "Among the psalms of triumph and thanksgiving this stands
> as pre-eminent, rising to the highest point of joy and grandeur."
> (Four Friends, *The Psalms*)

L A E T A T U S   S U M

Grad. 7.

Lae-tá-tus sum * in his quae dí-cta sunt

1 Laetátus sum in his
  Rejoiced I have at words

  quae dícta sunt míhi:
  which spoken were to me:

  In dómum Dómini íbimus.
  Into house of Lord we shall go.

I rejoiced at the words
which were spoken unto me:
"We shall go into the house of the Lord."

2 Stántes érant pédes nóstri,
  Standing were feet our,

  in átriis túis Jerúsalem.
  in courts your Jerusalem.

Our feet were standing
in your courts, O Jerusalem.

3 Jerúsalem, quae aedificátur ut cívitas:
  Jerusalem, which is built as city:

  cújus participátio éjus in id ípsum.
  whose sharing of it in it itself.

Jerusalem, which is built like a city
the parts of which are joined together.

136

4 Illuc   enim   ascendérunt   tríbus,
Whither   **for**   **ascended**   **tribes,**

For whither the tribes ascended,
the tribes of the Lord.

  tríbus   Dómini: testimónium   Israel
  tribes   **of Lord:**   **covenant**   **of Israel**

Israel's covenant is to profess
the name of the Lord.

  ad   confiténdum   nómine   Dómini.
  to   **professing**   **name**   **of Lord.**

5 Quia   illic   sedérunt   sédes   in   judício,
Because   **there**   **have sat**   **thrones**   **in judgement,**

Because there the thrones have sat in judgement,
the thrones of the house of David.

  sédes   super   dómum   Dávid.
  thrones   **above**   **house**   **of David.**

6 Rogáte   quae   ad   pácem   sunt   Jerúsalem:
Ask for   **what**   **for**   **peace**   **are**   **of Jerusalem:**

Pray for the peace of Jerusalem,
ask abundance for those that love you.

  et   abundántia   diligéntibus   te.
  and   **abundance**   **those loving**   **you.**

7 Fíat   pax   in   virtúte   túa:
Be   **peace**   **by**   **virtue**   **your:**

May there be peace within you
and abundance within your walls.

  et   abundántia   in   túrribus   túis.
  and   **abundance**   **within**   **towers**   **your.**

8 Propter   frátres   méos   et   próximos   méos,
For sake of   **brothers**   **my**   **and**   **neighbors**   **my.**

For the sake of my brothers and neighbors,
I have spoken peace unto you;

  loquébar   pácem   de   te:
  I bespoke   **peace**   **about**   **you.**

9 Propter   dómum   Dómini   Déi   nóstri,
For sake of   **house**   **of Lord**   **God**   **our,**

For the sake of the house of the Lord our God,
I have sought good for you.

  quaesívi   bóna   tíbi.
  I have sought   **good**   **for you.**

The first verse of **Laetatus sum** (Psalm 121 [122]) is employed on *Laetare* Sunday (the 4th Sunday of Quadragesima or Lent) as the psalm-verse for the Introit *Laetare Jerusalem* ("Rejoice Jerusalem, and come together all you that love her") from which this Sunday takes its name. Like *Gaudete* Sunday (the 3rd Sunday of Advent), this day is one of rejoicing during a time of penitence and preparation, and is marked by the wearing of rose-colored vestments and the use of the organ. The same verse of **Laetatus sum** is heard again as the Gradual for this Mass following the Lesson from Galatians 4:21-31 in which the children of Jerusalem are likened to Isaac as "children of promise," the children "not of the bond-woman, but of the free, by the freedom wherewith Christ hath made us free." Therefore: **Laetatus sum**, "I rejoiced at the words which were spoken unto me: We shall go into the house of the Lord."

Laetatus sum also serves as the Alleluia verse on the 2nd Sunday in Advent, a Sunday on which Jerusalem (Sion), a figure of the Church, is called upon to rejoice and prepare herself for the coming Messiah. The Gospel (Matthew 11:1-10) tells of John the Baptist who was sent to prepare the way for Christ's coming, and the Introit, Gradual, and Communion all mention the holy city Jerusalem as the place where the pilgrims shall gather:

> *Introit.* *Populus Sion:* "People of Sion, behold the Lord shall come [*Advent*] to save the nations and the Lord shall make the glory of his voice to be heard in the joy of your heart." (Isaiah 30) "Give ear, O thou that rulest Israel." (Psalm 79 [80] : 1)

> *Gradual.* *Ex Sion:* "Out of Sion the loveliness of his beauty: God shall come [*Advent*] manifestly. Gather ye together his saints to him; who have set his covenant before sacrifices." (Psalm 49 [50] : 2-3, 5)

> *Communion.* *Jerusalem, surge:* "Arise, O Jerusalem, and stand on high: and behold the joy that cometh [*Advent*] to thee from thy God." (Baruch 4:36, 5:5)

How perfectly fitting that **Laetatus sum** should be appointed 'as the jubilant Alleluia verse for this Mass.

Note: There are many problems with the Vulgate Latin translation from the original Hebrew that are essential to the proper historical and metaphorical interpretation of this psalm [see M. Buttenwieser, *The Psalms*, pp. 373-76]. The translation given above is faithful to the Latin text which composers have set throughout the centuries.

LAUDA JERUSALEM

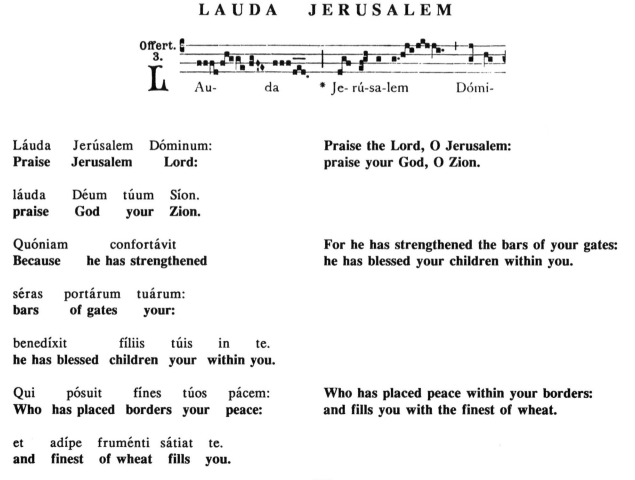

| Láuda | Jerúsalem | Dóminum: | Praise the Lord, O Jerusalem: |
| **Praise** | **Jerusalem** | **Lord:** | praise your God, O Zion. |

| láuda | Déum | túum | Síon. |
| **praise** | **God** | **your** | **Zion.** |

| Quóniam | | confortávit | For he has strengthened the bars of your gates: |
| **Because** | | **he has strengthened** | he has blessed your children within you. |

| séras | portárum | tuárum: |
| **bars** | **of gates** | **your:** |

| benedíxit | fíliis | túis | in | te. |
| **he has blessed** | **children** | **your** | **within you.** |

| Qui | pósuit | fínes | túos | pácem: | Who has placed peace within your borders: |
| **Who** | **has placed** | **borders** | **your** | **peace:** | and fills you with the finest of wheat. |

| et | adípe | fruménti | sátiat | te. |
| **and** | **finest** | **of wheat** | **fills** | **you.** |

Qui emíttit elóquium súum térrae:
Who sends forth commandment his on earth:

velóciter cúrrit sérmo éjus.
swiftly runs word his.

Who sends forth his commandment upon earth: his word runs swiftly.

Qui dat nívem sícut lánam:
Who gives snow like wool:

nébulam sicut cínerem spárgit.
hoarfrost like ashes scatters.

Who gives snow like wool: and scatters hoarfrost like ashes.

Míttit crystállum súam sícut buccéllas:
He sends ice his like morsels:

ante fáciem frigóris éjus quis sustinébit?
before face of cold his who will stand?

He sends his ice like morsels: who will stand before the force of his cold?

Emíttet vérbum súum,
He will send forth word his,

et liquefaciet ea:
and will melt them:

flábit spíritus éjus, et flúent áquae.
will blow wind his, and will flow waters.

He will send forth his word, and will melt them: his wind shall blow, and the waters shall flow.

Qui annúntiat vérbum súum Jácob:
Who proclaims word his to Jacob:

justítias et judícia súa Israel.
justices and judgements his to Israel.

Who proclaims his word to Jacob, his laws and justices to Israel.

Non fécit táliter ómni natióni:
Not he did such to each nation:

et judícia súa non manifestávit éis.
and judgements his not did manifest to them.

He did not do such to each nation: he did not make his judgements known to them.

Lauda Jerusalem is a psalm of praise and thanksgiving for the particular graces and favors that the Lord has shown to the children of Jerusalem. In the Vulgate it is numbered as a separate psalm: "Psalm 147." But in the Hebrew Psalter it is joined with the foregoing psalm and appears as the second half of Psalm 147, verses 12-20.

It is appointed to be sung as the fifth psalm at Lauds on Good Friday, along with the antiphon *Momento mei* ("Remember me, O Lord my God, when thou comest into thy kingdom"). In the votive Mass for Peace it appears as the Alleluia-Verse following the Lesson from II Machabees 1:1-5 and the Gradual from Psalm 121 [122] *Rogate* ("Pray for the peace of Jerusalem: and abundance for them that love thee"). And in the Solemnity of St. Joseph [the spouse of the Blessed Virgin Mary], which commemorates his title of Patron of the Universal Church, **Lauda Jerusalem** is the Offertory which follows the Gospel reading from St. Luke 3:21-23, the account of Jesus' baptism, the blessing he received from the Holy Spirit, and the beginning of his genealogy ("And Jesus himself, when he began his work, was about thirty years of age, being -- as was supposed -- the son of Joseph") which refers directly to the patron saint of the day.

LAUDA SION

Seq. 7.

L Auda Sí- on Salvatórem, Láuda dúcem et pastórem,

Láuda	Síon	Salvatórem,	
Praise	**Sion**	**Saviour,**	

Praise, O Sion, praise your Saviour,
Praise your leader and shepherd
In hymns and canticles.

Láuda	dúcem et	pastórem,
Praise	**leader and**	**shepherd,**

In	hýmnis et	cánticis.
In	**hymns and**	**canticles.**

Quantum	pótes,	tantum	áude:
As much as	**are able,**	**so much**	**dare:**

As much as you are able, so much dare:
For He is above all praise,
Nor can you praise Him enough.

5	Quia	májor ómni	láude,
	because	**greater all**	**praise,**

Nec	laudáre	súfficis.
Nor	**to praise**	**do you suffice.**

Láudis	théma	speciális,
Of praise	**theme**	**special,**

A special theme of praise
—the living bread of life—
is proposed today.

Pánis	vívus	vitális
Bread	**living**	**vital**

Hódie	propónitur.
Today	**is proposed.**

10	Quem in	sácrae	ménsa	coénae,
	Which at	**of sacred**	**table**	**supper,**

That which at the table of the sacred Supper
Was given to the group of twelve brethren
is not to be doubted.

Túrbae	frátrum	duodénae
To group	**of brethren**	**twelve**

Dátum	non	ambígitur.
Was given	**not**	**is doubted.**

Sit	laus	pléna, sit	sonóra,
Be	**praise**	**full, be**	**sonorous,**

Let our praise be full, let it be sonorous,
Let our mind's jubilation be pleasing,
Let it be fitting and becoming.

Sit	jucúnda, sit	decóra
Be	**pleasing, be**	**fitting**

15	Méntis	jubilátio.
	Of mind	**jubilation.**

Díes enim solémnis ágitur,
Day for solemn is happening,

In qua ménsae príma recólitur
On which of table first is recalled

Hújus institútio.
of this institution.

For a solemn day is being celebrated,
On which is recalled the first institution
Of this Table.

In hac ménsa nóvi Régis,
At this table of new King,

20 Nóvum Páscha nóvae légis,
New Pasch of new law,

Pháse vétus términat.
Period old ends.

At this Table of the new King,
The new Paschal rite of the new Law
Puts an end to the old Passover.

Vetustátem nóvitas,
Ancient new,

Umbram fúgat véritas,
Shadow puts to flight truth,

Nóctem lux elíminat.
Darkness light eliminates.

The new puts the old to flight,
As truth does to the shadow;
Light banishes darkness.

25 Quod in coéna Chrístus géssit,
What at supper Christ performed

Faciéndum hoc expréssit
To be done this he ordered

In súi memóriam.
In of him memory.

What Christ performed at the Supper
He ordered to be done
In remembrance of Him.

Dócti sácris institútis,
Taught by sacred institution,

Pánem, vínum in salútis
Bread, wine into of salvation

30 Consecrámus hóstiam.
We consecrate sacrifice.

Taught by His sacred institution,
We consecrate the bread and wine
Into the Sacrifice of salvation.

Dógma   dátur   christiánis,
Dogma   is given   to Christians,

Quod   in   cárnem   tránsit   pánis,
That   into   flesh   passes   bread,

Et   vínum   in   sánguinem.
And   wine   into   blood.

Quod non   cápis,   quod non   vídes,
What not   understand,   what not   see,

35   Animósa   fírmat   fídes,
Lively   confirms   faith,

Praeter   rérum   órdinem.
Beyond   of things   order.

A dogma is given to Christians:
That the bread becomes Flesh,
And the wine becomes Blood.

What you don't understand, what you don't see,
A lively faith confirms in a way
Which is beyond the natural order of things.

Sub   divérsis   speciébus,
Under   different   species,

Sígnis   tantum,   et   non   rébus,
Signs   only,   and   not   realities,

Látent   res   exímiae.
Lie hidden   things   wondrous.

40   Cáro   cíbus,   sánguis   pótus:
Flesh   food,   blood   drink:

Mánet   tamen   Chrístus   tótus
Remains   however   Christ   whole

Sub   utráque   spécie.
Under   each   species.

Under different species,
Different only in appearances, not in reality,
Wondrous things lie hidden.

Flesh is food, Blood is drink;
Yet Christ remains whole
Under each species.

A   suménte   non   concísus,
By   partaker   not   cut up,

Non   confráctus,   non   divísus:
Not   broken,   not   divided:

45   Integer   accípitur.
Whole   he is received.

Not cut up by the one partaking,
Not broken, not divided,
He is received whole.

Súmit únus, súmunt mille:
Partakes one, partake thousand:

One partakes, a thousand partake:
As much as a thousand partake, so much the one;
Nor is the One partaken of consumed.

Quantum ísti, tantum ílle:
As much this, so much that:

Nec súmptus consúmitur.
Nor partaken of is consumed.

Súmunt bóni, súmunt máli:
Partake good, partake evil ones:

The good partake, the evil ones partake:
But the effect is not the same:
One partakes of life, the other of ruin.

50 Sórte tamen inaequáli,
By effect however unequal,

Vítae vel intéritus.
Of life or of ruin.

Mors est mális, víta bónis:
Death is for evil, life for good:

There is death for the evil, life for the good:
Behold, of equal partaking,
How different the result is!

Víde páris sumptiónis
See from equal partaking

Quam sit díspar éxitus.
How is different result.

55 Frácto demum sacraménto,
Broken finally sacrament,

When the sacrament is finally broken,
Doubt not, but remember
That there is as much in the fragment
As is concealed in the whole.

Ne vacílles, sed meménto
Not doubt, but remember

Tantum ésse sub fragménto,
So much to be under fragment,

Quantum tóto tégitur.
As much whole is concealed.

Núlla réi fit scissúra:
No of reality happens division,

No division of the reality occurs,
There is only a fracture of the sign,
Whereby neither the state nor the stature
Of the One signified is diminished.

60 Sígni tantum fit fractúra,
Of sign only there is fracture,

Qua nec státus, nec statúra
Whereby neither state, nor stature

Signáti minúitur.
Of signified is diminished.

Ecce   pánis   Angelórum,
Behold   bread   of Angels,

Fáctus   cíbus   viatórum:
Made   food   of pilgrims:

65 Vere   pánis   filiórum,
Truly   bread   of children,

No   mitténdus   cánibus.
Not   to be given   to dogs.

In   figúris   praesignátur,
In   forms   it was prefigured:

Cum   Isaac   immolátur,
When   Isaac   was immolated,

Agnus   Páschae   deputátur,
Lamb   of Passover   was slain,

70 Dátur   mánna   pátribus.
Was given   manna   to forefathers.

Bóne   pástor,   pánis   vere,
Good   shepherd,   bread   true,

Jésu,   nóstri   miserére:
Jesus,   on us   have mercy:

Tu   nos   pásce,   nos   tuére,
Thou   us   feed,   us   protect,

Tu   nos   bóna   fac   vidére
Thou   us   goodness   make   to see

75 In   térra   vivéntium.
In   land   of living.

Tu   qui   cúncta   scis   et   váles,
You   who   all things   know   and   can do,

Qui   nos   páscis   hic   mortáles:
Who   us   guide   here   as mortals:

Túos   ibi   commensáles,
Your   there   table guests,

Coherédes   et   sodáles
Co-heirs   and   associates

80 Fac   sanctórum   cívium.
Make   of holy   citizens.

Behold the Bread of Angels
Is made the food of pilgrims;
Truly it is the bread of children,
Not to be cast to the dogs.

It was prefigured in other forms:
When Isaac was sacrificed,
When the Passover Lamb was slain,
When manna was given to our forefathers.

Good Shepherd, true Bread,
Jesus, have mercy upon us;
Feed us, protect us,
Make us to see good things
In the land of the living.

You, who know and can do all things,
Who feeds us mortals here below:
Make us there Your table-guests,
The co-heirs and associates
Of the holy citizens.

144

Lauda Sion was composed c.1264 by the Dominican friar and Italian theologian St. Thomas Aquinas (c.1225-1274) as part of a new Mass and Office for the institution of the Feast of Corpus Christi ("Body of Christ"). [see *O sacrum convivium*]

It is one of St. Thomas' four great Eucharistic hymns [along with *Pange lingua-corporis* (which contains *Tantum ergo*), *Sacris solemnis* (which contains *Panis angelicus*), and *Verbum supernum prodiens* (whose penultimate stanza is *O Salutaris Hostia*). "The Angelic Doctor took a single theme for his singing," states H.A. Daniel in his *Thesaurus Hymnologicus*; he was "the greatest singer of the venerable Sacrament." "It is in fact a doctrinal treatise in rhymed verse, setting forth the theory of Transubstantiation at length and in precise detail" (J. Mearns), similar to his comments on the Christian mysteries in his *Summa Theologica*. **Lauda Sion** also enjoys the honor of being one of the five sequences (out of thousands) to be retained in the Roman Missal, the equally great and uniquely beautiful others being *Dies irae, Stabat Mater, Veni Sancte Spiritus,* and *Victimae paschali laudes.*

The fascinating rhythmic and stanzaic form of **Lauda Sion** and its debt to the sequences of Adam of St. Victor (c.1110-1180) -- expecially his *Laudi crucis attollamus* and the Easter sequence *Zyma vetus expurgetus* -- is beautifully detailed by H.T. Henry in the *Catholic Encyclopedia*. Of particular interest, especially as it might relate to musical form and expression, is Adam's way of extending the stanzaic length toward the end of the poem, "as if the fervor of his theme had at length begun to carry the poet beyond his narrow [3-line] stanzaic limits." Thus we have 18 stanzas of 3 lines, followed by 4 of 4, and then 2 of 5, or, as Britt and Mearns more adroitly point out, 9 of 6, 2 of 8, and 1 of 10. *Nota Bene* how these groupings relate to content and the rhyme "couplings" of lines 3 and 6, 9 and 12, etc., 58 and 63, 66 and 70, and 75 and 80. Also note that this "fervent" extension not only relates to the number of lines in each stanza, but to the gradually increasing "rhymic jubilus": *Salvatorem, pastorem, canticis* (lines 1-3) becomes *sacramento, memento, fragmento, tegitur* (lines 55-58), and finally *vere, miserere, tuere, videre, viventium* (lines 70-74) -- a crescendo of musical euphony that leads from the commemoration of the first institution of the Blessed Sacrament to the anticipated participation in the final Messianic feast.

"It is impossible to say which is most to be admired -- its dogmatic accuracy, its sublime ideas, the variety of its rhymes, or the perfection of its rhythm. Devotion to the Holy Eucharist could hardly be expressed with greater fervour or in a more exquisite form. It is one of the most beautiful Canticles in the Catholic liturgy" (Abbot Cabrol, *Roman Missal*). "The saint 'writes with the full panoply under his singing-robes'; but always the melody is perfect, the condensation of phrase is of crystaline clearness, the unction is abundant and, in the closing stanzas, of compelling sweetness" (H.T. Henry, *Catholic Encyclopedia*).

Notes:

16. *Dies enim solemnis agitur . . .*
   Relates the sequence directly to the Mass of Corpus Christi.

20. *Novum Pascha . . .*
   "For Christ, our Passover, has been sacrificed for us" (I Corinthians 5:7). Christ is the new Paschal Lamb and the *Phases vetus* is the Old Testament sacrificial lamb.

22. *in sui memoriam.*
   Christ, to his disciples: "This is my body which is given for you; this do in remembrance of me" (Luke 22:19).

31. *Dogma datum christianis.*
   The doctrine of Transubstantiation, whereby the bread and wine are consecrated and the Real Presence of Christ exists whole under each appearance or species.

41. *Christus totus.*

The doctrine of the totality of the Real Presence under the appearance of <u>either</u> bread or wine, allowing the communicant to receive the <u>whole</u> Sacrament under either form.

48. *Nec sumptus consumitur.*

Even though thousands partake of Him, each communicant receives Christ whole, but He still remains whole and is not diminished, a mystery prefigured by the miracle of the feeding of the five thousand with the five loaves and two fishes (John 6:1-14).

52. *Mors est malis . . .*

For "whoever eats this bread or drinks the cup of the Lord unworthily, will be guilty of the body and the blood of the Lord. But let a man prove himself, and so let him eat of that bread and drink of the cup; for he who eats and drinks unworthily, without distinguishing the body, eats and drinks judgment to himself. (I Corinthians 11:27-29).

65. *panis filiorum . . . canibus.*

"It is not fair to take the children's bread [the children of Israel] and cast it to the dogs [the Gentiles]" (Matthew 15:26 [Douay]).

68. *Isaac.*

As a test of obedience and faith, Abraham is asked by God to offer his only son Isaac as a burnt offering to the Lord. With Isaac bound to the altar and Abraham lifting his sword to sacrifice his son, an angel of the Lord appears and stays him from the act (Genesis 22:1-14). Isaac, obedient unto death, prefigures Christ's offering of himself in obedience to His Father's will. [see Phillipians 2:8 and **Christus factus est**]

69. *Agnus Paschae.*

Central to the observance of the Jewish Feast of the Passover (the commemoration of their Exodus from Egypt) is the sacrificing of a lamb or kid, one which is unblemished and born in the preceding year; thus the first fruits were sacrificed in petition for an ensuing year of prosperity. Christ, the Lamb of God (**Agnus Dei**), is the the Paschal Lamb of the new rite, the single redeeming sacrifice for the sins of mortals. The new Passover Meal is the Lord's Supper, during which the sacrificial Lamb is consumed. [see **Victimae paschali laudes**]

70. *manna.*

(Heb *mān hu'*, "what is it?") The name is connected with the question the Israelites asked when they first found the edible substance during their forty years of wandering in the wilderness. "It was like coriander seed, white, and the taste thereof like to flour and honey" (Exodus 16:13-36). Also called "the bread of heaven" (Psalm 105: 40). Actually "manna" is produced by the excretions of scale insects; it contains three basic sugars and pectin. This prefigures Christ's proclaiming himself "the true bread," the living bread that has come down from heaven, not as your fathers ate manna, and died. He who eats this bread will live forever" (John 6:26-60).

76ff. *commensales, coheredes . . .*

The plea and hope that the faithful will be guests at the last, eternal feast: "The Spirit himself gives testimony to our spirit that we are sons of God. But if we are sons, we are heirs also: heirs indeed of God and joint heirs with Christ" (Romans 8:16-17).

Liturgical context: **Lauda Sion** is the sequence for the Mass of Corpus Christi.

LAUDATE DOMINUM IN SANCTIS EJUS

1. Laudá-te Dóminum in sánctis **é**-jus : * laudá-te é- um in

1 Laudáte Dóminum in sánctis éjus:
Praise Lord in sacred places his,

Praise the Lord in his sacred places,
praise him in the firmament of his power.

Laudáte éum in firmaménto virtútis éjus.
praise him in firmament of power his.

2 Laudáte éum in virtútibus éjus:
Praise him for mighty acts his,

Praise him for his mighty acts,
praise him according to his excellent greatness.

Laudáte éum secúndum
praise him according to

multitúdinem magnitúdinis éjus.
enormity of greatness his.

3 Laudáte éum in sóno túbae:
Praise him with sound of trumpet,

Praise him with the sound of the trumpet,
praise him with the psaltery and the harp.

Laudáte éum in psaltério et cíthara.
praise him with psaltery and harp.

4 Laudáte éum in týmpano et chóro:
Praise him with drum and dance,

Praise him with the timbrel and the dance,
praise him with strings and pipes.

Laudáte éum in chórdis et orgáno.
praise him with strings and pipes.

5 Laudáte éum in cýmbalis benesonántibus:
Praise him with cymbals high-sounding,

Praise him with high-sounding cymbals,
praise him with cymbals of joy.

Laudáte éum in cýmbalis jubilatiónis:
praise him with cymbals of joy.

ómnis spíritus láudet Dóminum.
Every spirit/breath let praise Lord.

Let everything that has breath praise the Lord!

147

Each of the books of the Hebrew Psalter (the Book of Psalms) ends with a concluding doxology (see the final verses of Psalms 40, 71, 88, and 105 [Vulgate]); but even the most extensive of these briefer doxologies, Psalm 71 [72]:18-19,

> "Blessed be the Lord God of Israel, who alone doth wonderful things. And blessed be the name of his majesty for ever: and the whole earth shall be filled with his majesty. So be it. So be it."

is greatly eclipsed by the great paean of praise which closes not only the fifth book, but the entire Psalter: Psalm 150, **Laudate Dominum in sanctis ejus.** Its superscription in the Vulgate is: *Doxologia solemnis et finalis.*

This, the greatest of the *Laudate* Psalms, has long been associated with Lauds, the Morning Office or Office of Aurora ("Dawn"), especially Lauds of Holy Saturday (where it appears near the conclusion of the office, just prior to the beginning of the Easter Vigil) and Lauds of the Office of the Dead.

Notes: It has been suggested that the different instruments named were those played by the various classes: the priests (trumpet), the Levites (psaltery and harp), the women (timbrel), and the men (strings, pipes, and cymbals).

3. *tubae.*

Trumpet, the shofar or booming ram's horn. *Ascendit Deus in jubilatione, et Dominus in voce tubae* (Psalm 46 [47] : 6, "God is ascended in jubilee, and the Lord to the sound of the trumpet").

3. *psalterio.*

A stringed instrument, a psaltery or harp; the Hebrew *naybel,* a harp-shaped instrument of which there were several varieties. *Confitemini Domino in cithara, in psalterio decem chordarum psallite illi* (Psalm 32 [33] : 2, "Give praise to God on the harp, sing to him with the 10-stringed psaltery").

3. *cithara.*

A stringed instrument, a harp. *Sumite psalmum, et date tympanum, psalterium jucundum cum cithara* (Psalm 80 [81] : 2, "Take up a psalm, and bring hither the timbrel and the sweet psaltery with the harp").

4. *tympano.*

A timbrel, a small hand drum or tambourine used to accompany a dance. *In tympano et psalterio psallant ei* (Psalm 149:3, "Sing praises to him with the timbrel and the psaltery"). "So Mary the prophetess, the sister of Aaron, took a timbrel in her hand: and all the women went forth after her with timbrels and with dances." (Exodus 15:20) "Princes went before joined with singers, in the midst of young damsels playing on timbrels." (Psalm 67 [68] : 26)

4. *chordis.*

The strings of a musical instrument. *In psalterio decem chordarum* (Psalm 32 [33] : 2, "Upon the psaltery of 10 strings").

4. *organo.*

Probably a shepherd's pipe, a reed-pipe. "His brother's name was Jubal; he was the father of them that play upon the harp and the organs." (Genesis 4:21) *Tenent tympanum et citharum, at gaudent ad sonitum organi* (Job 21:12, "They take the timbrel, and the harp, and rejoice at the sound of the organ").

5. *cymbalis.*

Cymbals, a pair of concave brass plates. The original Hebrew translation is "Praise Him with ringing cymbals/Praise Him with loud-crashing cymbals." The "high-sounding" or "ringing" cymbals may be the smaller finger cymbals used to accompany singing, and the "loud-crashing cymbals of joy" the much larger ones employed with other instruments when the singing was finished.

Incipite Domino in tympanis,	Begin ye to the Lord with timbrels,
cantate Domino in cymbalis.	Sing ye to the Lord with cymbals.

(Judith 16:2)

David et omnis Israel	David and all Isarel
ludebant coram Domino	played before the Lord
in omnibus lignis fabrefactis,	on all manner of instruments made of wood,
et citharis, et lyris, et tympanis,	on harps, and lyres, and timbrels,
et sistris, et cymbalis.	and cornets, and cymbals.

(II Kings [Samuel] 6:5)

5. *omnis spiritus laudet Dominum.*

One cannot help but recall Christopher Smart's litanies in *Jubilate Agno* and Bach's joyous *jubilus* on "Alles, was Odem hat, lobe den Herrn."

LAUDATE DOMINUM OMNES GENTES

Tract. 8.

Laudá- te * Dóminum ómnes géntes :

Laudáte	Dóminum	ómnes	géntes;	O praise the Lord, all ye nations;
Praise	**Lord**	**all**	**nations;**	**praise him, all ye peoples.**

laudáte	éum,	ómnes	pópuli.
praise	**him,**	**all**	**peoples.**

Quóniam	confirmáta	est	For his loving kindness
For	**bestowed**	**has been**	**has been bestowed upon us,**

super	nos	misericórdia	éjus,	
upon	**us**	**loving kindness**	**his,**	

et	véritas	Dómini	and the truth of the Lord
and	**truth**	**of Lord**	**endures for ever.**

mánet	in	aetérnum.	
endures	**for**	**eternity.**	

In the Mass for Holy Saturday, following the Epistle from Colossians 3:1-4, the joyous Easter *Alleluia* is heard for the first time after the long-imposed silence during the time of penitence and preparation for the great solemnity of Easter. Starting on a low, subdued pitch, the *Alleluia* rises with each of its three repetitions and continues its praise on the high *c* of the psalm verse *Confitemini Domino* ("Praise ye the Lord, for he is good"). The Tract **Laudate Dominum omnes gentes** with its joyful melismas immediately follows, offering further praise to God for the fulfillment of his promise to Israel.

The Mass continues, except that the Kiss of Peace is not given and the *Agnus Dei* and Postcommunion are omitted. Vespers, reduced to their most essential elements, are sung immediately following in the Choir. The psalm antiphon for Vespers of this day is the three-fold *Alleluia*, which is sung preceding and following the singing of **Laudate Dominum omnes gentes** (Psalm 116 [117]) and the customary appended doxology *Gloria Patri*. This succession of praise, unabated in its rising intensity since the first *Alleluias* of the Mass, culminates in the singing of the Canticle for Vespers, the Canticle of Mary, *Magnificat anima mea Dominum* ("My soul magnifies the Lord") which is itself preceded a most appropriate antiphon, the *Vespere autem sabbati* :

"In the evening of the sabbath, which dawns on the first day of the week, came Mary Magdalen, and the other Mary, to see the sepulchre. *Alleluia!*" (Matthew 28:1)

The same antiphon is also repeated after the *Magnificat*, and then the concluding prayer is offered, and the dismissal of the Mass of the greatest of the Church's solemnities again resounds with the Easter *Alleluias*:

Ite missa est, alleluia, alleluia.
Deo Gratias, alleluia, alleluia.

Laudate Dominum omnes gentes is one of the five Lucernal or Vesper psalms, long associated with the ancient office of Vespers. It is also employed as the Communion in the Mass for the Propagation of the Faith, as a psalm to be sung after Benediction of the Blessed Sacrament, and as a general antiphon of praise.

The brevity of this psalm suggests immediately that it must be a fragment or some lines omitted from another psalm. There is strong evidence [see Buttenwieser, *The Psalms*, pp. 359–361] that these two verses originally formed the conclusion of Psalm 148, *Laudate Dominum de caelis* ("Praise the Lord from the heavens"). The final verses of Psalm 148

"He has exalted the horn of his people. Glory has come to his faithful servants, to Israel, the people near him."

would fix the date of the two psalms as 583 B.C., the date of the rebirth of the Jewish nation, the occasion for which the original concluding verses, **Laudate Dominum omnes gentes**, gives appropriate praise and thanks.

LAUDATE PUERI

1	Laudáte	púeri	Dóminum,	O praise the Lord, ye children,
	Praise	**boys**	**Lord,**	praise the name of the Lord.
	laudáte	nómen	Dómini.	
	praise	**name**	**of Lord.**	

2	Sit nómen Dómini benedíctum ex hoc	Blessed be the name of the Lord
	Be name of Lord blessed from this	from hence forth now and for ever.
	nunc et usque in saéculum.	
	now and continually for generations.	

3	A sólis órtu usque et ad occásum,	From the rising of the sun
	From of sun rising even and to sunset,	even unto its setting,
	laudábile nómen Dómini.	the name of the Lord is praiseworthy.
	praiseworthy name of Lord.	

4	Excélsus super ómnes géntes Dóminus,	The Lord is high above all nations,
	High above all nations Lord,	his glory is above the heavens.
	et super coélos glória éjus.	
	and above heavens glory his.	

5	Quis sicut Dóminus Déus nóster,	Who is like the Lord our God,
	Who like Lord God our,	who dwells on high,
	qui in áltis hábitat,	
	who in highest dwells,	

					and yet he considers the lowly
6	et	humília	réspicit	in coélo	in heaven and on earth?
	and	lowly	looks down upon	in heaven	

	et	in	térra?	
	and	on	earth?	

7	Súscitans	a	térra	ínopem		Lifting up the needy from the dust,
	Lifting up	from	earth	needy		and raising the poor from the dungheap,

	et	de	stércore	érigens	páuperem:
	and	from	dungheap	raising up	poor,

8	Ut	cóllocet	éum	so that he may place him
	So that	he may place	him	with the princes of his people.

	cum	princípibus	pópuli	súi.
	with	princes	of people	his.

9	Qui	habitáre	fácit	stérilem	Who makes the sterile woman
	Who	to dwell	causes	sterile woman	to dwell in her house,
					the joyful mother of children.

	in	dómo,	mátrem	filiórum	laetántem.
	in	house,	mother	of children	rejoicing.

Laudate Pueri (Psalm 112 [113]) is one of the five Lucernal or Vesper psalms which, along with the *Magnificat*, have long been one of the characteristic features of the office of Vespers. On Sunday Vespers it is sung as the fourth psalm with the antiphon *Sit nomen Domini* ("Blessed be the name of the Lord for ever and ever").

The word *pueri* has suggested the use of this psalm in two Masses that relate directly to young children. This first is the Mass of the Holy Innocents which commemorates the deaths of the young male children of Bethlehem that an enraged Herod ordered to be killed. The Lesson for this Mass is from Apocalypse [Revelation] 14:1-5, the account of the forty-four thousand *innocents*, "they who were not defiled with women, [in whose] mouth there was found no lie; for they are without spot before the throne of God." The Gradual *Anima nostra* (from Psalm 123 [124]:7-8, "Our soul hath been delivered") is followed by the *Alleluia* and its psalm verse, **Laudate pueri**.

Laudate pueri is also sung at the home of a deceased child at the beginning of the burial rites for children, a service which concludes appropriately with the Canticle of the Three Children (Daniel 3:52-90).

Notes:

___

3. *A solis ortu.*

"From the rising of the sun even to the going down, my name is great among the Gentiles, and in every place where there is sacrifice, and there is offered to my name a clean oblation: for my name is great among the Gentiles, saith the Lord of hosts." (Malachias 1:11)

7. *Suscitans inopem . . . pauperum.*

"The Lord maketh poor and maketh rich, he humbleth and he exalteth. He raiseth up the needy from the dust, and lifteth up the poor from the dungheap." (I Kings [Samuel] : 7-8)

9. *sterilem.*

The barren wife is possibly the symbol of Israel in exile, made fruitful in the new Sion, as written in Isaiah's prophecy ("Give praise, O thou barren, that bearest not: sing forth praise, and make a joyful noise, thou that didst not travail with child" -- Isaiah 54:1) and recounted in Galatians 4:25-27 ("For Sinai ... corresponds to the present Jerusalem, and is in slavery with her children. But that Jerusalem which is above is free, which is our mother. For it is written: *Rejoice ye barren, that dost not bear; break forth and cry, thou that dost not travail; for many are the children of the desolate, more than of her that has a husband.*")

LOCUS ISTE

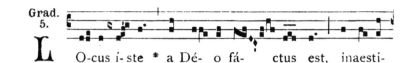

| Lócus | íste | a | Déo | fáctus | est, | **This place was made by God;** |
| **Place** | **this** | **by** | **God** | **made** | **was,** | |

| inaestimábile | sacraméntum, | **a priceless holy place,** |
| **priceless** | **holy place,** | |

| irreprehensíbilis | est. | **it is without fault.** |
| **without fault** | **it is.** | |

Locus iste is appointed as the Gradual for the Mass commemorating the Dedication of a Church. It is preceded and followed by the following appropriately selected texts:

Introit. *Terribilis est:* "Terrible is this place: it is the house of God, and the gate of heaven: and it shall be called the court of God." (Genesis 28:17,22) "How lovely are thy tabernacles, O Lord of hosts! my soul longeth and fainteth for the courts of the Lord." (Psalm 83 [84] : 1-2)

Lesson. *Vidi sanctam civitam:* "I saw the holy city, the new Jerusalem, coming down out of heaven from God . . . And I heard a great voice from the throne, saying: Behold the tabernacle of God with men; and he will dwell with them: and they shall be his people, and God himself with them shall be their God: and God shall wipe away all tears from their eyes." (Apocalypse [Revelation] 21:2-5)

Gradual. **Locus iste a Deo factus est.**

Alleluia-Verse. *Adorabo ad templum:* "*Alleluia. Alleluia.* I will worship towards thy holy temple, and I will give glory to thy name. *Alleluia.*" (Psalm 137 [138] : 2)

This Mass is said on the anniversary of the dedication of every consecrated church and on some universal feasts such as the dedication of other Roman basilicas (e.g., on November 18, those of St. Peter and St. Paul, etc.), but most especially it commemorates the dedication of the Archbasilica of the Saviour, the "Mother and Mistress of all churches throughout the world," the Cathedral church of the Pope, St. John Lateran in Rome (November 9).

MAGNIFICAT ANIMA MEA

1. Magní- fi-cat *   ánima *mé- a* Dóminum.
2. Et exsultávit *spí- ri-tus* mé- us * in Dé- o sa-lu- *tá-ri* mé-   o.

46	Magníficat	ánima	méa	Dóminum.	My soul magnifies the Lord.
	Magnifies	**soul**	**my**	**Lord.**	

47	Et	exultávit	spíritus	méus	And my spirit has rejoiced
	And	**has rejoiced**	**spirit**	**my**	in God my saviour.

in Déo salutári méo.
in God saviour my.

48	Quia	respéxit	humilitátem	For he has regarded the low estate
	Because	**he has considered**	**lowliness**	of his handmaiden:

ancíllae súae:
of servant his:

for behold, henceforth all generations
shall call me blessed.

ecce enim ex hoc
behold in fact from now

beátam me dícent ómnes generatiónes.
blessed me shall call all generations.

49	Quia	fécit	míhi	mágna	For he who is mighty
	Because	**he has done**	**to me**	**great things**	has done great things to me;

qui pótens est:
who mighty is;

and holy is his name.

et sánctum nómen éjus.
and holy name his.

50	Et	misericórdia	éjus	a	progénie	And his mercy is on them
	And	**mercy**	**his**	**from**	**generation**	who fear him from generation to generation.

in progénies timéntibus éum.
to generation for those fearing him.

51	Fecit	poténtiam	in	brácchio	súo:	He has shown strength with his arm;
	He has shown	**strength**	**in**	**arm**	**his;**	he has scattered the proud,

even the arrogant of heart.

dispérsit supérbos
he has dispersed proud

ménte córdis súi.
in spirit of hearts [their].

154

<table>
<tr><td>52</td><td colspan="4">Depósuit   poténtes   de   séde,
He has deposed mighty from seats,</td><td>He has deposed the mighty from their seats,
and exalted the humble.</td></tr>
</table>

52   Depósuit   poténtes   de   séde,   **He has deposed the mighty from their seats,**
     He has deposed mighty from seats,   **and exalted the humble.**

     et   exaltávit   húmiles.
     and   exalted   humble.

53   Esuriéntes   implévit   bónis: **The hungry he has filled with good things.**
     Hungry   he has filled   with good;   **and the rich he has sent empty away.**

     et   dívites   dimísit   inánes.
     and   rich   he has sent away   empty.

54   Suscépit   Israel   púerum   súum,   **He has helped his servant Israel,**
     He has helped   Israel   servant   his,   **in remembrance of his mercy.**

     recordatus   misericórdiae   súae.
     having remembered   of mercy   his.

55   Sicut   locútus   est   ad   pátres   nóstros,   **As it was spoken to our fathers,**
     As   spoken   was   to   fathers   our,   **to Abraham and his seed for ever.**

     Abraham   et   sémini   éjus   in   saécula.
     Abraham   and   seed   his   for   generations.

     Glória   Pátri,   et Fílio, et Spirítui Sáncto.   **Glory be to the Father, and to the Son,**
     Glory to Father, and Son, and Spirit Holy.   **and to the Holy Spirit.**

     Sicut érat in princípio, et nunc, et sémper,   **As it was in the beginning, is now,**
     As it was in beginning, and now, and always,   **and ever shall be, world without end, Amen.**

     et   in   saécula   saéculorum,   Amen.
     and for   generations   of generations,   Amen.

      The Canticle of the Blessed Virgin Mary (Luke 1:46-55) is one of the three evangelical canticles found in the first two chapters of the Gospel of St. Luke. Like the other two (the *Benedictus* or Canticle of Zachary, Luke 1:69-79, and the *Nunc dimittis* or Canticle of Simeon, Luke 2:29-32), it is to be interpreted as a personal expression of joy and thanksgiving and, symbolically, as the thanksgiving prayer and praise of all Israel for the Incarnation's fulfillment of God's promise of redemption. Mary, the Virgin Mother, is also "the highest and most perfect personification of Israel, the virgin daughter Sion" who rejoices at the inestimable favor bestowed on her (and Israel's) lowly estate. She sings praises to God her Saviour (verses 46-50), recalls the mercies shown to Israel (verse 51-53), and sings of the Incarnation's fulfillment of God's ancient promise to Abraham (verses 54-55). To this song of rejoicing sung by the Blessed Virgin during the Visitation to her cousin Elizabeth, the Roman liturgy appends the traditional doxology, the *Gloria Patri*.

Since the *Rule* of St. Benedict in 525 A.D. the **Magnificat** has been sung daily as the textual climax of the office of Vespers. Its daily use is made even more memorable by the censing of the altar which takes place during its singing (which requires that the **Magnificat** be sung at a slower tempo than the Vesper psalms) and its association with the *double* antiphons which precede and follow its singing, the most notable being the seven "O Antiphons" (*Antiphonae majores* or "Greater Antiphons") of the week preceding Christmas Eve.

The Marian authorship of the **Magnificat** has been seriously debated by scholars because three ancient Latin codices read: *"Et ait Elizabeth* (And <u>Elizabeth</u> said) : *Magnificat anima mea . . ."* Another consideration is the great similarity of the **Magnificat** and the Canticle of Anna (I Kings [Samuel] 2:1-10); for Anna, like Elizabeth, was aged and sterile, but miraculously conceived a son. But all the Greek manuscripts and centuries of scholarship and debate have strongly agreed and declared conclusively that the text is to be attributed to Mary.

Notes: (Passages from the Canticle of Anna, I Kings [Samuel] 2:1-10, will be quoted in italics in the following annotations.)

46. *Magnificat . . .*

My heart hath rejoiced in the Lord. "In the Lord shall my soul be praised: let the meek hear and rejoice. O magnify the Lord with me; and let us extol his name together" (Psalm 33 [34] : 3-4).

47. *Et exaltavit . . . in Deo salutari meo.*

My horn is exalted in my God . . . because I have joyed in thy salvation. "But my soul shall rejoice in the Lord; and shall be delighted in his salvation" (Psalm 34 [35] : 9). "But I will rejoice in the Lord: and I will joy in God my Jesus" (Habakkuk 3:18).

48. *respexit humilitatem . . . beatam me dicent*

"For the Lord is high, and looketh on the low" (Psalm 137 [138] : 6). "Who is as the Lord our God, who dwelleth on high: and looketh down on the low things in heaven and in earth?" (Psalm 112 [113] : 5-6). "And all nations shall call you blessed" (Malachias 3:12).

49. *fecit magna . . . et sanctum nomen ejus.*

The Lord has done great things for them. The Lord has done great things for us: we are become joyful" (Psalm 125 [126] : 2-3). *There is none holy as the Lord is: for there is no other beside thee.* "Sing ye to the Lord a new canticle; because he hath done wonderful things" (Psalm 97 [98] : 1).

50. *Et misericordia ejus . . . timentibus eum.*

"He hath sent redemption to his people: he hath commanded his covenant for ever. Holy and terrible is his name: the fear of the Lord is the beginning of wisdom" (Psalm 110 [111] : 9). *The adversaries of the Lord shall fear him: and upon them shall he thunder in the heavens.*

51. *Fecit potentiam in bracchio suo.*

There is none strong like our God. "The right hand of the Lord hath wrought strength; the right hand of the Lord hath exalted me" (Psalm 117 [118] : 16).

51. *Dispersit superbos in mente cordis sui.*

The pronoun *sui* ("his") is incorrect; it should be *suorum* ("their") and refer to the <u>proud</u>, not to God. "In the mind/thought/spirit of their hearts" would mean proud thoughts, even if only thought and not spoken; or, as the Jerusalem Bible translates it: "He has used the power of his arm, he has routed the arrogant of heart."

52. *Deposuit potentes . . . exaltavit humiles.*

The bow of the mighty is overcome, and the weak are girt with strength. . . He raiseth up the needy from the dust, and lifteth up the poor from the dunghill: that he may sit with princes, and hold the throne of glory. "The Lord bringeth to nought the counsels of nations; and he rejecteth the devices of people, and casteth away the counsels of princes" (Psalm 32 [33] : 10). "Wherefore will I pray to the Lord . . . who setteth up the humble on high" (Job 5:8,11).

53. *Esurientes implevit . . divites dimisit.*

They that were full before have hired out themselves for bread: and the hungry are filled . . . The Lord maketh poor and maketh rich, he humbleth and he exalteth.

54. *Suscepit Israel . . . recordatus.*

"He hath remembered his mercy and his truth toward the house of Israel" (Psalm 97 [98] : 3). "[The Lord] said unto me: Thou art my servant Israel, for in thee will I glory" (Isaiah 49:3). "But thou, Israel, art my servant, Jacob whom I have chosen, the seed of Abraham my friend . . . Thou art my servant, I have chosen thee, and have not cast thee away" (Isaiah 41:8,9).

55. *Sicut locutus est . . .*

"And God said to Abraham: Sara thy wife shall bear thee a son, and thou shalt call his name Isaac, and I will establish my covenant with him for a perpetual convenant, and with his seed after him . . . And I will multiply thy seed like the stars of heaven [*Abraham*, in the Hebrew, signifies the *father of the multitude*]: and I will give to thy posterity all these countries: and in thy seed shall all the nations of the earth be blessed" (Genesis 17:19; 26:4). "The Lord hath sworn truth to David, and he will not make it void: of the fruit of thy womb I will set upon thy throne" (Psalm 131 [132] : 11). "But the counsel of the Lord standeth forever: the thoughts of his heart to all generations" Psalm 32 [33] : 11).

"Steeped thus in Scriptural thought and phraseology, summing up in inspired ecstasy the economy of God with His Chosen People, indicating the fulfilment of the olden prophecy and prophesying anew until the end of time, the Magnificat is the crown of the Old Testament singing, the last canticle of the Old and the first of the New Testament." (H.T. Henry, *Catholic Encyclopedia*)

157

MIRABILE MYSTERIUM

8. G

M Mi-rá-bi-le mysté-ri- um * decla-rá-tur hó-di- e : in-

Mirábile	mystérium	declarátur	hódie:	A wonderful mystery is revealed today:
Wonderful	**mystery**	**is made known**	**today:**	
Innovántur	natúrae:			The two natures are renewed:
Renewed are	**natures:**			
Déus	hómo	fáctus	est.	God has become man.
God	**man**	**become**	**has.**	
Id,	quod	fúit,	permánsit,	That which he was, he remained,
That,	**which**	**he was,**	**he remained,**	
et	quod	nonérat	assúmpsit:	and that which he was not, he assumed:
and	**what**	**he was not**	**he assumed:**	
Non	commixtiónem	pássus,		suffering neither mixture nor division.
Not	**mixture**	**suffering,**		
néque	divisiónem.			
nor	**division.**			

"God, who at sundry times and in divers manners spoke in times past to the fathers by the prophets, last of all in these days has spoken to us by his Son, whom he appointed heir of all things, by whom also he made the world; who, being the brightness of his glory and the image of his substance, and upholding all things by the word of his power, has effected man's purgation from sin." (Hebrews 1:1–3)

"In the beginning was the Word, and the Word was with God; and the Word was God . . . In him was life, and the life was the light of men. And the light shines in the darkness; and the darkness comprehended it not . . . And the Word was made flesh, and dwelt among us. And we beheld his glory -- glory as of the only begotten Son of the Father -- full of grace and truth." (John 1:1,4–5,14)

MISERERE MEI, DEUS

Grad. 1.

Mise- rére * mé- i Dé- us,

1 Miserére   méi   Déus,
  Have mercy on me God,

  secúndum mágnam misericórdiam túam.
  according to great loving kindness your.

  Et secúndum multitúdinem miseratiónum tuárum
  And according to multitude of mercies your,

  déle iniquitátem méam.
  blot out iniquity my.

**Have mercy upon me, O God,
according to your great loving kindness.
And according to the multitude of your
mercies, blot out my iniquity.**

2 Amplíus láva me ab iniquitáte méa:
  More wash me from iniquity my,

  et a peccáto méo múnda me:
  and from sin my cleanse me.

**Wash me yet more from my iniquity,
and cleanse me from my sin.**

3 Quóniam inituitátem méam ego cognosco:
  Because iniquity my I acknowledge;

  et peccátum méum contra me est sémper.
  and sin my before me is always.

**For I acknowledge my transgression;
and my sin is ever before me.**

4 Tíbi sóli peccávi,
  To you only I have sinned,

  et málum córam te féci:
  and evil in presence of you done

  ut justificéris in sermónibus túis,
  that you may be justified in words your,

  et víncas cum judicáris.
  and be vindicated when you are judged.

**To you only have I sinned,
and done evil in your sight:**

**that you may be justified in your words,
and be vindicated when you are judged.**

159

5 Ecce   enim   in   iniquitátibus
  Behold **for**   **in**   **iniquities**

  concéptus   sum: et   in peccátis
  conceived   **I was;**   **and**   **in**   **sins**

  concépit   me   máter   méa.
  conceived   **me**   **mother**   **my.**

For behold, I was conceived in iniquities;
and in sins my mother conceived me.

6 Ecce   enim veritátem   dilexísti:
  Behold   **for**   **truth**   **you have loved;**

  incérta   et   occúlta   sapiéntiae túae
  obscure   **and**   **hidden**   **of wisdom**   **your**

  manifestásti   míhi.
  you have made known   **to me.**

For behold, you have loved the truth;
the obscure and hidden elements of
your wisdom you have made known to me.

7 Aspérges   me,   Dómine, hyssópo,
  You will sprinkle   **me,**   **Lord,**   **with hyssop,**

  et   mundábor: lavábis   me,
  and   **I shall be cleansed;**   **you will wash**   **me,**

  et   super   nivem   dealbábor.
  and   **more than**   **snow**   **I shall be made white.**

You will sprinkle me, O Lord, with hyssop,
and I shall be cleansed;

you will wash me,
and I shall be made whiter than snow.

8 Audítui   méo   dábis
  To hearing   **my**   **you will give**

  gáudium   et   laetítiam:
  gladness   **and**   **joy;**

  et   exsultábunt   óssa   humiliáta.
  and   **shall rejoice**   **bones**   **humbled.**

To my hearing you will give
gladness and joy;
and my humbled bones shall rejoice.

9 Avérte fáciem túam   a   peccátis méis:
  Avert   **face**   **your**   **from**   **sins**   **my;**

  et   ómnes iniquitátes méas   déle.
  and   **all**   **iniquities**   **my**   **blot out.**

Turn your face away from all my sins;
and blot out all my iniquities.

10 Cor   múndum   créa   in   me   Déus:
Heart   clean   create   in   me   God;

et   spíritum   réctum   innova
and   spirit   right   renew

in   viscéribus   méis.
in   innards   my.

Create in me a clean heart, O God;
and renew a right spirit within me.

11 Ne   projícias   me   a   fácie   túa:
Not   cast   me   from   face   your,

et   spíritum   sánctum   túum
and   spirit   holy   your

ne   áuferas   a   me.
not   take   from   me.

Cast me not away from your countenance,
and take not your holy spirit from me.

12 Rédde   míhi   laetítiam   salutáris   túi:
Restore   to me   joy   of salvation your;

et   spíritu   principáli   confírma   me.
and   spirit   steadfast   uphold   me.

Restore unto me the joy of your salvation;
and uphold me with a steadfast spirit.

13 Docébo   iníquos   vías   túas:
I will teach   sinners   ways   your;

et   ímpii   ad   te   converténtur.
and   wicked   to   you   shall be converted.

I will teach transgressors your ways:
and the wicked shall be converted unto you.

14 Líbera   me   de   sanguínibus   Déus,
Deliver   me   from   bloodguiltiness   God,

Déus,   salútis   méae: et   exsultábit
God,   of salvation   my;   and   shall extol

língua   méa   justítiam   túam.
tongue   my   justice   your.

Deliver me from bloodguiltiness, O God,
God of my salvation;
and my tongue shall extol your justice.

15 Dómine,   lábia   méa   apéries: et
Lord,   lips   my   you will open;   and

os   méum   annuntiábit   láudem   túam.
mouth   my   shall proclaim   praise   your.

O Lord, you will open my lips:
and my mouth shall proclaim your praise.

161

16 Quóniam si voluísses sacrifícium,
Because if you had desired sacrifice,

dedíssem utíque:
I would have given indeed;

holocáustis non delectáberis.
burnt offerings not you will delight in.

For if you had desired sacrifice,
I would indeed have given it:
you will not delight in burnt offerings.

17 Sacrifícium Déo spíritus contribulátus:
Sacrifice to God spirit broken;

cor contrítum et humiliátum,
heart contrite and humble,

Déus, non despícies.
God, not will despise.

A sacrifice to God is a broken spirit:
a humble and contrite heart, O God,
you will not depise.

18 Benígne fac, Dómine,
Kindness grant, Lord,

in bóna voluntáte túa Síon:
in good pleasure your to Zion;

ut aedificéntur múri Jerúsalem.
that may be built up walls of Jerusalem.

Grant kindness to Zion, O Lord,
according to your good pleasure:
that the walls of Jerusalem may be built up.

19 Tunc acceptábis sacrifícium justítiae,
Then you will accept sacrifice of righteousness,

oblatiónes et holocáusta:
oblations and whole-burnt offerings;

tunc impónent super
then they will lay upon

altáre túum vítulos.
altar your bullocks.

Then you will accept
the sacrifice of righteousness,
the oblations and the whole-burnt offerings;
then they will lay bullocks upon your altar.

As early as the 6th century the seven Penitential Psalms (Psalms 6, 31, 37, 50, 101, 129, and 142 in the Vulgate numbering) were considered as forming a class by themselves and especially suitable for the use of penitents in that they express sorrow for sin and desire for pardon. Pope Innocent III (1198-1216) ordered their recitation in Lent; Pius V (1605-1621) fixed the Fridays in Lent (except for Good Friday) as times when they should be said; and the number 7 is allegorically interpreted by Cassiodorus (d.565) to indicate the seven means by which sin is remitted: baptism, martyrdom, alms, forgiving others, conversion of a sinner, abundance of charity, and penance.

Miserere mei, Deus, known commonly as the "Miserere" (even though Psalms 55 [56] and 56 [57] also begin with the same word), is "the Church's classical act of contrition." It is the first psalm at Lauds in all the ferial Offices throughout the year, except during Paschaltide and the Sundays from Septuagesima to Palm Sunday inclusive. It occupies the same position in the Office of the Dead and, quite expectedly, is also very prominent in the ceremony of the Asperges [see *Asperges me, Domine* which is taken from this psalm]. The <u>many</u> other uses of this psalm are enumerated by H.T. Henry in his article in the *Catholic Encyclopedia*.

The Douay Version of the Old Testament (1609), the Church's official English translation of the Latin Vulgate, give the following heading for this Psalm:

PSALM 50
Miserere.

The repentance and confession of David after his sin.
The fourth penitential psalm.

1 Unto the end, a psalm of David,
2 when Nathan the prophet came to him,
after he had sinned with Bethsabee [Bathsheba].
(2 Kings [Samuel] 12.)

Notes:

4. *ut justificeris in sermonibus tuis.*

"For God is true, and every man is a liar, that thou mayest be justified in thy word, and mayest be victorious when thou art judged" (Romans 3:4).

5. *in iniquitatibus conceptus sum.*

"Who can make him clean that was conceived of unclean seed? is it not thou only who art?" (Job 14:4).

7. *Asperges me, Domine.*

See Leviticus 14 and Numbers 19. [also *Asperges me, Domine*]

7. *super nivem dealbabor.*

"If your sins be as scarlet, they shall be made as white as snow" (Isaiah 1:18).

9. *Averte faciem tuam a peccatis meis.*

"For my eyes are upon all their ways; they are not hid from my face, and their iniquity hat not been hid from my eyes" (Jermiah 16:17).

10. *Cor mundum . . .*

"And God, who knows the heart, bore witness by giving them the holy Spirit just as he did to us; and he made no distinction between us and them, but cleansed their hearts by faith" (Acts 15:8-9).

10. *et spiritum rectum innova.*

"And I will give you a new heart, and put a new spirit within you; and I will take away the stony heart out of your flesh, and will give you a heart of flesh" (Ezekiel 36:26).

11. *spiritum sanctum tuum ne auferas.*

"You, however, are not carnal but spiritual, if indeed the spirit of God dwells in you. But if anyone does not have the Spirit of Christ, he does not belong to Christ" (Romans 8:9).

14. *Libera me de sanguinibus.*

Bloodguiltiness, in Isael, was guilt incurred through bloodshed, slaying a man who did not deserve to die (*Christus factus est*). "The ancients of his city shall send, and take him out of the place of refuge, and shall deliver him into the hand of the kinsman of him whose blood was shed, and he shall die. Thou shalt not pity him, and thou shalt take away the *guilt* of Israel, that it may be well with thee" (Deuteronomy 19:12-13).

14. *exsultabit lingua mea justitiam tuam.*

"And my tongue shall meditate thy justice, thy praise all the day long" (Psalm 34 [35] : 28).

16. *holocaustis non delectaberis.*

"And Samuel said: Doth the Lord desire holocausts and victims, and not rather that the voice of the Lord should be obeyed? For obedience is better than sacrifices: and to hearken rather than to offer the fat of rams" (I Kings [Samuel] 15:32).

19. *sacrificium justitiae.*

The sacrifices of righteousness; those that are right, or correct ritually according to the Law of Moses.

19. *oblationes et holocausta.*

Offerings (oblations, gifts freely given) and whole-burnt offerings (in which the victim or sacrifice is wholly consumed by fire, symbolizing one's entire self-dedication to God).

19. *vitulos.*

Bullock, a young bull. "Do this, that they may be consecrated to me in priesthood. Take a calf from the herd, and two rams without blemish ... and offer them" (Exodus 29:1-3). "And they sacrificed victims to the Lord: and they offered holocausts the next day, a thousand bullocks, a thousand rams, a thousand lambs, with their libations, and with every thing prescribed most abundantly for all Israel" (I Chronicles 29:21).

Liturgical context: **Miserere mei, Deus**, the fourth Penitential Psalm, is the first psalm at Lauds in the Office of the Dead and in all the ferial Offices of the year except Paschaltide and the Sundays from Septuagesima to Palm Sunday inclusive. It is also prominent in the *Asperges*, or ceremonial sprinkling of the congregation with holy water as a symbolic cleansing of the soul as a preparation for the Mass.

MISERICORDIAS DOMINI

1. Mi-se-ricórdi-*as* **Dó**mini * in aeté*rnum cantá*- bo.

Misericórdias	Dómini	The mercies of the Lord
Mercies	**of Lord**	I shall praise for ever and ever;

in aetérnum cantábo:
into eternity I shall praise:

in generationem et generationem   **To generation and generation**
to generation and generation   **my mouth shall proclaim your truth.**

anuntiabo veritatem tuam in ore meo.
I will proclaim truth your in mouth my.

Quoniam dixisti: in aeternum   **For you have said:**
Because you have said: for eternity   **Mercy shall be built up for ever in the heavens:**
    your truth shall be prepared in them.

misericordia aedificabitur in coelis:
mercy shall be built up in heavens:

praeparabitur veritas tua in eis.
shall be prepared truth your in them.

Misericordias Domini (Psalm 88 [89]) is the first psalm appointed to the III. Nocturn of Matins *In Nativitate Domini* (on [the day] of the Birth of the Lord"). The great day of rejoicing is nigh; the steadfast faith in the perpetuity of the Church is about to find its reward.

The lessons for the office are from the Gospel according to St. Luke: the first is from Luke 2:1*ff* ("Now it came to pass in those days, that a decree went out from Caesar Augustus ... "), which is followed by a short homily by St. Gregory; the second is from Luke 2:15*ff* ("The shepherds were saying to one another, let us go up to Bethlehem and see ... "), which is also followed by a short homily, this one from St. Ambrose. The responsory *Verbum caro factum est* ("The Word was made flesh"), the third reading from John 1:1*ff* ("In the beginning was the Word ... "), a homily by St. Augustine, the singing of the *Te Deum*, the blessing, and the dismissal complete the office. The First Mass (the Midnight Mass) of Christmas Day immediately follows, ushered in by the thoughts of these great patron saints of the Church.

Liturgical context: **Misericordias Domini** is one of three psalms which are sung during the III. Nocturn of Matins of the Nativity, the office which immediately preceeds the first of the three Masses for Christmas Day.

MUSICA DEI DONUM OPTIMI

Música,	Déi	dónum	óptimi,
Music,	**of God**	**gift**	**highest,**

Music, gift of the highest God,
attracts mortals, it attracts the gods.

tráhit	hómines,	tráhit	Déos.
attracts	**men,**	**affects**	**gods.**

Música	trúces	móllit	ánimos
Music	**angry**	**calms**	**souls**

Music calms angry souls
and uplifts sad spirits.

tristesque	méntes	érigit.
and sad	**spirits**	**uplifts.**

Música	vel	ípsas	árbores
Music	**even**	**very**	**trees**

Music even moves the very trees
and the wild beasts.

et	hórridas	móvet	féras.
and	**wild**	**moves**	**beasts.**

The famous 6-part setting of this text by Orlando di Lasso has brought this appealing text to the attention of choral musicians throughout history. Who among us has not been calmed and uplifted by *Musica, Dei donum optimi*? "Du holde Kunst . . . ich danke dir."

Notes:

trahere -- to draw, attract, affect, fascinate, enchant, influence

mollire -- to soften, soothe, calm, "mollify," temper

truces / animos -- angry, savage / souls, hearts, spirits

erigere -- to cheer up, uplift, elevate, encourage, excite

tristes / mentes -- sad, mournful, aggrieved / minds, spirits, feelings

movere -- to move, stir, influence, affect

N I G R A   S U M

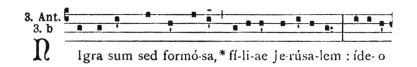

Nígra sum sed formó-sa, * fí-li-ae Je·rúsa-lem : íde- o

Nígra	sum,	sed	formósa,
Very dark	**I am,**	**but**	**comely,**

fíliae   Jerúsalem,
daughters   of Jerusalem,

sicut   tabernacula   Cedar,
like   tents   of Kedar,

sicut   pelles   Salomonis.
like   curtains   of Solomon.

I am very dark, but comely,
O daughters of Jerusalem,
like the tents of Kedar,
like the curtains of Solomon.

Nolite   me   considerare
Refuse   me   to gaze upon

quod   fusca   sim,
because   swarthy   I am,

quia   decoloravit   me   sol.
because has discolored   me   sun.

Do not gaze upon me
because I am swarthy,
because the sun has discolored me.

Filii   matris   meae
Sons   of mother   my

pugnaverunt   contra   me;
have fought   against   me;

posuerunt   me custodem in   vineis.
they have made   me   keeper in vineyards.

The sons of my mother
have fought against me;
They have made me the keeper
of the vineyards.

Ideo   diléxit   me   Rex,
Therefore   loved   me   King,

et   introdúxit   me
and   brought   me

in   cubículum   súum.
into   chamber   his.

Therefore the King loved me,
and brought me into his chamber.

Et   díxit   míhi:
And   he said   to me:

And he said to me:

Súrge	et	véni	amíca	méa,	
Arise	**and**	**come**	**love**	**my,**	

Arise, my love, and come:
for now the winter is past,
the rain is over and gone.

jam	híems	tránsiit,
now	**winter**	**is past,**

ímber	ábiit	et	recéssit.
rain	**is over**	**and**	**gone.**

Flóres	appáruerunt	in	térra	nóstra,
Flowers	**have appeared**	**in**	**land**	**our,**

The flowers have appeared in our land,
the time of pruning is come.   Alleluia!

témpus	putatiónis	advénit.	Allelúia.
time	**of pruning**	**is come.**	**Alleluia!**

Solomon, he who was "wiser than all men," "spake three thousand proverbs: and [whose] songs were a thousand and five" [I Kings 4:31-32], cannot be shown to be the author of the "Song of Songs" (*Canticum Canticorum*). The ascription in the title can have a variety of meanings -- "belonging to," "to," "for," or "concerning" Solomon -- and there is insufficient contextual evidence to determine which was intended. Indeed, the authorship and interpretation of the Song of Songs has been the subject of constant controversy among scholars.

Hebrew and Christian scholars have long debated its appropriateness in the canon and usually interpret it allegorically: as representing the love of Yahweh for his chosen Israel, the love of Christ for his bride the Church, and the love of God for the "Humanity of Jesus Christ," the Mother of God, and the adoring soul. Others read it as a drama, several scenes and songs depicting the love of Solomon for the Shulamite shepherdess. Some say the songs are from a Syrian wedding ritual; others argue that they are liturgies from an ancient fertility cult, replete with chorus (*filiae Jerusalem*) and the celebration of the reunion and marriage of the sungod and mother goddess, signifying the revival of life in nature (*flores apparuerunt*, "the winter is past, the time of pruning is come"). Still others see it as secular love poems "expressed in romantic and radiant language . . . folk poetry telling in passionate language of the devotion of a man and a maid."

Certain words and constructions date the text as coming from the 3rd century, but its subject matter "is altogether incongruous with [that century's] puritanical atmosphere." Most likely it is folk poetry that originated in Syria and northern Palestine, an anthology of liturgies that were preserved and passed down through centuries by repeated recitation and use. Rabbi Akiba (early 2nd century) called it "the holy of holies." "No day," he said, "outweighed in glory the one on which Israel received the Song of Songs."

The rustic beauty of the shepherdess is not royalty's fair white, but the deeply tanned swarthiness of the vineyard keeper, dark like the black goat's hair tents of Kedar (a Bedouin tribe of north Arabia), and sumptuous as Solomon's Oriental tapestries.

The text of Palestrina's setting is taken directly from Chapter 1, verses 4 and 5, while Pau Casals fashions his own (based mostly on the excerpts used in the Antiphon): *Nigra sum . . . -* Canticles 1:4a; *ideo dilexit . . . -* Canticles 1:3 (freely adapted); and *et dixit mihi . . . -* Canticles 2:10-12a.

Liturgical context: **Nigra sum** is the third Antiphon for II. Vespers of Feasts of the Blessed Virgin Mary; it is followed by the great hymn *Ave Maris Stella* ("Hail Star of the Sea").

NON NOBIS, DOMINE

Non	nobis,	Domine,	non	nobis,	**Not to us, O Lord, not to us,**
Not	**to us,**	**Lord,**	**not**	**to us,**	

sed	nomini	tuo	da	gloriam.	**but to your name give the glory.**
but	**to name**	**your**	**give**	**glory.**	

Conclusive evidence has not yet been found to prove that "the famous canon by William Byrd" was indeed from his pen. Although most of his works were published during his lifetime (1542–1623), this canon is first found in John Playford's *A Musicall Banquet* of 1651 and there are conflicting reports about the ascription of its authorship: Edmund Fellowes reports that "no composer's name is attached to it there," while Frank Howes cites "the inclusion of the canon under Byrd's name in Playford's *Musicall Banquet* of 1651" as "evidence ... pointing to Byrd's authorship." Hilton published it in 1652 in *Catch as Catch Can*, but again, no composer's name is given.

In 1730 Dr. Pepusch in no uncertain terms calls it "the famous canon by William Byrd" and William Boyce says of it: "His canon of *Non nobis Domine* will in particular remain a perpetual monument to his memory." But Fellowes again disagrees, finding "no reason to regard it as a work of outstanding merit, for the simple diatonic phrases lend themselves easily to canonical imitation." But he continues:

> "Nevertheless it is remarkable in how many ways this little canon may be solved and sung. There are solutions for two, three, and even four voices. It will also go in several ways by inversion, and, counting these, there are eleven known solutions."

NUNC DIMITTIS

Nunc	dimíttis	sérvum	túum, Dómine,	**Now let thy servant depart in peace,**
Now	**you dismiss**	**servant**	**your, Lord,**	**O Lord, according to thy word.**

secundum	verbum	tuum, in	pace.
according to	**word**	**your, in**	**peace.**

Quia	vidérunt	óculi	méi	**For my eyes have seen thy salvation,**
Because	**have seen**	**eyes**	**my**	

salutáre	túum,
salvation	**your,**

Quod	parásti	ante	fácem	**Which thou hast prepared**
Which	**have prepared**	**before**	**face**	**before the face of all peoples,**

ómnium	populórum,
of all	**peoples,**

Lúmen	ad	revelatiónem	géntium,	**A light as revelation to the Gentiles,**
Light	**to**	**as revelation**	**nations,**	**and a glory of thy people Israel.**

et	glóriam	plébis	túae	Israel.
and	**glory**	**of people**	**your**	**Israel.**

"And when the days of her purification were fulfilled according to the Law of Moses [which stated that a mother was unclean for seven days after the birth of a son and had to remain at home for another thirty-three days], they took the child Jesus up to Jerusalem to present him to the Lord." (Luke 2:21-22)

Simeon, a "just and devout" man, had been told by the Holy Spirit "that he should not see death before he had seen the Christ of the Lord. And he came by inspiration of the Spirit into the temple. And when his parents brought in the child Jesus, to do for him according to the custom of the Law, he also received him into his arms and blessed God, saying:

Nunc dimittis servum tuum, Domine, secundum verbum tuum

The Feast of the Purification of the Blessed Virgin Mary (February 2), established at Jerusalem in the 4th century, is perhaps the most ancient feast in honor of the Blessed Virgin. The words of the Canticle of Simeon which was sung to her on this occasion (*lumen ad revelationem gentium*) have given rise to the elaborate ceremony of the blessing of the candles, their solemn distribution to the clergy and laity, and the magnificent procession which has caused this day to be commonly known as *Candlemas* ("Candle Mass"). The **Nunc dimittis** is sung during the distribution of the candles, with the antiphon *Lumen ad revelationem* sung preceding and following each verse of Simeon's Canticle. During Septuagesima, the **Nunc dimittis** is sung as the Tract in place of the Alleluia-Verse of the Mass for this day.

This well-known canticle is also sung near the close of the concluding office of the day, the office of Compline. There it follows the Responsory from Psalm 30 [31] *In manus tuas* ("Into thy hands, O Lord, I commend my spirit"). It is sung with special significance at the close of Compline on All Saint's Day, November 2, the day on which all the departed saints and servants of God are honored by the universal Church.

Simeon's words recall those of *Viderunt omnes* (Psalm 97 [98]):
"The Lord hath made known his salvation ... he hath remembered his mercy and his truth toward the house of Israel [his promise to Simeon] ... All the ends of the earth have seen the salvation of our God." (Psalm 97:2-4)

and the *Dies sanctificatus:*
"Come ye nations and adore the Lord; for today a great light has descended upon the earth. *Alleluia.*"

and the opening chapter of the Gospel of St. John:

The light shineth in the darkness,
and the darkness comprehended it not.

O ADMIRABILE COMMERCIUM

O admirábile commércium! **O wondrous interchange!**	**O wondrous interchange!**
Creátor genéris humáni, **Creator of race human,**	**The Creator of the human race,** **assuming a living body,** **has deigned to be born of a virgin;**
animátum córpus súmens, **living body assuming,**	
de vírgine násci dignátus est: **of virgin to be born deigned has:**	
et procédens hómo sine sémine, **and coming forth man without seed,**	**and issuing forth unbegotten,** **he has bestowed upon us his divinity.**
largítus est nóbis súam deitátem. **bestowed has on us his divinity.**	

January 1, the beginning of the Civil Year, is both the octave day of Christmas and the day of the feast of the Circumcison in the Liturgical Year. The Roman Church especially honors the name of Jesus which was officially given to the Christ child on this day. It is during II. Vespers that **O admirabile commercium** is sung as the antiphon to the first Vesper psalm, Psalm 109 [110] *Dixit Dominus* ("The Lord said unto my Lord").

The mystery of the Incarnation is also addressed in the texts of *Mirabile Mysterium* and *Verbum caro factum est.*

O BONE JESU

O bóne Jésu, illúmina óculos méos, **O good Jesus, enlighten eyes my,**	**O blesséd Jesus, enlighten my eyes,** **lest I sleep the sleep of death,**
ne unquam obdórmiam in mórte, **lest at any time I fall asleep in death,**	
ne quándo dícat inimícus méus: **lest ever say enemy my:**	**lest my enemy ever say:** **I have prevailed against him.**
praeválui advérsus éum. **I have prevailed against him.**	

In mánus túas, Dómine,	Into your hands, O Lord,
Into hands your, Lord,	**I commend my spirit.**

commÉndo spíritum méum.	
I entrust spirit my.	

Redemísti nos, Dómine, Déus veritátis.	You have redeemed us, O Lord, God of truth.
You have redeemed us, Lord, God of truth.	

O Messías, locútus sum in língua méa;	O Messiah, I have spoken with my tongue;
O Messiah, spoken I have with tongue my;	

nótum fac míhi, Dómine, fínem méum.	make known to me, O Lord, my end.
known make to me, Lord, end my.	

This text is an interesting compilation of passages from the psalms, a penitent prayer of one of the faithful remembering various portions of the ancient Psalter as they relate to the present condition. The opening address is both emotional and Christological (*O bone Jesu*), following which the petitioner utters the Old Testament pleas from Psalm 12 [13], verses 4 and 5:

> "Enlighten my eyes,
> lest I sleep the sleep of death,
> lest my enemy ever say:
> I have prevailed against him."

and the next three lines (*In manus tuas . . .*) are from Psalm 30 [31], verse 6:

> "Into thy hands I commend my spirit:
> thou hast redeemed me [us],
> O God of truth."

which were probably suggested by verse 6 of the previously-quoted Psalm 12: "But I have trusted in thy mercy, my heart shall rejoice in thy salvation." The words *In manus tuas* ... are also, of course, the words spoken by the crucified Christ who "cried out with a loud voice and said, Father, into thy hands I commend my spirit." (Luke 2:46)

Christ's redeeming sacrifice may have occasioned the following address (*O Messias*) which precedes the final quotation from Psalm 38 [39] : 5, a passage well known to choral musicians from its setting in the Brahms *Requiem* :

> "I spoke with my tongue:
> O Lord, make me to know my end.
> And what is the number of my days:
> that I may know what is wanting in me."

O FILII ET FILIAE

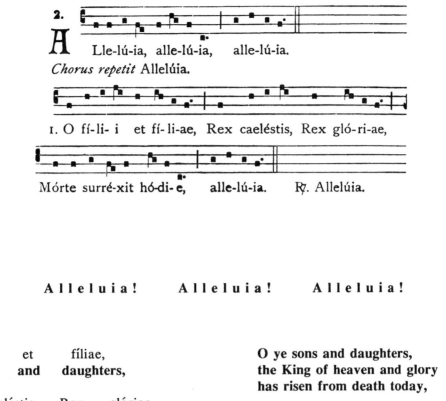

2.
Alle-lú-ia, alle-lú-ia, alle-lú-ia.
Chorus repetit Allelúia.

1. O fí-li- i et fí-li-ae, Rex caeléstis, Rex gló-ri-ae,

Mórte surré-xit hó-di- e, alle-lú-ia. ℞. Allelúia.

Alleluia! Alleluia! Alleluia!

O	fílii	et	fíliae,	
O	**sons**	**and**	**daughters,**	

O ye sons and daughters,
the King of heaven and glory
has risen from death today, alleluia!

Rex	caeléstis,	Rex	glóriae,
King	**of heaven,**	**King**	**of glory,**

Mórte	surréxit	hódie,	allelúia.
From death	**has risen**	**today,**	**alleluia.**

Et	mane	prima	sábbati,
And	**early**	**on first**	**sabbath,**

And early on the first sabbath,
the disciples came
to the entrance of the tomb, alleluia!

Ad	óstium	monuménti
to	**entrance**	**of tomb,**

Accessérunt	discípuli,	allelúia.
came	**disciples,**	**alleluia.**

Beáti	qui	non	vidérunt,
Blessed	**who**	**not**	**have seen,**

Blessed are they who have not seen,
and yet have firmly believed,
they shall have life eternal, alleluia!

Et	fírmiter	credidérunt,
yet	**firmly**	**have believed,**

Vítam	aetérnam	habébunt,	allelúia.
Life	**eternal**	**they shall have,**	**alleluia.**

In	hoc	fésto	sanctíssimo		In this most holy feast,
In	**this**	**feast**	**most holy**		let there be praise and jubilation,
					let us bless the Lord,
Sit	laus	et	jubilátio,		
be	**praise**	**and**	**jubiliation,**		
BENEDICÁMUS		DÓMINO,		allelúia.	
Let us bless		**Lord,**		**alleluia.**	

In this most holy feast,
let there be praise and jubilation,
let us bless the Lord,   alleluia.

De	quíbus	nos	humíllimas		For these reasons
For	**which**	**us**	**humble**		let us give humble, devout,
					and owing thanks to God, alleluia!
Devótas	atque	débitas			
devout	**as well as**	**owing**			
DÉO	DICÁMUS	GRÁTIAS,		allelúia.	
to God	**let us say**	**thanks,**		**alleluia!**	

Alleluia!   Alleluia!   Alleluia!

O Filii et Filiae, The "Joyful Canticle" -- so entitled by P. Guéranger because of the abundant *Alleluias* which accompany its singing -- is a 12-stanza hymn which celebrates various events of the Resurrection: the women at the tomb, the angel's message, John and Peter running to the tomb, Christ's appearance to the Apostles, and the doubt and confession of faith of Thomas [*Beati qui non viderunt*].

The *Alleluias* of Paschaltide are scarcely more abundant than when this hymn is sung with its triple *Alleluia* at the beginning and end and between each verse in addition to the single *Alleluia* which is sung at the close of each stanza.

The final two stanzas incorporate the well-known versicle and response from the end of Lauds and Vespers:

Benedicamus Domino,
Deo dicamus gratias.

174

O MAGNUM MYSTERIUM

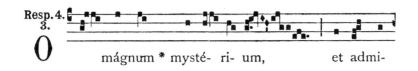

I O mágnum mystérium,
   O great mystery,

   et admirábile sacraméntum,
   and wondrous sacrament,

   ut animália vidérent Dóminum nátum,
   that animals should see Lord born,

   jacéntem in praesépio!
   lying in manger!

O great mystery,
and wondrous sacrament,

that animals should see the new-born Lord
lying in their manger!

II Beáta Vírgo, cújus víscera meruérunt
    Blessed Virgin, whose womb was worthy

    portáre Dóminum Chrístum. Allelúia!
    to bear Lord Christ. Alleluia!

Blessed is the Virgin whose womb was worthy
to bear the Lord Jesus Christ.   Alleluia!

III Dómine, audívi audítum túum
     Lord, I heard instruction your

     et tímui; considerávi ópera túa
     and I feared; I considered works your

     et expávi in médio duórum animálium.
     and I trembled in midst of two animals.

O Lord, I heard your oracle
and I was afraid;

I considered your works,
and I trembled
in the midst of the two animals.

I

Throughout the Old and New Testament the meek and lowly are assured of God's consideration and grace:

"Who is as the Lord our God, who dwelleth on high: and looketh down on the low things in heaven and earth?" (Psalm 112 [113] : 5-6) "Wherefore I will pray to the Lord ... who setteth up the humble on high." (Job 5:8,11) "Blessed are the poor in spirit ... Blessed are the meek ..." (Matthew 5:3-4) "The Lord maketh poor and maketh rich, he humbleth and he exalteth. He raiseth up the needy from the dust, and lifteth up the poor from the dungheap." (*The Canticle of Anna*, I Kings [Samuel] 2:7-8) "For he hath regarded the low estate of his handmaid ... He hath deposed the mighty from their thrones and exalted the lowly." (*The Canticle of the Blessed Virgin Mary*, the *Magnificat*, Luke 1:48,52)

O magnum mysterium, that he who was to be called the Son of the Most High, the heir of the throne of David, the king of the house of Jacob, of whose kingdom there will be no end (Luke 1:32-33) -- that this King should be born and laid in a manger, that lowly animals and shepherds should be the first to see the new-born Lord:

O admirabile sacramentum!

"And this shall be a <u>sign</u> unto you: you will find an infant wrapped in swaddling clothes and lying in a manger . . . And when they had seen they understood what had been told to them concerning the Child." (Luke 2:12,17)

O wondrous sacrament, sign and symbol of the nature of the coming kingdom.

II

The Annunciation.   "Blessed art thou among women ... Do not be afraid, Mary, for thou hast found grace with God" (Luke 1:28,30)

The Visitation.   Blessed art thou among women, and blessed is the fruit of thy womb." (Luke 1:42)

The Magnificat.   "My spirit has rejoiced in God my Saviour; because he hath regarded the low estate of his handmaid, for behold, henceforth, all generations shall call me blessed." (Luke 1:47-48)

The Te Deum.   "Thou art the King of Glory, O Christ. Thou art the eternal Son of the Father. To deliver us, you became man, and did not disdain the Virgin's womb."

III

The Angel's Annunciation to the Shepherds.   "And there were shepherds ... keeping watch over their flock by night. And behold, an angel of the Lord stood by them and the glory of God shone round about them, and *they feared exceedingly*. And the angel said unto them, Do not be afraid, for behold, I bring you good news of great joy ..." (Luke 2:8-10)

Le Sommeil de L'Enfant Jésus.   The reference to the "two animals" is found in various artistic portrayals of the Nativity (e.g., the text of the well-known Christmas Carol *The Sleep of the Infant Jesus*: "Here 'mid the ass and oxen mild ... ," or "'Twixt ox and ass in humble shed ... ," etc.). There is no biblical reference to the two animals being present at the Bethlehem manger, but the creative imaginations of monastics, folk poets, musicians and visual artists have depicted it thusly from very early on.

Psalm 47, the first psalm recited during the II. Nocturn of Matins for Christmas Day: "For behold, the kings of the earth assembled themselves: they gathered together. So they saw, and they wondered, they were troubled, they were moved: *trembling* took hold of them." (Psalm 47 [48] : 5-7)

Habakkuk, Chapter 3	*Tract for Good Friday*

O Lord, I have heard thy hearing
and was afraid;

O Lord, thy work, in the midst
of the years, bring it to life.
In the midst of the years
thou shalt make it known.

O Lord, I have heard thy hearing,
    and was afraid;
I considered thy works,
    and I trembled.

In the midst of two animals
    thou shalt be made known.

Liturgical context: **O magnum mysterium** is the Responsory following the 4th Lesson of the II. Nocturn of Matins for Christmas Day.

O NATA LUX

O   náta   lux   de   lúmine,
O   born   light   of   light,

O born light of light,
Jesus, redeemer of the world,

Jésu   redémptor   saéculi,
Jesus   redeemer   of age,

dignáre   clémens   súpplicum
to deem worthy   merciful   of supplicants

mercifully deem worthy and accept
the praises and prayers of your supplicants.

láudes   préces   que   súmere.
praises   prayers   and   to accept.

Qui   cárne   quondam   cóntegi
Who   in flesh   once   to be clothed

Thou who once deigned to be clothed in flesh
for the sake of the lost ones,

dignátus es   pro   pérditis,
you deigned   for   lost ones,

Nos   mémbra   confér   éffici,
Us   members   grant   to be made,

grant us to be made members
of your holy body.

túi   beáti   córporis.
of your   blessed   body.

177

The feast of August 6 commemorates the Transfiguration of Christ as recorded in the Gospel of Matthew:

> "Jesus taketh unto him Peter and James, and John his brother, and bringeth them up into a high mountain apart: and he was transfigured before them. And his face did shine as the sun, and his garments became white as snow ... And behold a bright cloud overshadowed them. And lo, a voice out of the cloud, saying: This is my beloved Son, in whom I am well pleased: hear ye him. And the disciples hearing, fell upon their face, and were very much afraid." (Matthew 17:1-9)

Various texts employed in the Mass for this day also refer to the Light of Light:

Introit. "Thy lightnings enlightened the world: the earth shook and trembled." (Psalm 76 [77] : 19)

Gradual verse. "He is the brightness of eternal light, the unspotted mirror, and the image of his goodness." (Wisdom 7:26)

Secret. "By the brightness of his glory in that revelation cleanse us from the stains of our sins."

How perfectly fitting that the hymn **O nata lux** ("O born light of light") should be appointed to be sung at Lauds (the Office of Aurora or Dawn) on the Feast of the Transfiguration.

O   QUAM   GLORIOSUM

Ad Magnif. Ant. 6. F

O quam gló-ri- ó-sum est régnum, * in quo

O	quam	gloriósum	est	régnum,
O	**how**	**glorious**	**is**	**kingdom,**

O how glorious is the kingdom, where all the Saints rejoice with Christ!

in	quo	cum	Christo
in	**which**	**with**	**Christ**

gáudent	ómnes	Sáncti!
rejoice	**all**	**Saints!**

amícti	stólis	álbis,
Clothed	**in robes**	**of white,**

Dressed in white robes, they follow the Lamb wheresoever he goes.   Alleluia!

sequúntur	Agnum
they follow	**Lamb**

quocumque	ierit.	Allelúia.
wheresoever	**he has gone.**	**Alleluia!**

178

The Feast of All Saints has existed since the 5th century. On May 13, 610, Pope Boniface IV converted the Pantheon, the "temple of all the gods," into a Christian Church in honor of the Blessed Virgin and the Holy Martyrs. This feast later became more general in character and was transfered to November 1 as the Feast of All Saints.

The Lesson for the Mass is the powerful passage from the seventh chapter of the Apocalypse of St. John:

> "Behold I saw a great multitude which no man could number, of all nations, and tribes, and peoples, and tongues, standing before the throne and in sight of the Lamb, clothed with white robes, and palms in their hands; and they cried with a loud voice, saying: Salvation to our God, who sitteth upon the throne, and to the Lamb. And all the angels stood round about the throne, and the ancients and the four living creatures, and they fell down before the throne upon tgheir faces, and adored God, saying: Amen. Blessing and honor, and wisdom and thanks, and glory and power, and strength be to our God for ever and ever. Amen." (from the Apocalypse [Revelation] 7:1-12)

and the Gospel reading is from Matthew 5:1-11, the Beatitudes from the Sermon on the Mount. The last three verses are particularly apporpriate for this feast and are employed again later in the service as the Communion:

> "Blessed are the clean of heart, for they shall see God: blessed are the peacemakers, for they shall be called the children of God: blessed are they that suffer persecution for justice sake, for theirs is the kingdom of heaven."

At the beginning of II. Vespers of this feast four of the traditional Lucernal or Vesper psalms are recited (*Dixit Dominus, Beatus vir, Confitebor,* and *Laudate Pueri*), the first two being accompanied by special antiphons for this day chosen from the passage from the Apocalypse quoted above (*Vidi turbam*, 7:9, and *Et omnes Angeli*, 7:11). The fifth psalm, *Credidi* (Psalm 115 [116] : 10-19), is specially appointed to this feast:

> "I have believed, therefore I have spoken; but I have been humbled exceedingly ... I will pay my vows to the Lord before all his people: precious in the sight of the Lord is the death of his saints." (Psalm 115 [116] : 10,14-15)

O Quam Gloriosum serves as the antiphon to the *Magnificat* which comes at the climactic close of this Vesper office.

Epilogue

> "And one of the elders spoke and said to me, These who are clothed in white robes, who are they? and whence have they come? And I said unto him, My Lord, thou knowest. And he said to me, These are they who have come out of the great tribulation, and have washed their robes and made them white in the blood of the Lamb. Therefore they are before the throne of God, and serve him day and night in his temple, and he who sits upon the throne will dwell with them. They shall neither hunger nor thirst any more, neither shall the sun strike them nor any heat. For the Lamb who is in the midst of the throne will shepherd them, and will guide them to the fountains of the waters of life, and God will wipe away every tear from their eyes." (Apocalypse [Revelation] 7:13-17)

O SACRUM CONVIVIUM

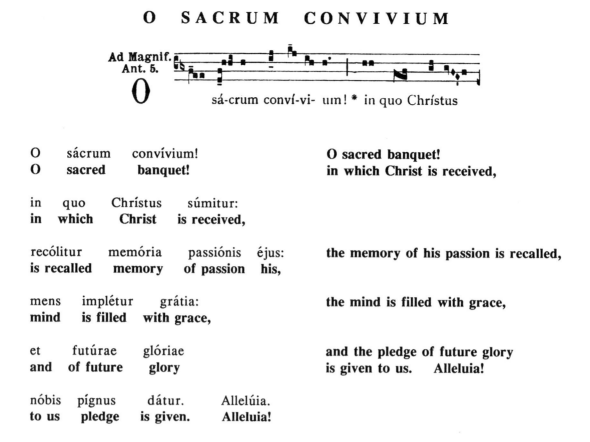

Ad Magnif. Ant. 5.

O sá-crum conví-vi- um! * in quo Chrístus

O sácrum convívium!	O sacred banquet!	**O sacred banquet!**
O sacred banquet!		**in which Christ is received,**
in quo Chrístus súmitur:	in which Christ is received,	
in which Christ is received,		
recólitur memória passiónis éjus:	is recalled memory of passion his,	**the memory of his passion is recalled,**
is recalled memory of passion his,		
mens implétur grátia:	mind is filled with grace,	**the mind is filled with grace,**
mind is filled with grace,		
et futúrae glóriae	and of future glory	**and the pledge of future glory**
and of future glory		**is given to us. Alleluia!**
nóbis pígnus dátur. Allelúia.	to us pledge is given. Alleluia!	
to us pledge is given. Alleluia!		

The Feast of Corpus Christi ("Body of Christ") amplifies Maundy Thursday's celebration of the Sacrament of the Holy Eucharist, giving it sole and extended focus without Holy Thursday's other rites and sorrowful associations. It originated in Belgium, at Liége, through the influence of an Augustinian nun, Juliana of Mont Carnillon, and was first celebrated in 1247 by order of Bishop Robert of Liége. In 1264 Pope Urban IV set aside the Thursday after Trinity Sunday for the celebration of the feast, but it was not universally celebrated until after the reaffirming decree of Pope Clement V in 1311.

There were several versions of the Office and the Mass: the first by an Augustinian, John of Mont Carnillon (as early as 1228), the Cistercian Offices (especially the one used at the Abbey of Villers near Liége), and the two offices usually attributed to St. Thomas Aquinas that were composed at Urban's request in 1264. The Office now in use "is the result of a fusion of elements drawn from various sources," including the afore-mentioned Cistercian office, anonymous lessons and repsonses, and a 12th century hymn of Adam of St. Victor. [see *Lauda Sion*] The custom of carrying the Host in procession following the Mass (the "Corpus Christi procession") first appeared in Cologne in 1279 and has been a prominent part of the celebration since the 14th century.

Texts for the Feast of Corpus Christi chosen from the Holy Scripture include the Introit (Psalm 80:17), the Lesson (I Corinthians 11:23–29), the Gradual (Psalm 144:14–15 and John 6:56–59), and the Communion (I Corinthians 11:26–27). These are combined with the great Sequence *Lauda Sion* ("Praise, O Zion, your Saviour") and the beautiful Eucharistic hymns *Verbum supernum prodiens* (which contains *O Salutaris Hostia*), *Pange lingua gloriosi* (which includes the *Tantum ergo*), and *Sacri solemnis* (which includes the *Panis angelicus*). Musical settings of the scriptural texts, the *Lauda Sion*, and the well-known portions of the three hymns can be meaningfully programmed with settings of **O sacrum convivium**.

The essence of the Feast of Corpus Christi is beautifully and succinctly expressed in **O sacrum convivium**: the sacramental partaking of the Real Presence, the memory of Christ's passion and the first institution of the sacrament, the present grace, and the promise of the future Messianic feast.

Liturgical context: **O sacrum convivium** is the Magnificat antiphon for II. Vespers of the Feast of Corpus Christi.

O   SALUTARIS   HOSTIA

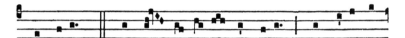

praémi- um. † 5. O SA- LU-TÁRIS HÓSTI-A, Quae caéli pán-

O	SALUTÁRIS	HÓSTIA,		O Redeeming Sacrifice,
O	Redeeming	Sacrifice,		which opens the gate of heaven:

Quae   caéli   pándis   óstium,
(You)who of heaven opens   gate,

Bélla   prémunt   hostília,   enemies threaten wars;
wars   threaten   enemies,   give us strength, send aid.

Da   róbur,   fér   auxílium.
give   strength,   send   aid.

O Salutaris Hostia is the last stanza of the hymn *Verbum Supernum prodiens, Nec Patris...* by St. Thomas Aquinas (c.1225–1274). The hymn was written c.1263 for the office for use on Corpus Christi, but this stanza has often been used, along with the concluding doxology, as a separate hymn (e.g., at the Benediction of the Blessed Sacrament). [see *O sacrum convivium*]

Liturgical context: As a part of the hymn *Verbum Supernum*, **O Salutaris Hostia** is a prescribed for use on Corpus Christi. Separately it is employed during the Office called Benediction, as a chant in honor of the Blessed Sacrament sung "*in elevatione corporis Christi* between the Sanctus and Benedictus. In some masses it serves as a replacement for the Benedictus.

O VOS OMNES

O vos ómnes,		**O all you**
O you all,		**who pass along this way,**
qui transítis	per víam,	
who pass	**along way,**	
atténdite	et vidéte	**behold and see**
attend	**and see**	**if there is any sorrow**
		like unto my sorrow.
si est	dólor,	
if there is	**sorrow,**	
sicut dólor	méus.	
like sorrow	**my.**	

The prophet Jeremias lived at the close of the 7th and the beginning of the 6th century B.C., turbulent and catastrophic times for the Jewish nation which eventually led to their defeat by King Nebuchadnezzar (586 B.C.) and the ensuing oppression of the Babylonian Captivity. In the superscription to the Lamentations in the in the Septuagint we read: "And it came to pass, after Israel was carried into captivity, and Jerusalem was desolate, that Jeremias the prophet sat weeping, and mourned with this lamentation over Jerusalem, and with a sorrowful mind, sighing, and moaning, he said" *O vos omnes ... attendite et videte si est dolor sicut dolor meus* (Lamentations 1:12). "Thus Jeremias, more than any other man was plainly called--it may be said, driven by an inner force--to lament the ruined city as threnodist of the great penitential period of the Old Covenant" (M. Faulhaber).

Portions of his five great songs of Lamentation, and the **O vos omnes** in particular, are appointed to some of the greatest solemnities of the liturgical year. On Holy Saturday, the eve of the Easter Resurrection, the I Nocturn of the Office of Matins takes its three Lessons from the Lamentations of Jeremias (Lamentations 3:22-30; 4:1-6; and 5:1-11). The sensitivity and care with which these texts were chosen makes the progression from Israel's hope in the third lament to the ravaging and destruction of the fifth very moving.

The II. Nocturn begins with the psalms, Psalm 23 [24] *Domini est terra* ("The earth is the Lord's") and Psalm 26 [27] *Dominus illuminatio mea* ("The Lord is my Light") -- images of bounty, fullness, and light that contrast dramatically with the *tenebrae* of the I. Nocturn: "Thou hast turned my mourning into joy ... I will give praise to thee forever" (Psalm 29:12,13). But Lesson V of this same Nocturn turns our thoughts to Christ's appearance before Pilate, and the later entombment. **O vos omnes** is the responsory to the fifth Lesson. Soon afterwards it appears again as the antiphon before the great *Laudate* psalm, Psalm 150 *Laudate Dominum in sanctis ejus* ("Praise the Lord in his sanctuary") which comes at the close of Lauds, just before the Easter Vigil begins.

On the Feast of the Seven Sorrows of the Blessed Virgin Mary (September 15) the **O vos omnes** is the verse of the Tract which preceeds "the tenderest and most pathetic hymn of the Middle Ages," the *Stabat Mater dolorosa*. And during the Feast of the Sacred Heart of Jesus (the second Friday after Corpus Christi) its function is similar to its position in the II Nocturn of Matins on Holy Saturday: it provides considerable contrast and serves as a reminder of the suffering and sorrow that occasioned the preceeding canticle of thanksgiving and praise (Isaiah 12:1-6, *Confitebor tibi, Domine* -- "I will give thanks to thee, O Lord, for thou was angry with me: thy wrath is turned away, and thou hast comforted me . . . ").

O M N E S   D E   S A B A

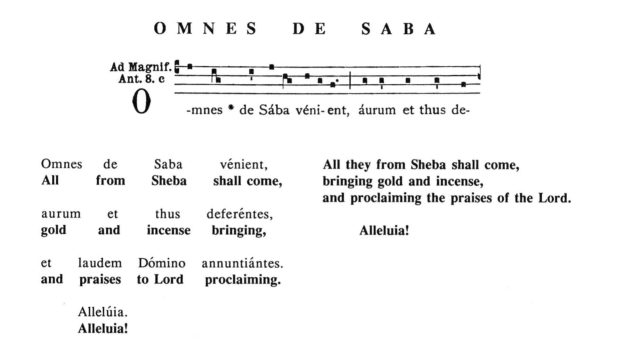

Omnes	de	Saba	vénient,	**All they from Sheba shall come,**
All	**from**	**Sheba**	**shall come,**	**bringing gold and incense,**
				and proclaiming the praises of the Lord.
aurum	et	thus	deferéntes,	
gold	**and**	**incense**	**bringing,**	**Alleluia!**
et	laudem	Dómino	annuntiántes.	
and	**praises**	**to Lord**	**proclaiming.**	
Allelúia.				
Alleluia!				

Saba, the Douay Version of Sheba, was an ancient country in South Arabia [now Yemen], a Semitic race of very ancient culture. The Sabeans were renowned as traders, especially of gold and incense, and are mentioned several times in the Old Testament, the best known reference being the account of the visit of the Queen of Saba to King Solomon (III Kings [I Kings]10:1-13).

Balaam's "vision of the Almighty" as a "Star" that "shall come out of Jacob" (Numbers 24:17) is echoed in Isaiah's prophecy:

> "Arise, be enlightened, for thy light is come, and the glory of the Lord is risen upon thee. For behold, the darkness shall cover the earth, and gross darkness the people: but the Lord shall arise upon thee, and his glory shall be seen upon thee. And the Gentiles will come to thy light, and kings to the brightness of thy rising. Lift up thine eyes round about, and see: all they gather themselves together, they come to thee: thy sons shall come from afar.
> "... all they from Sheba shall come: they shall bring gold and incense; and they shall shew forth the praises of the Lord." (Isaiah 60:1-4a, 6b)

Liturgical context: On the fifth day of the octave of the Epiphany **Omnes de Saba** is the antiphon which precedes the *Magnificat* in II. Vespers. The psalm of the day is Psalm 113 [114] : *In exitu* ("When Israel went out of Egypt").

PANGE LINGUA

Hymn. 3.

Pange língua glo-ri-ó-si Córpo-ris mysté-ri-um,

Pánge	língua	gloriósi
Sing	**tongue**	**of glorious**

Córporis	mystérium,
Body	**mystery,**

Sanguinísque	pretiósi,
and of blood	**precious,**

Quem	in	múndi	prétium
which	**as**	**of world**	**price;**

5 | Frúctus | véntris | generósi, |
|---|---|---|
| **fruit** | **of womb** | **noble,** |

Rex	effúdit	géntium.
king	**poured forth**	**of nations.**

Sing, O tongue, the mystery
Of the glorious Body,
And of the precious blood,
Which the King of all nations,
The fruit of a noble womb,
Poured forth as the ransom for the world.

Nóbis	dátus,	nóbis	nátus
To us	**given,**	**for us**	**born**

Ex	intácta	Vírgine,
of	**stainless**	**Virgin,**

Et	in	múndo	conversátus,
And	**on**	**earth**	**he abided,**

10 | Spárso | | vérbi | sémine, |
|---|---|---|---|
| **Having been sown** | **of word** | **seed,** |

Súi	móras	incolátus
His	**days**	**sojourning**

Míro	cláusit	órdine.
Wondrous	**he closed**	**way.**

Given to us, born for us
Of a stainless Virgin,
He abided on earth;
the seed of the word having been sown,
He concluded His earthly sojourn
In a wondrous way.

In	suprémae	nócte	cénae,
On	**last**	**night**	**of supper,**

Recúmbens	cum	frátribus,
Reclining	**with**	**brethren,**

On the night of the Last Supper,
Reclining with His brethren,
Having complied fully with the law
regarding legal foods,
He gives Himself with His own hands
As Food to the group of twelve.

15 Observáta   lége   pléne
Having observed   law   full

Cíbis   in   legálibus,
Foods of   law,

Cíbum   túrbae   duodénae
Food   to group of twelve

Se   dat   súis   mánibus.
Himself he gives with his hands.

Vérbum   cáro,   pánem   vérum
Word   flesh,   bread   true

Vérbo   cárnem   éfficit;
By word flesh   he makes;

Fítque   sánguis Chrísti mérum:
And becomes blood of Christ wine:

Et   si   sénsus déficit,
And if sense   fails,

Ad   firmándum   cor sincérum
To   assure   heart sincere

Sóla   fídes   súfficit.
Alone faith   suffices.

The Word (made) Flesh
Makes true bread Flesh by His word,
And wine becomes the blood of Christ;
And, if sense fails to perceive this,
Faith alone suffices
To assure a sincere heart.

25 Tántum   ergo   Sacraméntum
So great   therefore Sacrament

Venerémur   cérnui:
let us venerate bowing low;

Et   antíquum   documéntum
And ancient   document

Nóvo   cédat   rítui:
New let give way to rite:

Praéstet   fídes   suppleméntum
Let furnish faith   assistance

30 Sénsuum   deféctui.
of senses to deficiency.

Let us therefore, bowing low,
Venerate so great a Sacrament;
And let the old Law
Give way to the new rite;
Let faith afford assistance
To the deficiency of the senses.

Genitóri,	Genitóque		To the Begetter and the Begotten
To Begetter,	**to Begotten,**		**Let there be praise and jubilation,**

Genitóri,   Genitóque
To Begetter,   to Begotten,

Laus   et   jubilátio,
praise   and   jubilation,

Sálus,   hónor,   vírtus   quoque
salvation,   honor,   power   also

Sit   et   benedíctio:
be   also   blessing:

Procedénti   ab   utróque
To proceeding   from   both

Cómpar   sit   laudátio.
equal   be   praise.

To the Begetter and the Begotten
Let there be praise and jubilation,
Salvation and honor,
And power and blessing;
And to the One proceeding from both
Let there be equal praise.

Pange lingua − corporis was written by St. Thomas Aquinas (c.1225-1274) in c. 1264 for the institution of the new feast of Corpus Christi ("Body of Christ"). [see *O sacrum convivium*] The fifth stanza, *Tantum ergo*, along with the concluding doxology is sung as a separate hymn in the office of the Benediction of the Blessed Sacrament and during Mass at the Elevation of the Host. The meter and opening line are imitations of the hymn *Pange lingua − certamis* which is credited to St. Venantius Fortunatus (c.530-609), and *Genitori Genitoque/Procendi ab utroque* are borrowed from Adam of St. Victor's second sequence for Pentecost.

It is "one of the finest of the Medieval Latin hymns; a wonderful union of sweetness of melody with clear-cut dogmatic teaching" (W.A. Schoults, in Julian's *Dictionary of Hymnology*). James Mason Neale, the highly respected translator of *Medieval Hymns and Sequences*, offers equal praise:

> "This hymn contests the second place among those of the Western Church with the *Vexilla Regis*, the *Stabat Mater*, the *Jesu dulcis memoria*, the *Ad Regias Agni Dapes*, the *Ad supernam*, and one or two others, leaving the *Dies irae* in its unapproachable glory" (*Medieval Hymns*).

Notes:

5. *generosi.*

(from *genus*, of good or noble birth) The Blessed Virgin was of the house of David. [see *Virga Jesse floruit*]

16. *Cibus in legalibus.*

According to law the Jews were to eat the sacrificial lamb, unleavened bread, and wild lettuce as part of the Passover observance (Exodus 12:1-14); Christ ate this meal with his disciples prior instituting the Lord's Supper.

27. *Et antiquum . . . ritui.*

Let the sacrificial lamb of the Jewish Passover give way to the redeeming single sacrifice of Christ the Lamb of God. [see *Agnus Dei*]

PANIS ANGELICUS

Ut súmant, et dent cé-te-ris. † 6. PÁNIS ANGÉ-LI-CUS

Pánis angélicus, fit pánis hóminum,
Bread of angels, becomes bread of men,

Dat pánis coélicus figúris términum.
gives bread heavenly to forms end.

O res mirábilis mandúcat Dóminum,
O thing marvellous ingests Lord,

Páuper, sérvus, et húmilis.
poor man, slave, and humble one.

The bread of angels becomes the bread of men,
the heavenly bread
gives an end to (earthly) forms.

O marvellous and wondrous sacrament:
a poor man, a slave, and the humble one
all ingest the Lord.

The second line of this text is difficult to render. Translated literally, as above, the meaning is not immediately clear. The Heavenly Bread (Christ) takes on (during Communion) the figure (shape, dimension, and appearance) of the earthly bread; or, The Bread of Heaven takes on the earthly's shape. The shape of the bread does not have the sensible dimension of Christ's body, but "the bread of angels" becomes both the spiritual and physical nourishment of the faithful. "O wondrous thing! / Lowly and poor are fed, / Banqueting on their Lord and King."

Panis Angelicus, the sixth stanza of the hymn *Sacris Solémnis* by St. Thomas Aquinas (c.1225-1275), evidences an intricate internal rhyme scheme within its traditional four-line stanza form:

> *Panis angelicus,*
> > *fit panis hominum.*
> *Dat panis coelicus*
> > *figuris terminum.*
> > > *O res mirabilis!*
> > *manducat Dominum*
> > > *Pauper, servus, et humilis.*

Liturgical context: *Sacris Solemnis* is the hymn for the office of Corpus Christi and of the Votive Office of the Most Blessed Sacrament. **Panis Angelicus** is sometimes employed as a separate hymn at Benediction.

PATER NOSTER

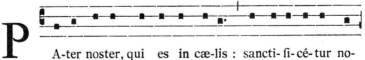

A-ter noster, qui es in cæ-lis : sancti-fi-cé-tur no-

Pater nóster, qui es in caélis:
Father our, who art in heaven:

sanctificétur nómen túum.
sanctified be name your.

Our Father, who art in heaven:

hallowed be thy name:

187

Advéniat régnum túum. **Let come kingdom your.**	**Thy kingdom come.**
Fíat volúntas túa, sicut **Be done will your, as**	**Thy will be done on earth** **as it is in heaven.**
in caélo, et in térra. **in heaven, so on earth.**	
Pánem nóstrum quotidiánum **Bread our daily**	**Give us this day our daily bread.**
da nóbis hódie. **give us today.**	
Et dimítte nóbis débita nóstra, **And forgive us debts our,**	**And forgive us our debts,** **as we forgive our debtors.**
sicut et nos dimíttimus **just as we forgive**	
debitóribus nóstris. **debtors our.**	
Et ne nos indúcas in tentatiónem. **And not us lead into temptation.**	**And lead us not into temptation.**
Sed líbera nos a málo. Amen. **But deliver us from evil one. Amen.**	**But deliver us from the evil one. Amen.**

Known in Latin as the **Pater Noster** ("Our Father") and called the "Lord's Prayer" (*oratio dominica*) because Jesus taught it to his disciples, this model prayer has produced more commentary than any other passage in the Bible and is, after baptism, the most common bond among Christians of every tradition. It consists of an address and seven petitions, the first three of which concern the things of God and the remaining four represent requests for divine assistance for the needs of humanity. The well-known closing line ("For Thine is the kingdom, and the power, and the glory, forever. Amen.") does not appear in the Vulgate or the Douay Version of the Bible. This doxology was used by the Jews at the time of Christ and could be found even earlier in a more elaborate form in I Chronicles 29:11-13. First employed as a liturgical embolismus or addition by Christians in the East, it was gradually introduced into the text of Matthew's gospel by Greek scribes. Two versions of the **Pater Noster** exist: the first is part of the Sermon on the Mount recorded in Matthew 6:9-13, and a shorter and significantly different version is found in Luke 11:2-4.

It was introduced into the liturgy by Pope Gregory I in c.595 A.D. who wrote to John of Syracuse: "We say the Lord's Prayer immediately after the Canon. . . It seems to me very unsuitable that we should say the Canon which an unknown scholar composed over the oblation and that we should not say the prayer handed down by our Redeemer himself over His body and blood." In addition to its place in the Mass, it originally concluded each service of Divine Office where it was said silently until the words *Et ne nos inducas in temptationem* when the priest raised his voice so that the people could respond *Sed libera nos a malo*.

Liturgical context: The **Pater Noster** is recited or sung after the Canon and prior to the Fraction of the Host during the Communion of the Roman Mass; formerly sung by the priest alone, it is now recited or sung by the priest and people. It is also a conspicuous feature of the baptismal liturgy and occurs repeatedly in the Divine Office.

PLORATE FILII ISRAEL

Ploráte	fílii	Israel:	O weep, you sons of Israel!
Weep	**sons**	**of Israel:**	

ploráte	ómnes	vírgines:	Weep, all you virgins, weep!
weep	**all**	**virgins:**	

et	fíliam	Jéphte	unigénitam	For the sake of Jephte's only daughter
and	**daughter**	**of Jephte**	**only-begotten**	sing your song of sorrow:

in	cármine	dolóris:
in	**song**	**of sorrow:**

lamentámini,	lamentámini,	lamentámini.	Bewail, bewail, bewail!
bewail,	**bewail,**	**bewail!**	

The name of Giacomo Carissimi (1605-1674) is almost synonymous with the emergence of the 17th century art form known as *oratorium* or *historia*. The texts of Carissimi's Latin oratorios (*Baltazar, Jephte, Jonas, Judicium Salomonis*) are derived from the Vulgate Bible, either directly quoted or freely paraphrased and adopted. Carissimi, called the "musical orator" of Italy, is best known for his development of the recitative style and the dramatically effective use of the chorus in his oratorios.

Plorate filii Israel is the final six-part chorus from *Jephte*, the story from Judges 11 of Jephte the Giliadite, the banished son of a harlot and prince of a band of robbers who was asked to return to Gilead and lead them in their war with the Ammonites. Jephte agrees and, after unsuccessful negotiations with the Ammonites, they enter into battle, and Jephte makes the following vow to the Lord:

> "If thou wilt deliver the children of Ammon into my hands, Whosoever shall first come forth out of the doors of my house, and shall meet me when I return in peace from the children of Ammon, the same will I offer a holocaust to the Lord. And Jephte passed over to the children of Ammon, to fight against them: and the Lord delivered them into his hands. . .
>
> And when Jephte returned into Maspha to his house, his only daughter met him with timbrels and with dances: for he had no other children. And when he saw her, he rent his garments, and said: Alas! my daughter, thou hast deceived me, and thou thyself art deceived: for I have opened my mouth to the Lord, and I can do no other thing. And she answered him: My father, if thou hast opened thy mouth to the Lord, do unto me whatsoever thou hast promised, since the victory hath been granted to thee, and revenge of thy enemies.
>
> And she said to her father: Grant me only this which I desire: Let me go, that I may go about the mountains for two months, and may bewail my virginity with my companions. And he answered her: Go. And he sent her away for two months. And when she was gone with her comrades and companions, she mourned her virginity in the mountains. And the two months being expired, she returned to her father, and he did to her as he had vowed, and she knew no man.
>
> From thence came a fashion in Israel, and a custom has been kept: That from year to year the daughters of Israel assemble together, and lament the daughter of Jephte the Giliadite for four days." (Judges 11:30-32;34-40)

Vows were not uncommon in Israel (cf. the vow of Jacob – Genesis 28:20-22, the vow of Anna – I Kings [Samuel] 1:11, and that of Absalom – II Kings [Samuel] 15:8). But once made, they were considered binding:

"If any man make a vow to the Lord, or bind himself by an oath: he shall not make his word void but shall fulfill all that he promised." (Numbers 30:3)

"When thou hast made a vow to the Lord thy God, thou shalt not delay to pay it: because the Lord thy God will require it. And if thou delay, it shall be imputed to thee for a sin. If thou wilt not promise, thou shalt be without sin. But that which is once gone out of thy lips, thou shalt observe, and shalt do as thou hast promised to the Lord thy God, and hast spoken with thy own will and with thy own mouth." (Deuteronomy 23:21-23)

Jephte's daughter expecially "bewails her virginity" because the bearing of children was most desirable for women living in Old Testament times. There was always the hope that some child of theirs might be the promised Messiah.

PSALLITE

Psállite   unigénito   Chrísto   Déi   Fílio!
Sing   to only begotten   Christ   of God   Son!

Sing to Christ the only begotten Son of God.
Sing to the Redeemer, our Lord,
the child lying in the manger.

Psállite   Redemptóri   Dómino,
Sing   to Redeemer   Lord,

puérulo,   jacénti   in   praesépio.
child,   lying   in   manger.

Ein kleines   Kindelein   liegt   in dem   Krippelein;
A   small   little child   lies   in   the   small crib;

A little child lies in the small crib;
All the lovely angels serve the child
and sing to him sweetly.

Alle   liebe   Engelein   dienen   dem   Kindelein,
All   lovely   angels   serve   the   little child,

und   singen   ihm   fein.
and   sing   to him   sweetly.

Singt   und   klingt!   Jesu,   Gottes   Kind
Sing   and   ring!   Jesus,   God's   child

Sing and ring! Jesus, the child of God
and Mary's little son!

und   Marien   Söhnelein!
and   Mary's   little son!

Unserm   lieben   Jesulein   im   Krippelein
Our   lovely   little Jesus   in the   little cradle

Our lovely little Jesus in the cradle,
surrounded by little oxen and sheep!

beim   Öchslein   und   beim   Eselein!
with   little oxen   and   with   little sheep!

190

The German composer Michael Praetorius (1571–1621) is generally credited as the composer of this delightful carol which was first published in 1609. The anonymous text (first published in 1582?) exhibits the technique of "farsing" (from *farcire*, to stuff): the interpolation or insertion of the vernacular into set texts, especially liturgical Latin texts. This procedure was sometimes defended as providing a vernacular exposition of the text for the benefit of the laity.

PUER NATUS EST

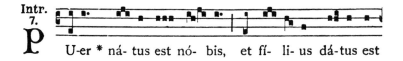

Intr. 7. P U-er * ná- tus est nó- bis, et fí- li- us dá-tus est

I

| Puer | nátus | est | nóbis, | A boy is born to us, |
| **Boy** | **born** | **is** | **to us,** | and a son is given: |

| et | fílius | dátus | est | nóbis: |
| **and** | **son** | **given** | **is** | **to us:** |

| cújus | impérium | super | húmerum | éjus: | whose government is upon his shoulder: |
| **whose** | **government** | **upon** | **shoulder** | **his:** |

| et | vocábitur | nómen | éjus, | and his name shall be called: |
| **and** | **shall be called** | **name** | **his,** | the Angel of great council. |

| mágni | consílii | Angelus. |
| **of great** | **council** | **Angel.** |

II

| Púer | nátus | est | in | Béthlehem, | A boy is born in Bethlehem, |
| **Boy** | **born** | **is** | **in** | **Bethlehem,** | wherefore Jerusalem rejoices, alleluia! |

| unde | gáudet | Jerúsalem, | allelúia. |
| **whence** | **rejoices** | **Jerusalem,** | **alleluia!** |

| Hic | jácet | in | praesépio, | Here lies in a manger, |
| **Here** | **lies** | **in** | **manger,** | he who reigns without end, alleluia! |

| qui | régnat | sine | término, | allelúia. |
| **who** | **reigns** | **without** | **end,** | **alleluia!** |

Réges	de	Sába	véniunt,	The Kings came from Sheba;
Kings	**from**	**Sheba**	**came,**	they offer him gold, frankincense,
				and myrrh, alleluia!

| áurum, | thus, | mýrrham | ófferunt, | allelúia. |
| **gold,** | **incense,** | **myrrh** | **offer,** | **alleluia!** |

| In hoc natáli gáudio, | In this natal joy, |
| **In this natal joy,** | **let us bless the Lord, alleluia!** |

| benedicámus Dómino, allelúia. | |
| **let us bless Lord, alleluia!** | |

| Laudétur sáncta Trínitas, | Let the Holy Trinity be praised, |
| **let be praised Holy Trinity,** | **Let us give thanks to God, alleluia!** |

| Déo dicámus grátias, allelúia. | |
| **To God let us say thanks, alleluia!** | |

I

The custom of having three Masses on Christmas Day dates from the 4th century. The first Mass is said at Midnight, the hour when the Angel appeared to the shepherds and brought the good tidings of the Saviour's birth. The second Mass, the Aurora Mass which is said at dawn, commemorates the Incarnation, the coming of light into a world of darkness ("Blessed is he who comes in the name of the Lord . . . Rejoice greatly, O daughter of Zion . . . thy king cometh.")

The Third Mass of Christmas Day begins with the Introit *Puer natus est* (Isaiah 9:6). Now the emphasis is on the *Puer/Filius* as the "Angel of great counsel" who bears the government upon his shoulder, the unchangeable abiding in a world of change and decay, the one whose salvation and justice have been revealed to the Gentiles and seen by "all the ends of the earth." [see *Viderunt omnes*]

II

The author and composer of the Christmas Carol **Puer natus est** ("A Babe is Born in Bethlehem," "Ein Kind Geborn zu Bethlehem," etc.) are unknown, but it is thought to have come from Germany, Bohemia, or Czechoslovakia about the 14th century.

PUERI HEBRAEORUM

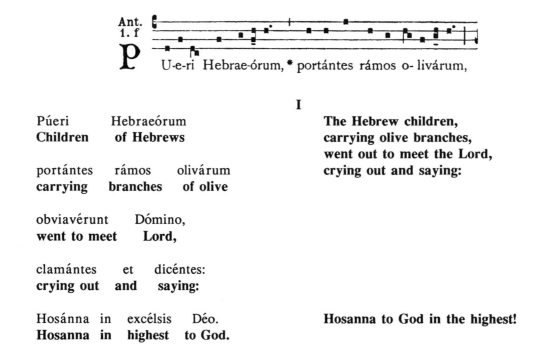

Ant. 1. f
PUe-ri Hebrae-órum, * portántes rámos o-livárum,

I

Púeri Hebraeórum	The Hebrew children,
Children of Hebrews	carrying olive branches,
	went out to meet the Lord,
portántes rámos olivárum	crying out and saying:
carrying branches of olive	

| obviavérunt Dómino, | |
| **went to meet Lord,** | |

| clamántes et dicéntes: | |
| **crying out and saying:** | |

| Hosánna in excélsis Déo. | Hosanna to God in the highest! |
| **Hosanna in highest to God.** | |

Púeri	Hebraeórum			The Hebrew children
Children	**of Hebrews**			spread their garments in his way, and cried out, saying:

vestiménta	prosternébant	in	via,
garments	**spread**	**in**	**way,**

et	clamábant	dicéntes:
and	**cried out**	**saying:**

Hosánna	fílio	Dávid:		Hosanna to the Son of David:
Hosanna	**to Son**	**of David:**		blessed is he who comes in the name of the Lord.

benedíctus	qui	vénit
blessed	**who**	**comes**

in	nómine	Dómini.
in	**name**	**of Lord.**

"And the children of Israel came into Elim, where there were twelve fountains of water, and seventy palm trees: and they encamped by the waters . . . And they set forward from Elim, and all the multitude of the children of Israel came into the desert of Sin, which is between Elim and Sinai . . . And the children of Israel said to [Moses and Aaron]: Would to God we had died by the hand of the Lord in the land of Egypt when we sat over the flesh pots, and ate bread to the full. Why have you brought us into this desert, that you might destroy all the multitude with famine? . . . And Moses and Aaron said to the children of Israel: In the evening you shall know that the Lord hath brought you forth out of the land of Egypt: And in the morning you shall see the glory of the Lord" (Exodus 15:27; 16:1,3,6-7).

These words are from the Lesson for the Blessing of the Palms, a rite which, along with the Procession of the Palms, was customary in Jerusalem as far back as the 4th century. These ceremonies precede the Mass for Palm Sunday, which commemorates Christ's triumphal entry into Jerusalem (*Hosanna!*) just days prior to his betrayal and death.

The two antiphons, **Pueri Hebraeorum portantes** (based on Matthew 21:8-9) and **Pueri Hebraeorum vestimentum** (based on Mark 11:8-10) are sung while the priest distributes the palms to the clergy and laity just prior to the great procession. The *Hosanna* is based on Psalm 117 [118]:26 ("Blessed is he that cometh in the name of the Lord.").

The significance of the palms and olive branches is explained in the prayers of the Blessing of the Palms found in the Roman Missal:

"Bless and sanctify this creature of the olive tree which thou didst cause to spring forth from the substance of the wood, and which the dove, returning to the ark, brought in his mouth: that all who receive it may find protection of soul and body . . .
"Grant, we beseech thee, that the devout hearts of the faithful may understand to their benefit the mystical meaning of that ceremony, when the multitude, by direction from heaven, going this day to meet our Redeemer,

strewed under his feet palms and olive branches: the palms represent his triumph over the prince of death, and the olive branches proclaim in a manner the coming of a spiritual unction. For that pious multitude knew that by them was signified, that our Redeemer, compassionating the misery of mankind, was to fight for the life of the whole world with the prince of death, and to triumph over him by his own death. And, therefore, in that action they made use of such things as might declare, both the triumph of his victory, and the riches of his mercy."

Liturgical context: **Pueri Hebraeorum portantes** and **Pueri Hebraeorum vestimenta** are the two antiphons sung while the priest distributes the palms at the conclusion of the Blessing of the Palms on Palm Sunday morning. The procession of the Palms follows.

QUEM VIDISTIS, PASTORES?

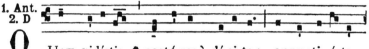

1. Ant.
2. D

Q Uem vidístis, * pastó-res? dí-ci-te : annunti- á-te

| Quem | vidístis, | pastóres, | dícite, | **Whom did you see? Shepherds, tell us!** |
| **Whom** | **did you see,** | **shepherds,** | **tell us,** | **Proclaim to us: who has appeared on the earth?** |

| annunciáte | nóbis, | in térris | quis | appáruit? |
| **proclaim** | **to us,** | **on earth** | **who** | **has appeared?** |

| Nátum | vídimus | et | chóros | angelórum | **We saw the new-born child** |
| **New-born** | **we saw** | **and** | **choirs** | **of angels** | **and choirs of angels praising the Lord.** |

| collaudántes | Dóminum. |
| **praising** | **Lord.** |

| Dícite | quídnam | vidístis? | **Tell us, what have you seen?** |
| **Tell us** | **what** | **have you seen?** | **Announce the Birth of Christ!** |

| et | annunciáte | Chrísti | Nativitátem. |
| **and** | **announce** | **of Christ** | **Birth.** |

Quem vidistis, pastores? would seem to be an imagined dialogue based on the well-known Christmas story found in the second chapter of the Gospel according to St. Luke:

> "And the angel said unto them, Fear not: for, behold, I bring you good tidings of great joy, which shall be to all people. For unto you is born this day in the city of David a Saviour, which is Christ the Lord . . . And suddenly there was with the angel a multitude of the heavenly host praising God, and saying, Glory to God in the highest, and on earth peace, good will towards men" (Luke 2:10-11,13-14). "And when [the shepherds] had seen it, they made know abroad the saying which was told them concerning this child. And all they that heard it wondered at those things which were told them by the shepherds" (Luke 2:17-18).

Liturgical context: **Quem vidistis, pastores?** is the first antiphon for Lauds [see *Angelus ad Pastores*] and the Responsory to the third Lesson of the first Nocturn of Matins of the Nativity.

REGINA COELI

Ant.
6.

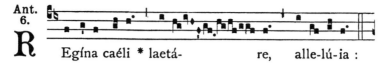

R Egína caéli * laetá- re, alle-lú-ia :

Regína coéli laetáre,	Queen of heaven, rejoice,
Queen of heaven rejoice,	
alleluia:	Alleluia!
Quia quem meruísti portáre,	For He whom you were worthy to bear,
For whom you did merit to bear,	
alleluia,	Alleluia,
Resurréxit,	Has risen,
He has risen,	
sicut dixit,	as He said,
as he said,	
alleluia.	Alleluia!
Ora pro nóbis Déum,	Pray for us to God,
Pray to for us God,	
alleluia.	Alleluia!

Regina coeli is the Marian Antiphon for Paschaltide, from Compline of Holy Saturday [*laetare!*] until None of the Saturday after Pentecost. Note the joyous Easter *Alleluias* that are so generously interspersed with the praises of the Blessed Virgin, the good news of the Resurrection, and the penitent plea for intercession. Since the decree of Pope Benedict XIV in 1742 it has also been used to conclude the *Angelus* in this same season.

It author and composer are unknown, but its earliest appearance is as the Magnificat antiphon for the octave of Easter in a manuscript of the local Roman chant tradition dating from c.1200. Legend has it that Pope Gregory the Great (d.604) heard the first three lines recited by angels on an Easter morning while he walked barefoot in a great religious procession and that he then added the fourth line: *Ora pro nobis Deum. Alleluia.* [see *Alleluia]

Liturgical context: **Regina coeli** is one of the four Marian Antiphons [the others being *Alma Redemptoris Mater, Ave Regina coelorum,* and *Salve Regina*]. It is sung at the conclusion of the hour of Compline during Paschaltide and also at the conclusion of the *Angelus* during this same season.

RESONET IN LAUDIBUS

Résonet   in   láudibus
Let resound   in   praises

Cum   jucúndis   pláusibus
with   joyous   acclaim

Síon   cum   fidélibus:
Zion   with   faithful:

Appáruit   quem   génuit   María.
He has appeared   whom   begot   Mary.

Sunt impléta   quae   praedíxit Gábriel.
Are   fulfilled   which   predicted   Gabriel.

Eja, eja!   Vírgo   Déum   génuit
Joy, joy!   Virgin   God   has begotten

quod   vóluit   cleméntia.
that which   has willed   clemency.

Hódie   appáruit   in   Israel,
Today   has appeared   in   Israel,

per   Maríam   Vírginam
by   Mary   Virgin

est   nátus   Rex.
was   born   King.

Mágnum   nómen   Dómini   Emánuel,
Great   name   of Lord   Emanuel,

quod   annunciátum   est   per   Gábriel.
which   announced   was   by   Gabriel.

Eja,   eja!
Joy,   joy!

**Let Zion resound in praises
with the joyful acclaim of the faithful:**

He whom Mary bore has appeared.

**The prophecies of Gabriel are fulfilled.
O joy, O joy!**

**The Virgin has given birth to God
that which divine mercy willed.**

**Today a king has appeared in Israel,
born of the Virgin Mary.**

**Great is the name of the Lord, Emanuel,
which was announced by Gabriel.
O joy, O joy!**

As is the case with many Christmas Carols that have come down to us from the Middle Ages, the author and composer of **Resonet in laudibus** are unknown. William Studwell (*Christmas Carols*) identifies it as a German carol from the the 13th or 14th century. The English translation by John Mason Neale ("Christ was born on Christmas Day") and the German text (*Joseph, lieber Joseph mein*) that uses the same tune are both well known.

SALVE REGINA

Ant. 1.

Sal-ve, Re-gí- na, máter mi-se-ricórdi- ae :

Sálve Regína, máter misericórdiae: **Hail Queen, Mother of mercy,**	Hail, O Queen, Mother of mercy; our life, our sweetness, and our hope: hail!
Víta, dulcédo, et spes nóstra, sálve. **life, sweetness, and hope our, hail.**	
Ad te clamámus, éxsules fílii Evae. **To you we cry, banished sons of Eve.**	To thee we cry, poor banished children of Eve. To thee we send up our sighs, groaning and weeping in this valley of tears.
Ad te suspirámus, geméntes et fléntes, **To you we sigh, groaning and weeping,**	
in hac lacrimárum válle. **in this of tears valley.**	
Eja ergo, Advocáta nóstra, **Quickly therefore, Advocate our,**	Hasten therefore, our Advocate, and turn your merciful eyes toward us.
íllos túos misericórdes óculos **those your of mercy eyes**	
ad nos convérte. **to us turn.**	
Et Jésum, benedíctum frúctum **And Jesus, blessed fruit**	And show us Jesus, the blessed fruit of your womb, after this exile.
véntris túi, **of womb your,**	
nóbis post hoc exílium osténde. **to us after this exile show.**	
O clémens: O pía: **O merciful, O pious,**	O merciful, O pious, O sweet Virgin Mary.
O dúlcis Vírgo María. **O sweet Virgin Mary.**	

Salve Regina is the Marian Antiphon sung formerly at Vespers during the Pentecost season, beginning with the Saturday before Trinity Sunday and ending with None of the Saturday before the First Sunday of Advent; since 1955, however, it occurs at the conclusion of the hour of Compline from Trinity Sunday through Friday before the First Sunday of Advent.

The author of **Salve Regina** is unknown, but the strongest candidate seems to be Adhemar (d.609), bishop of Le Puy-en-Velay, who is said to have composed it as a processional chant for the Crusades, and indeed there are 12th century references to the **Salve Regina** as the *Antiphona de Podio* ("Antiphon of Puy"). The more common attribution to Hermanus Contractus, monk of Reichenau, is probably erroneous. Legend credits the last two verses, *O clemens . . .*, to the Cistercian monk St. Bernard of Clairvaux (c.1090–1153), but earlier manuscripts with these words argue against this ascription.

Liturgical context: **Salve Regina** is one of the four Marian Antiphons [the others being *Alma Redemptoris Mater, Ave Regina coelorum,* and *Regina coeli*] which was first employed as a processional chant for the Feast of the Assumption (and other processions as well). Long sung at the close of Vespers during the Pentecost season, it now occurs at the close of Compline during that same season.

SICUT CERVUS DESIDERAT

Tract. 8.

Sicut cér- vus * de-sí-de-rat ad fóntes

| Sicut | cérvus | desíderat | | As the hart yearns for the water springs: |
| As | hart | desires | | |

| ad | fóntes | aquárum: | |
| for | springs | of waters: | |

| ita | desíderat | ánima | méa | so longs my soul for thee, O God! |
| so | longs | soul | my | |

| ad | te, | Déus. | |
| for | thee, | God. | |

| Sitívit | | ánima | méa | My soul has thirsted for the living God: |
| Has thirsted | | soul | my | |

| ad | Déum | vívum: | |
| for | God | living: | |

| quando | véniam | et | apparébo | When shall I come and appear before his presence? |
| when | shall I come | and | appear | |

| ante | fáciem | Déi | méi? |
| before | face | of God | my? |

| Fuérunt | míhi | lácrymae | méae | My tears have been my bread by day and also by night, |
| Were | for me | tears | my | |

| pánes | díe | ac | nócte, |
| bread | by day | and | night, |

| dum | dicitur | mihi | quotídie: | while it is said to me daily: Where is your God? |
| while | it is said | to me | daily: | |

| Ubi | est | Déus | túus? |
| Where | is | God | your? |

The service for Holy Saturday was originally a vigil which took place during the night between Saturday and Easter Sunday. The Mass which closes it was said at dawn on Easter Day. *Haec nox est*, "This is the night of which it is written: And the night shall be as the light of day." This was also the night on which the catechumens received Holy Baptism, the culmination of their initiation and the seven scrutinies which take place during the preceding forty days of Lent. It was also the occasion when the faithful recalled their own baptism.

Profound symbolism permeates the rites of this ancient liturgy: the blessing of the fire (the new fire that brings new light, the lighting of the Paschal candle, and the burning of incense); the singing of the magnificent *Exultet*; the reading of the twelve Prophecies from the Old Testament; the blessing of the water and the baptismal font; the Litanies of the Saints; and the concluding liturgy of the Mass that, on this day, is immediately followed by the Vespers which are reduced to their essential elements and recited following the Communion of the Mass.

Sicut cervus is the Tract sung during the procession to the baptismal font, following the Collect which concludes the twelfth and final Prophecy: "Almighty and eternal God ... *increase the desires* of thy people, since none of the faithful can advance to any virtue without thy inspiration."

Sicut cervus <u>desiderat</u> ad fontes aquarum ...

In the ancient preface for the blessing of the font which follows the symbolism of the water is made clear: "May it be a living fountain, a regenerating water, a purifying stream: that all those that are to be washed in this saving bath may obtain, by the operation of the Holy Ghost, the grace of a perfect purification." The "creature of water" is then blessed

> *in the name of God* "who in the beginning separated thee by his word from the dry land, whose spirit moved over thee. Who made thee flow from the fountain of paradise and commanded thee to water the whole earth with thy four rivers. Who, changing thy bitterness in the desert into sweetness, made thee fit to drink, and produced thee out of a rock to quench the thirst of the people."
> *and in the name of Christ his only Son* "who in Cana of Galilee changed thee into wine, by a wonderful miracle of his power. Who walked on thee dry foot, and was baptized in thee by John in the Jordan. Who made thee flow out of his side together with his blood, and commanded his disciples that such as believed should be baptized in thee, saying: Go teach all nations, baptizing them in the name of the Father, and of the Son, and of the Holy Ghost."
> *The priest later continues*: "Bless these clear waters: that besides their natural virtue of cleansing the body, they may also be effectual for purifying of the soul." Here the priest plunges the Paschal Candle in the water, three times, singing each time on a higher tone: "May the virtue of the Holy Ghost descend into all the water of this font ... and make the whole substance of this water fruitful, and capable of regenerating."

As the hart seeks the pure waters of the spring, the source of the flowing stream, so the heart seeks the purifying, regenerating waters of the spirit, the living stream, the fountain of life. One closing thought: Could *Sicut cervus / servus desiderat* possibly have had the same homonymic association in the original Latin as "hart / heart" does in English?

STABAT MATER

Séq.
2.

S Tábat Má-ter do-lorósa   Juxta crúcem lacrimósa,

Stábat	Máter	dolorósa
Stood	**Mother**	**grieving**

There stood the Mother grieving,
Beside the cross weeping,
While on it hung her Son.

Juxta	crúcem	lacrymósa,
next to	**cross**	**weeping,**

Dum	pendébat	Fílius.
while	**hung**	**Son.**

Cújus	ánimam	geméntem,
whose	**soul**	**sighing,**

Whose saddened soul,
Sighing and suffering,
A sword pierced through.

5
Contristátam	et	doléntem,
saddened	**and**	**suffering,**

Pertransívit	gládius.
pierced through	**sword.**

O	quam	trístis	et	afflícta
O	**how**	**sad**	**and**	**afflicted**

O how sad and how afflicted
Was that blessed Mother
Of the Only–Begotten!

Fúit	ílla	benedícta
was	**that**	**blessed**

Máter	unigéniti!
Mother	**of Only–begotten!**

10
Quae	moerébat	et	dolébat,
Who	**was grieving**	**and**	**was suffering,**

Loving Mother, who was grieving
And suffering, while she beheld
The torments of her glorious Son.

Pía	Máter,	dum	vidébat
loving	**Mother,**	**while**	**she beheld**

Náti	poénas	íncliti.
of Son	**torments**	**glorious.**

200

Quis est hómo qui non fléret,
Who is man who not would weep,

Mátrem Chrísti si vidéret
Mother of Christ if he should see

15 In tánto supplício?
in so much distress?

Who is the man who would not weep
If he should see the Mother of Christ
In such great distress?

Quis non pósset contristári,
Who not can be saddened,

Chrísti Mátrem contemplári
of Christ Mother to behold

Doléntem cum Fílio?
suffering with Son?

Who could not be saddened
If he should behold the Mother of Christ
Suffering with her only Son?

Pro peccátis súae géntis
For sins of his people

20 Vídit Jésum in torméntis,
she saw Jesus in torments,

Et flagéllis súbditum.
and whips subjected to.

For the sins of his people,
She saw Jesus in torments
And subjected to stripes.

Vídit súum dúlcem nátum
She saw her sweet begotten

Moriéndo desolátum,
(by)dying forsaken,

Dum emísit spíritum.
while he sent forth spirit.

She saw her own sweet Son,
Whose dying caused his desolation,
While he yielded up his Spirit.

25 Eja   Máter,   fons   amóris,
Oh   Mother,   fount   of love,

Me   sentíre   vim   dolóris
me   to feel   force   of grief

Fac,   ut   técum   lúgeam.
Make,   that   with you   I may mourn.

Fac,   ut   árdeat   cor   méum
Grant,   that   may burn   heart   my

In   amándo   Chrístum   Déum,
in   loving   Christ   God,

30 Ut   síbi   compláceam.
that   to him   I may be pleasing.

Oh Mother, fount of love,
Make me feel the force of your grief,
So that I may mourn with you,

Grant that my heart may burn
In loving Christ my God,
So that I may be pleasing to him.

Sáncta   Máter,   ístud   ágas,
Holy   Mother,   this   may you do,

Crucifíxi   fíge   plágas
of Crucified   fix   stripes

Córdi   méo   válide.
in heart   my   firmly.

Túi   náti   vulneráti,
Of your   begotten   wounded,

35 Tam   dignáti   pro   me   páti,
so   deigned   for   me   to suffer,

Poénas   mécum   dívide.
pains   with me   share.

Holy Mother, may you do this:
Fix the stripes of the Crucified
Deeply into my heart.

Share with me the pains
Of your wounded Son
Who deigned to suffer so much for me.

Fac   me   técum   píe   flére,
Make   me   with you   lovingly   to weep,

Crucifíxo   condolére,
with Crucified   to suffer,

Donec   égo   vixéro.
as long as   I   shall live.

40 Júxta   crúcem   técum   stáre,
Next to   cross   with you   to stand,

Et   me   tíbi   sociáre
and   myself   with you   to join

In   plánctu   desídero.
in   lament   I desire.

Make me lovingly weep with you,
To suffer with the Crucified
So long as I shall live.

To stand with you beside the cross,
And to join with you in deep lament:
This I long for and desire.

Vírgo   vírginum   praeclára,
Virgin   of virgins   most excellent,

Míhi   jam   non   sis   amára,
to me   now   not   be   bitter,

45 Fac   me   técum   plángere.
cause   me   with you   to mourn.

Fac,   ut   pórtem   Christi   mortem,
Grant,   that   I may bear   of Christ   death,

Passiónis   fac   consórtem,
of passion   make   sharer,

Et   plágas   recólere.
And   stripes   to be mindful of.

O Virgin all virgins excelling,
Be not inclement with me now;
Cause me to mourn with you.

Grant that I may bear the death of Christ;
Make me a sharer in His Passion
And ever mindful of his wounds.

Fac   me   plágis   vulnerári,
Make   me   by wounds   to be wounded,

50 Fac   me   crúce   inebriári,
cause   me   by cross   to be inebriated,

Et   cruóre   Fílii.
and   by blood   of Son.

Flámmis   ne   úrar   succénsus
By flames   lest   I burn   enkindled

Per   te,   Vírgo,   sim   defénsus
through thee,   Virgin,   may I be   defended

In   díe   judícii.
on   day   of judgement.

**Let me be wounded by His wounds,
Cause me to be inebriated by the Cross
And the Blood of your Son.**

**Lest I burn in flames enkindled,
May I, through thee, O Virgin,
Be defended on Judgement Day.**

55 Chríste,   cum   sit   hinc   exíre,
Christ,   when   it is   hence   to go,

Da   per   Mátrem   me   veníre
grant   through   Mother   me   to come

Ad   pálmam   victóriae.
to   palm   of victory.

**O Christ, when from here I must depart,
Grant that, through your Mother,
I may obtain the palm of victory.**

Quándo   córpus   moriétur,
When   body   shall die,

Fac,   ut   ánimae   donétur
Grant,   that   to soul   be given

60 Paradísi   glória.
of Paradise   glory.

**When my body perishes,
Grant that my soul be given
the glory of Paradise.**

The question of the authorship of this great sequence is still unresolved. It has been variously ascribed to Pope Gregory the Great (d.604), to St. Bernard of Clairvaux (d.1153), to Pope Innocent III (d.1216), to St. Bonaventura (d.1274), to Jacobus de Benedictus (Jacopone – d.1306), to Pope John XXII (d.1334), to Pope Gregory XI (d.1378), etc. James Mearns carefully considers the two most probable candidates, Innocent III and Jacopone, in his article in Julian's *Dictionary of Hymnology* (1915). Mearns feels that the ascriptions to Innocent III by Pope Benedict XIV, F.E. von Hurter, and Mone are strengthened by the "the great probability" that Innocent III was also the author of *Veni Sancte Spiritus*, and therefore capable of such depth of expression and pathos as is found in the *Stabat Mater dolorosa*; but recent scholarship has shown that the "most probable" author of *Veni Sancte Spiritus* is Stephen Langton, Archbishop of Canterbury (d. 1228) [see *Veni Sancte Spiritus*]. Mearns also points out that "certain of the expressions in stanzas vi–ix of the *dolorosa* have been thought to refer to the Stigmatisation of St. Francis of Assissi, the inference being drawn that the hymn was by a Franciscan. This, if true, would make it impossible that at least the current form should be by Pope Innocent III, for he died in 1216, and the date commonly assigned to the conferring of the Stigmas on St. Francis is Sept. 15, 1224."

The candidacy of Jacopone is more complex [the reader is again referred to Mearns' article]; but in summary one can say that (1) Mearns' conclusion that it is more likely that Jacopone wrote the *Stabat Mater speciosa* and not the **Stabat Mater dolorosa**, if indeed he wrote any Latin hymns at all [!], and (2) Mone's opinion that "the original form was by Pope Innocent III and that Jacopone may have made alterations and additions [i.e., those stanzas that are thought to refer to the Stigmatisation of St. Francis, being as Jacopone was a Franciscan] seem to be distinct possibilities.

In any case, the **Stabat Mater** was popularized by the 14th century when the Flagellants used to sing it on their travels from town to town, but it was much later that it found its way into the Roman liturgy. It was the Servites ("Servants of Mary") who in 1239 first devoted themselves to the sorrows of Mary standing under the Cross; later, a synod in Cologne (1413) established the *Compassio*, or *Commendatio, Lamentatio B.M.V.*, a devotion to the sorrows of Mary during the Crucifixion and Death of Christ, to atone for the crimes of the Hussites. This feast of the Compassion gradually spread over Europe until, in 1727, Pope Benedict XIII extended it to the universal Church under the title *Septem Dolorum BMV* ("The Seven Sorrows of the Blessed Virgin Mary") which was celebrated on the Friday after Passion Sunday. It was at this time that the singing of the **Stabat Mater** was added to both the Mass and Office of this feast. Later, in 1814, Pius VII established a second feast of the Dolours on the third Sunday of September, now September 15.

The enumeration of the Seven Sorrows of Mary's life is said to have evolved from the devotions of the Servites. They are: Simeon's prophecy (Luke 2:34–35), the flight into Egypt (Matthew 2:13–15), the three days' loss of the Holy Child at Jerusalem (Luke 2:41–50), meeting Christ carrying the Cross to Calvary, standing at the foot of the Cross (John 19:25–27), the descent of Christ from the Cross, and the entombment of Christ.

"The *Stabat Mater* is universally recognized as the tenderest and most pathetic hymn of the Middle Ages. In simple and vivid language, which cannot always be reproduced in prose, it represents the Mother of the Redeemer plunged in grief and weeping beneath the Cross on which He was suffering an unmerited and agonizing death. The historical event is narrated in the first, second, and fourth stanzas. The remaining strophes are made up of reflections, affections, petitions, and resolutions arising from the contemplation of Our Lord's bitter sufferings and death" (Britt, *Hymns of the Breviary and Missal*).

The early Notkerian sequences (Notker Balbulus, c.840–912) were basically unrhymed and of irregular meter. The **Stabat Mater**, however, has the verse form of the later metrical sequence which was brought to perfection by Adam of St. Victor: a regular meter (double versicles or couplets of 887 trochaic meter) and a consistent rhyme scheme of *aab ccb* which scholars date as coming from the latter half of the 12th century.

But it is its "pathos, its vividness of description, its devotional sweetness and unction" (H.T. Henry) that secures "the queen of sequences" (Daniel) its place in hearts and history. Schaff (*Literature and Poetry*) suggests that "the secret of the power of *Mater dolorosa* lies in the intensity of feeling with which the poet identifies himself with his theme, and in the soft, plaintive melody of its Latin rhythm and thyme, which cannot be transferred to any other language." And, in summation, James Mearns (in Julian, *Dictionary of Hymnology*) states that "this noble poem . . . has been, not unjustly, styled the most pathetic hymn of the Middle Ages. The vividness with which it pictures the weeping Mother at the Cross, its tenderness, its beauty of rhythm, its melodious double rhymes almost defying reproduction in another language, and its impressiveness when sung either to the fine plainsong melody or in the noble compositions which many of the great masters of music have set to it, go far to justify the place it holds, and has long held, in the Roman Catholic Church."

The text of the **Stabat Mater** is based on various passages from the Holy Scriptures: John 19:25, Luke 2:35, Zacharias 13:6, II Corinthians 4:10, and Galatians 6:17.

1. *Stabat Mater.*

"Now there were standing by the cross of Jesus his mother and his mother's sister, Mary of Cleophas, and Mary Magdalene. When Jesus, therefore, saw his mother and the disciple standing by, whom he loved [John; see John 13:23], he said to his mother: Woman, behold, thy son" (John 19:25-26).

6. *Pertransivit gladius.*

In accordance with the Law of Moses (Leviticus 12:1-8) Mary and Joseph took Jesus to the temple to present him and their sacrifice to the Lord. There they met Simeon, who was told by the Holy Spirit "that he should not see death before he had seen Christ the Lord." Mary, "marvelling" at the prophecy of Simeon's canticle (the *Nunc dimittis*, Luke 2:29-32), is then told by him: "Behold, this child is destined for the fall and for the rise of many in Israel, and for a sign that shall be contradicted. *And thine own soul a sword shall pierce*, that the thoughts of many hearts may be revealed." Is not this last phrase the effect of the pathos of this great poem and its musical settings?

19. *Pro peccatis suae gentis.*

"And she shall bring forth a son, and thou shall call his name Jesus; for he shall save his people from their sins" (Matthew 1:21).

20. *tormentis et flagellis.*

All four Gospels record the history of Christ's Passion. See Matthew 26-27, Mark 14-15, Luke 22-23, and John 18-19.

23. *desolatum.*

Betrayed by Judas, thrice denied by Peter, scourged and beaten by his captors, mocked and crucified, forsaken by all, even his Father: "My God, my God, why hast thou forsaken me?" (Matthew 27:46) "Despised and rejected, a man of sorrows, and acquainted with grief" (Isaiah 53:3).

24. *emisit spiritum.*

See Matthew 27:50 and John 19:30. Christ "gave up" or yielded up his spirit willfully. "The Father loves me because I lay down my life that I may take it up again. No one takes it from me, but I lay it down myself."

32. *plagas.*

Zacharias foretold of these wounds: "And they shall say to him: What are these wounds in the midst of thy hands? And he shall say: With these I was wounded in the house of them that loved me" (Zacharias 13:6). And Isaiah spoke of their healing power: "And with these stripes we are healed" (Isaiah 53:5). "Henceforth let no man trouble me: for I bear the marks of the Lord Jesus in my body" (Galatians 6:17).

46. *portem Christi mortem.*

"We endure persecution, but we are not forsaken; we are cast down, but we do not perish; always bearing about in our body the dying of Jesus, so that the life also of Jesus may be made manifest in our bodily frame" (II Corinthians 4:9-10).

50. *inebriari.*

Literally, "inebriated," filled to overflowing, "spiritually intoxicated"; said of the abundant goodness of God: "They shall be inebriated with the plenty of thy house: and thou shalt make them to drink of the torrent of thy pleasure" (Psalm 35 [36]:9).

52. *Flammis ne urar succensus.*

The translation retains the fervor of the redundant repetition of this pleonasm. This is the reason for the plea to the sorrowful Mother for intercession on Judgement Day.

55. *Christe.*

A dramatic change of address. Up to now the sorrows of the Mother and the suffering and torments of her Son have been described and she has been the object of address and appeal; and now, mindful of the *flammis* and *die judicii*, the penitent poet addresses Christ himself, considers the final moment of his mortality and asks that, through the Blessed Mother's intercession that his soul be given the *palmam victoriae*, eternal life in *gloria Paradisi.*

Liturgical context: **Stabat Mater dolorosa** is one of the five great sequences [the others being *Dies irae, Lauda Sion, Veni Sancte Spiritus,* and *Victimae paschali laudes*]. It was not one of the four to survive the reforms of the Council of Trent (1545-1563), but it was restored to the Mass in 1727. It is the sequence for the Mass for the two feasts of the Seven Sorrows of the Blessed Virgin Mary (*Septem Dolorum BMV*): the first on the Friday after Passion Sunday (the feast of the Compassion) and the second on September 15; it follows the Tract *O vos omnes* ("O all you that pass by the way, behold and see if there be any sorrow like unto my sorrow."). In Divine Office it is appointed as the "Hymn of the Compassion of the Blessed Virgin Mary" for use in Lent and as a hymn for the Friday after Passion Sunday, divided into three parts: *Stabat Mater dolorosa* (Vespers), *Sancta Mater, istud agas* (Matins), and *Virgo virginum praeclara* (Lauds).

SUPER FLUMINA BABYLONIS

Offert.
1.
S Uper flúmi- na * Baby- ló-

1 Super flúmina Babylónis,
   By streams of Babylon,

   By the streams of Babylon
   we sat down and we wept
   when we remembered you, O Zion.

   illic sédimus et flévimus,
   there we sat and we wept,

   dum recordarémur túi, Síon.
   when we remembered you, Zion.

2 In salícibus in médio éjus,
   Among willows in midst its,

   Among the willows on its banks
   we hung our harps;

   suspéndimus órgana nóstra;
   we hung instruments our;

3 quia íllic interrogavérunt nos,
   for there they asked us,

   for there they who have taken us captive
   asked us the words of our songs;

   qui captívos duxérunt nos,
   who captive have taken us,

   vérba cantiónum; et qui abdúxerunt nos:
   words of songs; and who have wasted us:

   they who had wasted us said:
   Sing a hymn for us from the songs of Zion.

   Hýmnum cantáte nóbis de cánticis Síon.
   Hymn sing for us from songs of Zion.

4 Quomodo cantábimus cánticum Dómini
   How shall we sing song of Lord

   How shall we sing the Lord's song
   in a strange land?

   in térra aliéna?
   in land strange?

Elegia de miseriis exilii
The lamentation of the people of God
in their captivity in Babylon

The superscription from the Vulgate and the Douay Version of the Bible immediately place Psalm 136 [137] in its historical context.

"As a human document the psalm is priceless. It is unparalleled for its realistic analysis of the emotions of a vanquished nation. The bitterness and the vindictiveness of the closing lines appear natural when it is remembered that the poet and his fellow-captives had lost all that was dear to them, all that made life worth while -- home and country." (M. Buttenwieser, *The Psalms*)

The texts for the Mass of the 20th Sunday after Pentecost can be read as beautifully appointed commentaries and elucidations of **Super flumina Babylonis**, the Offertory text for the day. The Introit from Daniel 3:27-30 is Azarias' prayer of praise offered as Shadrach, Meschach, and Abednego are cast into Nebuchadnezzar's fiery furnace: "All that thou hast done to us, O Lord, thou hast done in true judgement; because we have sinned against thee, and we have not obeyed thy commandments." The Lesson for the day contrasts the hedonistic Babylonians with the spiritual pursuits of the Hebrews: "And be not drunk with wine, wherein is luxury: but be ye filled with the Holy spirit, speaking to yourselves in psalms and hymns, and spiritual canticles, singing and making melody in your hearts to the Lord: giving thanks always for all things." (Ephesians 5:18-19)

The Gradual which follows speaks of maintaining hope during times of estrangement and despair: "The eyes of all hope in thee, O Lord; and thou givest them their meat in due season." (Psalm 144 [145] : 15) The lament of the Offertory **Super flumina Babylonis** is later followed by the appropriate prayer of the Communion: "Be mindful of thy word to thy servant, O Lord, in which thou hast given me hope; *this has comforted me in my humiliation*." (Psalm 118 [119] : 49-50)

Notes:

1. *flumina.*

Streams, rivers -- "by which is implied the Euphrates, its tributaries, and the network of canals which irrigated the whole valley" (E.J. Kissane); "an intensive plural" which refers to the river Euphrates (M. Buttenwieser).

1. *illic sedimus.*

"Say to the king, and to the queen: Humble yourselves, sit down: for the crown of your glory is come down from your head. The cities of the south are shut up and there is none to open them: All Juda is carried away captive with an entire captivity." (Jeremias 13:18-19)

1. *dum recordaremur tui, Sion . . . flevimus.*

Surrounded by the heathenism of Babylon, exiled, homeless, and without hope, Israel remembers the spirituality, the glory, the festivities and joyous songs of Sion -- and weeps a river of tears. "Behold the days come, saith the Lord, and I will send forth a famine into the land: not a famine of bread, nor a thirst of water, but of hearing the word of the Lord." (Amos 8:11)

2. *In salicibus . . . suspendimus organa nostra.*

The first line is a pleonasm, redundancy which gives intensity to the image of the silent harps hanging in the willows, an ancient symbol of sorrow and desolation.

3. *qui captivos duxerunt nos . . .*

Victors often require captives to entertain them with songs and play: "And the princes of the Philistines assembled together, to offer great sacrifices to Dagon their god, and to make merry, saying: Our god hath delivered our enemy Samson into our hands . . . And rejoicing in their feasts, when they had now taken their good cheer, they commanded that Samson should be called and should play before them. And being brought out of prison he played before them, and they made him stand between two pillars." (Judges 16:23,25)

4. *Quomodo cantabimus?*

"Not that they would have thought it a profanation but rather that to sing them would have seemed a mockery, for the world of belief told of in these songs had ceased to be, even as had their country." (Buttenwieser)

SURGE ILLUMINARE

Súrge illumináre Jerúsalem,   Arise, be enlightened, O Jerusalem,
Arise   be enlightened   Jerusalem,   for your light is come,

quia   vénit   lúmen túum,
because   is come   light   your,

et   glória   Dómini   and the glory of the Lord
and   glory   of Lord   is risen upon you.

super   te   órta   est.
upon   you   risen   is.

Quia écce   ténebrae   opérient térram,   For behold, darkness shall cover the earth,
For behold   darkness   shall cover   earth,   and a gloom shall come over the people:

et   calígo   pópulos:
and   gloom   peoples:

super   te   áutem   oriétur   Dóminus,   But the Lord shall arise upon you,
upon   you   however   shall rise   Lord,   and his glory shall be seen upon you.

et   glória   éjus   in   te   vidébitur.
and   glory   his   upon you   shall be seen.

Dies sanctificatus illuxit nobis
A holy day has dawned for us,
today a great light has descended to earth.

Surge illuminare. This familiar text from Isaiah 60:1-3 is probably best known from its solo settings in Handel's *Messiah*, but its rich contrasting images have inspired other composers as well (*N.B. surge* [see Palestrina and Byrd], *lumen, orta est, tenebrae, orietur, gloria ejus*). Note also: *illuminare*, be enlightened (not "shine"); and *caligo*, mist, fog, gloom, darkness, affliction.

On the island of Patmos in c. 96 A.D. St. John the Evangelist set down a similar vision of the new Jerusalem:

"And I saw a new heaven and a new earth . . . And I saw the holy city, New Jerusalem, coming down out of heaven from God . . . And the city has no need of the sun or moon to shine upon it. For the glory of God shall light it, and the Lamb is the light thereof. And the nations shall walk by the light thereof; and the kings of the earth shall bring their glory and honour into it" (Apocalypse [Revelation] 21 : 1-2, 23-24).

Haec dies quam fecit Dominus
This is the day which the Lord has made;
let us rejoice exceedingly and be glad in it.

SURGENS JESUS

S Urgens Je-sus Dó- mi-nus no- ster, stans in mé-

Surgens Jesus Domínus noster:
Rising Jesus Lord our,

stans in médio discipulórum suórum;
standing in midst of disciples his,

Dixit: "Pax vobis." Alleluia.
said: "Peace to you." Alleluia!

Gavísi sunt discipuli viso Dómino.
Rejoice did disciples at sight of Lord.

Allelúia.
Alleluia!

**Rising (from the dead), Jesus our Lord,
standing in the midst of his disciples,
said: "Peace be unto you." Alleluia!**

**The disciples rejoiced at the sight of the Lord.
Alleluia!**

This short motet text is derived from the following passage in the Gospel of St. John:

> "When it was late that same day, the first of the week, though the
> doors where the disciples gathered had been closed for fear of the Jews,
> Jesus came and stood in the midst and said to them, Peace be to you!
> And when he had said this, he showed them his hands and his side. The
> disciples therefore rejoiced at the sight of the Lord." (John 20:19-20)

Having first appeared to Mary Magdalen at the tomb (John 20:11-18), the risen Christ then manifested himself to his chosen Apostles. Eight days later he appeared again to them and convinced even the doubting Thomas that he was indeed the crucified Christ. (John 20:24-29) This epilogue follows:

> "Many other signs also Jesus worked in the sight of his disciples,
> which are not written in this book. But these are written that you may believe
> that Jesus is the Christ, the Son of God, and that believing you may have life in
> his name." John 20:30-31)

Liturgical context: **Surgens Jesus** is a motet for Paschaltide, especially the forty joyous days from Easter Sunday to the Feast of the Ascension.

SURREXIT PASTOR BONUS

S Urré-xit Pastor bo- nus, qui ánimam su-am pó-

				The good Shepherd has risen,
Surréxit	pástor	bónus,		he who laid down his life for his sheep,
Has risen	**Shepherd**	**good,**		
qui	ánimam	súam	pósuit	
who	**life**	**his**	**laid down**	
pro	óvibus	súis,		
for	**sheep**	**his,**		
et	pro	grége	súo,	who, for his flock, deigned to die.
and	**for**	**flock**	**his,**	**Alleluia!**
móri	dignátus est.	Allelúia.		
to die	**deemed it worthy.**	**Alleluia!**		

"For thus saith the Lord God: ... I will visit my sheep, and will deliver them out of the places where they have been scattered in the cloudy and dark day ... I will save my flock." (Ezechiel 34:11,12,22)

"He was wounded for our iniquities, he was bruised for our sins. The chastisement of our peace was upon him, and by his stripes are we healed ... He was offered because it was his own will ... If he shall lay down his life for sin, he shall see a long-lived seed, and the will of the Lord shall be prosperous in the land." (Isaiah 53:5,7,10)

"Greater love hath no man than this, that he lay down his life." (John 15:13) Thus all Christians, filled with gratutude in the joyous Eastertide season, give thanks and say: *Alleluia!*

TANTUM ERGO

5. Antum ergo Sacraméntum Vene-rémur cérnu-i :

Tántum ergo Sacraméntum
So great therefore Sacrament

Venerémur cérnui:
let us venerate bowing low;

Et antíquum documéntum
And ancient document

Nóvo cédat rítui:
New give way to rite:

Praéstet fídes suppleméntum
Furnish faith assistance

Sénsuum deféctui.
of senses to deficiency.

Genitóri, Genitóque
To Begetter, to Begotten,

Laus et jubilátio,
praise and jubilation,

Sálus, hónor, vírtus quoque
salvation, honor, power also

Sit et benedíctio:
be also blessing:

Procedénti ab utróque
To proceeding from both

Cómpar sit laudátio.
equal be praise.

Let us therefore, bowing low,
Venerate so great a Sacrament;
And let the old Law
Give way to the new rite;
Let faith afford assistance
To the deficiency of the senses.

To the Begetter and the Begotten
Let there be praise and jubilation,
Salvation and honor,
And power and blessing;
And to the One proceeding from both
Let there be equal praise.

Tantum ergo is a portion of St. Thomas Aquinas' hymn **Pange lingua – corporis** which was written c.1264 at the request of Pope Urban IV for use in the institution of the new Feast of Corpus Christi ("Body of Christ"). [see *O sacrum convivium*] The fifth stanza and the closing doxology form a separate hymn which has been prescribed for the Benediction of the Blessed Sacrament, a devotion consisting of the exposition of the Sacred Host on the altar, the singing of appropriate Eucharistic hymns [**Tantum ergo** is the only hymn specifically required], and a blessing with the sacred host.

The concluding doxology borrows *Genitori Genitoque* and *Procedenti ab utroque* from a Pentecost sequence of Adam of St. Victor. H.T. Henry, in the *Catholic Dictionary*, cites also a stanza of a sequence in honor of St. Agnes from Dreves' *Analecta hymnica:*

Genitori Genitoque
Psallat nostra concio;
Procedenti ab utroque
Compar sit laudatio;
Virginalis ipsum quoque
Laudet benedictio.

Concerning the appropriateness of musical settings of traditional texts, Pius X states in his Instruction on Sacred Music (1903): "In the hymns of the Church the traditional form of the hymn is to be preserved. It is not lawful, therefore, to compose, for instance, a *Tantum ergo* in such wise that the first strophe presents a *romanza*, a *cavatina*, an *adagio*, and the *Genitori* an *allegro*."

Notes:

Sacramentum.

The Holy Eucharist, the Lord's Supper. The Feast of Corpus Christi commemorates Christ's first institution of this Sacrament with his disciples on the eve of his crucifixion and death.

antiquum documentum . . . ritui.

The ancient document is the Old Law of the Jewish Passover which is become the new rite of the Christian Church; the sacrificial Passover Lamb is now the Lamb of God (*Agnus Dei*), the single redeeming sacrifice for all sinners; the Passover Meal of the immolated lamb, unleavened bread and wild lettuce is now the Blessed Sacrament in which the true bread and wine are consecrated into the Body and Blood of Christ.

Sensuum defectui.

If the doctrine of Transubstantiation is difficult for the senses to comprehend, if they see only the outward appearances of the bread and wine and not the Real Presence beneath each species, then <u>faith</u> must afford assistance; when sense is lost in mystery, faith alone confirms; or in Caswell's translation, which, as Dr. Neale (*Medieval Hymns*) points out, is "unshackled by rhyme" and "nearest" to the original Latin: "Faith for all defect supplying / When the feeble senses fail."

St. Thomas makes this point earlier in the hymn when he states: *Ad firmandum cor sincerum / Sola fides sufficit* (Faith alone suffices to assure a sincere heart") and also in his other great Eucharistic hymn *Lauda Sion*: *Quod non capis, quod non vides / Animosa firmat fides* ("What you don't understand, what you don't see, a lively faith confirms").

Genitori Genitoque . . . Procedenti ab utroque.

Father, Son, . . . and the Holy Spirit, the one proceeding from <u>both</u> (the Nicene Creed: *Qui cum Patre et Filio procedit* -- "Who proceeds from the Father <u>and</u> the Son") -- thus the schism of East and West.

214

TE DEUM

Hymn. 3.

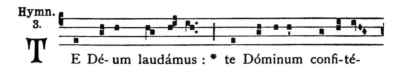

T E Dé-um laudámus : * te Dóminum confi-té-

1 Te   Déum   laudámus:
   Thee   God   we praise:

   te   Dóminum   confitémur.
   thee Lord   we acknowledge.

2 Te   aetérnum Pátrem
   Thee eternal   Father

   ómnis   térra   venerátur.
   all   earth   venerates.

3 Tíbi   ómnes   Angeli,
   To thee   all   Angels,

   tíbi   Caéli   et   univérsae Potestátes,
   to thee Heavens and   all   Powers,

4 tíbi   Chérubim et   Séraphim
   to thee Cherubim and Seraphim

   incessábili   vóce   proclámant:
   never ceasing   with voice   proclaim:

5 Sánctus: Sánctus: Sánctus:
   Holy,   Holy,   Holy,

   Dóminus Déus   Sábaoth.
   Lord   God   of Hosts.

6 Pléni   sunt   coéli   et   térra
   Full   are   heavens and earth

   majestátis glóriae   túae.
   majesty   of glory   thy.

7 Te   gloriósus Apostulórum chórus,
   Thee   splendid   of Apostles   chorus,

8 te   Prophetárum laudábilis númerus,
   Thee of Prophets   venerable   members,

9 te   Mártyrum candidátus láudat exércitus.
   Thee of Martyrs shining-robed praises army.

We praise thee, O God;
we acknowledge thee to be the Lord.

All the earth doth worship thee,
the Father everlasting.

To thee all Angels,
the Heavens, and all the Powers,

the Cherubim and Seraphim
proclaim without ceasing:

Holy, Holy, Holy,
Lord God of Hosts!
The heavens and the earth are full
of the majesty of thy glory.

The glorious chorus of the Apostles,
the admirable company of the Prophets,
the white-robed army of Martyrs praises thee.

10 Te   per   órbem   terrárum   Throughout the whole world
   Thee throughout whole of world   the holy Church gives praise to thee,
   sáncta confitétur Ecclésia: the Father of infinite majesty;
   holy   confesses   church,

11 Pátrem   imménsae majestátis:
   Father   of infinite   majesty;

12 Venerándum túum vérum, et únicum Fílium: they praise your admirable, true,
   Admirable   your true, and only   Son;   and only Son;
                                                           and also the Holy Spirit, our Advocate.

13 Sánctum quoque Paráclitum Spíritum.
   Holy   also   Paraclete   Spirit.

14 Tu   Rex   glóriae, Chríste.   You are the King of glory, O Christ.
   You King of glory,   Christ.   You are the eternal Son of the Father.

15 Tu   Pátris   sempitérnus es Fílius.
   You of Father   eternal   are   Son.

16 Tu   ad   liberándum susceptúrus hóminem,   To deliver us, you became human,
   You for   delivering   became   man,   and did not disdain the Virgin's womb.

   non   horruísti Vírginis úterum.
   not   disdain   of Virgin womb.

17 Tu   devícto   mórtis   acúleo,   Having blunted the sting of death, You
   You having blunted of death   sting,   opened the kingdom of heaven to all believers.

   aperuísti   credéntibus   régna   coelórum.
   you opened   to believing kingdom of heavens.

18 Tu   ad déxteram Déi   sédes,   You sit at the right hand of God,
   You at   right   of God you sit,   in the glory of the Father.

   in   glória   Pátris.
   in   glory   of Father.

19 Júdex   créderis   ésse   ventúrus.   You are believed to be the Judge
   Judge you are believed   to be   to come.   who will come.

20 Te   ergo   quaésumus,   Therefore, we beseech you,
   You   therefore   we beseech,   come to the aid of your servants, whom
                                                             you have redeemed by your precious blood.

   túis   fámulis   súbveni,
   of Thy   servants   come to aid,

   quos   pretíoso   sánguine   redemísti.
   whom   precious   by blood   you have redeemed.

21 Aetérna   fac   cum   sánctis túis   Make them to be numbered with thy saints
   Everlasting make with   saints thy   in glory everlasting.

   in   glória   numerári.
   in   glory   to be numbered.

22 Sálvum fac   pópulum túum, Dómine,
Safe   make   people   your,   Lord,

Save your people, O Lord,
and bless your inheritance.

et bénedic haereditáti túae.
and   bless   inheritance   your.

23 Et   rége   éos,   et   extólle   íllos
And   rule   them,   and   extol   them

Govern them, and extol them
from now into eternity.

usque   in   aetérnum.
continually   into   eternity.

24 Per   síngulos   díes, benedícimus té;
Through   every   day,   we bless   thee;

Day by day, we bless thee;
and we praise your name for ever,
yea, for ever and ever.

25 et   laudámus   nómen túum in saéculum,
and   we praise   name   your into eternity,

et   in   saéculum saéculi.
and into   ages   of ages.

26 Dignáre,   Dómine,   díe ísto
Vouchsafe,   Lord,   day this

Vouchsafe, O Lord, to keep us this day
without sin.

sine   peccáto nos custodíre.
without   sin   us   to keep.

27 Miserére   nóstri,   Dómine,
Have mercy   on us,   Lord,

Have mercy upon us, O Lord,
have mercy upon us.

miserére   nóstri.
have mercy   on us.

28 Fíat misericórdia túa, Dómine, super   nos,
Let be   mercy   thy,   Lord,   upon   us,

Let thy mercy be upon us, O Lord,
as we have trusted in thee.

quemádmodum   sperávimus   in   te.
just as   we have trusted   in   thee.

29 In   te Dómine,   sperávi:
In thee   Lord,   I have trusted:

In thee, O Lord, I have trusted:
let me never be confounded.

non   confúndar   in   aetérnum.
not may I be confounded   through   eternity.

The **Te Deum**, which is first mentioned in the *Rule of St. Caesarius*, A.D. 502, has been found in other manuscripts with many titles other than the familiar *"Te Deum"* or *"Te Deum laudamus"* by which it is known today. The other titles refer to its liturgical function, its character, or its possible authorship: *Hymnus ad matutina dicendus die domino* ("Hymn said at Matins on the day of the Lord," 7th century); *Ymnum in die dominica* (*Bangor Antiphonary*, 7th century); *Laudatio dei* ("The praises of God," *Book of Cerne*, 8th or 9th century); *Laus angelica* "Angelic praise"); *Hymnus quem S. Hilarius primus composuit* ("Hymn which St. Hilary first composed," 8th or 9th century); *Hymnus SS. Ambrosius et Augustini* or *Hymnus Ambrosianus* (St. Gall, 9th century); and *Canticum beati Niceti* ("Canticle of the blessed Nicetas [of Remesiana]), among many others.

The legendary tradition that the **Te Deum** was spontaneously composed and sung alternately by St. Ambrose and St. Augustine on the night of the latter's baptism (A.D. 387) is found in writings from the 9th century (Hincmar of Reims, *De praedestinatione*, 859) and in the so-called *Chronicle of Cacius* (Bishop of Milan, d. *circa* 555; this *Chronicle* is now thought to be a later 11th century forgery). Ten early Irish manuscripts attribute the authorship of this venerable hymn to "Bishop Nicet," which scholars (Morin, Burn) have identified with Nicetas (d. after 414), bishop and noted writer from Remesiana (now Bēla Palanka, near Nish, Yugoslavia). And, indeed, "parallel passages from his writings, although offering no direct quotation, exhibit similarity of thought and diction" (H.T. Henry). The hymn has also been ascribed to St. Hilary of Poitier and St. Ambrose, but the **Te Deum** is in rhythmical prose, and not in the classical meters of the hymns known to be written by them. Recent scholarship has rejected all of these ascriptions as inconclusive.

The tripartite structure of the **Te Deum** offers further insight into its origins. The first section is comprised of the first 10 verses (a hymn of praise to God the Father which contains, in verses 5 and 6, the *Tersanctus* of the Mass), and the concluding Trinitarian doxology in verses 11 to 13 (thought to be a later addition). The close parallels of verses 7-9 and portions of the following passage from St. Cyprian's *de Mortalite* (c. 252) seem to indicate that it was most likely the source of the wonderful progression of praise for the *Patrem immensae majestatis* (from the <u>12</u> Apostles, to the <u>company</u> of the Saints, and then to the <u>army</u> of Martyrs) :

> "*Illic <u>apostolorum gloriosus chorus</u>, illic <u>prophetarum</u> exultantium <u>numerus</u>, illic <u>martyrum</u> innumerabilis populus ob certaminis et passionis gloriam et victoriam coronatus, triumphantes virgines ... remunerati misericordes.*"

[See Julian's *Dictionary of Hymnology* for a side-by-side comparison of four different early manuscripts of the text [the Irish *Bangor Antiphonary*, the Milan Cathedral *Breviary*, the "Ordinary" Latin version from the early 10th century, and the Greek version (translation) of this opening section]

The second portion (verses 14-21 [or 23]), which was added in the 4th century, is Christological, a hymn in praise of Christ the Redeemer, the eternal Son, the coming Judge, which ends with the petition of the. faithful: that they be numbered *cum sanctis tuis*. [Verses 22 and 23 (from Psalm 28:9, *verbatim*) are sometimes grouped with the petition of verses 20 and 21, and sometimes cited as the beginning of the following section which is based on passages from the psalms.]

The third and concluding portion is derived almost exclusively from the psalms. And verse 24, *Per singulos dies, benedicimus te*, relates the hymn directly to its liturgical context: the close of the night office of Matins, just before Lauds, at the beginning of the day.

The following outline summarizes the above discussion:

I

verses 1-10:	an ancient hymn to God the Father
	verses 5-6: the Tersanctus (Trisagion, or Thrice Holy)
	verses 7-9: from St. Cyprian's *de Mortalite* (A.D. 252)
verses 11-13:	a later appended Trinitarian doxology

II

verses 14-21:	Christological hymn (added in the 4th century)

III

verses 22-29:	a series of petitions taken from passages in the psalms
	(Psalms 27:9, 114:2, 122:3, 33:22, and 30:2 [Vulgate])

Most scholars agree that the **Te Deum** was composed at the beginning of the 5th century, and that it was originally composed in Latin and is not translation from the Greek. Kähler (*Studien zum Te Deum*, 1958) further concludes that "the *Te Deum* originated before the middle of the 4th century as the preface, the Sanctus and the prayer following the Sanctus of an old Latin Mass of the Easter vigil, a Mass of baptism."

Notes:

1. *Te Deum laudamus: te Dominum confitemur.*

The traditional translation is given above. Actually, *Te* and *Deum* and *te* and *Dominum* are in apposition, and would literally translated as: "We praise Thee who art God; we acknowledge Thee who art the Lord."

5. *Sanctus . . . Dominus Sabaoth.*

The words of the cherubim from Isaiah 6:3 : "And one cried unto the other, and said, Holy, Holy, Holy is the Lord of hosts: the whole earth is full of his glory." And, from the Apocalypse [Revelation] : "And the four beasts had each of them six wings about him; and they were full of eyes within: and they rest not day and night, saying: Holy, Holy, Holy, Lord God Almighty, which was, and is, and is to come" (4:8).

Sabaoth is a title which ascribes majesty, referring mainly to God. It appears in the Old Testament no less than 282 times. The full ascription *yhwh 'ĕlōhê sebā'ôt yiśrā'ēl*, "Yahweh, the God of the armies of Israel" (I Kings [Samuel] 17:45), conveys the concept of Israel's God seen as the supreme commander of its armies, a warrior who led the hosts of Israel into battle. Later the term implies that Yahweh is also the God of the heavenly hosts and has sovereignty over all things.

7. *Apostulorum chorus.*

" ... and when thou shalt be come there into the city, thou shalt meet a company of prophets coming down from the high place, with a psaltery and a timbrel, and a pipe, and a harp before them and they shall be prophesying. . . . And they came to the foresaid hill, and behold a company of prophets met him: and the spirit of the Lord came upon him and he prophesied in the midst of them" (I Kings [Samuel] 10:5,10).

7-10. *Apostulorum ... Prophetarum ... Martyrum ... Ecclesia.*

The parallels of this passage with St. Cyprian's *de Mortalite* have been cited above; note the wonderful crescendo of praise that begins with the 12 Apostles who are joined by the company of Saints, then the noble army of Martyrs, and finally by the universal Church in praising the Father of *immensae majestatis.*

9. *Martyrum candidatus ... exercitus.*

"After this I saw a great multitude which no man could number, out of all nations and tribes and peoples and tongues, standing before the throne and before the lamb, clothed in white robes, and with palms in their hands" (Apocalypse [Revelation] 7:9).

14. *Rex gloriae.*

"... "Who is the King of Glory? the Lord of hosts, he is the King of Glory" (Psalm 23 [24] : 7–10).

17. *devicto mortis aculeo.*

"... "O death, where is thy victory? O death, where is thy sting?" (I Corinthians 15:55).

18. *ad dexteram Dei.*

"The Lord said to my Lord: Sit thou at my right hand" (*Dixit Dominus*, Psalm 109 [110] : 1). "So then the Lord, after he spoke to them, was taken up into heaven, and sits at the right hand of God" (Mark 16:19).

19. *sanguine redemisti.*

"You know that you were redeemed from the vain manner of life handed down from your fathers, not with perishable things, with silver or gold, but with the precious blood of Christ, as of a lamb without blemish and without spot" (I Peter 1:18–19).

22–23. *Salvum fac populum tuum ...*

Taken verbatim from the Vulgate Latin (Psalm 27 [28] : 9).

24–25. *Per singulos dies ...*

Again from the Vulgate Latin (Psalm 114 [115] : 2), with singular verbs made plural (*benedicam = benedicamus; laudabo = laudamus*). [cf. Psalm 144 [145] : 2]

27. *Miserere nostri ...*

Psalm 122 [123] : 3.

28. *Fiat misericordia tua ...*

Psalm 32 [33] : 22.

29. *In te Domine, speravi ...*

Psalm 30 [31] : 2.

Liturgical context: Since the 6th century the **Te Deum** has been sung at the end of Matins on Sundays and feast days except the Sundays of Advent and those Sundays from Septuagesima to Palm Sunday inclusive. It follows or replaces the last responsory and is followed immediately by Lauds, except on Christmas Day when it is followed by the prayer and the first Mass of the Nativity. It has also been employed as a thanksgiving hymn at consecrations, ordinations, following military victories, and at the close of some medieval mystery plays.

TENEBRAE FACTAE SUNT

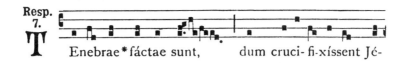

Resp. 7.
Tenebrae*factae sunt, dum cruci-fi-xíssent Jé-

Ténebrae   fáctae   sunt,
Darkness   made   was,

dum   crucifixíssent   Jésum   Judaéi:
when   had crucified   Jesus   Jews:

et   circa   hóram   nónam
and   about   hour   ninth

exclamávit   Jésus   vóce   mágna:
exlaimed   Jesus   voice   loud:

Déus méus, ut quid me   dereliquísti?
God   my, for what me have you abandoned?

Et   inclináto   cápite   emísit   spíritum.
And   inclined   head   he gave up   spirit.

Exclámans   Jésus   vóce   mágna,   áit:
Crying out   Jesus   voice   loud, he said:

Páter,   in   mánus   túas
Father,   into   hands   thy

comméndo   spíritum   méum.
I commend   spirit   my.

Darkness covered the earth
when the Jews had crucified Jesus:

and about the ninth hour
Jesus cried out with a loud voice:

"My God, why hast thou forsaken me?"
And, with his head inclined,
he gave up his spirit.

Jesus, crying out again with a loud voice, said:
"Father, into thy hands I commend my spirit."

Tenebrae factae sunt. "For, behold, the darkness shall cover the earth, and gross darkness the people" (Isaiah 60:2). "And it shall come to pass in that day, saith the Lord God, that I will cause the sun to go down at noon, and I will darken the earth in the clear day: and I will turn your feasts into mourning, and all your songs into lamentation" (Amos 8:9-10).

Mark's gospel records that Jesus was crucified at "the third hour" [about 9 a.m.]; and the gospels of Matthew (27:45), Mark (15:33), and Luke (23:44-45) all record that "there was darkness over the whole land from the sixth to the ninth hour" [12 noon to 3 pm] when Christ was crucified at Golgotha. Since a simple eclipse was impossible at this Paschal time, the fulfilling of the Old Testament prophecies by the darkening of the midday sun suggests that the cosmic implications of this occurence were felt and resonated by nature herself.

Christ's sense of dereliction and desolation are reflected in his utterance at the ninth hour: "Eli, Eli, lä'-mä sä-bặch'-thä-nī" ("My God, my God, why hast thou forsaken me?") (Matthew 27:46; Mark 15:34).

Since the usual time required for crucifixion was twelve hours, Pilate "marvelled" (Mark 15:44) that Christ's death came after only six hours on the cross. The final utterance (Luke 23:46) suggests that he voluntarily chose to "yield up," "give up," or "breathe forth" his spirit (cf. John 10:18). [N.B. Many translators and commentators read *voce magna* as a "great shout" of triumph.]

The fact that both these utterances are quotations from the Psalms (Psalm 22:1 and Psalm 31:5) has led some commentators to suggest that Christ may have been repeating and meditating on them during his great tribulation as Jews have often done in times of adversity.

Liturgical context: **Tenebrae Factae Sunt** is sung during the II. Nocturne of Matins on Good Friday as a Responsory to the fifth Lesson which concludes: *Si enim vere Filius Dei est, liberet eum* ("If indeed he is the true Son of God, let him save himself").

TIMOR ET TREMOR

Tímor et trémor vénerunt super me,
Fear and trembling have come over me,

et calígo cecídit super me.
and darkness has descended upon me.

Fear and trembling have taken hold of me,
and darkness has descended upon me.

Miserére méi, Dómine, miserére,
Have mercy on me, Lord, have mercy,

quonian in te confídit ánima méa.
because in you has trusted soul my.

Have mercy upon me, O Lord, have mercy,
for my soul has trusted in thee.

Exáudi Déus deprecatiónem méam,
Hear God supplication my,

quia refúgium méum es tu
because refuge my are you

et adjútor fórtis;
and helper strong;

Hear, O God, my supplication,
for thou art my refuge and strength;

Dómine, invocávi te,
Lord, I have called on you,

non confúndar.
not shall I be confounded.

O Lord, I have called upon thee,
let me never be confounded.

The motet text of **Timor et tremor**, a compilation of various passages from the Book of Psalms, is most appropriate for the season of Lent, the forty days of penitence and preparation for the joy of Easter. The weekly (and, in some cases, <u>daily</u>) recitation of the entire Psalter must have constantly suggested the relationships like the ones found here, parallels and similarities of thought and expression. The sources are quoted below so that the nature of the choices and the degree of adaptation can be better appreciated.

1. *Timor et tremor venerunt super me*
   et contexerunt me tenebrae.
   (Psalm 54:6 [55:5])

   Fear and trembling have taken hold of me
   and darkness has covered me.

2. *Miserere mei, Deus, miserere mei,*
   quoniam in te confidit anima mea.
   (Psalm 56:2 [57:1])

   Have mercy, upon me, O Lord, have mercy,
   For my soul has trusted in thee.

3. *Inclina ad me auram tuam ...*
   quoniam fortitudo mea et refugium es tu.
   (Psalm 30:3–4 [31:2–3])

   Incline thy ear to me . . .
   because thou art my strength and my refuge.

4. *Domine, non confundar,*
   quoniam invocavi te.
   (Psalm 30:18 [31:17])

   O Lord, let me not be confounded,
   for I have called upon thee.

This concluding verse also recalls the final lines of the *Te Deum*, the ancient hymn of praise and thanksgiving:

In te, Domine, speravi:
non confundar in aeternum.

In thee, O Lord, I have trusted:
let me never be confounded.

TOTA PULCHRA ES, AMICA MEA

T O-ta púlchra es, * amí-ca mé- a,   et mácu-la non

Tota	púlchra	es,	amíca	mea,
Wholly	**beautiful**	**are,**	**love**	**my,**

Thou art all fair, my love;
and there is no stain in you.

et	mácula	non	est	in	te.
and	**stain**	**not**	**is**	**in**	**you.**

Veni	de	Líbano,	sponsa	mea,
Come	**from**	**Lebanon,**	**spouse**	**my,**

Come from Lebanon, my spouse;
Come, and you will be greeted
from the peak of Amana,
from the summit of Shenir and Hermon,
from the lions' dens and mountains of leopards.

veni,	coronáberis;
come,	**you will be greeted;**

de	capite	Amana,
from	**peak**	**of Amana,**

de	vértice	Sanir	et	Hermon,
from	**summit**	**of Shenir**	**and**	**Hermon,**

de	cubílibus	leónum,
from	**dens**	**of lions,**

de	móntibus	pardórum.
from	**mountains**	**of leopards.**

This Marian motet takes its text from the Canticle of Canticles, chapter four, verses 7 and 8. The first verse is used to refer to the doctrine of the Immaculate Conception of the Blessed Virgin Mary, a feast which is celebrated during Advent on December 8. The second verse relates how Mary, the "fairest among women" (Canticle 1:7), she who is "full of grace" (Luke 1:28), the one "blessed by the Lord the most high God, above all women upon the earth" (Judith 13:23) will be greeted and crowned:

> *Ave Maria, gratia plena*
> *Tota pulchra es, Maria*
> *Salve Regina, mater misericordiae*
> *Ave Regina coelorum, Ave Domina Angelorum*
> *Regina coeli*
> *Alma Redemptoris Mater*
> *porta coeli et stella maris*

Note: Amana is the Anti-Lebanon range of the Lebanon mountains, of which Hermon is the highest peak -- "Mount Hermon, which the Sidonians call Sirion; and the Amonites call it Shenir." (Deuteronomy 3:9) Thus: "from the summit of Shenir (that is, Hermon)."

TOTA PULCHRA ES MARIA

OTA pulchra es Ma-rí- a, * et mácu-la o-ri-gi-

1 Tota   púlchra   es   María,
   Wholly   beautiful   thou art Mary,

    et   mácula   originális
    and stain   of original

    non   est   in   te.
    not is   in   thee.

Thou art all fair, O Mary,
and the stain of original sin
is not in thee.

2 Vestiméntum túum   cándidum   quasi nix,
   Vestments   your shining white as   snow,

    et   fácies   túa   sicut   sol.
    and face   your   like   sun.

Your vestments are as white as snow,
and your face is like the sun.

3 Tu   glória   Jerúsalem,   tu laetítia Israel,
   Thou glory of Jerusalem, thou joy of Israel,

    tu   honorificénti   pópuli   nóstri.
    thou honor   of people our.

Thou art the glory of Jerusalem,
the joy of Israel,
and the honor of our people.

4 Benedícta es   tu,   Vírgo María,
   Blessed   art thou, Virgin Mary,

    a   Dómino   Déo   excélso
    by   Lord   God   exalted

    prae   ómnibus   muliéribus   super térram.
    before of all   women   upon earth.

Thou art blessed, Virgin Mary,
by the exalted Lord God,
before all women on earth.

5	Tráhe	nos	Vírgo	immaculáta,
	Draw	**us**	**Virgin**	**unspotted,**

5 Tráhe nos Vírgo immaculáta,
  Draw us Virgin unspotted,

  post te currémus
  after thee we run

  in odórem unguentórum tuórum.
  amid fragrance of perfumes your.

**Draw us, Virgin unspotted,
we run after thee,
amid the fragrance of your perfumes.**

This text consists of the texts for the five antiphons of the Vesper psalms appointed to II. Vespers of the Feast of the Immaculate Conception of the Blessed Virgin Mary (December 8). The handmaid of the Lord is priased with beautiful, rapturous passages chosen most appropriately from the Canticle of Canticles and the Book of Judith.

1. Ant. *Tota pulchra es Maria.* "Thou art all fair, my love, and there is no spot in thee." (Canticle 4:7)

2. Ant. *Vestimentum tuum.* "Who is she that cometh forth as the morning rising, fair as the moon, bright as the sun?" (Canticle 6:9)

3. Ant. *Tu gloria Jerusalem.* "They all blessed her with one voice, saying: Thou art the glory of Jerusalem, thou art the joy of Israel, thou art the honor of our people." (Judith 15:10)

4. Ant. *Benedicta es tu.* "And Ozias, the prince of the people of Israel, said to her: Blessed art thou, O daughter, by the Lord the most high God, above all the women on the earth." (Judith 13:23)

5. Ant. *Trahe nos.* "Draw me: we will run after thee to the odor of thy ointments." (Canticle 1:3)

During the Mass for the Feast of the Immaculate Conception **Tota pulchra es Maria** is heard as the Alleluia verse following the Gradual *Benedicta es tu* which takes as its text the two passages from Judith quoted above. Other texts in the Mass relate 1) to the doctrine of the Immaculate Conception,

"The Lord possessed me in the beginning of his ways ... I was set up
for eternity, and of old, before the earth was made. The depths were not as
yet, and I was already conceived." (the Lesson, from Proverbs 8:22-35)

or 2) to the angel Gabriel's Annunciation (the Offertory *Ave Maria, gratia plena*), or 3) they recall portions of the *Magnificat*, the Canticle of Mary found in Luke 1:46-55.

"I will greatly rejoice in the Lord and my soul shall be joyful in God:
for he hath clothed me with the garments of salvation [*vestimentum candidatum*],
and with the robe of justice he hath covered me. I will extol thee, O Lord, for
thou hast upheld me." (the Introit, from Isaiah 61:10 and Psalm 144 [145]:1)
"Glorious things are told of thee, O Mary, for he who is mighty has done great
things unto thee." (the Communion)

And it is this same joyous Canticle, alluded to in the Mass, and preceded by the five Vesper psalms and their antiphons, that brings the later office of Vespers to its climactic conclusion on this day which so particularly celebrates the Virgin Mother.

225

TRISTIS EST ANIMA MEA

Resp. 8.

Rístis est * á-nima mé- a us- que ad

Trístis est ánima méa **Sorrowful is soul my**	My soul is sorrowful even unto death;
usque ad mórtem; **even unto death;**	
sustinéte hic, et vigiláte mécum: **stay here, and watch with me:**	stay here awhile, and watch with me:
nunc vidébitis túrbam, **now you shall see mob**	now you shall see the mob that will surround me.
quae circumdábit me. **that will surround me.**	
Vos fúgam capiétis, et égo **You flight shall take, and I**	You shall take flight, and I shall go to be sacrificed for you.
vádam immolári pro vóbis. **shall go to be offered for you.**	
Ecce appropínquat hóra, **Behold approaches hour,**	Behold the hour approaches, and the Son of man will be betrayed into the hands of sinners.
et Fílius hóminis trádetur **and Son of man will be betrayed**	
in mánus peccatórum. **into hands of sinners.**	

The Lessons for the I. Nocturn of Matins on Maundy Thursday are taken from the first chapter of the Lamentations of Jeremiah. Christ, on the day of his agony and betrayal and the eve of his crucifixion and death, is likened to Israel during the Babylonian Captivity.

The first Lesson, which is followed by the Responsory *In monte Oliveti,* recalls Christ's agony in the garden:

> "How doth the city sit solitary ... Weeping she hath wept in the night, and her tears are on her cheeks. There is none to comfort her among all them that were dear to her ... Her adversaries are become her lords ... her children are let into captivity."

The second Lesson suggests yet more Old Testament parallels to the Responsory **Tristis est anima mea** which is about to follow. Having accepted the will of the Father that this cup should not pass from him, Christ is "sorrowful, even unto death":

"And from the daughter of Zion all her beauty is departed ... she is cast down, not having a comforter: behold, O Lord, my affliction, because the enemy is lifted up."

This theme is brought to its moment of greatest despair in the text of the Third Lesson of this Nocturn:

"The enemy hath put out his hand to all her desirable things ... *O vos omnes, attendite, et vidéte si est dolor, sicut dolor meus* ... my strength is weakened: The Lord hath delivered me into a hand out of which I am not able to rise."

Note: The source of the text for **Tristis est anima mea** is to be found in Matthew 26:38 (Mark 14:34) and Matthew 26:45b (Mark 14:41b).

TU ES PETRUS

Tu	es	Pétrus,		Thou art Peter,
You	**are**	**Peter,**		**and upon this rock**
				I shall build my Church;

| et | super | hanc | pétram |
| **and** | **upon** | **this** | **rock** |

| edificábo | Ecclésiam | méam, |
| **I shall build** | **Church** | **my;** |

| et | pórtae | inféri | | and the gates of hell |
| **and** | **gates** | **of hell** | | **shall not prevail against it.** |

| non | prevalébunt | vérsus | éam. |
| **not** | **shall prevail** | **against** | **it.** |

| Et | tíbi | dábo | | And I shall give thee |
| **And** | **to you** | **I shall give** | | **the keys of the kingdom of heaven.** |

| cláves | régni | coelórum. |
| **keys** | **of kingdom** | **of heavens.** |

Jesus said unto his disciples: "Who do you say that I am? Simon Peter answered and said, Thou are the Christ, the Son of the living God. Then Jesus answered and said, Blessed art thou Simon Bar-Jona, for flesh and blood has not revealed this to thee, but my Father in heaven.

"And I say to thee, thou art Peter, and upon this rock I will build my Church, and the gates of hell shall not prevail against it. And I will give the the keys of the kingdom of heaven; and whatever thou shalt bind on earth shall be bound in heaven, and whatever thou shalt loose on earth shall be loosed in heaven." (Matthew 16:15-19)

Peter's profession of faith in the divinity of Christ brought him "the keys of the kingdom of heaven." Later his three denials required three affirmations before the powers of the primacy were bestowed upon him with the words: "Feed my lambs." (John 21:15-18)

Liturgical context: **Tu es Petrus** is the Alleluia psalm verse for the Mass in honor of Saints Peter and Paul (June 29). It follows the Gradual which is taken from Psalm 44: "Thou shalt make them princes over all the earth. They shall remember thy name throughout all generations. Therefore shall the people praise thee for ever." (Psalm 44 [45] : 17-18)

TU   PAUPERUM   REFUGIUM

Tu	páuperum	refúgium,	Thou art the refuge of the poor,
Thou	**of poor**	**refuge,**	thou art the remedy of the weak,
tu	languórum	remédium,	
thou	**of weak**	**remedy,**	
spes	exsúlum,	fortitúdo laborántium,	the hope of the exiled,
hope	**of exiled,**	**strength of heavy-laden,**	the strength of the heavy-laden,
vía	errántium,	véritas et víta.	the path of the errant,
path of errant,	**truth**	**and life.**	the truth and the life.

Et	nunc Redémptor,	Dómine,	And now, Redeemer Lord,
And	**now Redeemer,**	**Lord,**	to thee alone I come for aid;

ad	te sólum	confúgio,
to	**thee alone**	**I appeal,**

te	vérum Déum	adóro,	thee, true God, I worship;
thee	**true God**	**I worship,**	in thee I hope, in thee I trust,
			Jesus Christ, my salvation.

in	te spéro,	in te confído,
in	**thee I hope,**	**in thee I trust,**

sálus	méa,	Jésu Chríste.
salvation	**my,**	**Jesus Christ.**

Adjúva	me, ne	unquam	obdórmiat	Help me, lest at any time
Help	**me, lest**	**at any time**	**fall asleep**	my soul might die in sin.

in	mórte	ánima	méa.
in	**death**	**soul**	**my.**

Tu pauperum refugium is the *Secunda pars* (second part) of Josquin des Prez's four-part motet *Magnus es tu, Domine* ("Great are thou, O Lord"). "It shows an admirable combination of spirituality and expressiveness, of variety and clarity, of technical mastery and simplicity of means as well as close reciprocity between text and music." (Apel and Davidson, *Historical Anthology of Music*). The author of this equally exquisite text is unknown, but the beauty, precision, and hymn-like strength of its poetic prose are not soon forgotten.

UBI CARITAS

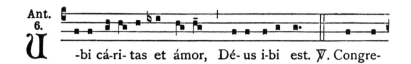

Ant. 6. U -bi cá-ri-tas et ámor, Dé-us i-bi est. ℣. Congre-

Ubi cáritas et ámor,	Where there is charity and love,
Where charity and love,	God is there.
Déus íbi est.	
God there is.	
Congregávit nos in únum Chrísti ámor.	The love of Christ has gathered us together.
Has gathered us into one of Christ love.	
Exsultémus et in ípso jucundémur.	Let us rejoice and be glad in it.
Let us rejoice and in it be glad.	
Timeámus et amémus Déum vívum.	Let us revere and love the living God.
Let us fear and love God living.	
Et ex córde diligámus nos sincéro.	And from a sincere heart let us love one another.
And from heart let us love us sincere.	

Ubi cáritas et ámor,	Where there is charity and love,
Where charity and love,	God is there.
Déus íbi est.	
God there is.	
Simul ergo cum in unum congregámur:	Likewise, therefore, when we come together
Also therefore when as one we come together:	let us be united as one;
Ne nos ménte dividámur, caveámus.	let us be careful,
Lest we in mind be divided, be careful.	lest we be divided in intention.
Céssent júrgia malígna, céssent lítes.	Let us cease all quarrels and strife.
Cease quarrels evil, cease strife.	
Et in médio nóstri· sit Chrístus Déus.	And let Christ dwell in the midst of us.
And in midst of us be Christ God.	

| Ubi cáritas et ámor, | Where there is charity and love, |
| **Where charity and love,** | **God is there.** |

| Déus íbi est. |
| **God there is.** |

| Simul quoque cum beátis videámus. | **May we also see, along with the blessed,** |
| **Along also with blessed may we see.** |

| Gloriánter vúltum túum, Chríste Déus. | **the glory of your face, O Christ.** |
| **Gloriously face your, Christ God.** |

| Gáudium quod est imménsum, atque próbum: | **And let there be immeasurable joy** |
| **Joy that is immense, and worthy:** |

| Saecula per infinita saeculorum. Amen. | **both now and for evermore. Amen.** |
| **ages through infinite of ages. Amen.** |

In the Mass for Maundy Thursday two special events are commemorated: Christ's institution of the Holy Eucharist and his washing of the disciple's feet. This latter rite, known as the *Mandatum* from the first word of the Introit (*Mandatum novum do nobis* - "A new commandment I give unto you, that you love one another, as I have loved you" (John 13:34)), is Christ's final lesson in charity, humility, and friendship.

During the Maundy, or washing of the feet, various antiphons are sung by the Choir, including the afore-mentioned *Mandatum*, the *Si ego Dominus* ("If I being your Lord and Master have washed your feet: how much more ought you to wash the feet of one another?" - John 13:14), *In hoc cognoscent omnes* ("By this all shall know that you are my disciples, if you have love for one another." - John 13:35), and *Maneant in vobis* ("Let these three, faith, hope, and charity, remain in you; but the greatest of these is charity." - I Corinthians 13:13). The antiphon **Ubi caritas** appears at the close of this rite.

Here in the Mass of Maundy Thursday, as in the institution of this rite, the *Mandatum* is intended as a preparation for the receiving of the Holy Eucharist.

Liturgical context: **Ubi caritas** is the final antiphon sung during the *Mandatum* on Maundy Thursday. Of the original hymn, which is very long, only three verses are now used. Its author is unknown, but it was most probably written in France during the 10th century.

VENI CREATOR SPIRITUS

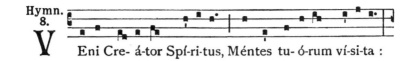

Hymn. 8.

Eni Cre- á-tor Spí-ri-tus, Méntes tu- ó-rum ví-si-ta :

Véni, Creátor Spíritus,
Come, Creator Spirit,

Méntes tuórum vísita,
Souls of yours visit,

Imple supérna grátia,
Fill supernal grace,

Quae tu creásti péctora:
Which you have created hearts:

Come, CREATOR SPIRIT,
Visit the souls of your devoted;
With your divine grace fill
The hearts which you have created.

5 Qui Paraclítus díceris,
(You)who Paraclete are called,

Dónum Déi altíssimi,
Gift of God most high,

Fons vívus, ígnis, cáritas,
Fount of life, fire, charity,

Et spiritális únctio.
And spiritual unction.

You are called Comforter,
Gift of the highest God,
Fount of life, fire, love,
And spiritual unction.

Tu septifórmis múnere,
You seven−fold gift,

10 Dígitus Déi déxterae,
Forefinger of God of right hand,

Tu ríte promíssum Pátris,
You duly promised by Father,

Sermóne dítans gúttura.
Speech enriching throats.

You are seven−fold in your gifts,
The finger of God's right hand,
You are the one duly promised by the Father,
Enriching our tongues with speech.

Accénde lúmen sénsibus,
Enkindle light to minds,

Infúnde amórem córdibus,
Infuse love into hearts,

15 Infírma nóstri córporis
Weaknesses of our body

Virtúte fírmans pérpeti.
Power strengthening perpetual.

Enkindle your light in our minds,
Infuse your love into our hearts;
Strengthen the frailties of our flesh
By your perpetual power.

Hóstem repéllas lóngius,
Enemy may drive far away,

May you drive our enemy far away,
And bestow abiding peace,
So that, with you leading before us,
We may shun all evil.

Pacémque dónes prótinus,
And peace may bestow continuously,

Ductóre sic te praévio,
Leader so you preceeding,

20 Vitémus ómne nóxium.
We may shun all evil.

Per te sciámus da Pátrem,
Through you we may know grant Father,

Grant that through you we may know the Father,
And that we might also come to know the Son;
And you, the Spirit of Them both,
May we trust at all times.

Noscámus atque Fílium,
We may come to know also Son,

Téque utriúsque Spíritum
And you of both Spirit

Credámus ómni témpore.
May we trust at every time.

25 Deo Patri sit gloria,
To God Father be glory,

Glory be to God the Father,
And to the Son,
Who rose from the dead,
And to the Comforter,
For ever and ever.

Et Filio, qui a mortuis
And to Son, who from dead

Surrexit, ac Paraclito,
Rose, and to Comforter,

In saeculorum saecula.
For of generations generations.

This great hymn, which "has taken deeper hold of the Western Church than any other hymn, the *Te Deum* alone excepted" (Dr. Gibson, in Julian *Dictionary of Hymnology*), appears in manuscript as early as the 10th century, but conclusive evidence about its authorship is yet unknown. Dr. Gibson's account shows the error of its ascription to Charlemagne by Ekkehard (c.1220) and assesses the various arguments that attribute its authorship to St. Ambrose, Gregory the Great, and Rhabanus Maurus as inconclusive. The earliest datable MS in which it is found is the Durham Hymnal, c.980. By the 11th century its use was widespread, and it is found in MSS representing England, France, Germany with Switzerland, Italy, and Spain.

The season of Pentecost (Whitsuntide) honors the Third Person of the Holy Trinity and has thus been the occasion for the liturgical use of this hymn since the 10th century. It has also been assigned to Terce on Whitsunday, to the three ferias following [see Acts 2:15], and, since the 11th century, to the Ordination Service. The Church also sings it at such solemn functions as the election of Popes, consecration of bishops, dedication of churches, coronations of kings, etc.

The terseness of its text, which makes translation difficult, becomes, ultimately, its abiding strength: in its five stanzas and doxology -- indeed, even single lines (e.g., *fons vivus, ignis, caritas*) -- a veritable panoply of history and doctrine are contained. The great poetic profundity which results has inspired the solemnity associated with its singing and occasioned numerous commentaries and translations. Other texts in this volume may also invite the reader to explore them in a manner similar to the following, but this hymn particularly requires a more thorough annotation in order to be understood and appreciated.

1. *Creator Spiritus.*

"The spirit of God hath made me, and the breath of the Almighty hath given me life." [Job 33:4]

"Send forth your spirit and they are created and you shall renew the face of the earth." [Psalm 104:30]

"*spiramen Dei omnipotentes qui fecit omnia, et scrutinat omnia absconsa in absconsis terrae*" (and the spirit of God Almighty who made all things, and scrutinizes the profundity of profundities of the earth") [IV Esdrae 16:63]

3. *imple.*

Note the strength of this opening stanza reflected in its three verbs: *veni, visita, imple* -- come, visit, fill.

5. *Paraclitus.*

Paraclete is the name used by Chirst himself for the Holy Spirit, the Comforter, our Advocate. "Notable as the only place in these latin hymns where we find the quantitative *Paraclitus* and not the accentual *Paráclitus*." [A.S. Walpole]

6. *donum.*

Jesus, to the Samarian woman: "If thou knewest the gift of God and who it is that saith to thee, Give me to drink. . . " [John 4:10]

Peter: "Repent . . . be baptized . . . and you shall receive the gift of the Holy Ghost." [Acts 2:38]

Peter, to Simon: "Thy money perish with thee, because thou had thought that the gift of God my be purchased with money." [Acts 8:18-20]

7. *fons vivus.*

Jesus, to the Samarian woman: "But whosoever drinketh of the water that I shall give him shall never thirst; but the water that I shall give him shall be in him a well of water springing up into everlasting life." {John 4:14]

7. *ignis.*

John the Baptist: "he shall baptize you with the Holy Ghost, and with fire." [Matthew 3:11]

Christ: "I am come to send fire on the earth." [Luke 12:49]

"For he is like a refiner's fire." [Malachi 3:2]

"When the Lord shall have ... purged the blood of Jerusalem ... by the spirit of burning." [Isaiah 4:4]

"And suddenly there came a sound from heaven as of a rushing mighty wind, and it filled all the house where they were sitting. And there appeared unto them cloven tongues like as of fire, and it sat upon each of them." [Acts 2:2-3]

7. *caritas.*

"the love of God is shed abroad in our hearts by the Holy Ghost which is given unto us." [Romans 5:5]

8. *unctio.*

"But ye have an unction from the Holy One, and ye know all things." [I John 2:20]

"Now he which stablisheth us with you in Christ, and hath annointed us, is God." [II Corinthians 1:21]

9. *septiformis.*

Et requiescet super eum spiritus Domini: spiritus sapientiae et intellectus, spiritus consilii et fortitudinis, spiritus scientiae et pietatis; et replebit eum spiritus timoris Domini. ("And the spirit of the Lord shall rest upon him: the spirit of wisdom and understanding, the spirit of counsel and might, the spirit of knowledge and devotion; and shall fill him with the spirit of the fear of the Lord.") [Isaiah 11:3-2]

"The seven seals, chambers, stars, angels, trumpets, and the seven spirits of God." [Apocalypse (Revelation) 3:1]

10. *Dei ... digitus.*

<u>Compare</u>: "But if I with the finger [*in digito*] of God cast out devils, no doubt the kingdom of God is come upon you." [Luke 11:20] <u>with</u>: "But if I cast out devils by the Spirit [*in spiritu*] of God, then the kingdom of God is come unto you." [Matthew 12:28]

Pharoah's magicians, unable to bring forth lice upon the land as Aaron had done with his rod, said: "This is the finger of God." [Exodus 8:19]

Moses, after 40 days and nights on Mt. Sinai: "And the Lord delivered unto me two tables of stone written with the finger of God." [Deuteronomy 9:10]

11. *promisso.*

"And, behold, I send the promise of my Father upon you: but tarry ye in the city of Jerusalem, until ye be endued with power from on high." [Luke 24:49]

12. *sermones.*

"And they were filled with the Holy Ghost and began to speak with other tongues, as the Spirit gave them utterance." [Acts 2:4]

"Whatsoever shall be given you in that hour, that speak ye: for it is not ye that speak, but the Holy Ghost." [Mark 13:11]

"For the Holy Ghost shall teach you in the same hour what ye ought to say." [Luke 12:12]

13. *lumen.*

"The Comforter, who is the Holy Ghost, shall teach you all things." [John 14:26] "And I will pray the Father, and he shall give you another Comforter, that he may abide with you for ever; Even the Spirit of truth; whom the world cannot receive, because it seeth him not, neither knoweth him: but ye know him; for he dwelleth with you, and shall be in you." [John 14:16-17]

"Nevertheless when it shall turn to the Lord, the vail shall be taken away. Now the Lord is that Spirit: and where the Spirit of the Lord is, there is liberty." [II Corinthians 3:16-17]

15. *infirma nostri corporis / virtute firmans perpeti.*

Even though these two lines are from the Christmas hymn by St. Ambrose (*Veni Redemptor gentium* , lines 27–28), hymnologists agree that this is insufficient evidence to assert that he is the author of *Veni creator Spiritus.*

16. *virtute firmans.*

"That [God] would grant you . . . to be strengthened with might by his Spirit in the inner man." [Ephesians 3:16]

"Strengthened with all might, according to his glorious power . . ." [Colossians 1:11]

19. *ductore . . . praevio.*

"Howbeit when he, the Spirit of truth, is come, he will guide you into all truth." [John 16:13] "Probably the reference is to the guiding cloud in the wilderness." [A.S. Walpole]

21-24. *The closing doxology.*

Even though this last stanza is itself a doxology, many MSS contain other doxologies that have been appended to this hymn. The two most common are:

> *"Sit laus Pátri cum Fîlio,*
> *Sáncto sîmul Paráclito . . . "*

which Dr. Gibson points out as "extraneous," "betrayed by the quantity of the penultimate of *Paraclītus* [see note for line 5]; and the obviously appropriate Eastertide doxology:

> *"Deo Patri sit gloria,*
> *Et Filio, Qui a mortuis*
> *Surrexit, ac Paraclito,*
> *In sempiterna saecula."*

21. *per te sciamus.*

"The Comforter, who is the Holy Ghost, shall teach you all things." [John 14:26]

23. *te utriusque Spiritum.*

Jesus: "[The Spirit of truth] shall glorify me: for he shall receive of mine, and shall shew it unto you. All things that the Father hath are mine: therefore said I, that he shall take of mine, and shall shew it unto you." [John 16:14-15]

"For it is not ye that speak, but the Spirit of your Father which speaketh in you." [Matthew 10:20]

A thorough reading and interpretative study of the descent of the Holy Ghost found in Acts 2:1-21 will shed further light on the season of Pentecost and its association with this most noble and famous hymn.

Liturgical context: **Veni Creator Spiritus** is sung at Vespers and Terce of Pentecost and throughout the octave. It is also used in the Ordination Service and on other solemn occasions such as the election of popes, consecration of bishops, dedications of churches, and the coronations of kings.

VENI SANCTE SPIRITUS

Seq. 1.
V Eni Sáncte Spí- ri-tus, Et emít-te caé- li-tus Lú-

Véni, Sáncte Spíritus,
Come, Holy Spirit,

Et emítte coélitus
And send forth from heaven

Lúcis túae rádium.
of light your ray.

Véni, páter páuperum,
Come, father of poor,

5 Véni, dátor múnerum,
Come, giver of gifts,

Véni, lúmen córdium.
Come, light of hearts.

Come, Holy Spirit,
Send forth from heaven
The ray of thy light.

Come, Father of the poor,
Come, giver of gifts,
Come, light of hearts.

Consolátur óptime,
Consoler best,

Dúlcis hóspes ánimae,
sweet guest of soul,

Dúlce refrigérium.
sweet refreshment.

10 In labóre réquies,
In labor rest,

In aéstu tempéries,
in heat tempering,

In flétu solátium.
In grief solace.

Thou best of Consolers,
Sweet guest of the soul,
Sweet refreshment.

In labor, thou art rest,
In heat, the tempering,
In grief, the consolation.

O lux beatíssima,
O light most blessed,

Réple córdis íntima
fill of hearts depths

15 Tuórum fidélium.
of your faithful.

O Light most blessed,
Fill the inmost heart
Of all thy faithful.

Sine   túo   númine,
Without your nod/consent,

Nihil est in hómine,
nothing is in man,

Nihil est innóxium.
nothing is not harmful.

Without your grace,
There is nothing in us,
Nothing that is not harmful.

Láva quod est sórdidum,
Cleanse what is sordid,

20 Ríga quod est áridum,
Moisten what is arid,

Sána quod est sáucium.
Heal what is hurt.

Cleanse what is sordid,
Moisten what is arid,
Heal what is hurt.

Flécta quod est rígidum,
Flex what is rigid,

Fóve quod est frígidum,
Warm what is frigid,

Rége quod est dévium.
Correct what is devious.

Flex what is rigid,
Fire what is frigid,
Correct what goes astray.

25 Da túis fidélibus,
Give to your faithful,

In te confidéntibus,
in you trusting,

Sácrum septenárium.
sacred seven-fold.

Grant to thy faithful,
Those trusting in thee,
Thy sacred seven-fold gifts.

Da virtútis méritum,
Give of virtue merit,

Da salútis éxitum,
Give of salvation passing,

30 Da perénne gáudium.
Give continuing joy.

Grant the reward of virtue,
Grant the deliverance of salvation,
Grant everlasting joy.

Veni Sancte Spiritus is the sequence for Whitsundtide and is sung daily at Mass from Pentecost Sunday until the following Saturday inclusive. Its authorship has been unconvincingly ascribed to Robert II of France and Hermann Contractus and by Ekkehard V of Sankt Gallen to Pope Innocent III (d.1216). But scholars today hold that the ascription in *Distinctiones monasticae et morales* (thought to be written by an English Cistercian) to Stephan Langton (d.1228), Archbishop of Canterbury, is the most probable, especially in light of evidence from the manuscript tradition which indicates that the Sequence spread from Paris, where Langton had taught and studied for several decades, rather than from the home of Innocent III in Rome.

This Sequence has not been found in manuscripts earlier than 1200 and its verse form is never found in the earlier Notkerian type of sequence; this dates **Veni Sancte Spiritus** as late 12th century, since its verse form is from the second period of sequence writing which has not been traced earlier than c.1150.

Praise for the "Golden Sequence" has been universal. Julian, in his *Dictionary of Hymnology* (1915), says that though "it is not distinguished by great and absolute originality of ideas . . . it combines a stately grace, a perfect rhythmic melody, and a faculty of saying just the right thing in just the fitting words." Julian cites two other opinions which are even more effusive, one by Archbishop Trench (*Sacred Latin Poetry*, 1864):

> "The loveliest . . . of all the hymns in the whole circle of Latin sacred poetry . . . it could only have been composed by one who had been acquainted with many sorrows, and also with many consolations."

and the other by Clichtovaeus (*Elucidatorium*, 1516):

> "Nor indeed, in my opinion, can this piece be sufficiently praised; for it is above all praise, whether by reason of its wonderful sweetness along with a most clear and flowing style, or by reason of its agreeable brevity along with wealth and profusion of ideas, especially as almost every line expresses one idea, of finally by reason of *the elegant grace of its structure, in which things contrasted are set over against each other, and most aptly linked together.* And I well believe that the author (whoever he was), when he composed this piece, had his soul transfused by a certain heavenly sweetness, by which, the Holy Spirit being it author, he uttered so much sweetness in so few words."

Indeed, this "elegant" structure merits closer observation. The ten stanzas are set as double versicles and the rhyme scheme is *aab ccb* ; in addition every third line throughout the sequence ends in *ium*, which not only obscures the antiphony of the versicles, but, especially when combined with all the other *um* and *us* endings, brings great sweetness of melody. [N.B. that in the first, fourth, and fifth double versicles <u>all</u> the lines close with *ium, um,* or *us.* Indeed, only three of the thirty lines do not contain the soothing, comforting *"u"* (*Consolatur*); many contain two (*Veni, l<u>u</u>men cordi<u>u</u>m*), and one has three (*L<u>u</u>cis t<u>u</u>ae radi<u>u</u>m.*]

The beginnings of each line -- in function as well as phonemic and expressive content -- contribute no less to the intricacy and beauty of the structure, the way in which these ideas are "so aptly linked together" -- see Example 1:

E X A M P L E   1

V eni _____	Come _____	C O M E
et emitte _____	send _____	
_____ radium	_____ ray	
V eni	Come	
V eni	Come	
V eni	Come	

C onsolatur	Consoler	C O M F O R T E R
D ulcis	Sweet	
D ulce	Sweet	
I n	In . . .	
I n	In . . .	
I n	In . . .	

O lux _____	Light	L I G H T
reple _____ intima	fill ___ depths	
_____	_____	
S ine	Without	D A R K N E S S
N ihil	Nothing	
N ihil	Nothing	

L ava	Cleanse	R E M E D Y
R iga	Nourish	
S ana	Heal	
F lecta	Flex	
F ove	Fire	
R ege	Guide	

D a _____	Grant _____	G R A N T
_____	_____	
_____ septenarium	_____ seven gifts	
D a	Grant	
D a	Grant	
D a	Grant	

Feel the urgency and need in the first six lines; the comfort and consolation of the next two stanzas; the antiphony of praise and emptiness of stanzas 5 and 6 followed by the six successive imperatives (*Lava, Riga, Sana, Flecta, Fove, Rege*) of 7 and 8; and then the petitions of the faithful in stanzas 9 and 10.

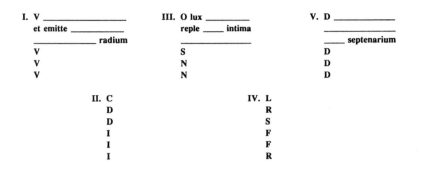

```
I.  V _____        III. O lux _____        V.  D _____
    et emitte _____        reple _____ intima           _____
    _____ radium         _____          _____ septenarium
    V                           S                             D
    V                           N                             D
    V                           N                             D

         II. C                       IV. L
             D                           R
             D                           S
             I                           F
             I                           F
             I                           R
```

Note (in Example 2) the subtle variations and parallels in I, III, and V, and the various verse forms used for addressing the Holy Spirit (I – *Sancte Spiritu*, II – *Consolatur*, III – *O lux*); the fact that S–N–N echoes C–D–D and not the expected V–V–V of I; the variation of C–D–D and S–N–N in the F–F–R of IV; the way in which I–I–I echoes V–V–V of I, but with prepositions, not the verbs of D–D–D of V; how the six strong imperatives of IV extends the V–V–V, I–I–I, D–D–D pattern to the whole double versicle by function (verb) rather than repetition of the word; that the Rondo-like structure of Example 2 (I – ii – III – iv – V) is contradicted and made stronger by the function and content groupings of   I – II – III / IV – V   of Example 3:

E X A M P L E   3

```
I.   V    Creator Spirit
          and send . . . .
          . . . . . . . . ray
     V    father
     V    giver              IV. L ava      cleanse
     V    light                  R iga      nourish
                                 S ana      heal
                                 F lecta    flex
                                 F ove      fire
II.  Consoler                    R ege      guide
     D    guest
     D    refreshment
     I    rest
     I    shade             V.  D    . . . . . . . . . . .
     I    solace                      . . . . . . . . . . .
                                     . . . . seven gifts
                                D    strength
                                D    deliverance
III. Light  . . . . . . . . .   D    joy
            fill . . depths
            . . . . . . . . . .
     S    without
     N    nothing
     N    nothing
```

and that the ascent from the depths of *sine/nihil/nihil* to *perenne gaudium* is reinforced and culminated by the structure of the final three lines: the crescendo from *now* (life/strength), to *then* (death/deliverance), and finally *forever* (eternity/joy!) -- even the syntactical change in the last line moves fervently forward:

Da   virtutis   meritum,

Da   salutis   exitum,

Da   perenne   gaudium.

But even with all these incredible subtleties and intricacies, "'art conceals art,' and the glow of devotion so transfuses and transfigures all that one is content to admire the beauty and hardly thinks of the skill" (Julian, *Dictionary of Hymnology*). "It is an incomparable hymn, exhaling the sweetness of Paradise, and regaling us with heaven's sweetest fragrance. Only a soul buried in deep recollection can suspect and taste the wealth of deep thought and affliction this Pentecost hymn contains, and that, too, in a form as remarkable for beauty as for brevity" (Gihr, *The Holy Sacrifice*). "The composer of this song was a veritable harp of God, on which the Holy Ghost Himself played."

"Not I, not I, but the wind which blows through me" (D.H. Lawrence).

Notes:

7. *Consolatur optime.*

"Best of Consolers," comforter, advocate; a Latin rendering of the Greek Παρακλητοσ (Latin *Paraclitus*), Paraclete.

16. *numine.*

Literally, a nod of the head; consent, grace.

19-24. *lava, riga, sana, flecta, fove, rege.*

Cleanse all our iniquities, remedy those conditions which inhibit the positive flow of the life–force, guide us back to the path when we go astray.

33. *Sacrum septenarium.*

"Sacred group of seven [gifts/graces]." "And the spirit of the Lord shall rest upon him [the Messiah]: the spirit of wisdom, and of understanding, the spirit of counsel, and of fortitude, the spirit of knowledge and of godliness. And he shall be filled with the spirit of the fear of the Lord" (Isaiah 11:2–3). [see *Veni Creator Spiritus*, line 9 and *note*]

Liturgical context: **Veni Sancte Spiritus** is one of the five great sequences of the Roman Church. [the others being *Dies irae, Lauda Sion, Stabat Mater,* and *Victimae paschali laudes*] It is sung at Mass from Pentecost Sunday until the following Saturday inclusive.

VERBUM CARO FACTUM EST

Resp. 8.
8.
V Er-bum * cáro fáctum est   et ha- bi-tá-

| Vérbum cáro fáctum est | The Word was made flesh |
| **Word flesh made was** | **and dwelt among us;** |

| et habitávit in nóbis; | |
| **and dwelt among us;** | |

| et vídimus glóriam éjus, | and we beheld his glory, |
| **and we beheld glory his,** | the glory as of the only–begotten by the Father, |

| glóriam quási unigéniti a Pátre, | full of grace and truth. |
| **glory as of only–begotten by Father,** | |

| plénum grátiae et veritátis. | |
| **full of grace and truth.** | |

241

The eighth Lesson for II. Vespers of the Nativity is from the Gospel of St. Luke: "And it came to pass, when the angels had departed from them into heaven, that the shepherds were saying to one onother, 'Let us go over to Bethlehem and see this thing that has come to pass, which the Lord has made known to us'" (Luke 2:15). **Verbum caro factum est** is the Responsory which follows.

"In the beginning was the Word, and the Word was with God; and the Word was God" (John 1:1).

"I write of what was from the beginning, what we have heard, what we have seen with our eyes, what we have looked upon and our hands have handled: of the Word of Life. And the Life was made known and we have seen, and now testify and announce to you, the Life Eternal which was with the Father, and has appeared to us" (I John 1:1-2).

"And I saw heaven standing open; and behold, a white horse, and he who sat upon it is called Faithful and True, and with justice he judges and wages war. And his eyes are as a flame of fire, and on his head are many diadems; he has a name written which no man knows except himself. And he is clothed in a garment sprinkled with blood, and his name is called The Word of God" (Apocalypse [Revelation] 19:11-13).

"And the glory of the Lord shall be revealed, and all flesh shall see it together, for the mouth of the Lord hath spoken it" (Isaiah 40:5).

"For the Law was given through Moses; grace and truth came through Jesus Christ" (John 1:17).

Liturgical context: **Verbum caro factum est** is the Responsory to the eighth Lesson of II. Vespers of the Nativity.

VERE   LANGUORES

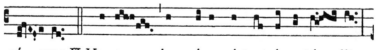

sú- mus. ℣. Ve-re   languóres nóstros ípse tú- lit,

Vére languóres nóstros, ípse túlit,   **Truly he alone has borne our infirmities,**
Truly weaknesses our, he alone has borne,

et dolóres nóstros, ípse portávit.   **and he himself has carried our sorrows.**
and sorrows our, he himself has carried.

"Despised, the most abject of men, a man of sorrows, and acquainted with grief ... Surely he hath born our infirmities and carried our sorrows: and we have thought him as it were a leper, and as one struck by God and afflicted. But he was wounded for our transgressions, he was bruised for our sins: the chastisement of our peace was upon him, and by his stripes we are healed." (Isaiah 53:3-5)

In the above passage from Isaiah's prophecy Christ's sufferings are foretold with compelling compassion. **Vere languores**, the fourth verse from this 53rd chapter, is most appropriately appointed as the verse for the Responsory to the Third Lesson of the I. Nocturn of Matins for Maundy Thursday. In the text of this Lesson, taken from verses 10–14 of the first chapter of the Lamentations of Jeremiah, the despair of Israel during the Babylonian Captivity is likened to Christ's despair and suffering on the night of his betrayal and arrest:

"The enemy hath put out his hand to all her desirable things ... *O vos omnes, attendite, et videte si est dolor, sicut dolor meus* ... my strength is weakened: the Lord hath delivered me into a hand out of which I am not able to rise."

The Responsory *Ecce vidimus eum* ("Behold we have seen him, and there is no beauty nor comeliness in him") follows, and is itself concluded by the verse **Vere languores**.

VICTIMAE PASCHALI LAUDES

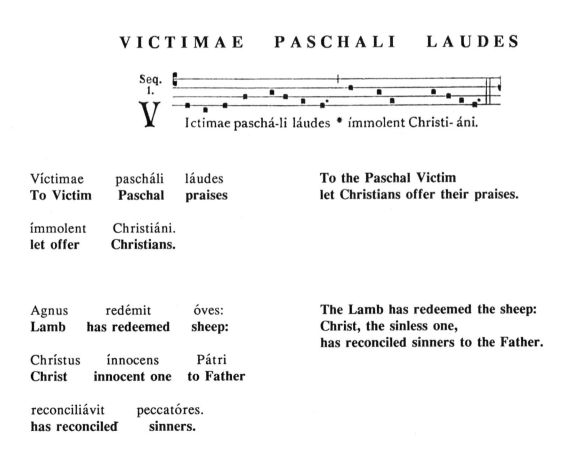

Seq. 1.

Victimae paschá-li láudes * immolent Christi-áni.

| Víctimae | pascháli | láudes: | To the Paschal Victim |
| **To Victim** | **Paschal** | **praises** | let Christians offer their praises. |

| immolent | Christiáni. | |
| **let offer** | **Christians.** | |

Agnus	redémit	óves:	The Lamb has redeemed the sheep:
Lamb	**has redeemed**	**sheep:**	Christ, the sinless one,
			has reconciled sinners to the Father.

| Christus | innocens | Pátri |
| **Christ** | **innocent one** | **to Father** |

| reconciliávit | peccatóres. |
| **has reconciled** | **sinners.** |

Mors et víta duéllo
Death and life duel

conflixére mirándo:
have engaged marvellous:

dux vítae mórtuus,
leader of life dead,

régnat vívus.
reigns alive.

Death and life have engaged
in a wondrous conflict:
the slain leader of life
reigns alive!

Dic nóbis María,
Tell to us Mary,

quid vidísti in vía?
what did you see on way?

Tell us Mary,
what did you see on your way?

Sepúlcrum Chrísti vivéntis,
Sepulchre of Christ living,

et glóriam vídi resurgéntis:
and glory I saw of rising:

I saw the sepulchre of the living Christ
and the glory of Him rising:

Angelícos téstes, sudárium,
Angelic witnesses, face-cloth,

et véstes.
and garments.

And I saw the angelic witnesses,
the napkin, and the linen clothes.

Surréxit Chrístus spes méa:
Has risen Christ hope my:

praecédet súos in Galilaéam.
He shall go before his into Galilee.

Christ my hope has risen:
he shall go before his own into Galilee.

[Credéndum est mágis sóli
Credence is greater alone

Maríae veráci quam Judaeórum
of Mary veracity than of Jews

túrbae falláci.]
crowd fallacious.

[Greater credence is to be placed
upon the veracity of Mary alone
than on the deceitful crowd of Jews.]

Scímus	Chrístum	surrexísse		
We know	**Christ**	**has risen**		

We know that Christ has truly risen
from the dead:
O thou, Victor, King,
have mercy upon us.

a	mórtuis	vére:
from	**dead**	**truly:**

tu	nóbis,	víctor	Rex,
Thou	**on us,**	**victor**	**King,**

miserére.
have mercy.

The early Notkerian period of sequence writing [Notker Balbulus (c.840-912)] was marked by a varying stanzaic form (which frequently contained, however, regular syllabic correspondences) and an "almost casual" assonance. This form gradually evolved, by the latter half of the 12th century, to the regular rhymic and stanzaic forms of the sequences of Adam of St. Victor (d. late 12th century). **Victimae paschali laudes** is an example of the transitional stage between the two periods: the first of its seven stanzas is unpaired, but the remaining six divide regularly into a strophe and antistrophe structure (with strict syllabic correspondence but irregular line lengths) and they display a significant increase in the frequency of rhyme. This has not always been clear to scholars due to various "revisions" and the reform of the Roman Missal by the Council of Trent (1545-1563) which omitted the sixth stanza (*Credendum est magis*) because of its uncomplimentary reference to the Jews.

As with many of these medieval texts, the authorship of this sequence has been ascribed to various writers, notably by Cardinal Bona to Notker Balbulus, to Robert II of France by Durandus, to Hermanus Contractus, and to Adam of St. Victor, even though it appears in a manuscript written before he was born. On the authority of an Einsiedeln manuscript of the 11th century, Schubiger (*Sängerschule St. Gallens*, 1858) ascribes it to Wipo (d.1048), a native of Burgundy who was a secular priest and poet. Thompson, however, thinks that the known poems of Wipo do not "show the fine ear for rhythm which the author of *Victimae paschali laudes* must have possessed" (in Duffield, *Latin Hymn Writers*). Julian likewise states that "there is nothing in the other pieces known as his which would lead us to connect the *Victimae paschali laudes* with his name" (*Dictionary of Hymnology*). On the other hand, M.I.J. Rousseay notes that the marked differences in style found in the two sections of the poem are similar to Wipo's "Song for the Lament of Conrad II" which "shows these same characteristics, a fact which strengthens his claim" (*New Catholic Encyclopedia*).

Martin Luther was particularly fond of this sequence, especially the *mors et vita duello* which he echoes in his *Christ lag in Todesbanden*: *"Es war ein wunderlicher Krieg/Da Tod und Leben rungen."* The sequence has also been a popular model for other writers who have imitated both its form and content.

Lastly, mention should be made of its use in the Easter Miracle or Mystery Plays and its influence on the development of liturgical drama. The intrinsic dramatic potential of the text was early recognized, both by authors and composers. "From this tiny seed, and not from the classical stage which perished centuries before, has grown the drama of today; first the miracle plays, then the moralities. From these it was by a short step to the plays of the modern stage" (Hughes, *Anglo-French Sequelae*, 1934).

Victimae paschali . . . Agnus redemit oves.

The sacrificial lamb of the Jewish Passover is now become the Paschal Victim; Christ, the Lamb of God (*Agnus Dei*), has redeemed the flock of sinners.

dux vitae mortuus regnat vivus.

The Prince of Life was crucified, yet, by his Resurrection, he again lives and reigns; "death is swallowed up in victory."

sudarium, et vestes.

Literally, "handkerchief, and clothes," rendered in King James as the "napkin" which covered his face during his entombment, and the "linen clothes" in which he was wrapped (John 20:6–7).

Liturgical context: **Victimae paschali laudes** is one of the five great sequences [the others being *Dies irae, Lauda Sion, Stabat Mater,* and *Veni Sancte Spiritus*]. It is sung daily at Mass during Eastertide, from Easter Sunday until the following Saturday, inclusive.

VIDENTES STELLAM

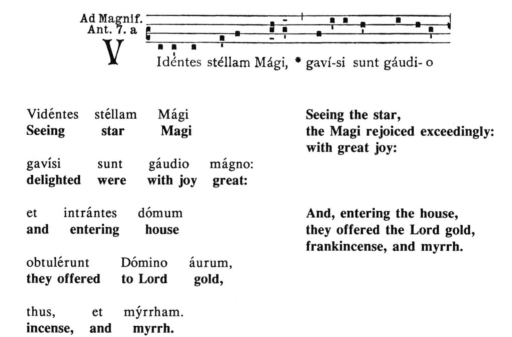

Vidéntes	stéllam	Mági		Seeing the star,
Seeing	**star**	**Magi**		the Magi rejoiced exceedingly:
				with great joy:
gavísi	sunt	gáudio	mágno:	
delighted	**were**	**with joy**	**great:**	
et	intrántes	dómum		And, entering the house,
and	**entering**	**house**		they offered the Lord gold,
				frankincense, and myrrh.
obtulérunt	Dómino	áurum,		
they offered	**to Lord**	**gold,**		
thus,	et	mýrrham.		
incense,	**and**	**myrrh.**		

The Epiphany or "manifestation" of Christ to the Gentiles in the person of the Magi is commemorated on January 6 or Twelfth Night (after Christmas). This is one of the oldest feasts of the Roman Church; it can be traced back to the end of the 3rd century. The Three Kings from the East and the Star they followed have caused the liturgy for this feast to be filled with images of rulers, kingdoms, dominion, and *light* :

Introit: "Behold the Lord the Ruler is come: and a kingdom in his hand, and power and dominion. (Malachias 3) Give to the king thy judgement, O God, and to the king's son thy justice." (Psalm 71 [72] : 1)

Lesson: *Surge, illuminare* -- "Arise, be enlightened, O Jerusalem, for thy light is come ... And the Gentiles shall walk in thy light, and kings in the brightness of thy rising ... *Omnes de Saba* -- All they from Saba shall come, bringing gold, and frankincense: and shew forth praise to the Lord." (Isaiah 60:1,3,6)

Gradual: Isaiah 60:6 and 60:1 as above; and additionally: "We have seen his star in the East and are come with gifts to adore the Lord." (Matthew 2:2)

Gospel: Matthew 2:1-12, the whole account of the Magi and their journey to Bethlehem to see the Christ child.

Offertory: "The kings of Tharsis and the isles shall offer gifts: the kings of the Arabians and of Saba shall bring presents: and all the kings of the earth shall adore him, and all nations shall serve him." (Psalm 71 [72] : 10-11)

Communion: Matthew 2:2, as above.

Liturgical context: **Videntes stellam** (Matthew 2:10-11) is the Magnificat antiphon during II. Vespers on the second day within the Octave of Epiphany.

VIDERUNT OMNES

| Vidérunt ómnes fines terrae | All the ends of the earth |
| **Have seen all ends of earth** | have seen the salvation of our God; |

| salutáre Déi nostri; | |
| **salvation of God our;** | |

| jubiláte Déo, omnis terra. | Sing joyfully unto God, all the earth. |
| **Sing joyfully to God, all earth.** | |

| Notum fecit Dóminus salutáre súum; | The Lord has made known his salvation; |
| **Known has made Lord salvation his;** | |

| ante conspéctum géntium | Before all nations he has revealed his justice. |
| **before sight of nations** | |

| revelávit justítiam súam. | |
| **he has revealed justice his.** | |

247

Three Masses are said on Christmas Day. The First Mass, at Midnight, celebrates the actual birth of Christ as it is described in the second chapter of St. Luke's Gospel. The Second Mass, the Aurora Mass at dawn, commemorates the coming of light into a world of darkness. And the Third Mass (of the Day) of the Nativity honors the eternal nature and the universal kingdom of the Word-made-flesh.

Viderunt omnes (Psalm 97 [98] : 3-4,2) is the Gradual for the Third Mass of Christmas Day. It follows the Introit (*Puer natus est*) and the Lesson from Hebrews 1:1-12 which tells of God's Son, "whom he hath appointed heir of all things ... [whose] throne is for ever and ever ... [who] shall continue ... the self-same; [whose] years shall not fail."

Viderunt <u>omnes</u> ... fines terrae ... omnis terra ... salutare Dei nostri.

The Alleluia-Verse which follows is *Dies sanctificatus* ("A holy day has dawned for us; come ye <u>nations</u>, and worship the Lord, for today a great light hath descended upon the earth"). The Gospel from the first chapter of John emphasizes that the kingdom of heaven is open to <u>all</u> believers: "To as many as received him, to them he gave the power to be made the sons of God"). The Offertory text reflects upon the universality of his kingdom once again: "Thine are the heavens, and thine is the earth: the world and the fullness thereof thou hast founded." (Psalm 88 [89] : 12) A shortened form of **Viderunt omnes** serves as the Communion antiphon near the close of this Third Mass of Christmas Day, affirming once more that "<u>All</u> the ends of the earth have seen the salvation of our God."

VIDI AQUAM

Ant. 8.

Vidi áquam *egre- di- éntem de tém-plo,

Vídi	áquam	egrediéntem	de		témplo,	I saw water flowing
I saw	**water**	**flowing**	**from**		**temple,**	from the right side of the temple, alleluia:

a	látere	déxtro,	allelúia:
from	**side**	**right,**	**alleluia:**

		And all to whom this water came were saved,
et	ómnes,	and they shall say: alleluia!
and	**all,**	

ad	quos	pervénit áqua	ísta,
to	**whom**	**came water**	**this,**

sálvi	fácti	sunt,	et	dícent,	allelúia.
saved	**made**	**were,**	**and**	**shall say,**	**alleluia.**

Since the 12th century the antiphon **Vidi aquam** has been sung during Paschaltide to accompany the ceremonial sprinkling of holy water which immediately precedes the principal Mass on Sundays. It replaces the *Asperges me, Domine* which is sung during this ceremony the rest of the liturgical year.

Ezekiel's vision of the waters issuing forth from the right side of the temple (Ezekiel 47:1-12), an Old Testament vision of Baptism, was fulfilled by Christ on the Cross when "one of the soldiers opened his side with a lance, and immediately there came out blood and water" (John 19:34). "And he showed me a river of the water of life, clear as crystal, coming forth from the throne of God and of the Lamb" (Apocalypse [Revelation] 22:1).

Liturgical context: **Vidi aquam** is the antiphon sung during the Paschal season (from Easter Sunday to Pentecost inclusive) at the sprinkling of holy water which preceeds the principal Sunday Mass. It replaces the *Asperges* which is sung at this time during the rest of the year.

VINEA MEA ELECTA

Resp. 8.
VI-ne-a mé-a * e-lé- cta, égo te plan-

Vinea méa elécta, égo te plantávi: Vineyard my chosen, I you planted:	O vineyard, my chosen one, I planted you:
Quomódo convérsa es in amaritúdinem, How have been changed you into bitterness,	How have you been changed into bitterness,
ut me crucifígeres et Barábbam dimítteres? that me would crucify and Barabbas dismiss?	that you would crucify me and set Barabbas free?
Sepívi te et lápides elégi I enclosed you and stones picked	I built a fence around you and picked the stones from you and built a watchtower.
ex te et aedificávit túrrim. from you and built up tower.	

In Psalm 80:8-16 Israel is "the vine brought out of Egypt" which flourishes but is eventually ravaged. In the parable of the vineyard found in Isaiah 5:1-7 (the source for most of the **Vinea mea electa** text), the "vineyard" is "the house of Israel, and the men of Judah [are] the plant of his pleasures." Jeremiah 2:21 echoes: "Yet I had planted thee a noble vine, wholly a right seed: how then art thou turned into the degenerate plant of a strange vine unto me?"

The unknown author of this text extends the metaphor into a New Testament context, asking not why the "chosen vine" was ravaged or brought forth the "wild grapes" of transgression, but how God's chosen Israel could become so embittered that they would be capable of crucifying Christ and freeing the thief Barabbas.

Liturgical context: **Vinea mea electa** appears during the I. Nocturn of Matins on Good Friday as a Responsory to the third Lesson from the third chapter of the Lamentations of Jeremiah which ends with the words:

> "He hath built against me round about, that I may not get out: he hath made my fetters heavy. Yea, and when I cry, and entreat, he hath shut out my prayer. He hath shut up my ways with square stones, he hath turned my paths upside down." (Lamentations 3:7-9)

VIRGA JESSE FLORUIT

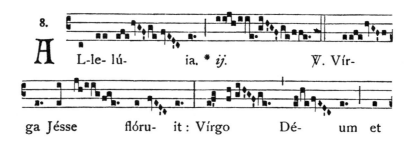

8. ᴀ Ll-le- lú-   ia. * *ij.*   ℣. Vír-

ga Jésse   flóru- it : Vírgo   Dé-   um et

| Vírga | Jésse | flóruit: | | | The rod of Jesse has blossomed: |
| **Rod** | **of Jesse** | **has blossomed:** | | | |

| Vírgo | Déum | et | hóminem | génuit: | a virgin has begotten One |
| **Virgin** | **God** | **and** | **man** | **has begotten:** | who is both God and man; |

| pácem | Déus | réddidit, | | | God has restored peace, |
| **peace** | **God** | **has restored,** | | | |

| in | se | reconcílians | íma | súmmis. | reconciling in himself the lowest to the highest. |
| **in** | **himself** | **reconciling** | **lowest** | **to highest.** | |

Allelúia.   Alleluia!
Alleluia!

"And there shall come forth a rod out of the root of Jesse, and a flower shall rise up out of his root.

"And the spirit of the Lord shall rest upon him: the spirit of wisdom, and of understanding, the spirit of counsel, and of fortitude, the spirit of knowledge, and of godliness.

"And he shall be filled with the spirit of the fear of the Lord. He shall not judge according to the sight of the eyes, nor reprove according to the hearing of the ears.

"But he shall judge the poor with justice, and shall reprove with equity for the meek of the earth: and he shall strike the earth with the rod of his mouth . . . " (Isaiah 11:1–4)

Mary, the Virgin Mother of God, was of the house and lineage of David who was the son of Jesse. Through heaven's portal the prophecy was fulfilled, the Word was made flesh *et Christus homo factus est.* The rod or sceptre of power blossomed forth; the fruit of the Blessed Virgin's womb, endowed with the Holy Spirit's sevenfold gifts of grace, has come to judge *omnes terra* with righteousness and equity. *O admirabile commercium* and *mirabile mysterium*: God has become man. That which he was, he remained; and that which he was not, he assumed: suffering neither mixture nor division. Thus reconciling within himself the lowest with the highest, he has restored peace to his people. *Alleluia!*

Liturgical context: **Virga Jesse floruit** is the Alleluia verse appointed for use in the Common Masses of the Blessed Virgin Mary from the Feast of the Purification (February 2) until Easter.

"Translation changes the character of a work and destroys its cultural unity. The presentation of works in their original language is a sign of rich culture in my opinion . . . Let librettos and texts be published in translation, let synopses and arguments of plots be distributed in advance, let imaginations be appealed to, but do not change the sound and stress of the words that have been composed to precisely certain music at precisely certain places."
(Igor Stravinsky)

Selected Settings
of
Sacred Latin Texts

"It should be a part of the choirmaster's business to translate and explain these texts to the choir, that they may be recited or sung with the understanding as well as with the voice." (H.T. Henry)

SELECTED SETTINGS OF LATIN TEXTS

This listing provides general information about the variety of composers, styles, and voicings associated with each of the translated texts. Performers are first encouraged to check the thorough listings in Musicdata's SACRED CHORAL MUSIC IN PRINT (Philadelphia, 1985; Supplement, 1988) for available editions and prices. In addition, consult the Complete Works and the listings in The New Grove Dictionary of Music and Musicians (1980) of specific composers as well as publisher's catalogs. If you still have questions, write to the publisher of this book and we will provide what information we have. [N.B. Some of these listings are only as good as our sources; considerable discretion has been exercised, but it has not been possible to verify the accuracy and authenticity of each entry. Our apologies for any spurious listings and any inconvenience this may occasion.]

Abbreviations:

satb/satb	double chorus
satb(ttbb)	optional voicing written by the composer
satb;O(2vn)	optional instruments
(2)satb	two different settings for satb
(arr)	a *few* often-performed arrangements are listed

A,a	alto	hrn	horn	str	strings
B,b	bass	hpsd	harpsichord	T,t	tenor
boy	boy soprano	inst	instruments	tr	treble solo
bc	basso continuo	kbd	keyboard	trb	trombone
br	brass	O	organ	trp	trumpet
bsn	bassoon	ob	oboe	v	voices
cb	contrabass	orch	orchestra	va	viola
cel	celesta	P	piano	vc	violoncello
cl	clarinet	perc	percussion	vib	vibraphone
fl	flute	S,s	soprano	vn	violin

ABSALOM, FILI MI

DES PREZ, J.	satb
JOHNSON, C.	T,ssaattbb
SCHUETZ, H.	B;4trb,bc

AD DOMINUM CON TRIBULARER

BYRD, W.	ssaattbb
HASSLER, H.L.	ssatb
HAYDN, M.	satb;2vn,2hrn,bc
OLSSON, O.	satb
SCARLATTI, A.	satb
SCHUETZ, H.	satb;bc

ADORAMUS TE, CHRISTE

AICHINGER, G.	ssaa
AICHINGER, G.	ssab
BENELLI, A.	satb
BRAHMS, J.	ssaa
BYRD, W.	ssatb
CLEMENS, J.	satb
CORSI, G.	satb
DUBOIS, T.	satb
GASPARINI, F.	satb
GESUALDO, C.	satttb
LASSUS, O.	(2)sss
LASSUS, O.	ssa(ttb)
LASSUS, O.	satb
LASSUS, O.	ssssa

LOTTI, A.	satb
MARTINI, G.	ssa(ttb)
MERULO, C.	ssattb
MONTEVERDI, C.	ssatbb;bc
MOZART (GASPARINI)	satb;O
PALESTRINA, G.P.	satb
PERTI, G.	satb
PITONI, G.	satb
RHEINBERGER, J.	ssa;O
ROSSELLI, F.	satb
RUFFO, V.	ttbb
SLOGEDAL, B.	satb
VIADANA, L.	satb
ZIELENSKI, N.	satb;O

ALMA REDEMPTORIS MATER

ANERIO, F.	satb
BERNABEI, G.	satb
BYRD, W.	satb
CAVALLI, F.	ssatb;bc
CHARPENTIER, M-A.	ss;bc
DAVIES, P.M.	canon a4
DES PREZ, J.	(2)satb
DUFAY, G.	(2)3v
DUNSTABLE, J.	att
GUERRERO, F.	satb
ISAAC, H.	4v
KOPRIVA, J.V.	SA,ssa;str,O
LASSUS, O.	ssatb
LASSUS, O.	(2)ssattb
LASSUS, O.	ssab/ssab
MARENZIO, L.	satb
OBRECHT, J.	3v
OCKEGHEM, J.	attb
PALESTRINA, G.P.	(2)4v
PALESTRINA, G.P.	(2)8v
PHILIPS, P.	5v
PHILIPS, P.	8v
VICTORIA, T.L.	5v
VICTORIA, T.L.	8v

ANGELUS AD PASTORES AIT

FRANCK, C.	ssatbb
GABRIELI, A.	7v
GABRIELI, G.	4v
GABRIELI, G.	7v
GABRIELI, G.	11v
HASSLER, H.L.	satb
HASSLER, H.L.	ssat/saatb

LASSUS, O.	satbb
MATTHIAS, W.	ssaa
MONTEVERDI, C.	ssa(ttb)
MOUTON, J.	4v
PINKHAM, D.	ssaa
SCHEIDT, S.	satb/satb
SWEELINCK, J.P.	ssatb;bc
VULPIUS, M.	ssatb/ttbb

ASCENDIT DEUS

BURKHART, F.	ttbb
BYRD, W.	ssatb
CLEMENS, J.	5v
ESTERHAZY, P.	satb;2tr,bc
GABRIELI, G.	4 choirs a4
HANDL, J.	satb
PALESTRINA, G.P.	ssaa
PALESTRINA, G.P.	sattb
PHILIPS, P.	5v
WILLIAMSON, M.	satb;O

ASPERGES ME, DOMINE

BRUCKNER, A.	satb
BRUCKNER, A.	(2)satb;O
CERTON, P.	4v
HAYDN, M.	satb;O
ISAAC, H.	4v
LASSUS, O.	(2)5v
MORALES, C.	4v
PALESTRINA, G.P.	(2)4v
SENFL, L.	satb
VICTORIA, T.L.	4v
ZELENKA, J.D.	satb;bc

ASSUMPTA EST MARIA

AICHINGER, G.	3v
BYRD, W.	ssatb
GESUALDO (STRAVINSKY)	sattbb
ISAAC, H.	4v
PALESTRINA, G.P.	5v
PALESTRINA, G.P.	6v
PHILIPS, P.	5v

AVE DULCISSIMA MARIA

GESUALDO, C.   sattb

AVE MARIA

AICHINGER, G.	satb
ANDRIESSEN, H.	satb
ARCADELT, J.	satb
AUBANEL, G.	satb
BACH–GOUNOD, C.	(arr)
BINKERD, G.	satb
BIZET, G.	satb
BRAHMS, J.	ssaa;orch
BRUCKNER, A.	SA,satb;vc,O
BRUCKNER, A.	saattbb
BRUCKNER, O.	A,satb;O
BRUML, A.	3v
BYRD, W.	atb
BYRD, W.	saatb
CANNICIORI, P.	satb
CASALI, G.B.	satb
CERTON, P.	3v
CHAUSSON, E.	satb;vc,hp,O
CHERUBINI, L.	ssa
CHIHARA, P.	satb
CLEMENS, J.	5v
DEERING, R.	5v
DES PREZ, J.	(2)satb
DES PREZ, J.	ssatbb
DETT, N.	satb
DONIZETTI, G.	S,satb;str
ELGAR, E.	satb;O
FAURÉ, G.	ttb;O
FAURÉ, G.	ss;O
FRANCK, C.	satb
FRANCK, C.	stb;O
FUX, J.	satb
GABRIELI, A.	ssa
GABURO, K.	satb
GLUCK, C.	ttbb
GOICOECHEA, V.	T,ttbb;O
GOMBERT, N.	ssattbb
GRETCHANINOV, A.	satb;O
GUERRERO, F.	satb
GUMPELTSHEIMER, A.	satb
HANDEL, G.F.	sa
HANDL, J.	attbb
HAYDN, J.	satb
HAYDN, M.	satb
HOLST, G.	ssaa div.
HOVHANESS, A.	ssaa;2ob,2hrn,hp
ISAAC, H.	4v

JANÁČEK, L.	satb
KODÁLY, Z.	ssa
LASSUS, O.	sattb
LISZT, F.	(3)satb;O
MENDELSSOHN, F.	SOLI,ssaattbb;O
MONTEVERDI, C.	ssa
MORALES, C.	5v
MOUTON, J.	satb
MOZART, W.A.	canon a4
OCKEGHEM, J.	4v
PALESTRINA, G.P.	(3)4v
PALESTRINA, G.P.	5v
PALESTRINA, G.P.	8v
PEETERS, F.	3v;O
PINKHAM, D.	sa
RAGNARSSON, H.	ssaattbb
RHEINBERGER, J.	satb
ROSSINI, G.	satb
SAINT-SAËNS, C.	satb
SCELSI, G.	unis
SCHUETZ, H.	SA,ssatb;inst,bc
SENFL, L.	ssatbb
SMITH, G.	ssa/satb;cel,O
STOUT, A.	satb
STRAVINSKY, I.	satb
VERDI, G.	satb
VICTORIA, T.L.	4v
VICTORIA, T.L.	8v
VIERNE, L.	satb;O
VILLA-LOBOS, H.	satb
WILLAERT, A.	attb
WITT, F.X.	satb;O
ZUCHINO, G.	satb/satb

AVE MARIS STELLA

ANERIO, F.	ttbb
BADINGS, H.	ttbb
BARDOS, L.	ssa
BYRD, W.	stb
CAVALLI, F.	atb;bc
CHAUSSON, E.	satb;vc,hp,O
CLEMENS, J.	5v
DES PREZ, J.	satb
DUFAY, G.	3v
DUNSTABLE, J.	att
ELGAR, E.	S,satb;O
GORCZYCKI, G.	satb
GRIEG, E.	satb
HASSLER, H.L.	satb
HOMILIUS, G.	satb
KVERNO, T.	satb
LISZT, F.	satb;O

LISZT, F.	ttbb;O
MARENZIO, C.	satb/satb/satb
MARTINI, G.	ssaa;4tr,str,bc
MASSENET, J.	2v;vc,O
MEYEROWITZ, J.	ttbb;br
MONTEVERDI, C.	2v/8v
OBRECHT, J.	3v
OLSSON, O.	ssattbb
PALESTRINA, G.P.	5v
PHILIPS, P.	5v
SALAS, E.	satb
SCARLATTI, A.	satb;bc
SWEELINCK, J.P.	canan a3
VICTORIA, T.L.	(2)4v
WESLEY, S.	ss

PALESTRINA, G.P.	(3)4v
PALESTRINA, G.P.	5v
PALESTRINA, G.P.	(2)8v
PERTI, G.	sattb
PHILLIPS, P.	ssatb
POWER, L.	atb
RHEINBERGER, J.	satb;O
RHEINBERGER, J.	ssa;O
SCARLATTI, A.	ss;bc
SURIANO, F.	satb
VICTORIA, T.L.	5v
VICTORIA, T.L.	8v
WILLAERT, A.	attb
ZELENKA, J.D.	satb;bc

AVE REGINA COELORUM

AICHINGER, G.	3v
AICHINGER, G.	satb
ANERIO, F.	sttb
BADINGS, H.	ttbb
BINKERD, G.W.	ssatb
BRUCKNER, A.	satb;O
BYRD, W.	satb
CAVALLI, F.	ssatb;bc
CERTON, P.	3v
CHARPENTIER, M.A.	ssa;bc
DES PREZ, J.	satb
DUFAY, G.	att
DUFAY, G.	satb
FUX, J.	satb
GABRIELI, A.	satb/attb
GESUALDO, C.	sattb
GOMBERT, N.	satb
GOMBERT, N.	attbb
GUERRERO, F.	satb
HASSLER, H.L.	satb
HAYDN, J.	S,satb;2vn,O
HAYDN, M.	satb/satb;2vn,O
INDY, V.	satb
KROMOLICKI, J.	satb;2trp,2trb,O
LA RUE, P.	satb
LASSUS, O.	3v
LASSUS, O.	4v
LASSUS, O.	5v
LASSUS, O.	(2)6v
LEONARDA, I.	satb;bc
LOTTI, A.	satb
MORALES, C.	5v
OBRECHT, J.	3v

AVE VERUM CORPUS

AUBANEL, G.	satb;O
BINCHOIS, G.	atb
BRUCKNER, A.	satb
BYRD, W.	satb
CHAUSSON, E.	satb;vn,O
CHERUBINI, L.	sss
CLEMENS, J.	sattb
DEERING, R.	sattb;O
DES PREZ, J.	sab
DES PREZ, J.	satb
ELGAR, E.	S,satb;O
FAURÉ, G.	sa(tb);O
FRANCK, C.	satb
FUX, J.	satb
GOUNOD, C.	ssatb
GRETCHANINOV, A.	satb;O
GUILMANT, A.	satb,O
JENNI, D.	sat
LASSUS, O.	ssattb
LISZT, F.	satb,O
MARTINI, G.	3v
MENDELSSOHN, F.	satb
MOZART, W.A.	satb;str,O
PALESTRINA, G.P.	5v
PEETERS, F.	satb;O
PERGOLESI, G.B.	unis;bc
PINKHAM, D.	satb;O
POULENC, F.	ssa
RAMINSH, I.	satb
SAINT-SAËNS, C.	satb;hrn,O
SCHUBERT, F.	satb
SÜSSMAYR, F.X.	satb;O,orch
VIADANA, L.	satb
VITTORIA, T.L.	satb
ZANINELLI, L.	satb

BEATUS VIR

BACH, J.C.	SATB,satb;orch
CAMPRA, A.	SOLI,5v;orch
CAVALLI, F.	atb;2vn,vc,bc
CHARPENTIER	SOLI,satb/satb;orch
COLONNA, G.	ssatb;O
COMES, J.B.	satb/satb
GALUPPI, B.	SA,satb;orch
HAYDN, M.	SS,ssa;2hrn,2vn,bc
LASSUS, O.	attb
LASSUS, O.	ssattb
LOTTI, A.	satb
MONTEVERDI, C.	sattb;bc
MONTEVERDI, C.	ssattb;2vn,bc
MONTEVERDI, C.	ssaattb;2vn,bc
MOZART, W.A.	(2)SATB,satb;orch
PERGOLESI, G.B.	satb;str,O
PERTI, G.	satb
SCARLATTI, A.	ssatb;O
STEFFANI, A.	8v;bc
VICTORIA, T.L.	satb
VICTORIA, T.L.	satb/satb
VIVALDI, A.	SOLI,satb/satb;orch
ZELENKA, J.D.	STB,satb;2ob,str,bc

BENEDICAMUS DOMINO

DUFAY, G.	(2)3v
HESELTINE, P.	satb
PRAETORIUS, M.	ssa
SCHEIDT, S.	5v;bc

CANTATE DOMINO

ALAIN, A.	satb
ANERIO, F.	satb
BANCHIERI, A.	satb
BUXTEHUDE, D.	ssb;bc
BYRD, W.	6v
CAMPRA, A.	2v
CARISSIMI, G.	ssb;bc
CROCE, G.	satb
CRÜGER, J.	sab
DEERING, R.	ssattb;O
DES PREZ, J.	ssatb
GABRIELI, A.	5v
GABRIELI, G.	satb
GABRIELI, G.	ssattb

GABRIELI, G.	satb/satb;bc
GRETCHANINOV, A.	satb;O
GUERRERO, F.	ssatb
HANDEL, G.F.	satb
HASSLER, H.L.	satb
HASSLER, H.L.	ssatb
HASSLER, H.L.	ssat/satb/ttbb
HAYDN, J.	3v
HAYDN, M.	satb;orch,O
INDY, V.	atb
LALANDE, M-R.	5v
LASSUS, O.	5v
LASSUS, O.	6v
LECHNER, L.	satb
LEWKOVITCH, B.	satb
MARENZIO, L.	ssaa/ttbb
MONTEVERDI, C.	ss(tt);bc
MONTEVERDI, C.	ssattb;bc
MOZART, W.A.	canon
PITONI, G.	satb
PRAETORIUS, M.	ssat/attb
SCHUETZ, H.	satb;bc
SERMISY, C.	4v
SLOGEDAL, B.	satb
SWEELINCK, J.P.	ssatb;bc
VECCHI, O.	satb
VIADANA, L.	satb
WILLIAMSON, M.	satb;O

CHRISTUS FACTUS EST

ANERIO, F.	satb
ASOLA, G.	satb
BRUCKNER, A.	ssaattbb
BRUCKNER, A.	ssaattbb;2vn,3trb
CARISSIMI, G.	atb;O
CASALI, G.	satb
COMES, J.B.	satb
DURANTE, F.	sab;O
EBERLIN, J.E.	satb
HANDL, J.	satb
HAYDN, M.	satb
JOMMELLI, N.	3v;bc
LEO, L.	sa;O
LEWKOVITCH, B.	satb
PALESTRINA, G.P.	4v
PETRASSI, G.	satbb
PITONI, G.	satb
STOUT, A.	satb;str
ZINGARELLI, N.	satb

CONFITEBOR TIBI DOMINO

BACH, J.C.	SATB,satb;orch
BINKERD, G.	satb
CALDARA, A.	S,satb;str,ob,O
CARISSIMI, G.	ssb;bc
CAVALLI, F.	ssaattbb;2vn,vc,bc
GABRIELI, G.	13v
HASSLER, H.L.	ssat/ttbb
HAYDN, M.	ssa;2vn,bc
LALANDE, M-R.	SATB,satb;2fl,str,bc
LASSUS, O.	4v
LASSUS, O.	6v
LASSUS, O.	8v
MONTEVERDI, C.	2v;2vn
MONTEVERDI, C.	3v
MONTEVERDI, C.	stb;2vn,bc
MONTEVERDI, C.	4v
MONTEVERDI, C.	ssatb;bc
MOZART, W.A.	S,satb;3trb,2vn,O,bc
MOZART, W.A.	SATB,satb;orch
OLSSON, O.	ssaattbb
PALESTRINA, G.P.	5v
PALESTRINA, G.P.	8v
PERGOLESI, G.B.	S,ssatb;orch,O
SCARLATTI, A.	ssatb;O
VIADANA, L.	satb
VIVALDI, A.	satb

CONFITEMINI DOMINO

CARISSIMI, G.	bb;bc
COSTANTINI, F.	ssa
HAYDN, M.	satb
KŘENEK, E.	ssa
LALANDE, M-R.	SATB,satb;orch
LASSUS, O.	sattb
LASSUS, O.	sattbb
PALESTRINA, G.P.	4v
SCHUETZ, H.	sst;bc
SCHUETZ, H.	satb;bc

DE PROFUNDIS

BERGER, J.	satb
BOULANGER, L.	A,satb;orch
CAMPRA, A.	SOLI,satb;orch
CHARPENTIER, M.A.	SOLI,satb;bc
CHORBAJIAN, J.	ssaattbb
CLARI, G.C.M.	SATB,satb;O
DES PREZ, J.	satb

DES PREZ, J.	satbb
DUDA, T.	satb
GABRIELI, A.	saatbb
GLUCK, C.	satb;orch
GOUNOD, C.	B,satb;orch
HAYDN, M.	SSA,ssa;2vn,bc
HOFFMANN, E.T.A.	satb
ISAAC, H.	(2)4v
KŘENEK, E.	ssa
LALANDE, M-R.	SOLI,5v,orch
LASSUS, O.	ssattb
LEWKOVITCH, B.	satb
LEVY, E.	satb;orch
LIDHOLM, I.	ssaatttbbb
LISZT, F.	B,ttbb;O
LULLY, J-B.	satb/satbb;orch
MARTINI, G.	4v
MORLEY, T.	6v
MOZART (REUTTER)	satb,O
NYSTEDT, K.	ssaattbbb
PALESTRINA, G.P.	4v
PALESTRINA, G.P.	5v
PÄRT, A.	ttbb;O,(perc)
REUTTER, C.G.	satb;O
SALIERI, A.	satb;vla,bsn,cb
SWEELINCK, J.P.	sattb
THOMSON, V.	satb
VIADANA, L.	satb
VLAD, R.	satb;orch
VULPIUS, M.	ssattb
WELLESZ, E.	satb
WITT, F.X.	satb
ZELENKA	AT,satb;2ob,3trb,str,O

DEO DICAMUS GRATIAS

HOMILIUS, G.A.	ssattb
PRAETORIUS, M.	satb

DIES SANCTIFICATUS

BYRD, W.	satb
CROCE, G.	sattb
EYBLER, J.	satb;orch
HANDEL, G.F.	satb
HANDL, J.	satb
ISAAC, H.	satb
KROEGER, K.	satb
PALESTRINA, G.P.	4v
PALESTRINA, G.P.	8v
SANTA CRUZ, D.	ssa
STOLZER, T.	satb

DIXIT DOMINUS

BACH, J.C.	SATB,satb;orch
BERNARDI, S.	S,satb;bc
CARISSIMI, G.	ssatb;bc
CAVALLI, F.	satb/satb;2vln,vc,bc
EBERLIN, J.	SATB,satb;br,str,bc
GALUPPI, B.	ssaa;str,bc
HANDEL, G.F.SSATB,ssatb;2vn,2va,bc
HAYDN, M.	SSA,ssa;2hrn,2vn,bc
LALANDE, M.R.	satb,SATB;O
LASSUS, O.	satb/satb
LOTTI, A.	SATB,satb;2ob,trp,O
MONTEVERDI, C.	4v
MONTEVERDI, C.	ssattb;bc
MONTEVERDI, C.	(2)ssaattbb;2vn,bc
MORALES, C.	4v
MOZART, W.A.	(2)SATB,satb;orch,O
PALESTRINA, G.P.	4v
PERGOLESI, G.B.	SSATB,satb,str,O
PERGOLESI	SATB,satb/satb;2orch
PERGOLESI	SSAAB,satb;2hn,str,O
SCARLATTI, A.	ssatb;O
SCARLATTI, A.	ssatb;ob,2vn,va,bc
SCARLATTI, A.	ssatb;O
SCARLATTI, A.	SATB,satb;3vln,bc
VIADANA, L.	satb
VITTORIA, T.L.	satb/satb
VIVALDI, A.	SOLI,satb/satb;orch
ZELENKA, J.D.	SATB,satb;orch

DIXIT MARIA

HASSLER, H.L.	satb

DUO SERAPHIM CLAMABANT

AICHINGER, G.	ssa
DEERING, R.	ssb;bc
GUERRERO, F.	ssat/satb/satb
HANDL, J.	satb/satb
HASSLER, H.L.	ssat/saat/ttbb
HASSLER, H.L.	ssat/ssab/aatb/atbb
MONTEVERDI, C.	3v
SCHEIDT, S.	ssat/atbb
VICTORIA, T.L.	ssaa

ECCE SACERDOS

BRUCKNER, A.	ssaattbb,3trb,O
HAYDN, M.	satb;O

ISAAC, H.	4v
JENNI, D.	satb;O
PALESTRINA, G.P.	6v
PORTA, C.	6v
VICTORIA, T.L.	satb

EXSULTATE DEO

ANDRIESSEN, W.	satb;O
CRÜGER, J.	sat
HANDL, J.	sattb
HASSLER, H.L.	ssatb
LEWKOVITCH, B.	satb
MENDELSSOHN, F.	satb
NAJERA, E.	satb;P
PALESTRINA, G.P.	saatb
POULENC, F.	ssattbb
SCARLATTI, A.	satb
SCARLATTI, D.	
WESLEY, S.	ssatb

EXSULTATE JUSTI

BANCHIERI, A.	sb(tb)
GABRIELLI, G.	satb/abbb
HASSLER, H.L.	ssat/satb/satb/atbb
LASSUS, O.	satb
VIADANA, L.	satb
VULPIUS, M.	satb

GLORIA PATRI

CALDARA, A.	S,sab;2vn,bc
CARISSIMI, G.	4v
DEERING, R.	ssb;bc
FRANCK, C.	4v/5v
LASSUS. O.	6v
LUBOFF, N.	satb
MORALES, C.	satb
PALESTRINA, G.P.	satb/satb
PALESTRINA, G.P.	satbb
PERGOLESI	satb;orch
TALLIS, T.	satb
VIVALDI, A.	satb/satb;orch

HAEC DIES

ARCADELT, J.	satb
BRUML, A.	4v
BYRD, W.	atb
BYRD, W.	ssatb

BYRD, W.	ssattb
DONATI, I.	satb;bc(vln)
HANDL, J.	satb/satb
INGENERI, M.A.	satb
KŘENEK, E.	ssa
LEONIN	sa
NANINI, G.	sattb
PALESTRINA, G.P.	satb
PALESTRINA, G.P.	ssattb
PALESTRINA, G.P.	satb/satb
VIADANA, L.	satb

HODIE CHRISTUS NATUS EST

ANDRIESSEN, H.	satb;O
BASSANO, G.	ssa/satb
BRITTEN, B.	unis,hp
BYRD, W.	satb
CLERAMBAULT	sa/satb;kbd(str)
ERBACH, C.	satb
GABRIELI, A.	7v
GABRIELI, G.	satb/satb
GABRIELI, G.	ssatb/abbbb
HANDL, J.	ssa/ttb
HASSLER, H.L.	saatb/sattb
MARENZIO, L.	satb
MONTEVERDI, C.	ssa(ttb)
NANINO, G.	satb
PALESTRINA, G.P.	satb
PALESTRINA, G.P.	satb/satb
POULENC, F.	satb
RORE, C.	ssattb
SANTA CRUZ, D.	ssaa
SCHUETZ, H.	ssattb;bc
SWEELINCK, J.P.	ssatb;bc
WILLAN, H.	satb

IN DULCI JUBILO

BACH, J.S.	satb
BUXTEHUDE, D.	sab;2vn,bc
ECCARD, J.	satb
HASSLER, H.L.	satb
LOEWE, C.	satb
NAJERA, E.	ssaattbb
PEARSALL, R.	SOLI,5v
PRAETORIUS, M.	satb;br
REGER, M.	ssattb
SCHEIDT, S.	ssat/atbb;2tr
TELEMANN, G	ATB,satb;orch
WILLIAMSON, M.	satb;P/O

IN ECCLESIIS

GABRIELI, G.	14v

IN MONTE OLIVETI

BRUCKNER, A.	satb
CROCE, G.	satb
GESUALDO, C.	sattbb
HAYDN, M.	satb;O
INGENERI, M.A.	satb
JOMELLI, N.	satb
LASSUS, O.	saatbb
MARTINI, G.	sab
PALESTRINA, G.P.	satb
RUBBRA, E.	satb
SCHUBERT, F.	satb
ZIELENSKI, M.	5v;O

JESU, DULCIS MEMORIA

BUXTEHUDE, D.	ss;2vn,va,bc
BUXTEHUDE, D.	atb;2vn,bc
DEERING, R.	5v
HANDL, J.	ssattbb
OLSSON, O.	B,ssattb
VICTORIA, T.L.	satb

JUBILATE DEO

AIBLINGER, J.	satbb
AICHINGER, G.	ssatb
ANDRIESSEN, H.	satb;O
BADINGS, H.	ttbb
BANCHIERI, A.	satb
CLEMENS, J.	6v
DEERING, R.	6v
DES PREZ, J.	satb
EYBLER, J.	satb;orch,O
GABRIELI, A.	8v
GABRIELI, G.	(2)8v
GABRIELI, G.	10v
GABRIELI, G.	15v
HANDEL, G.F.	AAB,ssaattbb;orch
HANDL, J.	satb
HASSLER, H.L.	ssatb
HASSLER, H.L.	ssat/attb
HASSLER, H.L.	satb/satb
HASSLER, H.L.	ssat/satb/atbb
HASSLER, H.L.	ssat/saatb/attbb

LAUDA SION

BRUML, A.	4v
BUXTEHUDE, D.	ssb;2vn,va,bc
DUFAY, G.	3v
HAYDN, J.	satb;str,O
LASSUS, O.	ssatbb
MENDELSSOHN, F.	SATB,satb;orch
MONTEVERDI, C.	ssa(sab)
PALESTRINA, G.P.	4v
PALESTRINA, G.P.	6v
PALESTRINA, G.P.	(2)8v
RUBBRA, E.	SB,satb/satb
SERMISY, C.	4v
VICTORIA, T.L.	satb/satb;bc

LAUDATE DOMINUM IN SANCTIS EJUS

AICHINGER, F.	satb/satb
BRUMEL, A.	satb
FRANCK, C.	satb;orch
GABRIELI, A.	10v
GINASTERA, A.	unis/satb;orch
HASSLER, H.L.	ssat/attb
KOKKONEN, J.	S,satb
LANGLAIS, J.	unis/satb;inst
LASSUS, O.	sattb
MARENZIO, L.	satb/4 inst
MARENZIO, L.	satb/satb
MECHEM, K.	satb
MONTE, P.	aatb/attb;bc
PALESTRINA, G.P.	8v
PITONI, G.	satb
ROGIER, P.	satb/satb
STRAVINSKY, I.	satb;orch
SWEELINCK, J.P.	satb

LAUDATE DOMINUM OMNES GENTES

BYRD, W.	ssatbb
CAVALLI, F.	satb/satb;br,str,bc
CHARPENTIER, M.A.	SOLI,4v;bc
CHARPENTIER, M.A.	SOLI,8v;fl,str,bc
CHARPENTIER, M.A.	atb;2trp,str,bc
CORBOZ, M.	satb
CROCE, G.	satb/satb
GABRIELI, A.	5v
GRETCHANINOV, A.	satb;O
HASSLER, H.L.	satb
HASSLER, H.L.	ssattb
HASSLER, H.L.	ssab/ttbb

LASSUS, O.	6v
LASSUS, O.	12v
LISZT, F.	satb;O
MONTEVERDI, C.	(2)8v;2vn,bc
MONTEVERDI, C.	ssaattbb;bc
MOZART, W.A.	S,satb;orch,O
MOZART, W.A.	S,satb;2vn,(bsn),bc
PALESTRINA, G.P.	8v
PITONI, G.	satb
PORTA, C.	satb/satb;O
PRAETORIUS, M.	ssattbb
PRAETORIUS, M.	satb/satb
RHEINBERGER, J.	ssattb
SCARLATTI, A.	sattb;str,bc
SERMISY, C.	4v
SWEELINCK, J.P.	ssatb;bc
TALLIS, T.	attbb
TELEMANN, G.	satb;2vn,bc
VICTORIA, T.L.	satb/satb
VIVALDI, A.	satb;str,bc

LAUDATE PUERI

BUXTEHUDE, D.	ss;5va,bc
BYRD, W.	sattbb
CALDARA, F.	S,satb;str,bc
CAVALLI, F.	ssatb;2vn,vc,bc
COUPERIN, F.	SB,3v;str,bc
DES PREZ, J.	satb
HANDEL, G.F.	S,ssatb;2ob,str,bc
HASSLER, H.L.	satb/satb
HAYDN, M.	ssa;bc
LASSUS, O.	ssaattbb
LOTTI, A.	ssa;str
MARTINI, G.	satb
MENDELSSOHN, F.	SSA,ssa;O
MONTEVERDI, C.	ssaattbb
MONTEVERDI, C.	(2)ssttb
MOZART, W.A.	(2)satb;orch
PALESTRINA, G.P.	4v
PALESTRINA, G.P.	8v
PERGOLESI, G.B.	S,satb;orch
TELEMANN, G.P.	satb;orch
VICTORIA, T.L.	satb/satb
VIVALDI, A.	(2)satb
VIVALDI, A.	satb/satb
WIDOR, C-M.	satb/satb;orch,(2)O
ZELENKA, J.D.	SOLI,ssab;O

LOCUS ISTE

AIBLINGER, J.	satb
BRUCKNER, A.	satb

MAGNIFICAT

ALBRECHTSBERGER, J.	(16)	MARTINI, G.	satb/satb;str,O
ANDRIESSEN, H.	satb,O	MENDELSSOHN, F.	satb;orch
ANDRIESSEN, J.	S,satb;orch	MONTE, P.	6v
BACH, C.P.E.	SATB,satb;orch	MONTE, P.	7v
BACH, J.C.	SATB,satb/satb;orch	MONTEVERDI, C.	4v
BACH. J.S.	(2)SSATB,ssatb;orch	MONTEVERDI, C.	6v;bc
BERIO, L.	SS,satb;2P,ww,br,perc,cb	MONTEVERDI, C.	7v;3trb,2vn,bc
BRUCKNER	SATB,satb;orch	MONTEVERDI, C.	8v
BRUML, A.	(2)3v	MORALES, C.	(16)4-6v
BRUML, A.	4v	MOZART, W.A.	(2)SATB,satb;orch
BUXTEHUDE	B,ssatb;str,bc	MOUTON, J.	(9)4v
BUXTEHUDE	ssatb;str,bc	OBRECHT, J.	4v
CARISSIMI	satb/satb;bc	PACHELBEL, C.T.	satb/satb;bc
CAVALLI	SATB,satb/satb;br,str,bc	PACHELBEL, J.	4v
CERTON	satb	PACHELBEL, J.	ssatb
CHARPENTIER	TBB,satb;2fl,str,bc	PACHELBEL, J.	(5)4v;inst
CHARPENTIER	SOLI,satb/satb;orch	PACHELBEL, J.	(6)5v;inst
CHIHARA, P.	sssaaa	PACHELBEL, J.	5v/5v;inst
CLEMENS, J.	(15)4v	PALESTRINA, G.P.	(26)satb
COMES, J.B.	ssat/satb	PALESTRINA, G.P.	(4)5v
CORNYSH, W.	satbb	PALESTRINA, G.P.	(4)6v
DES PREZ, J.	(2)satb	PALESTRINA, G.P.	8v
DUFAY, G.	4v	PENDERECKI, K.	SB,satb;orch
DUFAY, G.	(2)3v	PERGOLESI, G.B.	satb;orch
DUNSTABLE, J.	ssa	PETRASSI, G.	S,satb;orch
DURANTE, F.	SATB,satb;str,O	PINKHAM, D.	S,ssa;P
EBERLIN, J.	SATB,satb;br,str,bc	PORPORA, N.	ssaa;str
GABRIELI, A.	8v	PRADO, A.	ssattb
GABRIELI, A.	ssaa/satb/ttbb	PRAETORIUS, M.	satb/satb
GABRIELI, G.	satb/ttbb	RAUTAVAARA, E.	satb
GABRIELI, G.	(2)12v	RILEY, D.	satb
GABRIELI, G.	14v	SAMMARTINI, G.B.	SAT,satb;orch
GABRIELI, G.	17v	SCARLATTI, A.	ssatb;O
GABRIELI, G.	18v	SCARLATTI, D.	satb;bc
GABRIELI, G.	33v	SCHEIN, J.H.	st;bc
GOUNOD, C.	S,satb;O	SCHUETZ, H.	SOLI,satb;inst
GRAUPNER, C.	SATB,satb;orch	SCHUBERT, F.	SATB,satb;orch,O
HASSLER, H.L.	(2)satb	SENFL, L.	satb
HAYDN, M.	SSA,ssa;2hrn,2vn,bc	SERMISY, C.	(9)4v
HOVHANESS, A.	SATB,satb;orch	STEFFANI, A.	8v;O
JOMMELLI, N.	satb;orch	STEVENS, H.	satb;str,trp
KUHNAU, J.	SOLI,ssatb;orch	SWEELINCK, J.P.	5v;bc
LA RUE, P.	satb	TALLIS, T.	5v
LASSUS, O.	23(4v)	VECCHI, O.	5v
LASSUS, O.	34(5v)	VIADANA, L.	(4)satb
LASSUS, O.	32(6v)	VICTORIA, T.L.	(16)satb
LASSUS, O.	7v	VICTORIA, T.L.	satb/satb
LASSUS, O.	(6)8v	VICTORIA, T.L.	satb/satb/satb
LASSUS, O.	10v	VILLA LOBOS, H.	SATB,satb;orch
LECHNER, L.	satb	VIVALDI, A.	(2)satb;orch
LISZT, F.	(63)	VIVALDI, A.	SA,satb;str,O
LOPEZ Y CAPILLAS, F.	satb	ZELENKA, J.D.	AT,satb;orch
LOTTI, A.	satb	ZIMMERMANN, H.	ssatb;hpsd,cb,vib

MIRABILE MYSTERIUM

HANDL, J.	satbb
LASSUS, O.	5v
WELLESZ, E.	SATB,satb;orch
WILLAERT, A.	satb

MISERERE MEI, DEUS

AICHINGER, G.	8-12v
ALLEGRI, G.	satb div
BYRD, W.	5v
CHARPENTIER, M.A.	6v;2rec,str,bc
CHARPENTIER, M.A.	SSTB,7v;2fl,str,bc
CROCE, G.	8v
DELLO JOIO, N.	satb;br,str,perc
DES PREZ, J.	sattbb
DONIZETTI, G.	SOLI,satb;orch
GABRIELI, A.	6v
GABRIELI, G.	attbbb
GESUALDO, C.	sattbb
HASSE, J.	ssaa;orch
HASSLER, H.L.	ssa/attb(ttbb)
HASSLER, H.L.	satb/satb
JOHANSSON, B.	satb
KODÁLY, Z.	satb/satb
LANGLAIS, J.	unis/satb
LASSUS, O.	sattb
LASSUS, O,	ssattb
LASSUS, O.	9v
LEO, L.	satb/satb;bc
LOTTI, A.	satb
LULLY, J.B.	ssttb/sstbb;str,bc
MOUTON, J.	4v
MOZART, W.A.	atb(ttb);O
PALESTRINA, G.P.	(2)4v
PALESTRINA, G.P.	(2)5v
PALESTRINA, G.P.	6v
PALESTRINA, G.P.	12v
PENDERECKI, K.	satb/satb/satb
PERGOLESI, G.B.	satb
PERGOLESI, G.B.	SATB,satb;str,O
REUTTER, J.G.	satb;O(str)
SCARLATTI, A.	SATB,ssatb
SCARLATTI, A.	S,ssatb;2vn,va,bc
SCARLATTI, A.	satb;bc
SWEELINCK, J.P.	satb
SWEELINCK, J.P.	canon a4
TARTINI, G.	3v
TARTINI, G.	4v
TARTINI, G.	5v
VICTORIA, T.L.	satb/satb

MISERICORDIAS DOMINI

DES PREZ, J.	satb
DURANTE, F.	satb/satb
GABRIELI, G.	ssab/abbb
HASSLER, H.L.	ssaa/satb
LASSUS, O.	sattb
MOZART, W.A.	satb;orch,bc
PITONI, G.	
SERMISY, C.	4v

MUSICA DEI

CLEMENS, J.	satb
LASSUS, O.	ssattb

NIGRA SUM

CARISSIMI, G.	ss;bc
CASALS, P.	ssa(ttb);O
PALESTRINA, G.P.	sattb
VICTORIA, T.L.	6v

NON NOBIS

BYRD, W.	sab
HAYDN, J.	satb;O
MOUTON, J.	4v
PINKHAM, D.	ssa;O
QUILTER, R.	satb;orch
SODERHOLM, V.	satb

NUNC DIMITTIS

ARKHANGELSKY, A.	sab
BYRD, W.	ssatb
DES PREZ, J.	satb
GABRIELI, G.	ssatb/atbb/abbbb
GAVAERT, F.A.	satb
GRETCHANINOV, A.	ssaattbb
HASSLER, H.L.	sattb
LASSUS, O.	(6)4v
LASSUS, O.	(4)5v
LASSUS, O.	6v
LASSUS, O.	7v
OLSSON, O.	B,satbb
PALESTRINA, G.P.	(3)4v
PALESTRINA, G.P.	6v
PALESTRINA, G.P.	8v
PALESTRINA, G.P.	12v
PRAETORIUS, M.	satb/sttb

| STEVENS, H. | satb |
| STOUT, A. | satb;fl,str,cym,O |

O ADMIRABILE COMMERCIUM

BYRD, W.	satb
COSTANTINI, F.	satb
DES PREZ, J.	satb
HANDL, J.	ssaattbb
HASSLER, H.L.	ssattb
PALESTRINA, G.P.	ssatb
PALESTRINA, G.P.	8v

O BONE JESU

AGOSTINI, P.	satb
BRAHMS, J.	ssaa
CAVALLI, F.	sa;bc
COMPERE, L.	satb
DEERING, R.	sattb
INGEGNERI, M.A.	satb
LASSUS, O.	3v–4v
LEWKOVITCH, B.	satb
MONTEVERDI, C.	ssa
MONTEVERDI, C.	ss;bc
PALESTRINA, G.P.	(2)4v
PALESTRINA, G.P.	6v
PALESTRINA, G.P.	8v
PHILIPS, P.	2v
SCHUETZ, H.	ssaatb;str,bc
SURIANO, F.	satb

O FILII ET FILIAE

| GEVAERT, F.A. | ssa |
| LEISING, V. | 8v |

O MAGNUM MYSTERIUM

BYRD, W.	satb
CLEMENS, J.	6v
DAVIES, P.M.	satb
GABRIELI, G.	satb/atbb
HANDL, J.	satb/satb
HANDL, J.	ttbb/ttbb
HELLER, D.	S,satb/satb;2fl
MORALES, C.	satb

PAGE, R.	ssatb
PALESTRINA, G.P.	ssaatb
PINKHAM, D.	satb;2tr,2trb,O
POULENC, F.	satb
ROREM, N.	satb
SCARLATTI, A.	satb/satb
VICTORIA, T.L.	satb
WILLAERT, A.	satb

O NATA LUX

BYRD, W.	sattb
MATHIAS, W.	satb
TALLIS, T.	sattb

O QUAM GLORIOSUM

BYRD, W.	ssatb
ESQUIVEL, J.	satb
MARENZIO, L.	satb
VAET, J.	satb
VICTORIA, T.L.	satb

O SACRUM CONVIVIUM

AICHINGER, G.	sattb
ANERIO, F.	sttb
BERNABEI, G.	satb
BYRD, W.	satb
CARISSIMI, G.	sat
CHARPENTIER, M.A.	satb;O
CHERUBINI, L.	satb;orch
CROCE, G.	satb
GABRIELI, A.	sattb
GABRIELI, G.	7v
GESUALDO, C.	6v
GUERRERO, F.	saatbb
HANDL, J.	ssaa(ttbb)
HASSLER, H.L.	ssaattb
LASSUS, O.	sattb
LISZT, F.	A,sa;O
MARCELLO, B.	stb
MARENZIO, L.	satb
MESSIAEN, O.	satb
MORALES, C.	saatb
PALESTRINA, G.	5v
PERGOLESI, G.B.	satb
PHILIPS, P.	ssb
SWEELINCK, J.P.	sattb;bc

TALLIS, T.	attbb
VIADANA, L.	ttbb
VIADANA, L.	satb
VICTORIA, T.L.	4v
VICTORIA, T.L.	6v

O SALUTARIS HOSTIA

ANERIO, F.	satb
AUBANEL, G.	satb
BORTINIANSKY, D.	satb
BYRD, W.	satb
BYRD, W.	ssattb
CAPLET, A.	ssa(ttb)
CERTON, P.	4v
CHERUBINI, L.	ssaa(ttbb)
ELGAR, E.	satb;O
FRANCK, C.	S,satb;O
GABRIELI, A.	8v
GOUNOD, C.	4v
HANDL, J.	satb
HOWELLS, H.	ssattb
INDY, V.	ssa
ISAAC, H.	sab
LA RUE, P.	satb
LALO, E.	ssa;O
LASSUS, O.	sattb
LISZT, F.	ssaa;O
LISZT, F.	satb;O
MARTINI, P.	ssa
MASSENET, J.	S(satb);hp,O
MATHIAS, W.	ttbb
PALESTRINA, G.P.	4v
ROSSINI, G.	satb
SAINT-SAËNS, C.	(2)sab
SAINT-SAËNS, C.	tb(sa)
SCHUMANN, R.	SB,satb;orch
TALLIS, T.	satbb
VECCHI, O.	4v
VIADANA, L.	ssa(ttb)

O VOS OMNES

CASALS, P.	satb(ttbb)
CLAUSSEN, R.	S,satb/satb
COMPÈRE, L.	atb
COUPERIN, F.	sa;O
CROCE, G.	satb
DEERING, R.	5v
ESQUIVEL, J.	satb
GESUALDO, C.	sattb

GESUALDO, C.	sattbb
GINASTERA, A.	ssaattbb
INGEGNERI, M.A.	satb
JOMELLI, N.	satb
LOTTI, A.	satb
MARTINI, G.	ttb
MORALES, C.	satb
OBRECHT, J.	sab
PALESTRINA, G.P.	4v
PERTI, G.	satb
PRAETORIUS, H.	sattb
VAUGHAN WILLIAMS, R.	satb
VICTORIA, T.L.	satb

OMNES DE SABA

ASOLA, G.	ssaa(ttbb)
EYBLER, J.	satb;orch,O
HANDL, J.	sattb
LASSUS, O.	satb/satb

PANGE LINGUA

AICHINGER, G.	sattb
ASOLA, G.	satb
BELLINI, V.	2v;O
BRUCKNER, A.	(2)satb
BUXTEHUDE, D.	ssab;5str,bc
BYRD, W.	satb
DUFAY, G.	3v
KODÁLY, Z.	satb;O
PALESTRINA, G.P.	satb
PALESTRINA, G.P.	5v
PEARSALL, R.	4v;ww,O
PITONI, G.	satb
STRAUSS, R.	satb
TARTINI, G.	3v
WILLIAMSON, M.	satb
VICTORIA, T.L.	4v

PANIS ANGELICUS

CHARPENTIER, M-A.	unis
DEERING, R.	ssb;bc
FRANCK, C.	T,satb;P/O(arr)
MASSENET, J.	SOLO,satb;O
PALESTRINA, G.P.	4v
PHILIPS, P.	3v
SAINT-SAËNS, C.	satb

PATER NOSTER

ANDRIESSEN, H.	satb;O
BECKER, J.	satb
BERGER, J.	satb
CERTON, P.	6v
DES PREZ, J.	sattbb
GEVAERT, F-A.	ssa
GOUNOD, C.	SOLI,5v;O
GUERRERO, F.	ssaattb
HANDL, J.	ssaattbb
HASSLER, H.L.	satb/satb
JOHANSSON, B.	ssa
KŘENEK, E.	ssaa
LASSUS, O.	satb
LASSUS, O.	(2)saattb
LISZT, F.	ttbb;O
LISZT, F.	ssa;O
LISZT, F.	satb;O
MEYERBEER, G.	satb
MORALES, C.	5v
NICOLAI, O.	satb/satb
PALESTRINA, G.P.	(2)5v
PALESTRINA, G.	8v
PEETERS, F.	satb(sa)(tb);O
PHILIPS, P.	5v
PINKHAM, D.	satb;ob,Ehrn,bsn,O
PRAETORIUS, H.	ssaatbbb
SCELSI, G.	unis
SCHUBERT, F.	(mass in c)
SCHUETZ, H.	satb;bc
STRAVINSKY, I.	satb
TCHAIKOVSKY, P.I.	satb
VERDI, G.	ssatb
VILLA LOBOS, H.	satb
WILLAERT, A.	attb

PLORATE FILII ISRAEL

CARISSIMI, G.	ssatbb

PSALLITE

PRAETORIUS, M.	satb
SCHEIDT, S.	satb;O

PUER NATUS EST

BYRD, W.	satb
DIABELLI, A.	satb;orch,O
GEVAERT, F.	ssa;O
GUERRERO, F.	satb

HASSLER, H.L.	satb
ISAAC, H.	4v
LASSUS, O.	5v
LOEWE, C.	satb
MORALES, C.	sab
MOUTON, J.	satb
NEHLYBEL, V.	ssattb
PRAETORIUS, M.	satb
RHEINBERGER, J.	sa;O
SCHEIDT, S.	satb/satb
SERMISY, C.	4v

PUERI HEBRAEORUM

HANDL, J.	ssaa(ttbb)
PALESTRINA, G.P.	(2)4v
SCHUBERT, F.	satb
STOUT, A.	satb;str,hp,perc
THOMPSON, R.	ssaa/ssaa
VICTORIA, T.L.	satb

QUEM VIDISTIS PASTORES?

ASOLA, G.	ttbb/ttbb
DEERING, R.	ssattb
GABRIELI, A.	satb/satb
GABRIELI, G.	14v
HANDL, J.	satb/satb
HASSLER, H.L.	satb
LASSUS, O.	ssatb
NEHLYBEL, V.	ssattbb
PAGE, R.	ssa/ttb/satb
PINKHAM, D.	satb;br,O
POULENC, F.	saatb
ROGER-DUCASSE, J.	satb;O
VICTORIA, T.L.	ssatbb

REGINA COELI

AICHINGER, G.	satb
ALBRECHTSBERGER, J.	satb;O
ANERIO, F.	satb
BERKELEY, L.	ssatbb
BERNABEI, G.	satb
BRAHMS, J.	SA,ssaa
BRUML, A.	(2)4v
BYRD, W.	atb
CALDARA, A.	satb
CAVALLI, F.	atb;bc

CERTON, P.	(2)6v	CAVALLI, F.	satb;orch
CHARPENTIER, M-A.	2v	CERTON, P.	4v
CHERUBINI, L.	3v	CHARPENTIER, M-A.	SOLI,4v;bc
DES PREZ, J.	sattbb	CHERUBINI, L.	satb;orch
DUBOIS, T.		CHERUBINI, L.	tbb;orch
ERBACH, C.	satb	CIMAROSA, D.	S,satb;orch
GABRIELI, G.	satbbb/satbbb	CLEMENS, J.	4v
GUERRERO, F.	satb/satb	CORNELIUS, P.	ttbb
LALANDE, M.R.	satbb;orch	DAVID, J.N.	SATB,satb;orch
LASSUS, O.	satb	DES PREZ, J.	6v
LASSUS, O.	(3)5v	DONIZETTI, G.	(3)satb;orch
LASSUS, O.	(2)6v	DUBOIS, T.	SOLI,satb;orch
LASSUS, O.	7v	DURANTE, F.	8v
LOTTI, A.	satb	DURUFLÉ, M.	SOLI,satb;orch,O
MASCAGNI, P.	SAB,ssattb/ssattbb	DVOŘÁK, A.	SATB,satb;orch
MORALES, C.	satb	EYBLER, J.	8v;str,O
MORALES, C.	(2)6v	FAURÉ, G.	SB,satb;orch,O
MOUTON, J.	4v	GILLES, J.	5v;str,bc
MOZART, W.A.	(2)S,satb;orch,O	GOSSEC, F.J.	SATB,satb;orch
MOZART, W.A.	SATB,satb;orch,O	GOUNOD, C.	S,satb/satb;orch
OBRECHT, J.	2v	GUERRERO, F.	4v
PALESTRINA, G.P.	(2)4v	HAYDN, J.	SOLI,satb;orch
PALESTRINA, G.P.	(2)8v	HAYDN, M.	SATB,satb;orch
PERGOLESI, G.B.	satb	HEMBERG, E.	satb
PHILIPS, P.	5v	JOMMELLI, N.	SATB,satb;orch,bc
PHILIPS, P.	8v	KOKKONEN, J.	SB,satb;orch
PORTA, C.	ssaa(ttbb)	LA RUE, P.	2v-5v
PRAETORIUS, M.	3v	LASSUS, O.	4v
RHEINBERGER, J.	ssa;O	LASSUS, O.	5v
SERMISY, C.	5v	LEOPOLD I, P.	SOLI,5v;orch,O
STRAUSS, R.	satb	LIGETI, G.	SS,satb/satb;orch
SURIANO, F.	satb	LISZT, F.	TTBB,ttbb;O(br)
SWEELINCK, J.P.	3-5v;bc	LOTTI, A.	satb
VIADANA, L.	satb	MALIPIERO, G.	B,satb;orch
VICTORIA, T.L.	5v	MARTIN, F.	SATB,satb;orch
VICTORIA, T.L.	8v	MARTINI, G.	4v;inst,O
WIDOR, C.M.	sa;P	MASSENET, J.	4-8v;vc,cb,O
WILLAERT, A.	sttb	MORALES, C.	4v
WILLAN, H.	ssaa	MORALES, C.	5v
		MOZART, W.A.	SATB,satb;orch
		NUNES-GARCIA, J.M.	ATB,satb;orch
		OCKEGHEM, J.	2v-4v
REQUIEM		PALESTRINA, G.P.	5v
		PEARSALL, R.	4v;ww,O
ALAIN, J.	satb;O	PENDERECKI, K.	SATB,satb;orch
ALBRECHTSBERGER, J	(3)satb;inst,O	PERGOLESI, G.B.	satb;2hn,str,O
ANERIO, F.	satb	PINKHAM, D.	AT,satb;orch
BACH, J.C.	satb/satb;orch	PIZZETTI, I.	satb
BERLIOZ, H.	t,satb;orch	REDA, S.	SB,satb;orch
BIBER, H.	SSATB,ssatb;orch	REGER, M.	SATB,satb;orch,O
BONNO, G.	(2)SOLI,satb;orch	REUTTER, G.	SOLI,satb;orch
BRITTEN, B.	STB,boys/satb;orch	RHEINBERGER, J.	(3)settings
BRUCKNER, A.	SATB,satb;orch,O	RUTTER, J.	S,satb;orch
BRUMEL, A.	satb	SAINT-SAËNS, C.	SOLI,satb;orch
CAMPRA, A.	SOLI,satb;orch	SCARLATTI, A.	satb

SCELSI, G.	ssaattbb
SCHNITTKE, A.	satb;orch
SCHUBERT, F.	satb;orch
SCHUMANN, R.	satb;orch
SERMISY, C.	4v
SINOPOLI, G.	satb
STRAVINSKY, I.	AB,satb;orch
TAVENER, J.	satb/satb/satb;orch
THOMPSON, R.	satb/satb
THOMSON, V.	satb;orch
VAET, J.	5v
VECCHI, O.	5v
VERDI, G.	SATB,satb;orch
VIADANA, L.	satb
VICTORIA, T.L.	satb
VICTORIA, T.L.	ssattb
WARREN, E.R.	SB,satb;orch
WEBBER, A.L.	STtr,satb;orch

RESONET IN LAUDIBUS

ECCARD, J.	sattb;bc
ERBACH, C.	satb
HANDL, J.	satb
HASSLER, H.L.	satb
LASSUS, O.	sattb
PRAETORIUS, M.	sssatb

SALVE REGINA

AICHINGER, G.	satb
BELLINI, V.	satb/orch
BERKELEY, L.	unis;O
BROWNE, J.	satbb
BYRD, W.	satb
BYRD, W.	sattb
CARISSIMI, G.	ssb;bc
CARISSIMI, G.	SATB,satb;bc
CAVALLI, F.	attb;bc
CHARPENTIER, M-A.	atb;bc
CRESTON, P.	TTB,ttb;O
DES PREZ, J.	satb
DES PREZ, J.	sattb
FAURÉ, G.	satb;O
GOUDIMEL, C.	satb/satb/satb
GUERRERO, F.	attb
HAYDN, J.	satb;orch,O
HAYDN, M.	satb
HEILLER, A.	ssa
HOWELLS, H.	ssattb
LA RUE, P.	satb

LASSUS, O.	(2)4v
LASSUS, O.	5v
LASSUS, O.	(2)6v
LASSUS, O.	8v
LISZT, F.	satb;O
LOTTI, A.	satb
MARENZIO, L.	ssatb
MONTEVERDI, C.	2v
MONTEVERDI, C.	2v;2vn
MONTEVERDI, C.	3v
MORALES, C.	4v
MORALES, C.	5v
OBRECHT, J.	3v
OBRECHT, J.	6v
OCKEGHEM, J.	(2)4v
PALESTRINA, G.P.	4,8,12v
PALESTRINA, G.P.	5v
PALESTRINA, G.P.	6v
PALESTRINA, G.P.	(2)8v
PHILIPS, P.	5v
PERGOLESI, G.B.	ss;str
POULENC, F.	satb
PRAETORIUS, M.	satb
RHEINBERGER, J.	satb
RHEINBERGER, J.	ssa;O
SCARLATTI, A.	satb
SCARLATTI, A.	sa;2vn,bc
SCARLATTI, A.	satb;2vn,bc
SCHUBERT, F.	satb
SCHUBERT, F.	ttbb
TARTINI, G.	4v
TYE, C.	aatbb
VICTORIA, T.L.	(2)5v
VICTORIA, T.L.	6v
VICTORIA, T.L.	8v
VIVALDI, A.	A,satb/satb;orch

SICUT CERVUS

ANERIO, F.	satb
GOUNOD, C.F.	satbb
LA RUE, P.	satb
MARCELLO, B.	sab
OCKEGHEM, J.	4v
PALESTRINA, G.P.	satb
VAET, J.	sa(tb)

STABAT MATER

BONONCINI, A.M.	SATB,satb;str,bc
CALDARA, A.	SATB,satb;2trb,str,bc
DAVID, J.N.	ssa/ttb
DES PREZ, J.	sttbb

DOHNÁNYI, E.	SSA/ssa;orch
DVOŘÁK, A.	SATB,satb;orch
FRANCK, C.	SOLI, 3v
GOUNOD, C.	satb;orch
HAYDN, J.	SATB,satb;orch
HEILLER, A.	satb;orch
HOWELLS, H.	T,satb;orch
KODÁLY, Z.	ttbb
LASSUS, O.	8v
LEWKOVITCH, B.	ssaatbb
LISZT, F.	ssatb;O
LOUDOVÁ, I.	ttbb/ttbb
NAYLOR, B.	ssa/ssa;orch(O)
PALESTRINA, G.P.	4v
PALESTRINA, G.P.	8v
PALESTRINA, G.P.	12v
PENDERECKI, K.	satb/satb/satb
PERGOLESI, G.B.	SA,sa;2vn,2va,bc
PERSICHETTI, V.	satb;orch
PINKHAM, D.	S,satb;orch
POULENC. F.	S,satbb;orch
RHEINBERGER, J.	satb;O(str)
ROSSINI, G.	SSTB,satb;orch
SCARLATTI, A.	sa;2vn,bc
SCARLATTI, D.	SOLI,ssatb;bc
SCHUBERT, F.	STB,satb;orch,O
STEFFANI, A.	6v;str,bc
SZYMANOWSKI, K.	SAB,ssaatbb;orch
TARTINI, G.	3v
TŮMA, F.	satb;O
VERDI, G.	satb;orch
VIVALDI, A.	4v

SUPER FLUMINA BABYLONIS

CARISSIMI, G.	ssat;bc
CHARPENTIER, M-A.	sab;2fl,bc
FAURÉ, G.	satb;orch
GAVAERT, F.A.	satb
GOMBERT, N.	satb
GOUNOD, C.	satb;P
LASSUS, O.	satb
MARENZIO, L.	satb/satb/satb
NAJERA, E.	satb/satb
PALESTRINA, G.P.	satb
PALESTRINA, G.P.	5v
PERGOLESI, G.B.	satb;orch,O
SAINT-SAËNS, C.	satb
VICTORIA, T.L.	satb/satb

SURGE ILLUMINARE

BYRD, W.	satb

CLEMENS, J.	4v
PALESTRINA, G.P.	satb/satb
ROREM, N.	satb
SERMISY, C.	4v

SURGENS JESUS

LASSUS, O.	ssatb
MONTEVERDI, C.	ssa(sat)
PHILIPS, P.	ssatb

SURREXIT PASTOR BONIS

CARISSIMI, G.	sss;bc
GABRIELI, G.	ssaab/tbbbb
HANDL, J.	tttbb
HASSLER, H.L.	ssattb
INGEGNERI, M.A.	sttbb
LASSUS, O.	ssatb
MENDELSSOHN, F.	SSAA,ssaa;O
PALESTRINA, G.P.	4v
PALESTRINA, G.P.	8v
SCHEIDT, S.	ssat/atbb;str
SCHUETZ, H.	ssattb;2vn,3trb,bc
VICTORIA, T.L.	6v

TANTUM ERGO

AICHINGER, F.	sattb
ALAIN, A.	satb
ALBRECHTSBERGER, J.	satb
ANDRIESSEN, H.	satb
ANERIO, F.	satb
ASOLA, G.M.	satb
AUBANEL, G.	satb
BELLINI, V.	satb;orch
BORTINIANSKY, D.	satb
BRUCKNER, A.	(4)satb
BRUCKNER, A.	satb;O
BRUCKNER, A.	satb;2vn,2trp
BRUCKNER, A.	ssatb;O
BYRD, W.	(2)sttb
CARISSIMI, G.	ssa(ttb)
CHARPENTIER, M-A.	ttb
CORSI, G.	satb
COUPERIN, F.	ssb;bc
DUFAY, G.	atb
DUPRÉ, M.	satb;O
DURUFLÉ, M.	satb
FAURÉ, G.	S(T),satb;O
FAURÉ, G.	SOLI,ssa;O
FAURÉ, G.	T,5v;hp,O

FINCK, H.	sttb
FRANCK, C.	B,satb;O
GLUCK, C.	satb
GOUNOD, C.	3v;O
GRETCHANINOV, A.	satb;O
HANDL, J.	sattb
HEILLER, A.	(2)satb
LASSUS, O.	sssa
LISZT, F.	ttbb;O
LISZT, F.	ssaa;O
MATTHIAS, W.	satb
MENDELSSOHN, F.	satb
MOZART, W.A.	S,satb;orch
PACHELBEL, J.	satb
PALESTRINA, G.	(2)4v
PERTI, G.	satb
PITONI, G.	satb
REGER, M.	5v
SCHUBERT, F.	(6)satb;orch,O
SCHUMANN, R.	satb;O
TARTINI, G.	ssa
VICTORIA, T.L.	(3)satb
VIERNE, L.	satb;O
WIDOR, C-M.	satb;O
WILLIAMSON, M.	sat

TE DEUM

ALBRECHTSBERGER, J.	satb;inst,O
ANDRIESSEN, H.	satb;orch
ANERIO, G.F.	(2)satb
ARGENTO, D.	satb;orch
BACH, J.C.	SOLI,satb;orch
BADINGS, H.	ttbb;orch
BELLINI, V.	(2)satb;orch
BERLIOZ, H.	T,satb;orch
BERNAL JIMENEZ, M.	stb;O
BINCHOIS, G.	2v
BIZET, G.	ST,satb;orch
BRUCKNER, A.	SATB,satb;orch
BYRD, W.	ssattb
CALDARA, A.	SATB,satb/satb;orch
CAMPRA, A.	SOLI,satb;orch
CHARPENTIER	8v;orch
CHARPENTIER	SSATB,satb;orch
CIMAROSA, D.	ST,satb;orch
CLEMENS, J.	4v
DVOŘÁK, A.	SB,satb;orch
EBERLIN	SATB,satb;2trp,tmp,str,bc
ELGAR, E.	satb;orch
HAYDN, J.	(2)SATB,satb;orch
HAYDN, M.	(6)SATB,satb;orch,O
HEILLER, A.	satb;O

JOMMELLI, N.	SATB,satb;2hrn,str,O
JEPPESEN, K.	SATB,satb/satb;orch
KODALY, Z.	SATB,satb;orch
LALANDE, M.R.	SOLI,satb;orch
LASSUS, O.	ssattb
LISZT, F.	ttbb,O
LISZT, F.	satb;O(br)
LULLY, J-B.	SSATB,satb/satb;orch
MALMFORS, A.	satb;O
MENDELSSOHN, F.	satb/satb;bc
MOZART, W.A.	satb;orch,O
NICOLAI, O.	SOLI,satb;orch
PALESTRINA, G.P.	6v
PEETERS, F.	satb(ttb);O
PENDERECKI, K.	SATB,satb;orch
PEPPING, E.	satb;orch
PERSICHETTI, V.	satb;orch
PINKHAM, D.	sa(tb);3trp,O
REDA, S.	satb/satb;br
RUBBRA, E.	ssaattbb
SCARLATTI, A.	ssatb;2ob,str,bc
SCARLATTI, D.	satb/satb;O
SCHUMAN, W.	satb
STEVENS, H.	satb;br,O
SWEELINCK, J.P.	5v
VERDI, G.	S,satb/satb;orch
VIADANA, L.	satb
VICTORIA, T.L.	4v
ZELENKA, J.D.	SSATB,ssatb;orch

TENEBRAE FACTAE SUNT

ALBRECHTSBERGER, J.	satb
BIBER, C.H.	satb
CHARPENTEIR, M-A.	atb;bc
CROCE, G.	satb
EBERLIN, J.	satb
GESUALDO, C.	ssattb
HAYDN, J.	satb;bc
HAYDN, M.	satb
HAYDN, M.	ssa;O
INGENERI, M.A.	satb
JOMELLI, N.	satb
LEO, L.	satb;bc
PETRASSI, G.	sattb
POULENC, F.	S,satb
POULENC, F.	saatbb
RUBBRA, E.	ssaattbb
RUBBRA, E.	satb
VICTORIA, T.L.	satb
WEERBECKE, G.	satb
ZELENKA, J.D.	satb;bc

TIMOR ET TREMOR

CLEMENS, J.	4v
GABRIELLI, G.	satbbb
LASSUS, O.	ssattb
POULENC, F.	saatbb

TOTA PULCHRA EST MARIA

BRUCKNER, A.	T,satb;O
CASALS, P.	T,ssattb
CHAUSSON, E.	satb;vc,hp,O
CLEMENS, J.	5v
DURUFLÉ, M.	satb
ISAAC, H.	4v
LASSUS, O.	satb
MOUTON, J.	4v
MONTEVERDI, C.	ss;bc
PALESTRINA, G.P.	sattb

TRISTIS EST ANIMA MEA

CROCE, G.	satb
GESUALDO, C.	sattbb
HAYDN, M.	satb
INGEGNERI, M.A.	ssatb
KUHNAU, J.	ssatb
LASSUS, O.	sattb
LEO, L.	satb
MARTINI, G.	ttb(sab)
PALESTRINA, G.P.	satb
PETRASSI, G.	sattb
POULENC, F.	S,ssaattbb
RUBBRA, E.	satb

TU ES PETRUS

ALAIN, J.	3v
BYRD, W.	sattbb
CLEMENS, J.	satb
CORNELIUS, P.	satb
DURUFLÉ, M.	satb
FAURÉ, G.	B,satb;O
GRAUN, C.H.	satb
GRETCHANINOV, A.	B,satb;O
HASSLER, H.L.	satb
HASSLER, H.L.	ssatb
LASSUS, O.	satb
LISZT, F.	ttbb;O
MENDELSSOHN, F.	ssatb;orch
MONTEVERDI, C.	ssa(sab)
MORALES, C.	sab
MORALES, C.	5v
PALESTRINA, G.P.	6v
PALESTRINA, G.P.	7v

PHILIPS, P.	satb/satb
SAINT-SAËNS, C.	satb(ttbb)
SCARLATTI, A.	satb/satb;O
TARTINI, G.	(2)3v
VICTORIA, T.L.	ssattb
WIDOR, C-M.	satb/satb;(2)O

TU PAUPERUM REFUGIUM

DES PREZ, J.	satb

UBI CARITAS

BERKELEY, L.	satb
DURUFLÉ, M.	sattbb
EBEN, P.	ssatbb
LANGLAIS, J.	satb;O
PEETERS, F.	unis;O
PROULX, R.	satb;handbells

VENI CREATOR SPIRITUS

ANDRIESSEN, H.	satb;orch
ASOLA, G.	satb
BERLIOZ, H.	ssa;O
BERNABEI, G.	satb
BRUCKNER, A.	unis;O
CHARPENTIER, M-A.	(2)satb
DAVID, J.N.	satb/satb;orch
DUFAY, G.	3v
FINCK, H.	at;3inst
GESUALDO, C.	6v
GEVAERT, F.A.	satb
GIBBONS, O.	satb
GOUNOD, C.	ttbb
LASSUS, O.	ssatbb
LEWKOVITCH, B.	satb;6trb
MACHAUT, G.	4v
ORFF, C.	satb;3P,perc
PALESTRINA, G.P.	saatb
PEARSALL, R.	4v;ww,O
PHILIPS, P.	4v
PRAETORIUS, M.	satb
SAINT-SAËNS, C.	ttbb
RUBBRA, E.	satb;br,O
VICTORIA, T.L.	4v
ZANINELLI, L.	satb

VENI SANCTE SPIRITUS

ALLEGRI, G.	satb
BYRD, W.	ssttb
DAVIES, P.M.	SAB,satb;orch
DES PREZ, J.	saattb
DUDA, T.	satb div;perc

DUFAY, G.	(2)3v
DUNSTABLE, J.	tbb
FINCK, H.	at;3 inst
HANDL, J.	satb
HAYDN, M.	ssaattbb;bc
ISAAC, H.	satb
JANÁČEK, L.	ttbb
LASSUS, O.	6v
MOZART, W.A.	SATB,satb;orch,O
NYSTEDT, K.	ssaattbb
PALESTRINA, G.P.	4v
PALESTRINA, G.P.	(2)8v
SALIERI, A.	satb;P
SCHEIDT, S.	satb/satb
SCHUETZ, H.	16v;inst,bc
SERMISY, C.	4v
SHERLAW-JOHNSON, R.	satb;(perc)
VIADANA, L.	sab
VICTORIA, T.L.	satb/satb

VERBUM CARO

BÄCK, S.E.	satb
BYRD, W.	sttb
DES PREZ, J.	satbb
GEIST, C.	sa;str,bc
HASSLER, H.L.	ssattb
LASSUS, O.	ssaatb
MALMFORS, A.	satb
MOUTON, J.	6v
PALESTRINA, G.P.	satb
REGER, M.	satb;O
SCHEIN, J.H.	ssatbb
SCHUETZ, H.	ss(tt);bc
VICTORIA, T.L.	(2)3v
WALTER, J.	satb

VERE LANGUORES

CAMPRA, A.	3v
LOTTI, A.	ttb(ssa)
LOTTI, A.	satb
VICTORIA, T.L.	satb

VICTIMAE PASCHALI LAUDES

BYRD, W.	saatb
DAVID, J.N.	satb
DES PREZ, J.	satb
DES PREZ, J.	saatbb
DUFAY, G.	3v
HAYDN, M.	satb;orch

JOMMELLI, N.	6v;bc
LASSUS, O.	8v
MORALES, C.	4v
MATHIAS, W.	satb
PALESTRINA, G.P.	4v-8v
PALESTRINA, G.P.	(3)8v
VICTORIA, T.L.	satb/satb
WILLAERT, A.	ssattb

VIDENTES STELLAM

DES PREZ, J.	satttb
GABRIELI, A.	4v
GOUDIMEL, C.	satb
LASSUS, O.	ssatb
LASSUS, O.	ssattb
PALESTRINA, G.P.	8v
PHILIPS, P.	3v
POULENC, F.	ssaattbb

VIDERUNT OMNES

BYRD, W.	satb
HAYDN, M.	satb;orch
ISAAC, H.	4v
LASSUS, O.	ssatb
LEMACHER, H.	satb;O
LEONIN	2v
PEROTIN	tt;2inst
SERMISY, C.	3v

VIDI AQUAM

BRUML, A.	4v
LASSUS, O.	5v
MORALES, C.	4v
PALESTRINA, G.P.	4v
VICTORIA, T.L.	4v

VINEA MEA ELECTA

GESUALDO, C.	sattbb
INGEGNERI, M.A.	satb
JOMELLI, N.	satb
PALESTRINA, G.P.	satb
POULENC, F.	ssaatbb
VIADANA, L.	satb
ZELENKA, J.D.	satb;bc

VIRGA JESSE FLORUIT

BRUCKNER, A.	satb

INDEX
of
Titles and First Lines

TITLE AND FIRST-LINE INDEX

In this index you will find all the titles listed in the Table of Contents, the first lines when they differ from those titles, and the first lines of certain portions of the Mass, Requiem Mass, and Magnificat that are occasionally found in separate settings -- each accompanied by an identifying English translation.

277

"I believed, therefore have I spoken;
but I have been humbled exceedingly."
(Psalm 116:10)

EP31